Studies in World History Vol. 3

DR. JAMES STOBAUGH

The Modern Age
to Present
{1900 A.D. to Present}

GEOGRAPHY   GOVERNMENT   ECONOMICS   RELIGION   HISTORY   GEOGRAPHY

RELIGION   HISTORY   GOVERNMENT   GEOGRAPHY   ECONOMICS

Jr. High
STUDENT

First printing: April 2014
Second printing: February 2015

Master Books®, P.O. Box 726, Green Forest, AR 72638
Master Books® is a division of the New Leaf Publishing Group, Inc.

ISBN: 978-0-89051-786-4
Library of Congress Number: 2014931472

Cover by Diana Bogardus

Unless otherwise noted, Scripture quotations are from the New King James Version of the Bible.

Please consider requesting that a copy of this volume be purchased by your local library system.

Printed in the United States of America

Please visit our website for other great titles:
www.masterbooks.net

For information regarding author interviews, please contact the publicity department at (870) 438-5288

Master Books®
A Division of New Leaf Publishing Group
www.masterbooks.net

First Iwo Jima Flag Raising. Small flag carried ashore by the 2d Battalion, 28th Marines is planted atop Mount Suribachi at 1020, February 23, 1945 (USMarines).

Table of Contents

Studies in World History 3: The Modern Era to Present

Tommy Hawkins, a five year old, selling papers in St. Louis, Mo., 1910 (NARA).

Removal of liquor during prohibition (PD).

Table of Contents (cont)

Starved prisoners, nearly dead from hunger, in a concentration camp in Ebensee, Austria. The camp was reputedly used for "scientific" experiments. It was liberated by the 80th Division of the U.S. Army., May 7, 1945 (NARA).

Chimpanzee "Ham" in space suit is fitted into the biopack couch of the Mercury-Redstone 2 capsule #5 prior to its test flight which was conducted on January 31, 1961 (NASA).

The Sony canari (formerly AT&T building) in New York City, 1984, by Philip Johnson, illustrating a "Postmodern" spin with the inclusion of a classical broken pediment on the top that diverged from the boxy functional office towers common in Modern Architecture (CCA-SA3.0).

President Ronald Reagan (far left) and First Lady Nancy Reagan pay their respects to the caskets of the 17 US victims of the April 18, 1983 attack on the United States Embassy in Beirut (PD).

I visited the old tire swing that hangs from a huge, aged maple tree that grows in my yard. It is like any old tire swing. I imagine you have swung on one. Perhaps you still do. Now empty of bouncing children, this discarded tire was once a wild bucking horse, a twirling UFO, a charming Timbuktu prince. It was whatever my four children wanted it to be. My children were introduced to the universe on this old Michelin radial. They learned that they could soar to the end of the sky, yet return safely back to the sedentary loam of the ground. From that old tire they moved into history.

They gracefully wriggled their toes at passing mourning doves and plowed diminutive furrows through sensual pasture. They laughed at passing thunderstorms and frowned at interloping grasshoppers. They dodged maple leaves and smiled at rainbows.

At first they relied on me to launch them into their dreams, but as they matured and their legs grew longer and stronger they invaded the twilight below the tire on their own. They took control of their history and, in a way, my history. For we share history. We are one. My life and dreams that were stimulated on that tire swing go with them. On my swing they took solo trips to the horizon. They differentiated themselves from time, and pushed away from certainty and poise into a reckless iconoclasm.

They tried to twirl but could not. They still needed me to twirl them; that gave me silent pleasure. Something of their youth was captured in that old tire swing. It is there still. Something of them is resurrected as I walk to that tire swing and for one fleeting moment our halcyon souls kiss again. The grass grows wildly underneath the tire swing; there are no protruding appendages plowing my pasture. Where once pudgy starfighters attacked the cosmos, caterpillars wriggle through worn tire threads. I do not need the pasture but I still need the toes. If you drive by my farm you will see the tire swing. Stop and listen. Think of my children and their father who twirled his children into adulthood.

You know, history is that way. It is about people and time and differentiation (breaking away). It is not therapeutic — it is not something that exists to serve us. It is a glance back to the past and a road map into the future. But these are dangerous times.

America, in the beginning of the 21st century, is spinning out of control. We are stretching our wings adventurously but drifting further away from our God. We are in trouble.

As part of the symposium at the dedication of the Presbyterian Center, Louisville, Kentucky, October 28, 1988, the theologian Walter Brueggemann surprised the Presbyterian Church (USA) — as well as all Americans — by calling them to repentance. "We religionists [evangelicals] are caught in an odd endorsing and legitimating, when in our knowing, we may want to talk about the sovereign absence of God, an absence evident in the secularization of a society which seems to manage very well by itself." Brueggemann further suggests that we evangelical Christians are in exile and need to act accordingly.

Okay. We live in a post-Christian era. So what?

Deborah lived in a post-Jewish era, a time where worship of Yahweh was no longer practiced by her society. There was a great falling away — like now — and God called Deborah to make things right — like God is calling you now.

Deborah was a prophetess and the fourth judge of Israel. She was a warrior mom, a culture creator. The only female judge mentioned in the Bible, Deborah led a successful counter-attack against the forces of Jabin, king of Canaan, and his military commander Sisera.

> In the days of Shamgar son of Anath, in the days of Jael, the highways were abandoned; travelers took to winding paths. Villagers in Israel would not fight; they held back until I, Deborah, arose, until I arose, a mother in Israel. (Judges 5:6–7)

I want you to be Deborahs to this generation. I want you to capture the high culture of this land, and I want you to do that by being very smart. Be very, very smart!

I am persuaded that Deborah was not merely a great warrior — she was that — but she was much more. She won military victories, true, but she won a cultural war too.

> You who ride on white donkeys, sitting on your saddle blankets, and you who walk along the road, consider the voice of the singers at the watering places. They recite the victories of the Lord, the victories of his villagers in Israel. (Judges 5:10)

Deborah's Song, Judges 5. Wood engraving, circa 1866 (PD).

It was at the "watering places" that culture was created and maintained. The "watering places" were places of sustenance for body, mind, and spirit. It was the place where one came for gossip, for water, and for spiritual insight. In other words, the "watering places" were the universities of Deborah's time. There, insight was shared and policy was debated. This was the epistemological center of Jewish life.

I want you to go the place God is calling you, perhaps the universities, and make some high culture!

The term "high culture" was introduced into English largely with the publication in 1869 of *Culture and Anarchy* by Matthew Arnold. Arnold defined high culture as "the disinterested endeavour after man's perfection" and argued that having culture meant to "know the best that has been said and thought in the world." Arnold saw high culture as a force for moral and political good. I do, too. Arnold saw culture as that which promotes and creates the way of life that a civilization enjoys — the art that it views; the movies it enjoys; the books it reads. I am not talking about fads and superfluous external minutiae. I am talking about the things that determine the way we think, govern, and worship. The term is contrasted with popular or mass culture, as well as with traditional cultures. I want you to create a new, high culture — a wholesome, godly high culture.

You need to be the best you can be for our God. I want you to put the high culture creation epicenters of education, government, entertainment, health, law, and religion in your sights, go to those spheres, and be the best you can be.

I am excited! "Now, God be thanked Who has matched us with His hour, and caught our youth, and wakened us from sleeping." — Rupert Brooke (who died in WWI in 1915)

Using Your Student Textbook

How this course has been developed

1. Chapters: This course has 34 chapters (representing 34 weeks of study).

2. Lessons: Each chapter has five lessons, taking approximately 20 to 30 minutes each. There will be a short reading followed by discussion questions. Some questions require a specific answer from the text, while others are more open-ended, leading students to think "outside the box."

3. Weekly exams: The Teacher Guide includes two optional exams for the chapter.

4. Student responsibility: Responsibility to complete this course is on the student. Students are to complete the readings every day, handing their responses in to a parent or teacher for evaluation. This course was designed for students to practice independent learning.

5. Grading: Students turn in assignments to a parent or teacher weekly.

Throughout this book are the following components:

1. First thoughts: Background on the historical period.

2. Discussion questions: Questions based generally on Bloom's Taxonomy.

3. Concepts: Terms, concepts, and theories to be learned that are bolded for emphasis. Most are listed on the first page of the chapter.

4. History makers: A person(s) who clearly changed the course of history.

5. Historical debate: An examination of historical theories surrounding a period or topic.

What the student will need:

1. Notepad: For writing assignments.

2. Pen/pencil: For answers and essays.

3. The Teacher Guide for weekly exams and/or to record daily assignments.

As the *Titanic* sank, lifeboat No. 15 was nearly lowered onto lifeboat No. 13 (depicted by Charles Dixon in *The Graphic*) (PD).

Chapter 1

Modernism: To Rule the Earth

First Thoughts

British writer Virginia Woolf's assertion that "on or about December 1910, human character changed"[1] is all so true. About that time, modernism emerged as the primary social and worldview in human history. Modernism aims at that radical transformation of human thought in relation to God, man, the world, life, and death, which was presaged by humanism and 17th-century philosophy (e.g., Immanuel Kant), and violently practiced in the French Revolution. French philosopher J.J. Rousseau was the first to use the term, but it would not blossom fully until the 20th century.

Chapter Learning Objectives

Chapter 1 examines the social, religious, and intellectual movement called modernism. We will define the movement and discuss its genesis. Then we will look at examples in art and in literature. Finally, we will examine a tragic example of the limitations of modernism: the sinking of the *Titantic*.

As a result of this chapter you should be able to:

1. Understand the essence of modernism

2. Explain why the transatlantic cable was the ultimate representation of modernism

3. Analyze modernism in literature

4. Analyze modernism in art

5. Discuss why the sinking of the *Titanic* was an example of the limits of modernism.

Concepts

Deism

Pragmatism

Epistemology

Avant-garde

Surrealism

Moral relativism

---

1. Dr. Bryony Randall, University of Glasgow, " 'On or about December 1910 human character changed' Centenary reflections and contemporary debates: modernism and beyond," December 10–12, 2010, University of Glasgow, UK, http://call-for-papers.sas.upenn.edu/node/34848.

Modernism

Epistemology is the study of knowledge.

If the worldview **deism** suggested that God was out to lunch, modernism, a cousin of naturalism, suggested that God was absent altogether.

Modernism, in its broadest definition, is a cultural tendency originally arising from wide-scale and far-reaching changes to Western society in the late 19th and early 20th centuries. The world, including America, had rapidly changed from an agrarian to an urban society in one short generation.

Modernism fervently believed in science and technology. It was an optimistic vision of the future. It was also a revolt against the conservative values of limitation and **pragmatism**. The trademark of modernism was its rejection of tradition. Modernism rejected the lingering certainty of Enlightenment **epistemology** and also rejected the existence of a compassionate, all-powerful Creator God in favor of human progress. The first casualty of this quixotic thinking was Judeo-Christian morality.

Modernism was universal in its rejection of everything conventional. Literature, art, architecture, religious faith, social organization, and daily life were all targets of this surprisingly arrogant movement. Perhaps no social movement has been as confident in its moral ambiguity as modernism was.

The poet Ezra Pound's 1934 injunction to "Make it new!"[2] was paradigmatic of the movement's approach toward the obsolete. And Pound is a good example of the paradoxes inherent in modernism. Pound embraced a new understanding of human liberty and free expression while also embracing nascent totalitarianism and anti-Semitism. Pound, like so many modernists, felt he could separate his ethics from his worldview. This delusion would have disastrous consequences. Adolf Eichmann had a similar view in Nazi Germany and designed and implemented the Holocaust.

The modernist movement, at the beginning of the 20th century, marked the first time that the term "**avant-garde**," which the movement was labeled until the word "modernism" prevailed, was used for the arts. Surrealism was the "the **avant-garde** of modernism."

A sculpture called "Sylvette" by Pablo Picasso, an intriguing painter and sculptor of the modern period (PD).

Discussion Question

Art historian Clement Greenberg states, "The essence of modernism lies, as I see it, in the use of characteristic methods of a discipline to criticize the discipline itself, not in order to subvert it but in order to entrench it more firmly in its area of competence. The philosopher Immanuel Kant used logic to establish the limits of logic, and while he withdrew much from its old jurisdiction, logic was left all the more secure in what there remained to it."[3] Modernism, in its attempt to attack everything traditional, created an autocratic liberalism. Explain.

2. www.stanford.edu/dept/DLCL/cgi.../make_it_new_stanford.docx.

3. Clement Greenberg, "Avant-Garde and Kitsch," http://www.sharecom.ca/greenberg/modernism.html.

The Transatlantic Cable

To modernism, science and technology assured the ultimate unity of mankind and the ultimate salvation of mankind. No technological feat of the late 19th and early 20th century evidenced this more than the transatlantic cable. Twenty-two years after the completion of the first telegraph line between Washington and Baltimore, in 1844, the first transatlantic cable was stretched to Europe. It only lasted a few weeks, but it was soon replaced.

American historian and poet Rossiter Johnson wrote the following poem to celebrate this momentous event.

The Victory
When Man, in his Maker's image, came
To be the lord of the new-made earth,
To conquer its forests, its beasts to tame,
To gather its treasures and know their worth,
All readily granted his power and place
Save the Ocean, the Mountain, and Time, and Space;
And these four sneered at his puny frame,
And made of his lordship a theme for mirth.

Whole ages passed while his flocks he tended,
And delved and dreamed, as the years went by
Till there came an age when his genius splendid
Had bridged the river and sailed the sky,
And raised the dome that defied the storm,
And mastered the beauties of color and form;
But his power was lost, his dominion ended,
Where Time, Space, Mountain, or Sea was nigh.

The Mountains rose in their grim inertness
Between the peoples, and made them strange,
Save as in moments of pride or pertness
They climbed the ridge of their native range,
And, looking down on the tribe below,
Saw nothing there but a deadly foe,
Heard only a war-cry, long and shrill,
In echoes leaping from hill to hill.

The Ocean rolled in its mighty splendor,
Washing the slowly wasting shore,
And the voices of nations, fierce or tender,
Lost themselves in its endless roar.
With frail ships launched on its treacherous surge,
And sad eyes fixed on its far blue verge,
Man's hold of life seemed brittle and slender,
And the Sea his master forevermore.

The new transatlantic cable was laid by the ship *Great Eastern* captained by Sir James Anderson. Her immense hull was fitted with three iron tanks for the reception of 2,300 nautical miles of cable (PD).

11

Communication aross the ocean opened up endless possibilities for the modern age (PD).

And Space and Time brought their huge dimensions
To separate man from his brother man,
And sowed between them a thousand dissensions,
That ripened in hatred and caste and clan.
So Sea and Mountain and Time and Space
Laughed again in his lordship's face,
And bade him blush for his weak inventions
And the narrow round his achievements ran.

But one morning he made him a slender wire,
As an artist's vision took life and form,
While he drew from heaven the strange, fierce fire
That reddens the edge of the midnight storm;
And he carried it over the Mountain's crest,
And dropped it into the Ocean's breast;
And Science proclaimed, from shore to shore,
That Time and Space ruled man no more.

Then the brotherhood lost on Shinar's plain
Came back to the peoples of earth again.
"Be one!" sighed the Mountain, and shrank away.
"Be one!" murmured Ocean, in dashes of spray.
"Be one!" said Space; "I forbid no more."
"Be one!" echoed Time, "till my years are o'er."
"We are one!" said the nations, as hand met hand
In a thrill electric from land to land.[4]

Discussion Question

Why did a transatlantic cable have such importance to modernists?

Lesson 3

Modernism and Literature

The ordered, stable, and inherently meaningful worldview of the 19th century could not, wrote T.S. Eliot, connect with "the immense panorama of futility and anarchy which is contemporary history."[5] Modernism created a profound break with Victorian stable morality. This break led to **moral relativism**, a worldview no more evident than in the literary arts.

---

4. http://history-world.org/Laying%20Of%20The%20Atlantic%20Cable.htm.
5. This comment is related to T.S. Eliot's criticisms of James Joyce's *Ulysses*, people.virginia.edu/~jdk3t/eliotulysses.htm.

In literature, the movement is associated with the works of (among others) T.S. Eliot, James Joyce, Virginia Woolf, W.B. Yeats, Ezra Pound, Gertrude Stein, Albert Camus, Franz Kafka, and Jean Paul Sartre. As literary critic John Barth explains, "In their attempt to throw off the aesthetic burden of the realist novel, these writers introduced a variety of literary tactics and devices: the radical disruption of linear flow of narrative; the frustration of conventional expectations concerning unity and coherence of plot and character and the cause and effect development thereof; the deployment of ironic and ambiguous juxtapositions to call into question the moral and philosophical meaning of literary action; the adoption of a tone of epistemological self-mockery aimed at naive pretensions of bourgeois rationality; the opposition of inward consciousness to rational, public, and objective discourse; and an inclination to subjective distortion to point up the evanescence of the social world of the 19th century bourgeoisie."[6]

Elizabeth Barrett Browning (PD).

Modern authors would generally abandon content in order to investigate new forms. Essentially, novelists and poets revolutionized literature as completely as artists revolutionized orthodox art forms. Nothing like this had ever happened to literature.

Modernism, however, in its headlong pursuit of the "unusual" or "avant-garde" views took adherents in to nihilism and worse. Many of the chief Modernists either flirted with **fascism** or openly supported it (e.g., Eliot, Yeats, Hamsun, and Pound). There was a sort of inherent elitism in literature that bothered many critics. For instance, most readers can't make heads or tails of James Joyce. This obscure elitism was a way to save literature, in their minds, from mediocrity.

It could be argued that the achievements of the modernists have had little impact on world literature in general. Arguably, very few people read these novelists and poets. The problem is, the people who mostly read them, and were influenced greatly by them, were university students who quite literally formed the next emerging elite in the world and more or less made social and political policies for the world for the 20th century.[7]

Discussion Question

Which passage has modernist tendencies and why?

> How do I love thee? Let me count the ways.
> I love thee to the depth and breadth and height
> My soul can reach, when feeling out of sight
> For the ends of my Being and ideal Grace.
> I love thee to the level of everyday's
> Most quiet need, by sun and candlelight.
> I love thee freely, as men strive for Right;
> I love thee purely, as they turn from Praise.
> I love thee with the passion put to use
> In my old griefs, and with my childhood's faith.
> I love thee with a love I seemed to lose
> With my lost saints—I love thee with the breath,

---

6. John Barth, *The Friday Book: Essays and Other Non-Fiction*, "The Literature of Replenishment" (London: The John Hopkins University. Press, 1984.), p. 68.

7. http://www2.iath.virginia.edu/elab/hfl0255.html.

Smiles, tears, of all my life! And, if God choose,
I shall but love thee better after death.
— Elizabeth Barrett Browning

That is the worst moment, when you feel you have lost
The desires for all that was most desirable,
Before you are contented with what you can desire;
Before you know what is left to be desired;
And you go on wishing that you could desire
What desire has left behind. But you cannot understand.
How could you understand what it is to feel old?
— From T.S. Eliot, "The Cocktail Party" (1949)

Lesson 4

Modern Art: Tamed by the Middle Class

Art For Art's Sake is a view that art should not be analyzed or judged for its composition, form, or worldview.

Perhaps the most radical departure from traditionalism occurred in the arts.

The roots of modern art lie in the 16th century, initiating what is called the Early Modern Period, which extends up to the 18th century. The intellectual underpinnings of modernism emerged during the Renaissance when, through the study of the art, poetry, philosophy, and science of ancient Greece and Rome, humanists revived the notion that the pleasure of man is the goal of all things, and promoted this notion through education and government. Art was soon to follow. It then, should also be created to please man, not God.

The Renaissance also gave rise to utopian visions of a perfect society, beginning with Sir Thomas More's *Utopia*, written in 1516, in which is described as a perfect island community. In retrospect, Renaissance humanism was an expression of that modernist confidence in the potential of humans to shape their future and the future of the world. Also present is the belief that humans can understand and control natural forces, and even grasp the nature of the universe.

By the early 20th century, modernism dominated the art scene in Europe. Early modern artists presented images that contained or reflected good, conservative moral values, served as examples of virtuous behavior, or offered inspiring Christian sentiment. In this sense they were traditional in their subject matter.

Jean-Paul Laurens's painting, *Last Moments of Maximilian, Emperor of Mexico* (1882; Hermitage, St. Petersburg), for example, shows the emperor before his execution by firing squad. This depiction is in contrast to Manet's broadly painted, "unfinished" picture, which depicts the event in unheroic terms. Laurens presents the emperor as a noble hero calmly consoling his distraught confessor while a faithful servant on his knees clings to his left hand. His Mexican executioners stand waiting at the door admiring the emperor's composure.

"Art for Art's Sake" was a rallying cry, a call for art's freedom from the demands that it possess meaning and purpose. From a progressive modernist's point of view, it was a further exercise of freedom.

In his book *The Gentle Art of Making Enemies*, published in 1890, modernist painter James Abbott McNeill Whistler, argued, "Art should be independent of all claptrap —should stand alone, and appeal to the artistic sense of eye and ear, without confounding this with emotions entirely foreign to it, as devotion, pity, love, patriotism, and the like. All these have no kind of concern with it."

Last Moments of Maximilian, Emperor of Mexico, a painting by Jean-Paul Laurens, shows him moments before his death by firing squad (PD).

However, "Art for Art's Sake" backfired. The same middle class to whom Whistler was selling his art quickly turned the call of "Art for Art's Sake" into a formal art. From now on, art was to be discussed in formal terms — color, line, shape, space, and composition. This effectively removed the question of meaning and purpose from consideration but also put limits on modern art to the extent that it would now be discussed and analyzed by professionals and amateurs alike.

This approach became pervasive to the extent that artists were as tyrannical about their modernist style as earlier traditionalists (e.g., Baroque artists) were about theirs!

Eventually there emerged the notion that modernist art is to be practiced entirely within a closed formalist sphere. The formalist critic Clement Greenberg, in an article first published in 1965 entitled "Modernist Painting," saw modernism as having achieved a self-referential autonomy. The work of art came to be seen as an isolated phenomenon governed by the internal laws of stylistic development. Art stood separate from the materialistic world and from the mundane affairs of ordinary people. And very quickly no one liked it and no one bought it.[8]

Discussion Question

The underlying assumptions at work in modern art represent, in microcosm, the problem with modernism in general. Modern art insists that the artist, by virtue of special dispensation, should express the finer things of humanity through a purely abstract and entirely personal understanding and mode of expression. This purely visual art made it an autonomous sphere of activity, completely separate from the everyday world of social and political life. Also, it was separate from history and the lessons learned from history. The self-determining nature of visual art meant that questions asked of it could be properly put, and answered, only in its own terms. Modernism's "history" was constructed through reference only to itself. Why did this spell trouble for modernism?

8. http://arthistoryresources.net/Modernism/artsake.html.

The Sinking of the *Titantic*

Secondary Source: *New York Times*, April 15, 1912

CAPE RACE, N.F., April 15. — The White Star liner Olympic reports by wireless this evening that the *Cunarder Carpathia* reached, at daybreak this morning, the position from which wireless calls for help were sent out last night by the *Titanic* after her collision with an iceberg. The *Carpathia* found only the lifeboats and the wreckage of what had been the biggest steamship afloat.

The *Titanic* had foundered at about 2:20 A.M., in latitude 41:46 north and longitude 50:14 west. This is about 30 minutes of latitude, or about 34 miles, due south of the position at which she struck the iceberg. All her boats are accounted for and about 655 souls have been saved of the crew and passengers, most of the latter presumably women and children. There were about 1,200 persons aboard the *Titanic*.

The Leyland liner *California* is remaining and searching the position of the disaster, while the *Carpathia* is returning to New York with the survivors.

It can be positively stated that up to 11 o'clock to-night nothing whatever had been received at or heard by the Marconi station here to the effect that the *Parisian*, *Virginian* or any other ships had picked up any survivors, other than those picked up by the *Carpathia*.

RMS *Titanic* departing Southampton on April 10, 1912 (PD).

The first news of the disaster to the *Titanic* was received by the Marconi wireless station here at 10:25 o'clock last night (as told in yesterday's *New York Times*.) The *Titanic* was first heard giving the distress signal "C. Q. D.," which was answered by a number of ships, including the *Carpathia*, the *Baltic* and the *Olympic*. The *Titanic* said she had struck an iceberg and was in immediate need of assistance, giving her position as latitude 41:46 north and longitude 50:14 west.

At 10:55 o'clock the *Titanic* reported she was sinking by the head, and at 11:25 o'clock the station here established communication with the Allan liner *Virginian*, from Halifax to Liverpool, and notified her of the *Titanic's* urgent need of assistance and gave her the *Titanic's* position.

The *Virginian* advised the Marconi station almost immediately that she was proceeding toward the scene of the disaster.

At 11:36 o'clock the *Titanic* informed the *Olympic* that they were putting the women off in boats and instructed the *Olympic* to have her boats read to transfer the passengers.

Photograph of the front page of *The World*, April 16, 1912 headlining the sinking of the *Titanic* (LOC).

The *Titanic*, during all this time, continued to give distress signals and to announce her position.

The wireless operator seemed absolutely cool and clear-headed, his sending throughout being steady and perfectly formed, and the judgment used by him was of the best.

The last signals heard from the *Titanic* were received at 12:27 A.M., when the *Virginian* reported having heard a few blurred signals which ended abruptly.[9]

Discussion Question

The sinking of the *Titanic* was a severe blow to modernism. The engineering feat of the 20th century, the unsinkable *Titanic*, was the poster boy of modernism. It combined the latest technological advances of the age and the exorbitant luxuries of the same age. On the *Titanic*, one traveled in luxury in technology unrivaled in human history. Yet, ironically, in a little over two hours it sank with the loss of thousands of lives. What lessons can we learn from such a tragedy?

---

9. http://www.nytimes.com/learning/general/onthisday/big/0415.html.

Acts of Honor and Dishonor

Honor is a theme for many involved in the *Titanic* disaster. The ship's captain, Edward Smith, who despite ignoring the dangers sent the ship full speed toward its doom, did not seek shelter on the lifeboats but instead spent his final moments aboard the vessel he commanded. Beyond his encouragement of the crew to "be British," Captain Smith's last moments are unknown, yet his decision to stay onboard is remembered as one of honor.

Even today, his decision is cited as a rebuke to those more recent examples of the MS *Costa Concordia* and the MTS *Oceanos*, both cruise liners in peril of sinking that had their captains, and even some of the crew, take to the lifeboats while abandoning passengers to uncertain fates.

History also records the honor of Captain Rostron of the RMS *Carpathia*, applauded as without hesitation, he bravely sent his ship rushing through the dangerous waters beyond what was thought its top speed into the darkness in a desperate race to rescue as many as possible despite the distance it had to overcome to reach *Titanic*.

History has also not forgotten what many rightly or wrongly felt was the dishonor of Captain Stanley Lord and the crew of the SS *Californian*. As the scope of the *Titanic* disaster became known, it was revealed that a ship nearby failed to come to its aid. Despite initial denials and claims of being too far away, investigations over the last 100 years have done little to change the perception of their dishonor, and the missed opportunity to save perhaps hundreds more of *Titanic's* passengers. As one author noted "the crime of Stanley Lord was not that he may have ignored the *Titanic's* rockets, but that he unquestionably ignored someone's cry for help."[1]

Edward J. Smith, captain of the *Titanic* who died at sea (PD).

Mrs. J.J. "Molly" Brown presenting trophy cup award to Capt. Arthur Henry Rostron, for his service in the rescue of the *Titanic* (LOC).

Collision of *Costa Concordia*, 2012 (CCA-SA3.0).

1   http://en.wikipedia.org/wiki/SS_Californian

Two eight-year-old newsboys in Philadelphia, PA, 1910 (LOC).

Chapter 2

Progressivism: Newsies and Muckrakers

First Thoughts

Progressivism began as a political movement that represented the interests of ordinary people in their roles as taxpayers, consumers, employees, citizens, and parents. In that sense, it was a populist movement. However, as progressivism unfurled its true colors in the early 20th century, its real agenda emerged. Progressives became the economic elites, and economic elites inevitably seek to promote their own interests. Progressives enjoyed great wealth and influence, literarily abandoned their populist agenda — by the people and for the people — and embraced a modernist tendency toward exclusive elitism. They became a formidable enemy of Judeo-Christian, godly traditionalists who sought to preserve the unique, viable traditions of Western culture.

Chapter Learning Objectives

Chapter 2 will examine the rise of progressivism. We will look at Herbert Croly's immensely popular and very important book *The Promise of American Life* and its impact on American history. We will examine how Hollywood has popularized this era and evaluate its veracity. Next, we will examine the impact of the very colorful president Teddy Roosevelt, and end with an examination of the first federal income tax.

As a result of this chapter you should be able to:

1. Evaluate government's penchant toward elitist paternalism

2. Summarize Herbert Croly's views

3. Watch the *Newsies* movie and compare it to what actually happened in the 1899 labor strike

4. Understand how Roosevelt expanded the power of the presidency and why such a president was wildly popular in the progressive era

5. Predict which problems would result from an income tax over the next few decades

CONCEPTS

Deism

Pragmatism

Epistemology

Avant-garde

Surrealism

Moral relativism

A New Age

In the wake of modernism, world leaders witnessed, and in some cases, encouraged, a social, political, and economic revolution. These practitioners were called **Progressives**. Progressives blatantly challenged the status quo in every aspect of life.

Margaret Sanger in 1922 (LOC).

Of all the changes that took place in women's lives during the 20th century, the most significant was women's increasing ability to control fertility. In 1916, the controversial and racist **Margaret Sanger** opened the country's first birth control clinic in Brooklyn, New York. Police shut it down ten days later. Margaret Sanger coined the phrase "birth control" and eventually convinced the courts that the government had every right, indeed, was obligated to disseminate birth control information and devices. As the founder of Planned Parenthood, she aided in the development of the birth control pill, which appeared in 1960, and eventually championed the abortion cause. Sanger is, without a doubt, one of the most malicious characters in all of world history.

Meanwhile, racial relations had stalled. No major progress was occurring in civil rights. The publication of W.E.B. DuBois' *The Souls of Black Folk*[1] heralded a new, more confrontational approach to civil rights. "The problem of the 20th century," DuBois' book begins, "is the problem of the color line." In his book, DuBois, the first African American to receive a Ph.D. from Harvard, condemns Booker T. Washington's philosophy of accommodation and his idea that African Americans should confine their ambitions to manual labor. DuBois was the first African American activist, whose views would encourage later reformers like Malcolm X to embrace **racial separatism vs. racial accommodation**.

For the first time, too, conservation became part of public policy. Until the modern era, most people thought that American resources were inexhaustible. During Roosevelt's presidency, 148 million acres were set aside as national forest lands and more than 80 million acres of mineral lands were withdrawn from public sale.

In 1902, President Theodore Roosevelt also became the first president to intervene on the side of workers in a labor dispute. He threatened to use the army to run the coal mines unless mine owners agreed to arbitrate the strike. **"One Big Union for All"** was the goal of the radical labor leaders and Socialists who met in Chicago in 1905. This group also formed the International Workers of the World (IWW). Rejecting the approach of the American Federation of Labor, which only admitted skilled craft workers to its ranks, the IWW opened its membership to any wage earner regardless of occupation, race, creed, or sex.

Religious ideas and institutions have always been among the wellsprings of the American reform impulse. Progressive reformers were heavily influenced by the body of religious ideas known as the **Social Gospel**, the philosophy that the churches should be actively engaged in social reform. Dwight L. Moody and William Booth (Salvation Army) had been doing this for many years. But new liberal theologians, encouraged by German theologians who challenged the inspiration of Scripture, held that Christian

1   W.E.B. Du Bois, *The Souls of Black Folk* (Chicago, IL: A.C. McClurg & Co., 1903).

principles needed to be applied to social problems and that efforts needed to be made to bring the social order into conformity with Christian values. Again, modernism, and progressivism in particular, had an irritating habit of claiming that what it embraced and advocated was unique and unprecedented. Most of the time (as in the case of social welfare) this was simply not true.

Newspaper circulation, in particular, expanded significantly during this era. Modern, cheap papermaking made newspapers affordable to all Americans, and was a powerful social instrument. A new fad would be pictured in one syndicated newspaper in New York City and it would be copied by Americans in Toledo, Dallas, and Seattle within the next week. Newspapers were later replaced by television as the major culture creators of the 20th century, but that would not occur until 50 years later.

Muckraking reporters, exploiting mass circulation journalism, attacked malfeasance in American politics and business. They embraced lost, obscure causes, championed aberrant positions, and created conflict and confusion, all in order to increase circulation. President Theodore Roosevelt gave them the name "muckrakers" after a character in the book *Pilgrim's Progress*, "the Man with the Muckrake," who was more preoccupied with filth than with heaven above.

They did some good. Popular magazines such as *McClure's, Cosmopolitan,* and *Collier's* published articles exposing the evils of American society. Upton Sinclair's *The Jungle* exposed unsanitary conditions in the meat-packing industry.

But a dangerous precedent was set: the media, immune to the electorate, or any other controls, was committed to sensationalism over truth, if it increased circulation. For the first time, the media felt no obligation to embrace any standard but its own (a modernist tendency). Furthermore, it accepted no policy that would force it to show any objectivity. The media abandoned all facade of altruism and fairness, and became a parochial, chauvinistic profit-making machine, answerable to no one.[2]

Advertisement for Margaret Sanger's book, *Woman and the New Race* appearing in *Science & Invention*, January 1922 (PD).

Discussion Question

Despite the fact that a majority of Americans, who were very active in their pro-life, anti-abortion Protestant and Roman Catholic churches, opposed Sanger's intervention in the private affairs of citizens, the government allowed for Sanger's agenda anyway. Why?

2. http://www.digitalhistory.uh.edu/era.cfm?eraid=11&smtid=1.

The Promise of American Life
by Herbert Croly

Herbert Croly was a political theorist and journalist who founded the magazine *The New Republic*.

If any one book summarized progressive beliefs, it was Herbert Croly's *The Promise of American Life* (1909). Croly (1869–1930) was progressivism's preeminent philosopher. Published in 1909, his book argued that Americans had to overcome their Jeffersonian heritage, with its emphasis on minimal government, decentralized authority, and the sanctity of individual freedom, in order to deal with the unprecedented problems of an urban and industrial age. Industrialism, he believed, had reduced most workers to a kind of "wage slavery," and only a strong central government could preserve democracy and promote social progress:

Chapter 1

The average American is nothing if not patriotic. "The Americans are filled," says Mr. Emil Reich in his "Success among the Nations," "with such an implicit and absolute confidence in their Union and in their future success that any remark other than laudatory is inacceptable to the majority of them. We have had many opportunities of hearing public speakers in America cast doubts upon the very existence of God and of Providence, question the historic nature or veracity of the whole fabric of Christianity; but never has it been our fortune to catch the slightest whisper of doubt, the slightest want of faith, in the chief God of America — unlimited belief in the future of America." Mr. Reich's method of emphasis may not be very happy, but the substance of what he says is true. The faith of Americans in their own country is religious, if not in its intensity, at any rate in its almost absolute and universal authority. It pervades the air we breathe. As children we hear it asserted or implied in the conversation of our elders. Every new stage of our educational training provides some additional testimony on its behalf. Newspapers and novelists, orators and playwrights, even if they are little else, are at least loyal preachers of the Truth. The skeptic is not controverted; he is overlooked. It constitutes the kind of faith which is the implication, rather than the object, of thought, and consciously or unconsciously it enters largely into our personal lives as a formative influence. We may distrust and dislike much that is done in the name of our country by our fellow-countrymen; but our country itself, its democratic system, and its prosperous future are above suspicion.

Of course, Americans have no monopoly of patriotic enthusiasm and good faith. Englishmen return thanks to Providence for not being born anything but an Englishman, in churches and ale-houses as well as in comic operas. The Frenchman cherishes and proclaims the idea that France is the most civilized modern country and satisfies best the needs of a man of high social intelligence. The Russian, whose political and social estate does not seem enviable to his foreign contemporaries, secretes a vision of a mystically glorified Russia, which condemns to comparative insipidity the figures of the "Pax Britannica" and of "La Belle France" enlightening the world. Every nation, in proportion as its nationality is thoroughly alive, must be leavened by the ferment of some such faith. But there are significant differences between the faith of, say, an Englishman in the British Empire and that of an American in the Land of Democracy. The contents of an Englishman's national idea tends to be more exclusive. His patriotism is anchored to the historical achievements of Great Britain and restricted thereby. As a good patriot he is bound to be more preoccupied with the inherited fabric of national institutions and traditions than he is with the ideal and more than national possibilities of the future. This very loyalty to the national fabric does, indeed, imply an important ideal content; but the national idealism of an Englishman, a German, or even a Frenchman, is heavily

The election of 1912 was one of controversy. Having lost the Republican nomination because of a party split between conservatives and progressives, former President Theodore Roosevelt choose to become part of a third party, the Progressive Party, which was then re-named the Bull Moose party in hopes of being re-elected. Herbert Croly is credited for having influenced both this new party and Roosevelt himself (LOC).

mortgaged to his own national history and cannot honestly escape the debt. The good patriot is obliged to offer faithful allegiance to a network of somewhat arbitrary institutions, social forms, and intellectual habits — on the ground that his country is exposed to more serious dangers from premature emancipation than it is from stubborn conservatism. France is the only European country which has sought to make headway towards a better future by means of a revolutionary break with its past; and the results of the French experiment have served for other European countries more as a warning than as an example.

The higher American patriotism, on the other hand, combines loyalty to historical tradition and precedent with the imaginative projection of an ideal national Promise. The Land of Democracy has always appealed to its more enthusiastic children chiefly as a land of wonderful and more than national possibilities. "Neither race nor tradition," says Professor Hugo Münsterberg in his volume on "The Americans," "nor the actual past, binds the American to his countrymen, but rather the future which together they are building." This vision of a better future is not, perhaps, as unclouded for the present generation of Americans as it was for certain former generations; but in spite of a more friendly acquaintance with all sorts of obstacles and pitfalls, our country is still figured in the imagination of its citizens as the Land of Promise. They still believe that somehow and sometime something better will happen to good Americans than has happened to men in any other country; and this belief, vague, innocent, and uninformed though it be, is the expression of an essential constituent in our national ideal. The past should mean less to a European than it does to an American, and the future should mean more. To be sure, American life cannot with impunity be wrenched violently from its moorings any more than the life of a European country can; but our American past, compared to that of any European country, has a character all its own. Its peculiarity consists, not merely in its brevity, but in the fact that from the beginning it has been informed by an idea. From the beginning Americans have been anticipating and projecting a better future. From the beginning the Land of Democracy has been figured as the Land of Promise. Thus the American's loyalty to the national tradition rather affirms than denies the imaginative projection of a better future. An America which was not the Land of Promise, which was not informed by a prophetic outlook and a more or less constructive ideal, would not be the America bequeathed to us by our forefathers. In cherishing the Promise of a better national future the American is fulfilling rather than imperiling the substance of the national tradition.

When, however, Americans talk of their country as the Land of Promise, a question may well be raised as to precisely what they mean. They mean, of course, in general, that the future will have something better in store for them individually and collectively than has the past or the present; but a very superficial analysis of this meaning discloses certain ambiguities. What are the particular benefits which this better future will give to Americans either individually or as a nation? And how is this Promise to be fulfilled? Will it fulfill itself, or does it imply certain responsibilities? If so, what responsibilities? When we speak of a young man's career as promising, we mean that his abilities and opportunities are such that he is likely to become rich or famous or powerful; and this judgment does not of course imply, so far as we are concerned, any responsibility. It is merely a prophecy based upon past performances and proved qualities. But the career, which from the standpoint of an outsider is merely an anticipation, becomes for the young man himself a serious task. For him, at all events, the better future will not merely happen. He will have to do something to deserve it. It may be wrecked by unforeseen obstacles, by unsuspected infirmities, or by some critical error of judgment. So it is with the Promise of American life. From the point of view of an immigrant this Promise may consist of the anticipation of a better future, which he can share merely by taking up his residence on American soil; but once he has become an American, the Promise can no longer remain merely an anticipation. It becomes in that case a responsibility, which requires for its fulfillment a certain kind of behavior on the part of himself and his fellow-Americans. And when we attempt to define the Promise of American life, we are obliged, also, to describe the kind of behavior which the fulfillment of the Promise demands.

The distinction between the two aspects of America as a Land of Promise made in the preceding paragraph is sufficiently obvious, but it is usually slurred by the average good American patriot. The better future, which is promised for himself, his children, and for other Americans, is chiefly a matter of confident anticipation. He looks upon it very much as a friendly outsider might look on some promising individual career. The better future is understood by him as something which fulfills itself. He calls his country, not only the Land of Promise, but the Land of Destiny. It is fairly launched on a brilliant and successful career, the continued prosperity of which is prophesied by the very momentum of its advance. As Mr. H.G. Wells says in "The Future in America," "When one talks to an American of his national purpose, he seems a little at a loss; if one speaks of his national destiny, he responds with alacrity." The great majority of Americans would expect a book written about "The Promise of American Life" to contain chiefly a fanciful description of the glorious American future — a sort of Utopia up-to-date, situated in the land of Good-Enough, and flying the Stars and Stripes. They might admit in words that the achievement of this glorious future implied certain responsibilities, but they would not regard the admission either as startling or novel. Such responsibilities were met by our predecessors; they will be met by our followers. Inasmuch as it is the honorable American past which prophesies on behalf of the better American future, our national responsibility consists fundamentally in remaining true to traditional ways of behavior, standards, and ideals. What we Americans have to do in order to fulfill our national Promise is to keep up the good work — to continue resolutely and cheerfully along the appointed path.

The reader who expects this book to contain a collection of patriotic prophecies will be disappointed. I am not a prophet in any sense of the word, and I entertain an active and intense dislike of the foregoing mixture of optimism, fatalism, and conservatism. To conceive the better American future as a consummation which will take care of itself, — as the necessary result of our customary conditions, institutions, and ideas — persistence in such a conception is admirably designed to deprive American life of any promise at all. The better future which Americans propose to build is nothing if not an idea which must in certain essential respects emancipate them from their past. American history contains much matter for pride and congratulation, and much matter for regret and humiliation. On the whole, it is a past of which the loyal American has no reason to feel ashamed, chiefly because it has throughout been made better than it was by the vision of a better future; and the American of to-day and to-morrow must remain true to that traditional vision. He must be prepared to sacrifice to that traditional vision even the traditional American ways of realizing it. Such a sacrifice is, I believe, coming to be demanded; and unless it is made, American life will gradually cease to have any specific Promise.

The only fruitful promise of which the life of any individual or any nation can be possessed, is a promise determined by an ideal. Such a promise is to be fulfilled, not by sanguine anticipations, not by a conservative imitation of past achievements, but by laborious, single-minded, clear-sighted, and fearless work. If the promising career of any individual is not determined by a specific and worthy purpose, it rapidly drifts into a mere pursuit of success; and even if such a pursuit is successful, whatever promise it may have had, is buried in the grave of its triumph. So it is with a nation. If its promise is anything more than a vision of power and success, that addition must derive its value from a purpose; because in the moral world the future exists only as a workshop in which a purpose is to be realized. Each of the several leading European nations is possessed of a specific purpose determined for the most part by the pressure of historical circumstances; but the American nation is committed to a purpose that is not merely of historical manufacture. It is committed to the realization of the democratic ideal; and if its Promise is to be fulfilled, it must be prepared to follow whithersoever that ideal may lead.

No doubt Americans have in some measure always conceived their national future as an ideal to be fulfilled. Their anticipations have been uplifting as well as confident and vainglorious. They have been prophesying not merely a safe and triumphant, but also a better, future. The ideal demand for some sort of individual and social amelioration has always accompanied even their vainest flights of patriotic prophecy. They may never have sufficiently realized that this better future, just in so far as it is better, will have to be planned and constructed rather than fulfilled of its own momentum; but at any rate, in seeking to disentangle and emphasize the ideal implications of the American national Promise, I am not wholly false to the accepted American tradition. Even if Americans have neglected these ideal implications, even if they have conceived the better future as containing chiefly a larger portion of familiar benefits, the ideal demand, nevertheless, has always been palpably present; and if it can be established as the dominant aspect of the American tradition, that tradition may be transformed, but it will not be violated.

The four-way race - the election of 1912 highlights a period of change among American society, encompassing philosophical ideals, governmental realities, and personal values. The race included Democrat Woodrow Wilson who would win, Progressive Theodore Roosevelt, Republican William Taft, and Socialist Eugene Debs (LOC).

Furthermore, much as we may dislike the American disposition to take the fulfillment of our national Promise for granted, the fact that such a disposition exists in its present volume and vigor demands respectful consideration. It has its roots in the salient conditions of American life, and in the actual experience of the American people. The national Promise, as it is popularly understood, has in a way been fulfilling itself. If the underlying conditions were to remain much as they have been, the prevalent mixture of optimism, fatalism, and conservatism might retain a formidable measure of justification; and the changes which are taking place in the underlying conditions and in the scope of American national experience afford the most reasonable expectation that this state of mind will undergo a radical alteration. It is new conditions which are forcing Americans to choose between the conception of their national Promise as a process and an ideal. Before, however, the nature of these novel conditions and their significance can be considered, we must examine with more care the relation between the earlier American economic and social conditions and the ideas and institutions associated with them. Only by a better understanding of the popular tradition, only by an analysis of its merits and its difficulties, can we reach a more consistent and edifying conception of the Promise of American life.[3]

Discussion Question

Summarize Herbert Croly's views.

Lesson 3

Newsies

Arguably, my second favorite Disney film (after *Sword in the Stone*) is *Newsies*. It is a 1992 Disney musical film starring Christian Bale, David Moscow, and Bill Pullman. Robert Duvall and Ann-Margret also appeared in supporting roles. Besides having a great story, and essentially historically correct story, it contains 12 songs and multiple dance sequences. Musical highlights include "Carrying the Banner," "Santa Fe," "Seize the Day," "The World Will Know," and "King of New York."

Newsies is based on the true story of the Newsboys Strike of 1899 in New York City. Thousands of homeless and orphaned children who were selling newspapers to make money to buy food lived in newsboys' lodging houses, including 17-year-old Manhattan newsboy Jack "Cowboy" Kelly (Christian Bale), who is a regular newsboy selling newspapers for Joseph Pulitzer (Robert Duvall) and his paper, the *New York World*.

In 1866, Charles Loring Brace, a Christian social reformer, described the condition of homeless newsboys in New York City: "I remember one cold night seeing some 10 or a

---

3. http://www.gutenberg.org/files/14422/14422-h/14422-h.htm#CHAPTER_I.

Newsboys first appeared on city streets in the mid-19th century with the rise of mass circulation newspapers. They were often extremely poor, homeless children who typically worked well into the night and slept on the street. There were lodging houses for them, but these were few and far between.

dozen of the little homeless creatures piled together to keep each other warm beneath the stairway of *The [New York] Sun* office. There used to be a mass of them also at *The Atlas* office, sleeping in the lobbies, until the printers drove them away by pouring water on them. One winter, an old burnt-out safe lay all the season in Wall Street, which was used as a bedroom by two boys who managed to crawl into the hole that had been burned."[4]

In 1872, James B. McCabe Jr., a member of the Salvation Army, wrote: "There are 10,000 children living on the streets of New York. . . . The newsboys constitute an important division of this army of homeless children. You see them everywhere. . . . They rend the air and deafen you with their shrill cries. They surround you on the sidewalk and almost force you to buy their papers. They are ragged and dirty. Some have no coats, no shoes and no hat."[5]

As in the movie, in 1899, several thousand newsboys — who made about 30 cents a day — called a strike, refusing to handle the newspapers of William Randolph Hearst and Joseph Pulitzer. Competing papers took advantage of the competing *New York World* woes and covered the strike extensively. *The New York Tribune* quoted Kid Blink's speech to 2,000 strikers: "Friens and feller workers. Dis is a time which tries de hearts of men. Dis is de time when we'se got to stick together like glue. . . . We know wot we wants and we'll git it even if we is blind.[6]

While the strike did not bring immediate results, conditions began to improve as urban child-welfare practices took root, and publishers began competing for newsies by giving them prizes and trips.

Discussion Question

Watch the *Newsies* movie and compare it to what actually happened in the 1899 labor strike.

4. http://www.digitalhistory.uh.edu/disp_textbook.cfm?smtID=2&psid=3136.
5. Ibid.
6. Ibid.

Theodore Roosevelt

The **Rough Riders** were Roosevelt's Spanish American troops who took San Juan Hill.

Theodore Roosevelt, one of the most colorful presidents in American history, was essentially able to speak some sanity into the progressive/modernist mind.

Born in New York City in 1858, Roosevelt was, in his own words, "nervous and timid" as a youth. He was also a little wimpish. However, he was anything but "timid" as an adult. By then, he was rough and ready. In 1912, for instance, he was shot in the chest by an assassin, but delivered an hour-long speech before having the bullet removed.

At the age of 23, Roosevelt began his political career in the New York state legislature. Then, in 1884, his wife and his mother died on the same day. He was crushed. So he retreated to a 25,000-acre ranch in North Dakota's Badlands and became a cowboy. He wore spurs and carried a pearl-handled revolver from Tiffany, the New York jewelers. This image — the cowboy and the expensive, stylish revolver, is a fitting metaphor for what Roosevelt became.

He returned to politics and became assistant secretary of the Navy and governor of New York before his election as vice president in 1900. Lacking any military experience whatsoever, and looking very much the part, Roosevelt wore an outlandish uniform custom-tailored by Brooks Brothers during the **Spanish American War**. Roosevelt served as second-in-command of the **Rough Riders**, a volunteer cavalry unit that fought in Cuba. He led the epic charge up San Juan Hill that brought him fame, glory, and the vice-presidency.

Col. Theodore Roosevelt stands triumphant on San Juan Hill, Cuba, after his "Rough Riders" captured this hill and its sister Kettle Hill during the Spanish American War (LOC).

This photo shows a friendly meeting in a military context with Theodore Roosevelt (center) with his son Kermit (left) and the German Emperor Kaiser Wilhelm II near the town of Döberitz. Roosevelt had visited European capitals like Rome and Vienna before recieving his honorary doctorate in Berlin on May 12, 1910 (PD).

With William McKinley's assassination, he became, at the age of 42, the youngest president in American history.

Roosevelt was a Republican but had definite progressive tendencies. As president, he made anti-trust, conservation of natural resources, and consumer protection national priorities. He forced coal operators to recognize the United Mine Workers.

Historian Steve Mintz writes, "Roosevelt's life was filled with contradictions. He was a member of one of the country's 20 richest families, yet he denounced business magnates as 'malefactors of great wealth.' The first president born in a big city, he was a hunter as a well as a conservationist. He was a bellicose man who boxed in the White House. He was also the first American to receive the Nobel Peace Prize for brokering peace between Russia and Japan."[7]

Roosevelt represented the emerging optimism of an age. He was brilliant and energetic, a potent combination. He was "a steam engine in trousers" who somehow found time to write three dozen books on topics ranging from history to hunting, and in languages ranging from Italian and Portuguese to Greek and Latin. He was the first celebrity president known simply by his initials.

Roosevelt greatly expanded the powers of the presidency. He was the first president who fully grasped the power of the media. Thus he called the White House a "bully pulpit" from which he could preach his ideas about the need for an assertive government, the inevitability of bigness in business, and an active American presence in foreign policy. He also made a dramatic public state-ment about race when he invited Booker T. Washington to dine at the White House. No African American had been invited into the White House except as a servant.

Discussion Question

How did Roosevelt expand the power of the presidency, and why was such a president wildly popular in the progressive era?

Theodore Roosevelt speaking from the balcony of the Hotel Allen, Allentown, Pennsylvania, 1914 (PD).

U.S. President Theodore Roosevelt (left) and nature preservationist John Muir, founder of the Sierra Club, on Glacier Point in Yosemite National Park, 1906 (LOC).

---

7. http://www.digitalhistory.uh.edu/disp_textbook.cfm?smtID=2&psid=3140.

The Income Tax

Federal Income Tax was the first federal tax based on income.

Period: 1900s

The **federal income tax** was introduced in 1913. It has now become the main source of revenue for the federal government.

From 1866 to 1893, the federal government ran surpluses, thanks to revenues from tariffs and excise taxes. Northern Republicans defended protective tariffs as a positive good. They claimed that a high tariff encouraged industrialization and urbanization, generated high wages and profits, and created a rich home market for farmers and manufacturers. Beginning in 1887, the Democrats, led by Grover Cleveland, argued that the tariff was a tax on consumers for the benefit of rich industrialists. They claimed that the tariff raised prices, encouraged foreign countries to retaliate against American farm exports, and stimulated the growth of economic trusts.

In 1894, the government ran the first deficit since the Civil War and enacted a short-lived income tax, which was declared unconstitutional in 1895. The Supreme Court ruled that it violated a constitutional provision that taxes had to be apportioned among the states.

In April 1909, Southern and Western congressmen sponsored another income tax bill, hopeful that the Supreme Court with a new membership might approve it. The Senate vote was 77 to 0 votes; the House vote was 318 to 14 votes.

The problem of the Supreme Court still remained. It was apparently unconstitutional to have an income tax. But during the 1912 election, Democrat Woodrow Wilson and third-party candidate Theodore Roosevelt supported an income tax, a constitutional amendment that was passed. The income tax was here to stay.

The new federal income tax was modest and affected only about .5 percent of the population. It taxed personal income at 1 percent and exempted married couples earning less than $4,001. A graduated surtax, beginning on incomes of $20,000, rose to 6 percent on incomes of more than $500,000. As late as 1939, only 3.9 million Americans had to file taxes. But just six years later, 42.6 million Americans filed. That number would increase considerably in the next 75 years, but a majority of Americans never paid a federal income tax.

Proposed amendment to the Constitution stating that Congress "shall have power to lay and collect taxes" (PD).

Discussion Question

Predict what problems would result from an income tax over the next few decades.

The HMS *Audacious*, a dreadnought, sinks after hitting a mine, October 1914 (CCA-SA3.0).

Chapter 3

1900–1914: On the Brink

First Thoughts

"What is this war? It is mud, trenches, blood, rats, lice, bombs, pain, barbed wire, decaying flesh, gas, death, rain, cats, tears, bullets, fear and a loss of faith in all that we once believed in."[1] This quote from contemporary artist Otto Dix captures the disillusionment and disaster that World War I was. It was more than a killing field. It was a place where mankind lost all hope in God and in themselves. It was a macabre turning point in world history and had significant consequences for all of history that followed it. How did the entire world find itself in this conflagration that was, without a doubt, an unmitigated world disaster? It decided nothing; it accomplished nothing; it solved nothing; it pleased no one.

Chapter Learning Objectives

Chapter 3 looks more closely at the causes of the catastrophe that was World War I. We see how the modernist vision failed miserably in the face of human selfishness. We look at these myths and determine to what degree they precipitated World War I. Of course, we discover, no one could really predict what World War I became. We see that militarism and ineffectual national governments were two major causes, with culpability lying mostly in German hands.

As a result of this chapter you should be able to:

1. Explain why it was so ironic that World War I occurred at all

2. Know why Germany was the primary cause of World War I

3. Understand why World War I was unlike any other previous European war

4. Analyze European governments and explain why they were so ineffectual in 1914

5. Evaluate whether or not our nation could handle the same crisis as the one that occurred in 1914

CONCEPTS

Kulturkampf

Dreadnoughts

---

1. http://history-world.org/world_war_one.htm.

The Loss of Faith in All That We Once Believed In

The badly shelled main road to Bapaume through Pozieres, showing a communication trench and broken trees, 1916 (PD).

Most of the nations of Europe, as well as the United States, the Middle East, and other regions, were involved in World War I. The four-year war pitted the Central Powers — mainly Germany, Austria-Hungary, and Turkey — against the Allies — mainly France, Great Britain, Russia, Italy, Japan, and from 1917, the United States. It ended with the defeat of the Central Powers. The war was nearly unprecedented in the slaughter, carnage, and destruction it caused. It was unprecedented in the barbaric practices it unleashed.

World War I was one of the great watersheds of 20th-century geopolitical history. It led to the fall of four great dynasties (in Germany, Russia, Austria-Hungary, and Turkey), resulted in the Communist Revolution in Russia, and, in its destabilization of European society, laid the groundwork for World War II.

As in the later Korean War, Vietnam War, and Gulf War, by the time World War I ended, no one knew why it had been fought. Nor could what caused it really be understood. One thing seems certain. As historian Robert Guisep explains, "The nationalism that prevailed at the time combined with the incompetent ruler of Germany, Kaiser Wilhelm and a poorly conceived system of alliances, lay at the heart of it all."[2]

Certainly Germany was at the heart of the cause, but was not the only cause. European national pride, when combined with the alliance system in place in 1914, made war inevitable.

The Austrian Empire was well on its way to becoming a second-rate power, yet its emperor refused to admit this and insisted on maintaining its dominance over at least the lowly Balkans. Thus, when the archduke of Austria was assassinated, Austria used it as an excuse to declare war on the Serbs. Serbia was aligned with Russia, who declared war on Austria. Germany was allied with Austria, so that meant war between Germany and Russia. Russia had a treaty with France, so war with Russia meant war with France. War with France, who had a treaty with England, meant war with England. The world, in macabre irony, was caught in its own trap, and went to war.

The German kaiser seemed not to understand the system of alliances, which had been created before his taking the throne, and he removed from power the only man in Germany who did, Otto Van Bismarck. Bismarck once said that it would be some d--n fool thing in the Balkans to throw Europe into war, and it did.

This was a war which had no purpose, was fought without good reason, and by the time it was over, ten million would be dead, four empires destroyed and the stage set for World War II. It was a tragic war fought that produced a futile peace.[3]

---

2. http://history-world.org/world_war_one.htm.
3. Ibid.

Discussion Question

Why was it so ironic that World War I occurred at all?

The Spirit of the Modern World

Ironically, the spirit of the modern world, the very hopefulness and optimism that so commended modernity, ultimately caused its violent demise. It was as if mankind built its Tower of Babel and invited the gods to destroy it.

Modris Eksteins, in his book *The Rites of Spring: The Great War and the Birth of the Modern Age* argues that the First World War was the pivotal moment in modern history and consciousness. Eksteins' argument is that in our modern world, life and art have blended together, and aesthetics have become more important than ever. In other words, modernists are not sure what is real and what isn't. He then points to Germany before the Great War as the nation in which these ideals were the most pronounced, the modernist nation *par excellence*, which served as a model for our world. For Eksteins, the First World War was a conflict between the old established world order (based on Enlightenment ideals of reason, logic, and tradition, and represented primarily by Great Britain and, to some extent, by France) and the new ideas of the modern world struggling for liberation and emancipation from the old order, as represented by Germany. While Germany lost the war, many of the ideas and attitudes that characterized German society eventually won out and are characteristic of the modern consciousness. In other words, Germany lost the shooting war but won the culture war.[4]

A posed group of dancers in the original production of Igor Stravinsky's ballet *The Rite of Spring*, showing costumes and backdrop by Nicholas Roerich, 1913 (PD).

New York Times journalist Christopher Lehmann-Haupt (March 13, 1989) points out that Eksteins uses the 1913 Russian ballet *The Rites of Spring* as a metaphor for the war. He then proceeds to examine the climate of opinion immediately preceding the war, particularly in Germany. His analysis of the First World War focuses almost exclusively on the attitudes and ideas expressed by common people in the lead-up to the war, as well as throughout the duration of the brutal trench warfare period. Following the war, he focuses on two cultural phenomena that shed insight on the way the war had changed the world: the reception of Lindbergh as a hero after his transatlantic flight and the success of Erich Maria Remarque's war book *All Quiet on the Western Front*.

---

4. Modris Eksteins, *Rites of Spring, The Great War and the Birth of the Modern Age* (Toronto: Key Porter Books, 1989), discussed in http://www.allempires.com/article/index.php?q=The_Rites_of_Spring.

Finally, he wraps it all up with an analysis of how the ideals and attitudes represented by Germany created the ideologies of fascism and national socialism (nazism).[5]

Ekstein hits the nail on the head. He points out the unreasonable expectations both sides had about the duration of the war, as well as the enthusiasm that greeted the news of the impending conflict. The beginning months of the war did not mark an abrupt end to the prevalent romantic view of the world, as many believe. The Christmas truce of 1914 is indicative of the attitudes both sides still held: the Germans celebrating Christmas in the trenches with lights (despite the potential danger that represented), the ad-hoc truce between the two sides, and the tendency of the British to regard the war as sport. It was only after the war raged on in the trenches that attitudes began to change. But the change came, and it spelled the end of modernism as it once existed. After World War I, modernism took a decidedly nasty, cynical turn that led directly to the counterculture rebellion of the 1960s.

The truth is, it was this nasty, post-World War I modernism that caused so much misery for Christianity. Witness the Scopes Trial and the general rejection of everything Christian. In effect, World War I killed the baby in the bath water, but no one could see it. And while the rhetoric of modernism espoused guarded optimism, there in fact emerged a profound, malevolent, genuine hopelessness that pervades American society even today.

Discussion Question

A critic argues, "Ours is a society which no longer firmly believes in anything as certain; it is a society which has lost its confidence in itself as the most advanced civilization in the world. Ours is the age of uncertainty in which all theories and sets of values hold a kernel of truth, but none of them is absolute. The emancipation that Eksteins focuses on is not solely the result of the German spirit that demanded emancipation, but rather the result of our society losing confidence in itself and being forced to accept new (or old) ideas, lifestyles, and values as being equally valid with those of the Enlightenment, which constituted the bedrock of society throughout the 19th century. Our obsession with death, movement (or change), and newness can as well be seen as a result of the modern man's uncertainty and desire to find some answers in an unclear world. Myths are more important than ever because they compensate for the mystique and meaning which has been drained out of the modern people's lives, who longer know what to believe in."[6] What are myths, and what myths motivate us today?

5. Christopher Lehmann-Haupt, "Books of The Times; Modernism: Rites of Spring, Rites of Destruction," March 13, 1989, http://www.nytimes.com/1989/03/13/books/books-of-the-times-modernism-rites-of-spring-rites-of-destruction.html.

6. http://www.allempires.com/article/index.php?q=The_Rites_of_Spring.

The German Empire

With some justification, many historians blame Germany for World War I.

By 1914, the German Empire, as it was called, had existed since the end of the Franco-German War of 1875. Germany won the war handily and now embarked on a rather successful overseas colonial expansion spree.

In a way, Germany was a constitutional monarchy like England. However, democracy never really caught on in Germany. Germany's government had a parliament much like that of England. One house was full of appointed officials while another was full of elected officials. Otto von Bismarck would allow members in the one house to be elected by men over the age of 25. The German empire was run by the kaiser, who was the king of Prussia. Otto von Bismarck's policies were very popular among traditional land-owners as well as the ever-growing class of businessmen.

Germany had the most efficient, the best equipped, and, apart from Russia, the largest military, which received most of its funding through the Reichstag. The main factor in Germany's efficient military was its military head staff, which was second to none.

Otto von Bismarck and Napoleon III after the Battle of Sedan in 1870 (PD).

Germany's territory was the Germany we know today: Silesia, East Prussia, West Prussia, South Prussia, Alsace-Lorraine, and part of Belgium. Colonies were also created in Africa in Togo, Namibia, Tanzania, and north of the Congo. There were colonies spread throughout the Pacific as well.

Germany's economy was arguably the most robust in the world. From 1871 to 1914, German industries were jumping by leaps and bounds. Prior to 1914, Germany was producing more steel than the entire British Empire, previously the largest steel-producing nation. This bothered the British a great deal, and they were very threatened by the German surge.

From 1871 to 1914, Germany's population rose to 65 million. German industries boomed and the arts flourished. Nationalism soared as Germany was seen more and more as a single nation. The Socialist Party and the National Liberal progressive parties, which represented the middle class, became important in the German Empire. Between 1872 and 1879, Otto von Bismarck instituted a series of reforms within Germany as an attempt to dilute the impact of the Roman Catholic Church. This was known as the **Kulturkampf** (cultural struggle).

Bismarck, realizing that Germany was weak and vulnerable despite her daunting military and exploding economy, created a series of questionable alliances. Some felt that the alliances were like tying the nation to dying animals — the declining Ottoman and Austro-Hungarian Empires — but these alliances worked well for Bismarck, who had no intention of entering war with anyone he knew he could not conquer. It is certain that Bismarck, if he were in power, would not have allowed World War I to occur!

But when World War I came, the kaiser felt obligated to maintain his hegemony over Europe, even if he was tied to weak allies. This he did to everyone's regret.[7]

Discussion Question

Why was Germany, arguably, the primary cause of World War I?

Militarism

The Argentine *Rivadavia*, first of her class, under construction in a US shipyard at Quincy, 1912 (LOC).

In 1914, Europe thought of war as an extension of foreign policy. Short, effective wars had effectively advanced national interests for a millennium. There were a few wars that were too long, such as the Thirty Years War, and a few that were expensive in human loss and money, like the French and Indian War. Nonetheless, most wars were short, sweet, and relatively effective. The Franco-Prussian war, for instance, was painless to both the victor and the vanquished, and while Prussia (Germany) gained little, France lost even less. Mostly, wars were fought for prestige, and this could easily be regained if lost. Generally speaking then, no one in Europe could imagine the train wreck of a catastrophe that was coming down the track. World War I, it was imagined by most at the beginning, would be another splendid war full of low casualties, colorful flags and stirring charges, and stories of valor for all to tell their grandchildren.

The problem was that military hardware had superseded military strategy. The same thing had occurred in the American Civil War where the rifle and rifled canon killed one out of five combatants. The American soldier lined up in neat rows and was slaughtered. This worked in the American Revolution when the inaccurate musket and smooth-bore canon was used, but was disastrous in the American Civil War.

But that was America and this was Europe, and it was really shocking that European military planners did not pick up on this. The main problem was the machine gun, originally invented by the Germans. This nasty machine could kill 50 to 60 men in one minute. This was not war; this was slaughter.

Militaries, though, did not create tactics and strategies to match their weapons. Not yet at least.

The fact is, European countries liked their armies. They made them feel invulnerable and safe, and fed into the rampant nationalism that was storming across Europe. All

---

7. http://history-world.org/world_war_one.htm.

the nations of Europe were militaristic, but the governments of Germany and Austria-Hungary were especially so.

My goodness! It was peacetime and there were almost six million soldiers in tiny Europe! As one country increased its armies, so all the others felt obliged to increase their armed forces to keep the "balance of power." Once they had their militaries, they felt they needed to use them.

The Royal Navy's HMS *Dreadnought*, the world's first dreadnought, or massive battle ship, 1906 (US Navy).

Germany touched a raw nerve when it challenged Britain's sea power. The island nation found this unacceptable. A strong navy would allow Germany to threaten British colonies overseas. Britain made an alliance with Japan in 1902 so as not to have to worry so much about the Pacific.

Britain also began to build **Dreadnoughts**, huge monster battle ships. The British government had planned to build four Dreadnoughts in 1909, but when Germany refused to limit the number of ships it was building, the British public protested, demanding: "We want eight and we won't wait." Britain and Germany thus had a naval arms race. This was a destabilizing force in the region.

Another mitigating factor was that the countries of Europe had huge numbers of trained reservists who could greatly enlarge their armies in one or two weeks. One historian has estimated the total number of men (including reservists) that the countries could thus call upon as:

- Germany: 8.5 million men
- Russia: 4.4 million
- France: 3.5 million
- Austria-Hungary: 3 million[8]

Finally, in 1914 the German army was the biggest and best in the world yet the Russian army was growing the fastest, and German generals were worried that, in a few years' time, they would not be able to defeat Russia so easily. Better a nice Franco-Prussian War in 1914 instead of a long, drawn out war in 1924. What everyone got, however, was an entirely different matter.

Discussion Question

Why was World War I unlike any other previous European War?

All the countries of Europe built up their armies and navies. In 1914, their peacetime armed forces were:

- Germany: 2,200,000 soldiers, 97 warships

- Austria-Hungary: 810,000 soldiers, 28 warships

- Italy: 750,000 soldiers, 36 warships

- France: 1,125,000 soldiers, 62 warships

- Russia: 1,200,000 soldiers, 30 warships

- Great Britain: 711,000 soldiers, 185 warships[1]

1. http://www.johndclare.net/causes_WWI2.htm.

8. Ibid.

The Failure of Government

A **constitutional monarchy** is in effect a democracy, and in Britain's case it also had a huge empire.

The governments in Europe, even the democratic governments, were fairly ineffective in diplomacy and politics. Modernism and progressivism had disoriented governments and they were ill prepared to handle the crisis that occurred in June 1914. Socialism, Bolshevism, and anarchy, in particular, had weakened European governments and they simply could not effectively defuse the crisis that exploded in the Balkans.

In spite of the liberal, nationalist revolutions of the past one-half century, very few of the countries of Europe were democracies. It is hard for a democracy to go to war because the people (not just an individual ruler or small group of ministers) need to agree to go to war. The autocracies and monarchies needed no such popular support.

As I mentioned in the previous lesson, no European government could even imagine what would happen if it followed its alliance-driven, militarist foreign policy. Germany, for one, could not muster enough moral courage to say no to its ally, Austria-Hungary, even though Kaiser Wilhelm had genuine misgivings (that he communicated to the Russian czar, his cousin).

If that wasn't bad enough, Germany was shackled with another weak, dysfunctional partner. The Ottoman Empire, Turkey, was the sick man of Europe. Once, Turkey had ruled all of the Balkans, and brought stability and Islam. As Turkey declined, ethnic and religious wars broke out that continue until today.

Things were about the same in the Austro-Hungarian Empire that had not really been healthy since before the railroad was invented. Italy's problem was that it was too new. Thus, it was still not unified and had a weak government and pathetic army. Mother Russia, the big bear, was huge but backward. Czar Nicholas II was a weak and ineffectual ruler, henpecked by his wife and her lackey, Rasputin.

France was the best hope for Europe. It had a massive army and was pretty savvy in diplomacy. In addition, it was a democracy; regardless, the French government was also weak. In 1870–1871, when Germany was trying to become a united country, France had gone to war to try to stop it. The Germans won the war easily and the French were now desperate for revenge. Fighting another little war in 1914 seemed like a minor price to pay for lost prestige.

Britain was an enigma. It was constitutional monarchy that, for the most part, stayed out of European affairs. But the pesky Huns (i.e., Germany) were messing up the "balance of power" that the nation-building English so desperately wanted to maintain. They fought the Crimean War in the 1850s to do just that, and were prepared to fight this local war in the Balkans to do the same in 1914.

It is fair to say, then, that one major cause of World War I was Europe's dysfunctional political order that was simply too confused, or weak, or vengeful, to compromise when the assassin's bullet felled the archduke in June 1914.

Discussion Question

A. Why were European governments so ineffectual in 1914?

Two United States soldiers run toward a bunker, 1917-1918 (LOC).

Chapter 4

World at War: World War I Memoirs

First Thoughts

War is more than a compilation of battles and strategy. War is about people. From 2 to 3 million Russians died in World War I. Among the other major participants, almost 2 million Germans, over 1.5 million French, close to a million English, a half-million Italians, 1.2 million from Austria-Hungary, and 325,000 from Turkey died in battle. These figures do not count the wounded, whose lives may have been shortened as a result of their injuries. It is estimated that Germany and France each lost over 15 percent of their young men. Estimates of the financial drain of the war range between $250 billion and $300 billion, considering the value of the dollar in the early 1920s. These figures do not bring home the depth of the war's impact on trade, shipping, and monetary stability. How does one analyze the psychological expense of the conflict? How does one calculate the cost of taking 75 million men who were mobilized away from their jobs and their homes?

Chapter Learning Objectives

Chapter 4 examines World War I from the perspective of the participants. This horrible war changed everything. Yet, in the midst of the carnage, there is quiet courage and fortitude. It is amazing how peaceful these five souls are. The young German ace who loves flying and his brother who flies with him. The young French artist who seems too sensitive and gentle to be a soldier. The young nurse who uses understatement and mild sarcasm to survive. The brave father and husband who willingly lives with his men in the trenches and dies with them in a charge.

As a result of this chapter you should be able to:

Examine the lives of five participants of World War I and assess the impact that this war had on their lives.

1. Oswald Bölcke, a German flyer

2. An unknown French infantryman

3. An unknown English nurse

4. Lt. Col. George Laurie, a Canadian infantryman

5. Chaplain George McCarthy, an American chaplain

CONCEPTS

Oswald Bölcke

Biplanes

Field hospitals

Lt. Col. George Brenton Laurie

Chaplain George T. McCarthy

An Aviator's Field Book

The Field Reports of Oswald Bölcke, from August 1, 1914, to October 28, 1916

Oswald Bölcke was a renowned pilot, a victor of 40 aerial battles, who died in a plane crash at the young age of 25 (PD).

Oswald Bölcke was born on the 19th of May, 1891, in Giebichenstein, Germany. He joined the German Air Corps in 1914 and fought in every major engagement until he went missing in action in 1916.

By chance, I witnessed a great military spectacle. As I did not have to fly in the afternoon, I went to the artillery observer's post with our Captain. About four o'clock we reached V.; from here we had another half hour's walk ahead of us. From a distance we could see there was heavy firing going on. The Major, in the company's bomb-proof, told us that the artillery would hardly have time now to avail themselves of airplanes to find the range for them. The French were just at the time trying to get revenge for an attack we made the day before, and the artillery was very busy. From there we went to the observer's post and were very lucky. Our batteries were just firing at the enemy's, our airplanes finding the range for them. Suddenly the non-commissioned officer at the double-periscope yelled over to us that the French were bringing up reinforcements through the communicating trenches. The Lieutenant of Artillery ran over to the field artillery and showed them the beautiful target. Soon after that a few of our shrapnel burst over these positions. Bang! And the enemy was gone. Suddenly a ball of red fire appeared in the first French trench. This meant — shells fall ahead of trenches; place shots further back. Just then, over a front of one and a half kilometers, a whole brigade of Frenchmen rose from the trenches, shoulder to shoulder, a thing I had never seen before. We have to admire them for their courage. In front, the officers about four or five steps in the lead; behind them, in a dense line, the men, partly negroes, whom we could recognize by their baggy trousers. The whole line moved on a run. For the first four hundred meters (in all they had seven hundred meters to cover) we let them come without firing. Then we let them have our first shrapnel. As the artillery knew the exact range, the first shots were effective. Then came the heavier shells. We now opened a murderous fire; it was so loud that we could not hear each other at two paces. Again and again our shells struck the dense masses and tore huge gaps in them, but, in spite of this, the attack continued. The gaps were always quickly closed. Now our infantry took a hand. Our men stood up in the trenches, exposed from the hips up, and fired like madmen. After three or four minutes the attack slackened in spots; that is, parts of the line advanced, others could not. After a quarter of an hour the French on our left wing, which I could see, reached our trenches, shot and stabbed from above, and finally jumped in. Now we could plainly see the hand-to-hand combat: heads bobbing back and forth, guns clubbed (they seemed to be only trying to hit, not kill), glistening bayonets, and a general commotion. On the right wing, things progressed slower, almost at a standstill. In the middle a group jumped forward now and then, and into them the artillery fired with telling effect. We could see men running wildly about, they could not escape our artillery fire. The whole slope was strewn with bodies. After about a quarter of an hour the Frenchmen started to retreat. First one, then two, then three, came out of our trenches, looked all around, and started for their own trenches. In the meantime more troops came up from the rear. But after the first few started to run more came out of the trenches, until finally all were out and retreating. Our men also got out to be able to fire at the retreating enemy to better advantage. Again and again the French officers tried to close up their ranks, rally their men, and lead them anew to the attack.

A German biplane shot down by American machine gunners in France. From October 1918 (PD).

But in vain, for more and more sought safety in flight. Many dropped — I think more than in the advance. In the center, the French had advanced to within fifty meters of us, and could get no closer. As the retreat started on the left, some in the center also lost heart, and fled like frightened chickens. But almost all were killed. I saw six running away when a shell exploded near them. The smoke disappeared; there were only four left. A second shell, and only one was left. He was probably hit by the infantry. The following proves how completely we repelled their attack: Four Frenchmen rose, waved their arms and ran toward our trench. Two of them carried a severely wounded comrade. Suddenly they dropped their burden and ran faster toward us. Probably their comrades had fired on them. Hardly were these four in our trenches when fifty more of them got up, waved their caps and ran toward us. But the Frenchmen didn't like this, and in a second four well-placed shells burst between them and us; probably they were afraid that there would be a general surrender on the part of their men. The retreat was now general. At 6:15 the main battle was over. Afterward we could see here and there a few Frenchmen running or crawling to their trench. I was very glad I had the opportunity to see this. From above, we aviators don't see such things.

Letter of October 8, 1916

With some of my men I attacked a squadron of F.-E. biplanes on the way back from C. Of these, we shot down six out of eight. Only two escaped. I picked out the leader, and shot up his engine so he had to land. It landed right near one of our kite-balloons. They were hardly down when the whole airplane was ablaze. It seems they have some means of destroying their machine as soon as it lands. On September 19th six of us got into an English squadron. Below us were the machines with lattice-work tails, and above were some Morans, as protection. One of these I picked out, and sailed after him. For a moment he escaped me, but west of B. I caught up with him. One machine gun jammed, but the other I used with telling effect. At short range, I fired at him till he fell in a big blaze. During all this, he handled himself very clumsily. . . . Everything goes well with me; healthy, good food, good quarters, good companions, and plenty to do.

Discussion Question

Though Oswald Bölcke's body was recovered from a plane crash, many soldiers disappeared and were never heard from again. Research your own community and find out if there are MIAs (missing in action) in the Vietnam War or more recent wars. If there are, research who one of these men was.

Unknown French Soldier, 1914–1915

French soldiers guarding a subway entrance in Paris, France at the beginning of World War I, 1914-1915 (LOC).

Preface by André Chevrillon

The letters that follow are those of a young painter who was at the front from September [1914] till the beginning of April [1915]; at the latter date he was missing in one of the battles of the Argonne. Are we to speak of him in the present tense or in the past? We know not: since the day when the last mud-stained paper reached them, announcing the attack in which he was to vanish, what a close weight of silence for those who during eight months lived upon these almost daily letters! But for how many women, how many mothers, is a grief like this today a common lot!

In the studio and amid the canvases upon which the young man had traced the forms of his dreams, I have seen, piously placed in order on a table, all the little papers written by his hand. A silent presence — I was not then aware what manner of mind had there expressed itself — revisiting this hearth: a mind surely made to travel far abroad and cast its lights upon multitudes of men.

It was the mind of a complete artist, but of a poet as well, that had lurked under the timid reserves of a youth who at thirteen years of age had left school for the studio, and who had taught himself, without help from any other, to translate the thoughts that moved him into such words as the reader will judge of. Here are tenderness of heart, a fervent love of Nature, a mystical sense of her changing moods and of her eternal language: all those things of which the Germans, professing themselves heirs of Goethe and of Beethoven, imagine they have the monopoly, but of which we Frenchmen have the true perception, and which move us in the words written by our young countryman for his most dearly beloved and for himself.

*****

My very dear Mother, — These are my first days of life at war, full of change, but the fatigue I actually feel is very different from what I foresaw. I am in a state of great nervous tension because of the want of sleep and exercise. I lead the life of a government clerk. I belong to what is called the dépôt, I am one of those doing sedentary work, and destined eventually to fill up the gaps in the fighting line.

What we miss is news; there are no longer any papers to be had in this town.

August 13, 1914

We are without news, and so it will be for several days, the censorship being of the most rigorous kind. Here life is calm. The weather is magnificent, and all breathes quiet and confidence. We think of those who are fighting in the heat, and this thought makes our own situation seem even too good. The spirit among the reservists is excellent.

August 16, 1914

Today a walk along the Marne. Charming weather after a little rain. A welcome interlude in these troubled times. We are still without news, like you, but we have happily a large stock of patience. I have had some pleasure in the landscape, notwithstanding the invasion of red and blue. These fine men in red and blue have given the best impression of their moral. Great levies will be made upon our dépôts, to be endured with fortitude. The monotony of military life benumbs me, but I don't complain. After nine years these types are to be rediscovered, a little less marked, improved, and leveled down. Just now everyone is full of grave thoughts because of the news from the East. The ordinary good-fellowship of the mess has been replaced by a finer solidarity and a praise-worthy attempt at adaptation. One of the advantages of our situation is that we can, as it were, play at being soldiers with the certainty of not wasting our time. All these childish and easy occupations, which are of immediate result and useful-ness, bring back calm to the mind and soothe the nerves. Then the great stay which supports the men is a profound, vague feeling of brotherhood which turns all hearts towards those who are fighting. Each one feels that the slight discom-fort which he endures is only a feeble tribute to the frightful expense of all energy and all devotedness at the front.

A French soldier using a periscope during trench warfare in 1915. Periscopes used mirrors to allow one to view the enemy without being put in the line of fire (PD).

August 25, 1914

This letter will barely precede our own departure. The terrible conflict calls for our presence close to those who are already in the midst of the struggle. I leave you, Grandmother and you, with the hope of seeing you again, and the certainty that you will approve of my doing all that seems to me my duty. Nothing is hopeless, and, above all, nothing has changed our idea of the part we have to play. Tell all those who love me a little that I think of them. I have no time to write to anyone. My health is of the best. After such an upheaval we may say that our former life is dead. Dear mother, let us, you and I, with all our courage adapt ourselves to an existence entirely different, however long it may last. Be very sure that I won't go out of my way to do anything that endan-gers our happiness, but that I'll try to satisfy my conscience, and yours. Up till now I am without cause for self-reproach, and so I hope to remain. A second letter to tell you that, instead of our regiment, it was Pierre's that went. I had the joy of seeing him pass in front of me when I was on guard in the town. I accompanied him for a hundred yards, then we said good-bye. I had a feeling that we should meet again. It is the gravest of hours; the country will not die, but her deliverance will be snatched only at the price of frightful efforts. Pierre's regiment went covered with flowers, and singing. It was a deep consolation to be together till the end. It is fine of Andréto to have saved his drowning comrade. We don't realize the reserve of heroism there is in France, and among the young intellectual Parisians. In regard to our losses, I may tell you that whole divisions have been wiped out. Certain regiments have not an officer left. As for my state of mind, my first letter will perhaps tell you better what I believe to be my duty. Know that it would be shameful to think for one instant of holding back when the race demands the sacrifice. My only part is to carry an undefiled conscience as far as my feet may lead.

December 1, 1914

I remember the satisfaction I felt in my freedom when I was exempted from my military duties. It seemed to me that if, at twenty-seven years old, I had been obliged to return to the regiment, my life and career would have been irretrievably lost. And here I am now, twenty-eight years old, back in the army, far from my work, my responsibilities, my ambitions — and yet never has life brought me such a full measure of finer feelings; never have I been able to record such freshness of sensibility, such security of conscience. So those are the blessings arising out of the thing which my reasonable human foresight envisaged as disaster. And thus continues the lesson of Providence which, upsetting all my fears, makes good arise out of every change of situation.

The two last sunrises, yesterday and today, were lovely. . . . I feel inclined to make you a little sketch of the view from my window. . . . It is done from memory; in your imagination you must add streaks of purple color, making the most dramatic effect, and an infinite stretch of open country to right and left. This is what I have been able again and again to look upon, during this time. At this moment, the soft sky brings into harmony the orchards where we work. My little job dispenses me from digging for the time. Such are the happinesses which, from afar, had the appearance of calamities.

I have just received your letters of the 25th, 26th, and 27th, as well as a dear letter from Grandmother, so valiant, so full of spirit, and so clear-minded. It gave me great pleasure, and brings me a dear hope, of which I accept the augury with joy. Each one of your beloved letters, too, gives me the best of what life holds for me. My first letter of today replies to what you say about the acceptation of trials and the destruction of idols.

You will see that I think absolutely as you do, and I trust that there is in this hour no impeding idol in my heart. . . . I think that my last prayer is in fact very simple. The spirit of the place could not have borne to be clothed in an art that was overloaded. God was everywhere, and everywhere was harmony: the road at night, of which I speak to you so often, the starry sky, the valley full of the murmuring of water, the trees, the Calvaries, the hills near and far. There would not have been any room for artifice. It is useless for me to give up being an artist, but I hope always to be sincere and to use art as it were only for the clothing of my conscience.

December 5, 1914

We have come out of our burrows, and three days of imprisonment are followed by a morning in the open. It would be impossible to imagine such a state of mud.

Your pretty aluminum watch is the admiration of everybody. Is André's wound serious? The mothers endure terrible agony in this war, but courage — nothing will be lost. As for me, I get on all right, and am as happy as one may be. A terrific wind today, chasing the fine clouds. Keen air, in which the branches thrive. Beautiful moonlight on all these nights, all the more appreciated if one has been cheated of the day. Dear, I am writing badly today because we are bewildered by the full daylight after those long hours of darkness, but my heart goes out to you and rests with you. Let us bring to everything the spirit of courage. Let us have confidence in God always, whatever happens. How much I feel, as you do, that one can adore Him only with one's spirit! And like you I think that we must avoid all pride, which condemns the ways of other people. Let our love lead us in union towards the universal Providence. Let us, in constant prayer, give back our destiny into His hands. Let us humbly admit to Him our human hopes, trying at every moment to link them to eternal wisdom. It is a task which now seems full of difficulty, but difficulty is in everything in life.

April 4, Easter Eve

Darling Mother, — A time of anxious waiting, big with the menace of near things. Meanwhile, however, idleness and quiet. I am not able to think, and I give myself up to my fate. Beloved, don't find fault with me if for a month past I have been below the mark. Love me, and tell our friends to love me. Did you get my photograph? It was taken at the fortunate time of our position here, when we were having peaceful days, with no immediate enemy except the cold. A few days later I was made corporal, and my life became hard enough, burdened with very ungrateful labours. After that, the storm; and the lights of that storm are still bright in my life. Dear Mother, — We are again in the immediate care of God. At two o'clock we march towards the storm. Beloved, I think of you, I think of you both. I love you, and I entrust the three of us to the Providence of God. May everything that happens find us ready! In the full power of my soul, I pray for this, on your behalf, on mine: hope through all; but, before all else, Wisdom and Love. I kiss you, without more words. All my mind is now set upon the hard work to be done.

April 6, 1915

Dear beloved Mother, — It is midday, and we are at the forward position, in readiness. I send you my whole love. Whatever comes to pass, life has had its beauty.

[It was in the fight of this day, April 6, that the writer of these letters disappeared. His body was never recovered.][1]

Discussion Question

Clutton-Brock, a comrade in arms, writes: "These letters reveal to us a new type of soldier, a new type of hero, almost a new type of man; one who can be brave without any animal consolations, who can endure without any romantic illusions, and, what is more, one who can have faith without any formal revelation. For there is nothing in the letters more interesting than the religion constantly expressed or implied in them. . . . He seems afraid to give any artistic expression to his own faith, lest he should falsify it by over-expression, lest it should seem to be more accomplished than it is. He will not even try to take delight in it; he is almost fanatically an intellectual ascetic; and yet again and again he affirms a faith, which he will hardly consent to specify by uttering the name of God. He is shy about it, as if it might be refuted if it were expressed in any dogmatic terms. So many victories seem to have been won over faith in the modern world that his will not throw down any challenge. If it is to live, it must escape the notice of the vulgar triumphing skeptics, and even of the doubting habits of his own mind. Yet it does live its own humble and hesitating life; and in its hesitations and its humility is its strength. Any eager bishop as a lost sheep returning repentant to the fold could not acclaim him; but he is not lost, nor is the universe to him anything but a home and the dear city of God even in the trenches."[2] Do you agree with Brock's assessment of his comrade? Why or why not?

1. Anonymous, *Letters of a Soldier, 1914–1915*, Project Gutenberg; http://www.gutenberg.org/files/17316/17316-h/17316-h.htm.
2 Ibid.

Anonymous, *Diary of a Nursing Sister on the Western Front*, 1914–1915

Monday, May 10th, 9.30 a.m. — We have had a night of it. Every Field Ambulance, barge, Clearing Hospital, and train [is] blocked with them. The M.O.'s neither eat nor sleep. I got up early yesterday and went down to the barge to see if they wanted any extra help (as the other two were coping with the wounded officers), and had a grim afternoon and evening there. One M.O., no Sisters, four trained orderlies, and some other men were there. It was packed with all the worst cases — dying and bleeding and groaning. After five hours we had three-fourths of them out of their blood-soaked clothes, dressed, fed, hemorrhage stopped, hands and faces washed, and some asleep. Two died, and more were dying. They all worked like bricks. The M.O., and another from the other barge which hadn't filled up, sent up to the O.D.S., when my hour for night duty there came, to ask if I could stay, and got leave. At 11 p.m. four Sisters arrived

A group of nurses aboard the *Red Cross* bound for Europe in mid September, 1914 at the beginning of World War I (LOC).

. . . two for each barge; so I handed over to them and went to the O.D.S. to relieve the other two there for night duty. The place was unrecognizable: every corner of every floor filled with wounded officers — some sitting up and some all over wounds, and three dying and others critical; and they still kept coming in. They were all awfully good strewing about the floor — some soaked to the skin from wet shell holes — on their stretchers, waiting to be put to bed. One had had "such a jolly Sunday afternoon" lying in a shell hole with six inches of water in it and a dead man, digging himself in deeper with his trench tool whenever the shells burst near him. He was hit in the stomach. One officer saw the enemy through a periscope sniping at our wounded.

4 p.m. — In bed. It seems quiet today; there are so few guns to be heard, and not so many ambulances coming. All except the hopeless cases will have been evacuated by now from all the Field Hospitals. There was a block last night, and none could be sent on. The Clearing Hospitals were full, and no trains in. Those four Sisters from the base had a weird arrival at the barge last night in a car at 11 p.m. It was a black dark night, big guns going, and a sudden descent down a ladder into that Nelson's cockpit. They were awfully bucked when we said, "Oh, I am glad you have come." They buckled to and set to work right off. The cook, who had been helping magnificently in the ward, was running after me with hot cocoa (breakfast was my last meal, except a cup of tea), and promised to give them some. One wounded of the Munsters there said he didn't mind nothing now, — he'd seen so many dead Germans as he never thought on. As always, they have lost thousands, but they come on like ants. They have only had about seven new cases today at the O.D.S., but two of last night's have died. A Padre was with them.

They had no market this morning, for fear of bombs from aeroplanes. There's been no shelling into the town.

Tuesday, May 11th, 6.30 p.m. — In bed. I went to bed pretty tired this morning after an awful night (only a few of the less seriously wounded had been evacuated yesterday, and all the worst ones, of course, left), and slept like a top from 10.30 to 5, and feel as fit as anything after it. The fighting seems to have stopped now, and no more have come in today. Last night a stiff muddy figure, all bandages and straw, on the stretcher was brought in. I asked the boy how many wounds? "Oh, only five," he said cheerfully. "Nice clean wounds, — machine-gun, — all in and out again!" The Padre came at 7.30 and had a Celebration in each ward, but I was too busy to take any notice of it. A German shell hit one of these officers on Sunday morning early, soon after our bombardment began. He crawled about till he was hit again twice by other shells, and then lay there all that day and all that night, with one drink from another wounded's water-bottle; everyone else was either dead or wounded round him. Next morning his servant found him and got stretcher-bearers, and he got here. I don't know how they live through that.

Wednesday, May 12th, 11 p.m. — Just heard a shell burst, first the whistling scream, and then the bang—wonder where? There was another about an hour ago, but I didn't hear the whistle of that — only the bang. I shouldn't have known what the whistle was if I hadn't heard it at Braisne. It goes in a curve. All the men on the top floor have been sent down to sleep in the cellar; another shell has busted. The sky on the battle line to-night is the weirdest sight; our guns are very busy, and they are making yellow flashes like huge sheets of summer lightning. Then the star-shells rise, burst, and light up a large area, while a big searchlight plays slowly on the clouds. It is all very beautiful when you don't think what it means.

5 a.m. — Daylight — soaking wet, and no more shells since 2 a.m. We have admitted seven officers tonight; the last — just in — says there have been five people wounded in the town by this peppering — one killed. I don't know if civilians or soldiers.

That bombardment on Sunday morning was the biggest any one has ever heard, — more guns on smaller space, and more shells per minute.[3]

Elsie Knocker and Mairi Chisholm outside their advanced dressing station in Pervyse, Belguim, 1917 (PD).

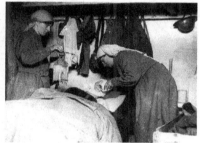

Mairi and Elsie tend to a wounded Belgian soldier (PD).

Discussion Question

Pretend that you are this nurse's pastor. What would you say to comfort her?

Wounded soldiers waiting on stretchers on Menin Road near Hooge, Germany 1917 (PD).

3 http://archive.org/stream/diarynursesisterwestfront00blacuoft/diarynursesisterwestfront00blacuoft_djvu.txt.

Letters of Lt.-Col. George Brenton Laurie (Commanding 1st Battn. Royal Irish Rifles)

George Brenton Laurie (1867-1915) fought in both the Boer War and the First World War, where he died in battle.

November 4th, 1914-March11th, 1915

George Brenton Laurie was born at Halifax, Nova Scotia, on October 13th, 1867. He was the eldest surviving son of the late Lieut.-General John Wimburn Laurie, C.B., M.P., of 47 Porchester Terrace, London, and of Mrs. Laurie, of Oakfield, Nova Scotia.

He was grandson of the Hon. Enos Collins, M.L.C., of Gorse Brook, Halifax, and great-grandson of Sir Brenton Haliburton, Chief Justice of Nova Scotia. He was educated at Galt Collegiate Institute, Ontario, and at the Picton Academy, from whence he passed into the Royal Military College, Kingston, Canada, in 1883. He joined the Royal Irish Rifles as a Lieutenant in September, 1885, going with them to Gibraltar in 1886, and on to Egypt in 1888. He took part in the Nile Campaign in 1889, but, contracting smallpox at Assouan, he was sent home to recover, and spent two years at the Depot at Belfast, rejoining his battalion in Malta. He was promoted Captain in 1893, and when the Rifles came back to home service he obtained an Adjutancy of Volunteers in Devonshire in October, 1896, and from that date until March, 1901, by ceaseless energy he brought the battalion to full strength and high efficiency.

In March, 1901, he was appointed a special service officer, including the command of a mounted infantry battalion for the South African War. He was present at operations in the Transvaal, Orange River Colony, and Cape Colony, between April, 1901, and May, 1902, having been Mentioned in Despatches for his services (London Gazette, July 29th, 1902), also receiving the Queen's Medal with five clasps. After peace was signed he served in Ireland, and in October, 1904, obtained his majority. Afterwards he served in England till, becoming Lieut.-Colonel in 1912, he went out to India to take command of the 1st Battalion Royal Irish Rifles. He was deeply engaged at this time in writing the History of his Regiment, a work soon officially accepted and highly praised. He had previously written a history of "The French in Morocco," compiled from many sources during his years in the Mediterranean. When the European War broke out in August, 1914, he was at Aden with his battalion, and until anxiety in Somaliland was allayed, the Irish Rifles were detained there, only reaching France in November. They spent the winter in the trenches, taking their share in the fierce fighting in December. On March 10th, 1915, they took part in the attack on Neuve Chapelle, and were the first battalion to reach the village, but losses were heavy. A sergeant-major wrote: "Our Colonel was everywhere, encouraging his men, and seeming to bear a charmed life. He knew no fear, and walked quietly in front of us as if no bombardment were going on." On Friday evening, March 12th, a fresh assault was ordered. Lieut.-Colonel Laurie rallied his exhausted men, and, calling out "Follow me! I will lead you!" he sprang over the parapet, revolver in hand. A moment later he fell shot through the head. He was buried with his fallen officers and men in a garden near Neuve Chapelle.

November 20th, 1914

I am now in the trenches in the snow, and it was very cold indeed last night. Can you picture such conditions, lying out in it after dark? All my poor men feel the change very much, coming from the heat of Aden. However, it is business. We are supposed to go out to-morrow night for three days' rest after six nights in the trenches, during which I have not washed or shaved! Yesterday a bullet pierced our splinter-proof roof. Major W—— had his cap cut by one, greatly to his surprise! I was up half the night with orders, etc., coming in. Whilst I was going round quite a pretty little fight developed. Fifty Germans attacked a few of our men; I stood revolver in hand and watched it, as we gradually drove them back. This morning at daybreak our men are reported to have shot two men of a burying party, so there must have been casualties. Still, one is sorry for the burial party. Their guns are knocking things about here; big guns, too. Our Brigadier, General Lowry Cole, asked me if Mrs. L.C. might write to you about comforts for the troops, and I said certainly. If you have any gloves or waistcoats, send them along, please. We thought our friends had arranged to take away their guns, and for one day we did not see them; then they opened again this afternoon. I shall not be sorry to get relieved to-morrow, when we march all night and go into billets, taking our boots off, which will be a great relief. I have caught several local men inhabitants here and sent them off under escort, since which time "sniping" has gradually decreased. Well, I did not write to you yesterday; was too busy. I am inclined to think that Germany has shot her bolt.

> "Fifty Germans attacked a few of our men; I stood revolver in hand and watched it, as we gradually drove them back."

In Trenches. November 21st, 1914

Very cold, and more snow — I wonder how we can stand it! Fortunately, the Germans are equally badly off. I have had a chequered life. Last night, after a meagre dinner of tinned beef, I found an officer of the Royal Engineers waiting for me, who announced that he and a party of men had come to put my wire entanglements into order. Having done that, they were to go home. Passing along a deep drain, led by myself, we got to the end of a huge mound of earth. Three of my men popped over it in the dark, within 100 yards of some Germans who were lying down firing at us. Then over went the Sappers, whilst I flew off to see that our own men did not fire on them. Back again to my hole in the ground to put other things "in train." Up at 11.30 p.m. to repulse an attack. That driven off, I rolled up in blankets to shiver until 1 a.m., when messages began to pour in from everywhere as to all sorts of things. Up again at 4, and at 5.30 for good, back to the trenches, followed by five officers who are relieving us. This procession was a walk with stooping heads, bullets raining in through the loopholes, and frantic runs along ditches

A French infantrymen bayonet charge, 1914 (PD).

beside hedges (just like the "shallows" at Carlton). I crawled completely doubled up. Suddenly a sniper would see some part of me showing, and would then let drive at me. I had to duck, and then run like a hare until I got to a bank which gave some protection. Needless to say, my coat and riding things are already in holes. Please send me another large packet of chocolate; the last was much appreciated; also some soup squares.

In Billets. November 23rd, 1914

We are back again in billets now. Such a business as it was getting out of the trenches. Of course, my men could not leave until the others were in their places; then they had to change back to their roads through the trenches, practically so narrow that they could not pass without stepping over each other, and these three miles long. Well, the result of all was that, moving off at 4.30 p.m., we collected at a road two miles back at 2 in the morning. Just think of it! There was snow and 15 degrees of frost, and we were awfully cold. We got to our billets about 3 a.m., and the General was in my room at 5 o'clock to see me. I was very tired after my week's work, but I think it was successful. My casualties I am not allowed to state, but they were more than I like to count; also, alas! the number of men killed in action recently. . . . Well, following on from that, you will quite understand that I had much to think about; funerals, wounded men, rations and everything, shivering with cold the whole time. Then I had to go into my returns, and I

A ration party of the Royal Irish Rifles in a communication trench during the Battle of the Somme. The date is believed to be July 1, 1916 (Imperial War Museums PD).

was even asked to make up maps and sketches. I believe one of my officers had a bullet through his clothes whilst trying to sketch the enemy's position at night. Still, we did our work. One particular night, for instance, I had four officers — patrols — in the enemy's lines. It cost me one man killed and one man wounded, though I heard that Capt. Stevens died too the day after he was hit, poor fellow! Colonel Napier was not wrong when he said it would be a terrible war, but Germany must surely be very nearly at the end of her tether. After all, I must return my boots, as the pair sent, though quite large enough in an ordinary way, are much too small now that I wear two pairs of socks and do not remove them for a week! Did it ever occur to you how difficult it is to feed 1,000 men in a trench 3 miles long when you can only get in at the ends? It took from 5 p.m. to 10 o'clock to get and give them their teas, and then from 3 a.m. to half-past six to give them their breakfast and their food for the day, whilst all the time the enemy was fighting and shooting, and one had to judge to a nicety where to keep everyone until the rations were issued, so that in case the Germans should suddenly rush us we should have enough to repel them. I wonder where you are now — at Rostrevor or at Carlton — and whether I am fated to get home before Christmas or not. In any case, best of luck. . . .

In Billets. November 24th, 1914

Off to the trenches again to-night, and please God we shall not lose so many men as before. I had the clergyman up Today and Holy Communion administered for officers and men. Quite a lot of the former attended. You remember we were together last at Winchester. What a difference between that day and now! . . . Then, the most stately pile in the world; here a little room in a French farmer's house, with the table pushed into the corner and a few broken chairs to sit upon. An evil-looking bin stands in the corner containing our rations, a pistol on the mantelpiece, and some boots at the fireplace drying, which latter I hastily removed. However, the service was really just the same as at Winchester, excepting that you were not with me. If anything happens to me on this expedition, I should like that small window looking on our pew, representing the Bishop of York's figure, etc., etc., to be filled in to my memory; and, curiously enough, I think the Penitent Thief always one of the greatest heroes in the Bible; for he must have had enormous faith to believe when he was in such a bad way himself. The snow is fast melting, and, on the whole, it is much warmer than yesterday. Well, beyond this I have no news to give you, excepting that, of course, though Germany may put up a long fight, yet, in my opinion, she is being strained to death to keep herself going, and I believe that she cannot last long at this rate.

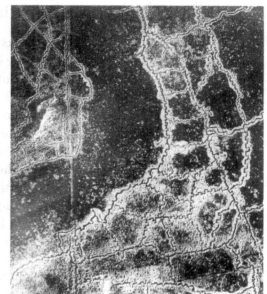

An aerial reconnaissance photograph of the opposing trenches and "no-man's land" between Loos and Hulluch in Artois, France, taken July 22, 1917. German trenches are at the right and bottom, and British trenches are at the top left. (Imperial War Museums PD).

November 25th, 1914

Back in the trenches, and very busy indeed, as apparently we intend to stay here for some time, and we are doing our best to make them habitable for the winter. Our own dug-out, which was 3 feet deep, we have deepened to 4 feet, but just at this moment the roof beams of Major Baker's half have been carried away, whilst a sniper prevents our getting on the top of the roof to shovel off the earth and renew the beams. Altogether a cheerful problem. However, like many others we shall gradually get this right. I was told that the Germans made a great attack in the afternoon two days ago on the Brigade to our right, but were beaten back. I have warned all my men to be ready for a rush at any time. We made an amusing attack two nights ago with 8 men and one officer, all of whom were wrapped in sheets to avoid being seen in the snow. It took place from one of my trenches. The officer got to the German trench, where a man looked into his face. He fired his revolver at one yard, and his men following dashed forward and fired right and left down the trenches. A great scamper ensued, as you may imagine, and then from each German trench burst out a heavy rifle fire. Our guns were ready, and immediately opened on them in the darkness, and presumably caused the enemy many casualties. I must say that I should never be surprised at the war coming to a sudden conclusion, or for it to last a very long time; but I fancy that a great deal depends upon the result of this battle in Poland. The sniping gentleman is tremendously busy at present, but I hope he will not catch me on my way to luncheon. I have to go there very shortly. You see, I believe they have rifles fixed in clumps, and then they fire them by a sentry pulling a trigger. Of course, the shots are erratic to a certain extent, but they find out from spies where the general line of advance to our trenches is, scour them regularly, and now and then bag someone or other. Last night passed quietly enough; we had our scrap about one o'clock. I was out, but nothing serious happened, I am glad to say. The weather has turned to rain again, and the country is losing the snow, whilst the trenches accumulate the rain and mud badly. Please God this war will soon be over.

Camel-mounted infantry brigades were raised in during the First World War for service in the Middle East. 1915 (LOC).

March 9th, 1915

Many thanks for your letter. My new puttees will be most useful, as my old ones are full of holes. We have, during the last day or so, had a strong wind, and the ground is drying up wonderfully, so it will not be so hard on puttees for the future. As a rule, when one walks across country, and struggles through muddy trenches without one's horse, one wears puttees if one is not wearing long gum boots; these latter keep the legs and feet drier, but the difficulty is that they are too heavy to walk very far in them. I had a long letter from Meta, which I enclose. I am sending two badges to the children from my old coat. I thought they might like them. I look forward very much to the cake you are sending, as the last parcel went astray. My new coat came last night. It is made out of very thick cloth, and altogether loose and useful. There always has been a battalion of the London Irish Rifles (Volunteers), now a territorial corps. The War Office would not allow them to belong to us, because Irish Regiments have no territorial Bns. In S. Africa, that Bn. (London Irish Rifles) sent us a company which was attached to our regiment throughout the war. I leave the Irish visit in your hands at present. The only leave I shall receive will be if I am wounded. There will be a lot of fighting of a bad sort from now on. It would never be surprising if one were hit. I have been mercifully preserved up to now; and, again, one must put one's trust in Providence. . . .

[Lt. Colonel Laurie was killed in action on March 11, 1915][4]

Discussion Questions

It was highly irregular for an officer of a rank higher than a captain to lead a charge, yet, on March 11, Lt. Colonel Laurie chose to do this. Why?

Lesson 5

The Greater Love

Chaplain George T. McCarthy, U. S. Army, 1917–1918

Gallant Pershing was even then maneuvering his masterly all-American offensive in the San Michel. Our Seventh Division, with the 28th on the left and the 92d on the right, now reached the high full tide of martial responsibility; merging from the reserve into the attack; and taking its place with the Immortal Combat Divisions of proud Old Glory.

The front line sector, which that night we took over, extended in a general westerly direction from north of Pont à Musson on the Moselle river to Vigneulles — a distance of ten kilometers.

---

4. http://www.gutenberg.org/files/24862/24862-h/24862-h.htm.

Approximate positions found the 55th Infantry at Thiacourt, the 64th at Vieville, the 37th at Fay-en-Haye, and the 56th at Vilcey-sur-Trey, with Machine Gun Battalions distributed equally among them. During September, Division Headquarters was at Villers-en-Haye; moving in echelon to Noviant and Euvezin October 24th.

Although Villers-en-Haye was mostly in ruins, the Sacristy of the village church was in good shape, and this I at once occupied. On the preceding Sunday, good Father Harmon of Chicago had said Mass in this church, as a note, fastened to its front door, announced.

Chaplain George T. McCarthy.

Thoroughly tired, I spread my blanket on the floor and fell quickly to sleep. I dreamed I was tied to a railroad track with a train rushing towards me. With a start I awoke, just as a siren voiced shell came screaming across the fields, bursting at the foot of the hill on which the church stood.

The gas alarm was at once sounded and every trooper sought refuge in the dugouts. It was then half-past eight. At four-minute intervals and with the most deadly regularity these shells came at us for four nerve-racking hours.

Boom! You could hear it leave the eight-inch howitzer six miles away, then in a high tenor pitch, it rushed toward you with a crescendo of sound, moaning, wailing, screaming, hissing, bursting with frightful intensity apparently in the center of your brain. Falling here, there, and everywhere in the ruins and environs of the village, mustard gas, flying steel and mortar, levied cruel toll on six boys, whose mangled bodies I laid away the following afternoon at Griscourt under the hill. One of these, I now recall, was Corporal Donald Bryan of the 7th Engineers, a most handsome and talented young man who, before the war, had won fame in the field of movie drama.

German field chaplain burying a French Officer who died in a hospital, 1914 (LOC).

"Where were you last night?" inquired gallant Colonel Cummings of Missouri, our Machine Gun Regimental Commander.

"In the sacristy," I replied.

"The worst possible place for you!" he exclaimed; "you would find it far safer in a dugout."

I preferred the sacristy, however, for its convenience to the altar, where I could say daily Mass, and so won my point.

Chaplain and burial work had been meanwhile growing tremendously. Burial details to be organized, equipped and dispatched far and wide along the front; conferences with Chaplains; forwarding to them of Departmental Orders; receiving their weekly reports, and compiling these in daily reports to the Graves Registration Service; with monthly reports to be prepared for Bishop Brent at Chaumont, Monsignor Connolly at Paris, and Archbishop Hayes at New York.

At this time welfare workers joined us and we had thirty Y. M. C. A. secretaries under Rev. Mr. Todd; eight American Red Cross secretaries under Mr. Kolinski of Chicago; six Salvation Army lady secretaries under Adjutant Mr. Brown, and ten Knights of Columbus secretaries under Mr. McCarthy of Kansas City, who joined us at Bouillonville.

All these workers rendered most valuable and devoted service; especially at a time and place when we were far afield in ruined shell-swept areas, and completely cut off from every vestige of ordinary comforts. How good a bar of chocolate, a stick of Black Jack, a "dash" of despised inglorious "goldfish" tasted to Buddie, lying cold, hungry, dirty and "cootified" in his dugout!

A distinct contribution to modern civilization, and a form of national and international altruism making for the betterment, not only of him who receives but as well of him who gives, was organized welfare work. The need of such work always existed; and the organization of trained and equipped auxiliary forces intelligently to perform it must have ever been apparent. It remained for the World War, conceived, at least in the American mind in unselfish motive, to create and give flesh and blood expression to so Divine a vocation; and assign it honored rank among National institutions eminently to be desired, and, without invidious comparison, devotedly to be maintained.

Female workers in the Salvation Army making pies for the soldiers and wearing helmets (Ansonville, France) (CCA-SA2.0).

One day, timing and dodging dropping shells, I came to ruined, bombarded Essey. A single piece of bread had been my only fare for many trying hours and I was hungry to the point of exhaustion.

Above the door of a dugout I saw the welcome sign "Salvation Army," and, making my way to the door, I knocked. It was at once opened by two lady secretaries.

The savory odor of fresh, crisp fried cakes greeted me, and in the center of the room beyond, I saw a table heaped high with the precious viands themselves! Truly it was Angel Food! Not the lily-white sort served and known as such at home, but the golden ambrosial kind angels dream of — and surely were the Salvation Army ladies who saved me that day from starving, angels. Not only did they kindly point to the table of delight and generously say, "Help yourself, Chaplain," but Adjutant Brown, husband of one of them, entering at that moment, cheerily remarked:

"Chaplain, won't you join us? We are just sitting down to dinner."

Having no other dinner engagement just then, I accepted! The table was placed under a stairway, just room for the four of us. Outside, the air was filled with the spume and shriek of bursting shells. The windows were tightly barricaded, and a candle, placed in the mouth of a bottle, gave the only light.

"Chaplain, will you offer Grace?"

Reverently all four bowed our heads in prayer; and may the good God who brought us there together, join us some future day in his heavenly home above!

The problem of transportation was most insistent and difficult. The Division being far below its quota of automobiles and motorcycles, Chaplains and burying details were compelled frequently to journey on foot, with possible aid from some passing truck.

Under these conditions I found "Jip" truly "bonne chance." "Jip" was the horse assigned me by my good friend, Lieutenant Davis, of Headquarters Troop, and whom I named after my faithful dog "Jip" of Harvey. He was a noble animal, utterly without fear; broken by chasseurs-a-cheval to gun fire. My only comrade on many a long, lone ride, we grew fond of each other to a degree only he can appreciate who has spent days and weeks of solitude and danger with a devoted horse. All the pet names and phrases "Jip" of Harvey knew, I lavished on him, leaning forward to whisper in his ear. Although it was not the familiar French he heard, it seemed to please him, and obediently he bore me on, little heeding the danger of the trail, so that he shared my sorrows and pleasures.

One beautiful day in mid-October, he carried me many miles through Bois de Puvinelle, deep in whose solitudes, at Jung Fontaine the 20th Machine Gun Battalion was camped; passing on our way ruined Martincourt, then heavily shelled, to the borders of grim Bois-le-Pretre.

Before starting on this mission, which had for its object inspecting of front line conditions and burial work, I had talked over the situation thoroughly with Colonel P. Lenoncle, French Army, who, during two years, had fought over every foot of Bois-le-Pretre, and won there his Croix de Guerre.

"Monsieur le Chaplain," he said, "this forest is a household word for danger and death throughout all Germany. I know, in your goodness, you will not fail to bury any of my brave poilu whose bodies you there may find."

Glorious was our canter down the dim leafy aisles of the Bois oak, maple, ash, and pine flamed with the glorious coloring of autumn. Crimson ivy festooned each swaying limb, weaving canopies against a mottled sky of blue and white; morning-glories nodded

Catholic service in Austrian military hospital, Ratisbon, Germany, 1916 (LOC).

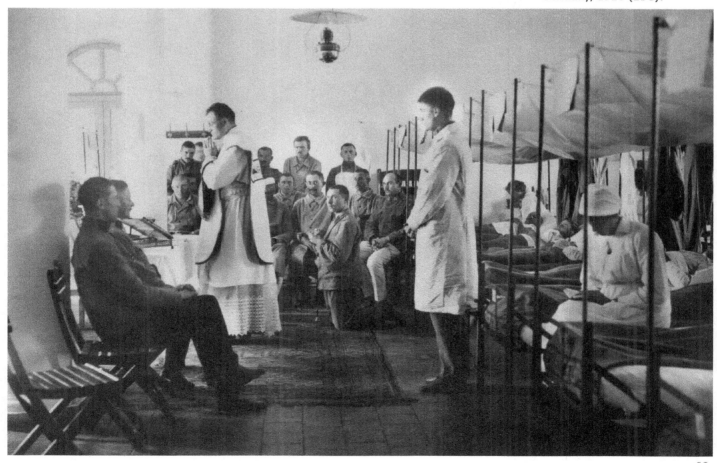

A British chaplain writing a letter for a wounded soldier in World War I. This was just one way that chaplains helped bring the Lord's peace to a world torn apart by war (PD).

greeting from the hedges, while forest floors were carpeted with the red of geranium, yellow of marigold and purple of aster.[5]

Discussion Questions

One of the high points of this memoir was the moment when this Roman Catholic chaplain is invited to dine with Salvation Army workers. Indeed, the priest is asked to say grace! In peacetime England, the Protestant Salvation Army and the Roman Catholic Church were tacit enemies. Yet, on the front lines, they were great friends. Why?

5. George T. McCarthy, *The Greater Love* (Chicago, IL: Extension Press, 1920), chapter 6, http://www.gutenberg.org/files/24889/24889-h/24889-h.htm.

Chicago Ferris Wheel, 1893 (PD).

Chapter 5

Modern America: The Cultural Revolution

First Thoughts

The first half of the 20th century witnessed the birth of modern America. These years saw several fascinating new inventions: the phonograph, the telephone, the moving picture, and the radio. For the first time, Americans also experienced mass-circulation newspapers and magazines, best-selling novels, and expensive national advertising campaigns. These years saw the rise of commercialized entertainment, including the amusement park. Many modern sports, including baseball, became popular. New transportation technologies, like the automobile, electric trains, and trolleys, and, in 1903, the airplane, were transforming America faster than most Americans could comprehend.

Chapter Learning Objectives

Chapter 5 examines the first 20th-century cultural revolution. We examine mass communication and how it changed the complexion of American life. Next we look at the rise of the theme park and commercialized entertainment. We see a national malaise arising that may be imagined or real, but has captured the imagination of a generation. Next, we briefly examine the changes in the national university, then finish by reflecting on what the loss of the American university will mean to the future of the world.

As a result of this chapter you should be able to:

1. Discuss the impact mass communication had on American society

2. Predict what problems communal entertainment will bring in the future

3. Evaluate whether or not there really is a stress disorder caused by too much change in too little time

4. Analyze how the American university changed in the early part of the 20th century

5. Pray about the sort of university God might be calling you to attend

CONCEPTS

Vaudeville

Neurasthenia

Morrill Act

Mass Communication

Yellow journalism is sensational, salacious writings to persuade an audience to buy into a lie.

The 20th century saw the emergence of mass communication — the mass-circulation newspaper, the mass-market magazine, and national advertising campaigns. American culture also made a critical shift to community forms of entertainment — e.g., the theme park, the baseball game.

From the beginning, objectivity was a casualty of mass communication. Social historian Irving Fang writes, "Because a cooperative news agency existed to serve client newspapers and thrived by acquiring still more clients, it followed that the agency would try to please all its customers, or at least as many as possible, which covered a multitude of political leanings on every conceivable issue. Pleasing as many customers as possible translated itself into transmitting facts that were colored as little as humanly possible by the agency reporter's point of view. Objective reporting, something rather new, was born. In a profession that prided itself on the brilliant essay, it took some effort of will to hold facts high and opinion low. Yet, it had to be done if full advantage were to be taken of the transmission of news dispatches by electricity."[1]

Hearst's treatment was effective and focused on the enemy who set the bomb — and offered a huge reward to readers February 17, 1898 (PD).

Newspapers, in particular, were cheap. And in order to turn a profit, editors had to publish news reports and editorials that appealed to as wide an audience as possible. At first this spawned a sort of objectivity. The so-called penny press wanted to appeal to everyone's interests and thus, logically, it stood opposed to anyone's "special" interest —except, of course, its own interests, which presumably corresponded to its expressed policy of indifference.[2]

It wasn't long, though, before journalists discovered a truism that corrupted modern media forever: the fact is Americans would buy most anything if it included sensational, salacious, interesting facts. For instance, before the Spanish American War, the Hearst Press wrote highly partisan, at times inaccurate, sensationalized reports about Spanish atrocities in Cuba. This so-called "yellow journalism" was very popular among Americans, therefore the Hearst news organization sold a lot of newspapers. The power of this medium was so thorough and ubiquitous that when the USS *Maine* exploded in Havana Harbor, the Hearst press said that the Spanish did it, and everyone believed the press, including the U.S. government.

We went to war because the Hearst people wanted to make some money. Years later, it was discovered that the Spanish had nothing to do with the *Maine* disaster. An internal explosion in the coal boiler caused it. It was merely an accident.

At the same time, politicians, government officials, and others learned how to "spin" the news to suit their own agenda.

The world of magazine publishing was also revolutionized by the rise of the country's first mass circulation national magazines. After the Civil War, the magazine field was

---

1. Irving Fang, *A History of Mass Communication: Six Information Revolutions* (Boston, MA: Focal Press, 1997), p. 52, books.google.com/books?isbn=0240802543.
2. Ibid.

dominated by a small number of magazines, like *The Atlantic, Harper's Weekly,* and *Scribner's,* written for the intellectual elite. These magazines informally enforced a media code that said that nothing should be published that did not encourage Judeo-Christian morality. Poet James Russell Lowell said that no man should describe any activity that would make his wife or daughter blush.

All this changed with the emergence of the weekly tabloid. By running popular articles, editors sought to maximize circulation, which, in turn, attracted advertising that kept the magazine's price low. By 1900, the nation's largest magazine, *The Ladies' Home Journal,* reached 850,000 subscribers — more than eight times the readership of *Scribner's* or *Harper's.*

The 20th century also marked a critical turning point in the history of book publishing, as marketing wizards like Frank Doubleday organized the first national book promotional campaigns, created the modern best seller, and transformed popular writers like Jack London and Mark Twain into celebrities. The flip side of this was that mass production of literature encouraged mediocrity. No matter how artistically perfect a literary piece might be, no publisher would publish it if it would not sell.

A social historian wrote, "In 1898, the National Biscuit Company (Nabisco) launched the first million dollar national advertising campaign. It succeeded in making Uneeda biscuits and their water-proof 'In-er-Seal' box popular household items. During the 1880s and 1890s, patent medicine manufacturers, department stores, and producers of low-priced packaged consumer goods (like Campbell Soups, H.J. Heinz, and Quaker Oats), developed modern advertising techniques. Where earlier advertisers made little use of brand names illustrations or trademarks, the new ads made use of snappy slogans and colorful packages. As early as 1900, advertisements began to use psychology to arouse consumer demand by suggesting that a product would contribute to the consumer's social and psychic well-being. To induce purchases, observed a trade journal in 1890, a consumer 'must be aroused, excited, terrified.' Listerine mouthwash promised to cure 'halitosis.' Scott tissue claimed to prevent infections caused by harsh toilet paper. By stressing instant gratification and personal fulfillment in their ads, modern advertising helped undermine an earlier Victorian ethos emphasizing thrift, self-denial, delayed gratification, and hard work. In various ways, it transformed Americans from 'savers' to 'spenders' and told them to give in to their desire for luxury."[3]

The desire for and convenience of toilet paper readily available in homes was obvious. Though the Great Depression was devastating to the overall economy, the Scott Paper Company never had to lay off one worker. The need and demand for toilet paper kept their factories operating at full capacity, with people even hoarding it in the 1950s because it had become so necessary.

Discussion Questions

Why was objectivity an early casualty of mass communication?

3. Ibid., p. 64–65.

The Theme Park

The original Chicago Ferris Wheel, 1893 (PD).

Of all the differences between the 19th and 20th centuries, one of the most striking involves the rapid growth of commercialized entertainment. Quite literally, entertainment moved from Central Park, to Coney Island, and into the home, in one generation.

With advances in technology, and social labor reform, Americans had more leisure time than ever before. They were looking for resources to help them enjoy it.

For much of American history, commercial amusement — corporate entertainment offered by separate industries — was viewed as somehow suspect. And for good reason. The most popular commercial amusement industry in America was the pub or bar. Millions of Americans were squandering their financial resources on one-shot drinks and other entertainment in these establishments. Quite literally, there were hundreds of bars in American cities — far more bars than churches. These businesses spawned other immoral, and in some cases, illegal, industries, including prostitution.

In the beginning of the 20th century there were wholesome, alternative commercial entertainment industries for the first time. During the first 20 years of the new century, attendance at professional baseball games doubled. **Vaudeville**, too, increased with entertainment previously found only at county fairs: comical acts, group dances, and one-act plays. Amusement parks, penny arcades, dance halls, and other commercial amusements flourished. Movies also entered the picture in a big way.

The rise of these new kinds of commercialized amusements radically reshaped the nature of American society. At Asbury Park or Coney Island, people of all genders and nationalities commingled. Commercial amusements and the Roman Catholic Church were the only places in American society that commingled the classes.

Ironically, the commingling of different social groups had an ameliorating effect on commercial entertainment. Coney Island, for instance, had to remove some of the less family-oriented activities to attract the more lucrative family-oriented market. Coney Island, with its technological marvels — Ferris wheels and other daredevil rides — represented a new era in entertainment.

Discussion Question

Amusement parks, in the short run, offered an alternative to beer halls and bars. Predict what sort of problems might arise in the future.

The Sandow Trocadero Vaudevilles. Promotional poster for the vaudeville act showing dancers, clowns, trapeze artists and dogs in costume, 1894 (LOC).

National Anxiety

There were two major cultural revolutions in the 20th century. The last was in the 1960s with the explosion of counterculture individualism. The first was in the first 20 years of the 20th century.

There was a real fear that too much change in too short a time was causing mental illness in the United States.

At the end of the 19th century, a New York physician, George M. Beard, coined the term "**neurasthenia**" to describe a psychological ailment that afflicted a growing number of Americans. Neurasthenia's symptoms included "nervous dyspepsia, insomnia, hysteria, hypochondria, and nervous exhaustion." According to expert medical opinion, neurasthenia's underlying cause was "over-civilization." Nervous overstimulation, stress, and emotional repression produced debilitating bouts of depression, anxiety attacks, and nervous prostration. Fears of over-civilization actually worried sociologists. The rise of social Darwinism, which posited that American society was growing stronger through natural selection and survival of the fittest, saw soft urban life, with all of its stimulus overload, as an absolute threat to the survival of the species! Social critics worried that urban life was producing a generation of wimps. We heard the same discussion at the beginning of the 21st century when television announcer Tom Brokaw talked about the Greatest Generation (the World War II generation).[4]

More frequent entertainment and advances in technology conspired to create a national anxiety. Americans were looking for all sorts of things to worry about. For instance, a sharply falling birth rate was blamed on a type of national neurasthenia. A host of therapies promised to relieve the symptoms of neurasthenia, including Dr. Hammond's Nerve and Brain Pills, which was a mild anti-depressant. Sears even sold an electrical contraption called the Heidelberg Electric Belt, designed to reduce anxiety by sending electric shocks to male private parts![5] The point is, progress of any sort caused, and is still causing, some anxiety.

> **Neurasthenia:** nervous overstimulation, stress, and emotional repression produced debilitating bouts of depression, anxiety attacks, and nervous prostration.

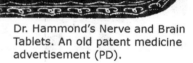

Dr. Hammond's Nerve and Brain Tablets. An old patent medicine advertisement (PD).

Discussion Question

Future Shock is a book written by the futurist Alvin Toffler in 1970.[6] In the book, Toffler defines the term "future shock" as "too much change in too short a period of time." All this change causes stress and disorientation. Was Toffler right? If so, can you give an example?

4. http://www.webmd.com/mental-health/neurasthenia.
5. www.museumofquackery.com/ephemera/heidelberg.htm.
6. Alvin Toffler, *Future Shock* (New York: Random House, 1970).

The University

Colleges underwent profound changes after the Civil War. Before the war, they were mostly religious institutions that attracted only the elite of the world. These colleges relied heavily on drill and rote memorization. The "college lecture" was rare. These institutions prescribed almost all of a student's course of study. There were very few electives. Practical subjects, like accounting, were excluded from the curricula.

The Flemish Renaissance Revival building at 899 Tenth Avenue was originally built as DeWitt Clinton High School in 1903-1906, designed by C.B.J. Synder. It was rebuilt and expanded for John Jay College of Criminal Justice of the City University of New York in 1988, designed by Rafael Vinoly.

The 1862 **Morrill Act** granted land for higher education in each state. The Morrill Act specifically directed that the endowed institutions were "to teach such branches of learning as are related to agriculture and the mechanic arts." The underlying idea was that educational institutions should support occupations in industry and the professions. This was an entirely novel idea in higher education but one that was readily embraced — principles are one thing, federal money is another. Higher education shamelessly pursued funding by immediately changing its course offerings to attract federal dollars.

At the same time, the concept of "graduate school" emerged. Modeled on German universities, these institutions did not simply train undergraduates. They also provided graduate and professional training in law, medicine, engineering, and divinity.

Suddenly, the "elective" was offered as well. The elective system made universities more attractive to a broader range of students and expanded the skills that they acquired.

At the same time, with a growing demand for higher education, the Scholastic Aptitude Test, or SAT, was created to help colleges in the growing, competitive admission process.[7]

Discussion Question

How did the American university change in the early part of the 20th century?

---

7. www.columbia.edu/cu/univprof/jcole/greatamerican.html.

Harvard or Heaven: The Decline of the Evangelical University

James P. Stobaugh

This article is about the secular colleges we will attend: how they got to be the way they are and how we can prosper in such a place.

First, to most evangelical Christians, the modern, secular university is a hostile place. It was not always so. In fact, the American university was built solidly on evangelical principles. There were no so-called official "secular" colleges until the rise of the land grant colleges in the middle of the 19th century. An early brochure, published in 1643, stated that the purpose of Harvard University (the oldest American university) was "To advance Learning and perpetuate it to Posterity; dreading to leave an illiterate Ministry to the Churches." Harvard's motto for 300 years was *Veritas Christo et Ecclesiae* (Truth for Christ and the Church). In fact, most of the U.S. universities founded before the 20th century had a strongly religious, usually Protestant evangelical Christian character. Yale, Princeton, Chicago, Stanford, Duke, William and Mary, Boston University, Michigan, and the University of California had a decidedly evangelical Christian character in their early years, but abandoned it by the 20th century. By the 1920s, the American university had stepped back completely from its evangelical roots. This was true of almost every American university founded in the first 200 years of the nation's existence.

Readers would be surprised to see how evangelical and Christ-centered early universities were. They had pastors as presidents. These men closely tied the identity of their university to a strong Christian worldview. The core curriculum included Bible courses and Christian theology. These were mandatory Bible courses. All American universities insisted on doctrinally sound content for sensitive courses and often required that faculty be born-again Christians! Imagine this: the famous historian Frederick Jackson Turner was refused a professorship at Princeton because he was a Unitarian! And chapel attendance was required at Harvard and Yale! It is more than coincidental that the architects who designed early universities designed them to look like churches. At the University of Pittsburgh, for instance, the most prominent building on campus is the Cathedral of Learning.

Universities were founded because early Americans earnestly believed that American society should be governed by evangelical Christian people. They believed that American industry should be run by evangelical Christian entrepreneurs. They believed that American culture should be created by evangelical artists. The early American university was committed to making sure that this happened.

The Cathedral of Learning. This is the angle that, according to architectural historian Franklin Toker, best reveals its Gothic tracery, setbacks and corner pinnacle (CCA-SA3.0).

The marriage of spiritual maturity and elite education is a potent combination which, to a large degree, assured the success of the American experiment. Its divorce may presage America's demise.

Today the university is not even loosely a Christian institution. Religion in the university and in public life has been relegated to the private experience. So-called "academic freedom" has become a sacrosanct concept and precludes anything that smacks of religiosity, especially orthodoxy that evangelicals so enthusiastically embrace. Religion is represented on campus in sanitary denominational ministries and token chapel ministries that are hardly more than counseling centers.

To a large degree, then, the American university abandoned the evangelical, and the evangelical abandoned the American university.

This created a crisis in the American university and in the evangelical community. The secular American university compromised its "soul" for naturalism; evangelicalism compromised its epistemological hegemony for ontological supremacy. In other words, the secular university became a sort of academic hothouse for pompous rationalism. Evangelicals abandoned the secular university, and until recently, more or less compromised their academic base. Evangelicals even founded their own universities, but they were poor academic substitutes for secular offerings. Even as I write this article, this is changing.

The university, if it has any value, must be involved in the communication of immutable, metaphysical truth. The American secular university is not about to accept such limits. It recognizes no citadel of orthodoxy, no limits to its knowledge.

Most secular universities have concluded that abstract concepts like grace, hope, and especially faith are indefinable, immeasurable, and above all unreasonable. Not that God or the uniqueness of Jesus Christ can be proved, or disproved. There are certain issues that the order of the intellect simply cannot address, so we must rise above that to the

Claverly Hall, Harvard University, Cambridge, Massachusetts, USA (PD).

order of the heart. Faith is our consent to receive the good that God would have for us. Evangelicals believe God can and does act in our world and in our lives. They also believe human needs are greater than this world can satisfy; therefore, it is reasonable to look elsewhere. The university has either forgotten or ignores this fact.

That is all changing — and partly due to the popularity of the American homeschooling movement. In massive numbers, the American homeschooling movement — initially and presently primarily an evangelical Christian movement — is depositing some of the brightest, most capable students in our country into the old, august institutions like Harvard. And, what is more exciting, the flashpoint of cultural change is shifting from Harvard, Princeton, and Stanford to Wheaton, Grove City, Calvin, and Liberty (all evangelical universities). Before long, the new wave of elite culture creators will be graduating from American secular universities and Christian universities, and they will be a great deal different from the elite of which I was a part in the mid-1970s. I am not saying that the secular university will change quickly — intellectual naturalistic reductionism makes that extremely difficult. However, I do see the whole complexion of university graduates changing significantly in the next 20 years. Never in the history of the world has such a thing happened.

Young people, make sure you know who you are and who your God is. "By faith, Moses, when he had grown up refused to be known as the son of Pharaoh's daughter" (Heb. 11:24). Theologian Walter Brueggemann calls American believers to "nurture, nourish, and evoke a consciousness and perception alternative to the consciousness and perception of the dominant culture around us."[8]

Blanchard Hall in Wheaton College, Illinois (PD).

Refuse to be absorbed into the world but choose to be a part of God's Kingdom. There is no moderate position anymore in American society — either we are taking a stand for Christ in this inhospitable culture or we are not.

You are a special and peculiar generation. Much loved. But you live among a people who do not know who they are. A people without hope. You need to know who you are — children of the Living God — and then you must live a hopeful life. Quoting C.S. Lewis, we "are half-hearted creatures, fooling about with drink and sex and ambition when infinite joy is offered us, like an ignorant child who wants to go on making mud pies in a slum because he cannot imagine what is meant by the offer of a holiday at the sea."[9]

Take responsibility for your life. Moses accepted responsibility for his life. "He chose to be mistreated along with the people of God rather to enjoy the fleeting pleasures of sin" (Heb. 11: 25). If you don't make decisions for your life, someone else will.

Get a cause worth dying for. Moses accepted necessary suffering even unto death. You need a cause worth dying for (as well as living for). "He [Moses] regarded disgrace for the sake of Christ as of greater value than the treasures of Egypt, because he was looking

8. Walter Brueggemann, *The Prophetic Imagination* (Philadelphia, PA: Fortress Press,1978), p. 13.
9. C.S. Lewis, *The Weight of Glory and Other Addresses* (Grand Rapids, MI: Eerdmans, 1965), p. 1–2. This quote is referenced in John Piper, *Desiring God* (Portland, OR: Multnomah Press, 1986), p. 16.

ahead to his reward" (Heb. 11: 26). "I have been crucified with Christ and I no longer live, but Christ lives in me" (Gal. 2:20).

Finally, never take your eyes off the goal. "By faith he left Egypt, not fearing the king's anger; he persevered because he saw him who is invisible" (Heb. 11:27). What is your threshold of obedience?

Young people, if you are part of this new evangelical elite, you have immense opportunities ahead of you. A new godly generation is arising. You will be called to guide this nation into another unprecedented revival. We shall see.

Discussion Questions

Do you feel that God may be calling you to a secular university? Why or why not? If so, what can you do to prepare?

Russians demonstrate on October 17, 1905 (PD).

Chapter 6

The Russian Revolution: Fighting with No Ethics

First Thoughts

Vladimir Lenin was fond of saying, "A lie told often enough becomes the truth." The Bolshevik Revolution of 1917 was a grand vision built on false premises. In many ways, it was the ultimate dream envisioned by Modernists. But it was the death of reason — something that modernism had sought fervently since the turn of the century. But what replaced reason was a hellish nightmare unprecedented in world history. An estimated 15 million Russians died in the Revolution, but that number pales in comparison to the carnage that Communist leader Stalin inflicted in his 1930 purges. Arthur Koestler, a Russian poet, wrote a fictional piece about a man who supported, then was an opponent of, the Bolsheviks. In this scene the character, Rubashov, is waiting in a prison cell to be executed by the Bolsheviks:

> When he asked himself, For what actually are you dying? He found no answer. It was a mistake in the system; perhaps it lay in the precept which until now he had held to be uncontestable, in whose name he had sacrificed others and was himself being sacrificed: in the precept, that the end justifies the means. It was this sentence, which had killed the great fraternity of the Revolution and made them run amuck. What had he once written in his diary? "We have thrown overboard all conventions, our sole guiding principle is that of consequent logic; we are sailing without ethical ballast."[1] — Arthur Koestler, *Darkness at Noon*

Chapter Learning Objectives

Chapter 6 looks closely at the causes and results of the Russian Revolution. It looks at the 1905 Revolution and then traces further developments to the October 1917 Revolution. Next, we will compare communism and democracy. We will read a primary source report from a sympathetic American reporter. Finally, we will examine Dr. King's criticism of communism.

As a result of this chapter you should be able to:

1. Analyze the 1905 Revolution

2. Understand the causes of the 1917 Revolution

3. Compare and contrast communism and democracy

4. Evaluate where John Reed's sympathies lie

5. Summarize Martin Luther King Jr.'s views of communism

Concepts

Crew of battleship *Potemkin*

Czar Nicholas II

Soviet

Duma

Lenin

Bolshevism

---

1. Arthur Koestler, *Darkness at Noon* (New York: Scribner, 2009), http://www.goodreads.com/work/quotes/881601-darkness-at-noon.

Russian History, 1905–1917

Czar Nicholas II was Czar when the Russian Revolution arrived.

Since the reign of Peter the Great, Russia had tried its best to define itself as a European nation. Its defeat in the Russo-Japanese War, therefore, was particularly galling since it came at the hands of an Asian nation. The British would have a similar humiliation when the Japanese captured Singapore in World War II.

To make things worse, in 1905, when the war ended, the economic situation in Russia was abysmal. Much of the land still belonged to the gentry. Furthermore, much of Russia was still steeped in feudalism and the serfs/peasants had had enough. But it was not the peasants who would start the 1905 Revolution. The conditions in which industrial workers lived were equally depressing. Both in 1905 and in 1917, the workers started the revolution.

Tsar Nicholas II (1915) (PD).

First, the workers tried peaceful, legal methods to show their displeasure. Strikes paralyzed factories in several parts of the Empire, and a Peasants' Union was established to voice the demands of the peasants. In large areas, the peasants took up arms and occupied the land they demanded. The **crew of battleship *Potemkin*** mutinied. However, army and navy overall remained loyal to **Czar Nicholas II**.

On January 9, 1905, a peaceful demonstration marched toward the Winter Palace, in St. Petersburg, in order to hand a petition to the czar. It was fired upon, an event which turned a peaceful demonstration into an outright revolution. In December 1905 the revolutionaries attempted to take control of St. Petersburg outright, but failed.

In October, the first **Soviet** or elected council was established in St. Petersburg, soon to be followed by Soviets in other cities all over Russia. Nonetheless, the revolution failed to create a national organization. To appease his people, the czar established the **Duma**, the Russian Parliament. He also granted freedom of speech, outlawed arbitrary arrest, and granted almost universal adult manhood suffrage. The government, however, was not to be elected. It was to be appointed by the czar and to represent him.

Nothing worked, and eventually Czar Nicholas II resorted to violence to quell the revolt.

Until 1905, political parties had been prohibited; some parties had been founded illegally before the revolution, while others emerged now. The most important party was the Bolzheviks. There was also a conservative Union of the Russian People, organized by state officials, nobles, and priests loyal to the autocratic state. The establishment of these political parties, no doubt a necessary measure in light of the 1905 Revolution, set the stage for the Bolshevik Revolution 12 years later.

Discussion Question

Is there anything at this point in 1905 that Czar Nicholas could have done to stop the later 1917 Russian Revolution from occurring?

Summary

The 1917 Russian Revolution was not one well-organized event in which Czar Nicholas II was overthrown and Lenin and the Bolsheviks took power. It was a series of events that took place during 1917. It really was two separate revolutions in February and October which eventually plunged the nation into Civil War before leading to the founding of the Communist State.

Attacking the Tzar's police during the first days of the March Revolution, March 1917 (PD).

Arguably, World War I was the cause of the Russian Revolution. In many ways Russia's disastrous participation in World War I was the final blow to czarist rule. In the very first engagement with the Germans at the Battle of Tannenberg, the Russian army was comprehensively beaten, suffering 120,000 casualties to Germany's 20,000. A continuing series of losses and setbacks meant that Nicholas left St. Petersburg in the autumn of 1915 to take personal control of the army. By this time, Russia was sending conscripts and untrained troops to the front, with little or no equipment, and fighting in an almost continual retreat. The spirit of the nation was broken.

On February 23, 1917, the International Women's Day Festival in St. Petersburg turned into a city-wide demonstration, as exasperated women workers left factories to protest against food shortages. Men soon joined them, and on the following day the entire populace went on strike. Nicholas ordered the police and military to intervene. However, the military was no longer loyal to the czar, and many mutinied or joined the people in demonstrations. Fights broke out, and the whole city was in chaos. On October 28, over 80,000 troops mutinied from the army, and looting and rioting was widespread. Faced with this untenable situation, Czar Nicholas II abdicated his throne. He should have also left the country.

A provisional government was formed but it also collapsed in October 1914. The Germans secretly allowed **Lenin** to return to Russia, and he led the next phase of the revolution.

Despite being allowed to seize power so easily, Lenin soon discovered that his support was far from absolute. His Peace Policy with the Germans was particularly unpopular as it ceded large amounts of Russian territory. Shortly after the October Revolution, the Russian Civil War broke out between the "Reds" (Communists) and the "Whites" (Nationalists, Conservatives, and other anti-Bolshevik groups). After a bloody four-year struggle, Lenin and the Reds won, establishing the Soviet Union in 1922 at an estimated cost of 15 million lives. In 1923, Lenin died and Stalin took over the Communist Party, which continued to rule Russia until 1991 when the USSR was dissolved.

As time would tell, the Communist regime was far more oppressive than any monarchy the Russian people had ever endured.[2]

Discussion Question

What caused the 1917 Russian Revolution?

---

2. http://www.st-petersburg-life.com/st-petersburg/1917-russian-revolution.

Communism Vs. Democracy

Communism is a political ideology that is based on common ownership.

The symbol of the hammer and sickle, which became synonymous with the Soviet Union, and the desired unity of both peasants and workers.

Communism and democracy are two opposite political ideologies. Communism is a socioeconomic structure that attempts to establish an egalitarian society. Democracy is a political system of governance either carried out by the people directly or by elected representatives.

In communism (in theory), power lies in a group of people who decide the course of action. Communism is suspicious of strong tertiary leadership of any sort. It prefers to govern by the whole group. To this end, communism has no scruples about interfering in the public life of others.

On the other hand, democracy, which also stands for equality, is governed by a group of elected people. Democracy is a rule by the people, and the elected representatives are duty bound to honor the wishes of the people who elected them.

There are other differences. Democracy and communism have entirely different economic systems. In communism, the government has complete control over the production and distribution of goods and all the resources and it is shared in the society equally. But in democracy, private parties own and control all economic entities. In communism, it is the community or the society that holds the major resources and production. Democracy thrives on free enterprise.[3]

Discussion Question

Compare and contrast communism and democracy.

Lesson 4

Ten Days that Shook the World
by John Reed

This book is a slice of intensified history — history as I saw it. It does not pretend to be anything but a detailed account of the November Revolution, when the Bolsheviki, at the head of the workers and soldiers, seized the state power of Russia and placed it in the hands of the Soviets.

Naturally most of it deals with "Red Petrograd," the capital and heart of the insurrection. But the reader must realize that what took place in Petrograd was almost exactly

3. http://www.differencebetween.net/miscellaneous/difference-between-communism-and-democracy/#ixzz1ms7FA6B7.

duplicated, with greater or lesser intensity, at different intervals of time, all over Russia.

In this book, the first of several which I am writing, I must confine myself to a chronicle of those events, which I myself observed and experienced, and those supported by reliable evidence, preceded by two chapters briefly outlining the background and causes of the November Revolution. I am aware that these two chapters make difficult reading, but they are essential to an understanding of what follows.

Many questions will suggest themselves to the mind of the reader. What is **Bolshevism**? What kind of a governmental structure did the Bolsheviki set up? If the Bolsheviki championed the Constituent Assembly before the November Revolution, why did they disperse it by force of arms afterward? And if the bourgeoisie opposed the Constituent Assembly until the danger of Bolshevism became apparent, why did they champion it afterward?

These and many other questions cannot be answered here. In another volume, "Kornilov to Brest-Litovsk," I trace the course of the Revolution up to and including the German peace. There I explain the origin and functions of the Revolutionary organisations, the evolution of popular sentiment, the dissolution of the Constituent Assembly, the structure of the Soviet state, and the course and outcome of the Brest- Litovsk negotiations. . . .

John Reed, American journalist and Communist activist, between about 1910 and about 1915 (LOC).

In considering the rise of the Bolsheviki it is necessary to understand that Russian economic life and the Russian army were not disorganized on November 7th, 1917, but many months before, as the logical result of a process which began as far back as 1915. The corrupt reactionaries in control of the Tsar's Court deliberately undertook to wreck Russia in order to make a separate peace with Germany. The lack of arms on the front, which had caused the great retreat of the summer of 1915, the lack of food in the army and in the great cities, the break-down of manufactures and transportation in 1916 — all these we know now were part of a gigantic campaign of sabotage. This was halted just in time by the March Revolution.

For the first few months of the new régime, in spite of the confusion incident upon a great Revolution, when one hundred and sixty millions of the world's most oppressed peoples suddenly achieved liberty, both the internal situation and the combative power of the army actually improved.

But the "honeymoon" was short. The propertied classes wanted merely a political revolution, which would take the power from the Tsar and give it to them. They wanted Russia to be a constitutional Republic, like France or the United States; or a constitutional Monarchy, like England. On the other hand, the masses of the people wanted real industrial and agrarian democracy.

William English Walling, in his book, Russia's Message, an account of the Revolution of 1905, describes very well the state of mind of the Russian workers, who were later to support Bolshevism almost unanimously:

They (the working people) saw it was possible that even under a free Government, if it fell into the hands of other social classes, they might still continue to starve. . . .

The Russian workman is revolutionary, but he is neither violent, dogmatic, nor unintelligent. He is ready for barricades, but he has studied them, and alone of the workers of the world he has learned about them from actual experience. He is ready and willing to fight his oppressor, the capitalist class, to a finish. But he does not ignore the existence of other classes. He merely asks that the other classes take one side or the other in the bitter conflict that draws near. . . .

They (the workers) were all agreed that our (American) political institutions were preferable to their own, but they were not very anxious to exchange one despot for another (i.e., the capitalist class). . . .

The workingmen of Russia did not have themselves shot down, executed by hundreds in Moscow, Riga and Odessa, imprisoned by thousands in every Russian jail, and exiled to the deserts and the arctic regions, in exchange for the doubtful privileges of the workingmen of Goldfields and Cripple Creek. . . .

And so developed in Russia, in the midst of a foreign war, the Social Revolution on top of the Political Revolution, culminating in the triumph of Bolshevism.

Mr. A. J. Sack, director in this country of the Russian Information Bureau, which opposes the Soviet Government, has this to say in his book *The Birth of the Russian Democracy*:

The Bolsheviks organized their own cabinet, with Nicholas Lenin as Premier and Leon Trotsky — Minister of Foreign Affairs. The inevitability of their coming into power became evident almost immediately after the March Revolution. The history of the Bolsheviki, after the Revolution, is a history of their steady growth. . . .

Foreigners, and Americans especially, frequently emphasize the "ignorance" of the Russian workers. It is true they lacked the political experience of the peoples of the West, but they were very well trained in voluntary organization. In 1917 there were more than twelve million members of the Russian consumers' Cooperative societies; and the Soviets themselves are a wonderful demonstration of their organising genius. Moreover, there is probably not a people in the world so well educated in Socialist theory and its practical application.

William English Walling thus characterizes them:

The Russian working people are for the most part able to read and write. For many years the country has been in such a disturbed condition that they have had the advantage of leadership not only of intelligent individuals in their midst, but of a large part of the equally revolutionary educated class, who have turned to the working people with their ideas for the political and social regeneration of Russia. . . .

Many writers explain their hostility to the Soviet Government by arguing that the last phase of the Russian Revolution was simply a struggle of the "respectable" elements against the brutal attacks of Bolshevism. However, it was the propertied classes, who, when they realised the growth in power of the popular revolutionary organisations, undertook to destroy them and to halt the Revolution. To this end the propertied classes finally resorted to desperate measures. In order to wreck the Kerensky Ministry and the Soviets, transportation was disorganised and internal troubles provoked; to crush the Factory-Shop Committees, plants were shut down, and fuel and raw materials diverted; to break the Army Committees at the front, capital punishment was restored and military defeat connived at.

This was all excellent fuel for the Bolshevik fire. The Bolsheviki retorted by preaching the class war, and by asserting the supremacy of the Soviets.

Between these two extremes, with the other factions which whole-heartedly or half-heartedly supported them, were the so-called "moderate" Socialists, the Mensheviki and Socialist Revolutionaries, and several smaller parties. These groups were also attacked by the propertied classes, but their power of resistance was crippled by their theories.

Roughly, the Mensheviki and Socialist Revolutionaries believed that Russia was not economically ripe for a social revolution — that only a *political* revolution was possible. According to their interpretation, the Russian masses were not educated enough to take over the power; any attempt to do so would inevitably bring on a reaction, by means of which some ruthless opportunist might restore the old régime. And so it followed that when the "moderate" Socialists were forced to assume the power, they were afraid to use it.

They believed that Russia must pass through the stages of political and economic development known to Western Europe, and emerge at last, with the rest of the world, into full-fledged Socialism. Naturally, therefore, they agreed with the propertied classes that Russia must first be a parliamentary state — though with some improvements on

Russian Tsarevich Alexei Nikolaevich was the youngest child and only son of Czar Nicholas II, the last czar of Russia who was forced to abdicate his reign during the February Revolution of 1917. A mischievous child, he was born with hemophilia, an inability for his blood to clot which he got from his mother. Held captive with his family for the next year, he would be carried into a cellar by his father, where he would watch his mother and father be killed, and then, helpless and trapped in a wheelchair because of an injury, he was shot and stabbed multiple times, dying a month shy of his 14th birthday - dead along with his parents, four sisters, and their closest servants. The mystery of his burial was finally solved in 2008 when remains of he and one of his sisters were finally recovered (PD).

the Western democracies. As a consequence, they insisted upon the collaboration of the propertied classes in the Government.

From this it was an easy step to supporting them. The "moderate" Socialists needed the bourgeoisie. But the bourgeoisie did not need the "moderate" Socialists. So it resulted in the Socialist Ministers being obliged to give way, little by little, on their entire program, while the propertied classes grew more and more insistent.

And at the end, when the Bolsheviki upset the whole hollow compromise, the Mensheviki and Socialist Revolutionaries found themselves fighting on the side of the propertied classes. . . . In almost every country in the world to-day the same phenomenon is visible.

Instead of being a destructive force, it seems to me that the Bolsheviki were the only party in Russia with a constructive program and the power to impose it on the country. If they had not succeeded to the Government when they did, there is little doubt in my mind that the armies of Imperial Germany would have been in Petrograd and Moscow in December, and Russia would again be ridden by a Tsar. . . .

It is still fashionable, after a whole year of the Soviet Government, to speak of the Bolshevik insurrection as an "adventure." Adventure it was, and one of the most marvellous mankind ever embarked upon, sweeping into history at the head of the toiling masses, and staking everything on their vast and simple desires. Already the machinery had been set up by which the land of the great estates could be distributed among the peasants. The Factory-Shop Committees and the Trade Unions were there to put into operation workers' control of industry. In every village, town, city, district and province there were Soviets of Workers', Soldiers' and Peasants' Deputies, prepared to assume the task of local administration.

No matter what one thinks of Bolshevism, it is undeniable that the Russian Revolution is one of the great events of human history, and the rise of the Bolsheviki a phenomenon of world-wide importance. Just as historians search the records for the minutest details of the story of the Paris Commune, so they will want to know what happened in Petrograd in November 1917, the spirit which animated the people, and how the leaders looked, talked and acted. It is with this in view that I have written this book.

In the struggle my sympathies were not neutral. But in telling the story of those great days I have tried to see events with the eye of a conscientious reporter, interested in setting down the truth.[4]

Discussion Question

John Reed was an American journalist who experienced firsthand the Bolshevik Revolution. Where do his sympathies lie?

---

4. http://www.marxists.org/archive/reed/1919/10days/10days/preface.htm.

"How Should a Christian View Communism," by Martin Luther King Jr.

"Let judgment run down as waters, and righteousness as a mighty stream" (Amos 5:24).

Few issues demand a more thorough and sober discussion than that presented by Communism. For at least three reasons every Christian minister should feel obligated to speak to his people on this controversial theme. The first reason recognizes that the widespread influence of Communism has, like a mighty tidal wave, spread through Russia, China, Eastern Europe, and now, even to our own Hemisphere. Nearly one billion of the peoples of the world believe in its teachings, many of them embracing it as a new religion to which they have surrendered completely. Such a force cannot be ignored.

A second reason is that Communism is the only serious rival to Christianity. Such great world religions as Judaism, Buddhism, Hinduism, and Mohammedanism are possible alternatives to Christianity, but no one conversant with the hard facts of the modem world will deny that Communism is Christianity's most formidable rival.

A third reason is that it is unfair and certainly unscientific to condemn a system before we know what that system teaches and why it is wrong.

Let me state clearly the basic premise of this sermon: Communism and Christianity are fundamentally incompatible. A true Christian cannot be a true Communist, for the two philosophies are antithetical and all the dialectics of the logicians cannot reconcile them. Why is this true?

Martin Luther King Jr. in 1964 (LOC).

I.

First, Communism is based on a materialistic and humanistic view of life and history. According to Communist theory, matter, not mind or spirit, speaks the last word in the universe. Such a philosophy is avowedly secularistic and atheistic. Under it, God is merely a figment of the imagination, religion is a product of fear and ignorance, and the church is an invention of the rulers to control the masses. Moreover, Communism, like humanism, thrives on the grand illusion that man, unaided by any divine power, can save himself and usher in a new society —

> I fight alone, and win or sink,
> I need no one to make me free;
> I want no Jesus Christ to think,
> That He could ever die for me.

Actor Lionel Stander testifies before the House Committee on Un-American Activities. Although he asked to testify to clear his name after associates linked him to the Communist Party, he was blacklisted and kept from working in Hollywood several times from the 1940s to 1965. The appearance or hint of a communist connection was enough to kill your career and lose friends in a time when a fear of communism was almost epidemic in the country. Stander sealed his fate when during his testimony, he refused to waffle or deny anything he might have said, telling committee members instead "I am not a dupe, or a dope, or a moe, or a schmoe...I was absolutely conscious of what I was doing, and I am not ashamed of anything I said in public or private." With his career essentially ended, he was able to eventually move overseas and find work as an actor. (LOC).

Cold atheism wrapped in the garments of materialism, Communism provides no place for God or Christ.

At the center of the Christian faith is the affirmation that there is a God in the universe who is the ground and essence of all reality. A Being of infinite love and boundless power, God is the creator, sustainer, and conserver of values. In opposition to Communism's atheistic materialism, Christianity posits a theistic idealism. Reality cannot be explained by matter in motion or the push and pull of economic forces. Christianity affirms that at the heart of reality is a Heart, a loving Father who works through history for the salvation of his children. Man cannot save himself, for man is not the measure of all things and humanity is not God. Bound by the chains of his own sin and finiteness, man needs a Savior.

Second, Communism is based on ethical relativism and accepts no stable moral absolutes. Right and wrong are relative to the most expedient methods for dealing with class war. Communism exploits the dreadful philosophy that the end justifies the means. It enunciates movingly the theory of a classless society, but alas! Its methods for achieving this noble end are all too often ignoble. Lying, violence, murder, and torture are considered to be justifiable means to achieve the millennial end. Is this an unfair indictment? Listen to the words of Lenin, the real tactician of Communist theory: "We must be ready to employ trickery, deceit, lawbreaking, withholding and concealing truth." Modem history has known many tortuous nights and horror-filled days because his followers have taken this statement seriously.

In contrast to the ethical relativism of Communism, Christianity sets forth a system of absolute moral values and affirms that God has placed within the very structure of this universe certain moral principles that are fixed and immutable. The law of love as an imperative is the norm for all of man's actions. Furthermore, Christianity at its best refuses to live by a philosophy of ends justifying means. Destructive means cannot bring constructive ends, because the means represent the-ideal-in-the-making and the-end-in-progress. Immoral means cannot bring moral ends, for the ends are preexistent in the means.

Third, Communism attributes ultimate value to the state. Man is made for the state and not the state for man. One may object, saying that in Communist theory the state is an "interim reality," which will "wither away" when the classless society emerges. True — in theory; but it is also true that, while it lasts, the state is the end. Man is a means to that end. Man has no inalienable rights. His only rights are derived from, and conferred by, the state. Under such a system, the fountain of freedom runs dry. Restricted are man's liberties of press and assembly, his freedom to vote, and his freedom to listen and to read. Art, religion, education, music, and science come under the gripping yoke of government control. Man must be a dutiful servant to the omnipotent state.

All of this is contrary, not only to the Christian doctrine of God, but also to the Christian estimate of man. Christianity insists that man is an end because he is a child of God, made in God's image. Man is more than a producing animal guided by economic forces; he is a being of spirit, crowned with glory and honor, endowed with the gift of freedom. The ultimate weakness of Communism is that it robs man of that quality which makes him man. Man, says Paul Tillich, is man because he is free. This freedom is expressed through man's capacity to deliberate, decide, and respond. Under Communism, the individual soul is shackled by the chains of conformity; his spirit is bound by the manacles of party allegiance. He is stripped of both conscience and reason. The trouble with Communism is that it has neither a theology nor a Christology; therefore it emerges with a mixed-up anthropology. Confused about God, it is also confused about man. In spite of its glowing talk about the welfare of the masses, Communism's methods and philosophy strip man of his dignity and worth, leaving him as little more than a depersonalized cog in the ever-turning wheel of the state.

Clearly, then, all of this is out of harmony with the Christian view of things. We must not fool ourselves. These systems of thought are too contradictory to be reconciled; they represent diametrically opposed ways of looking at the world and of transforming it. We should as Christians pray for the Communist constantly, but never can we, as true Christians, tolerate the philosophy of Communism.

Yet, something in the spirit and threat of Communism challenges us. The late Archbishop of Canterbury, William Temple, referred to Communism as a Christian heresy. He meant that Communism had laid hold on certain truths which are essential parts of the Christian view of things, although bound to them are theories and practices which no Christian could ever accept.

II.

The theory, though surely not the practice, of Communism challenges us to be more concerned about social justice. With all of its false assumptions and evil methods, Communism arose as a protest against the injustices and indignities inflicted upon the underprivileged. The Communist Manifesto was written by men aflame with a passion for social justice. Karl Marx, born of Jewish parents who both came from rabbinic stock, and trained, as he must have been, in the Hebrew Scriptures, could never forget the words of Amos: "Let judgment roll down as waters, and righteousness as a mighty stream." Marx's parents adopted Christianity when he was a child of six, thus adding to the Old Testament heritage that of the New. In spite of his later atheism and antiecclesiasticism, Marx could not quite forget Jesus' concern for "the least of these." In his writings, he champions the cause of the poor, the exploited, and the disinherited.

Communism in theory emphasizes a classless society. Although the world knows from sad experience that Communism has created new classes and a new lexicon of injustice, in its theoretical formulation it envisages a world society transcending the superficialities of race and color, class and caste. Membership in the Communist party theoretically is not determined by the color of a man's skin or the quality of blood in his veins.

Christians are bound to recognize any passionate concern for social justice. Such concern is basic in the Christian doctrine of the Fatherhood of God and the brotherhood of man. The Gospels abound with expressions of concern for the welfare of the poor. Listen to the words of the Magnificat: "He hath put down the mighty from their seats, and exalted them of low degree. He hath filled the hungry with good things; and the rich he hath sent empty away." No doctrinaire Communist ever expressed a passion for the poor and oppressed such as we find in the Manifesto of Jesus which affirms: "The Spirit of the Lord is upon me, because he hath anointed me to preach the gospel to the poor; he hath sent me to heal the brokenhearted, to preach deliverance to the

When the concept of communism was formed, many successful and elite people joined the Communist Party or attended meetings, having an interest in the idea. These interests and associations would come back to haunt many, including a number of Hollywood professionals, after an effort to blacklist or shun those who were felt to have or take part in "un-American" ideas or activities. A product of the ongoing Cold War, it was felt that Communist supporters were spies and could be dangerous to the future of the country. This fear has been connected to Senator Joe McCarthy who took part in special Senate hearings and investigations to uncover subversives and it referred to as McCarthyism. The House of Representatives also had their own anti-communist efforts with the House Committee on Un-American Activities from 1938 to 1975. (LOC).

captives, and recovering of sight to the blind, to set at liberty them that are bruised, to preach the acceptable year of the Lord."

Christians are also bound to recognize the ideal of a world unity in which all barriers of caste and color are abolished. Christianity repudiates racism. The broad universalism standing at the center of the gospel makes both the theory and practice of racial injustice morally unjustifiable. Racial prejudice is a blatant denial of the unity which we have in Christ, for in Christ there is neither Jew nor Gentile, bond nor free, Negro nor white.

In spite of the noble affirmations of Christianity, the church has often lagged in its concern for social justice and too often has been content to mouth pious irrelevancies and sanctimonious trivialities. It has often been so absorbed in a future good "over yonder" that it forgets the present evils "down here." Yet the church is challenged to make the gospel of Jesus Christ relevant within the social situation. We must come to see that the Christian gospel is a two-way road. On the one side, it seeks to change the souls of men and thereby unite them with God; on the other, it seeks to change the environmental conditions of men so that the soul will have a chance after it is changed. Any religion that professes to be concerned with the souls of men and yet is not concerned with the economic and social conditions that strangle them and the social conditions that cripple them is the kind the Marxist describes as "an opiate of the people."

Honesty also impels us to admit that the church has not been true to its social mission on the question of racial justice. In this area it has failed Christ miserably. This failure is due, not only to the fact that the church has been appallingly silent and disastrously indifferent in the realm of race relations, but even more to the fact that it has often been an active participant in shaping and crystallizing the patterns of the race-caste system. Colonialism could not have been perpetuated if the Christian Church had really taken a stand against it. One of the chief defenders of the vicious system of apartheid in South Africa today is the Dutch Reformed Protestant Church. In America slavery could not have existed for almost two hundred and fifty years if the church had not sanctioned it, nor could segregation and discrimination exist today if the Christian Church were not a silent and often vocal partner. We must face the shameful fact that the church is the most segregated major institution in American society, and the most segregated hour of the week is, as Professor Liston Pope has pointed out, eleven o'clock on Sunday morning. How often the church has been an echo rather than a voice, a taillight behind the Supreme Court and other secular agencies, rather than a headlight guiding men progressively and decisively to higher levels of understanding.

The judgment of God is upon the church. The church has a schism in its own soul that it must close. It will be one of the tragedies of Christian history if future historians record that at the height of the twentieth century the church was one of the greatest bulwarks of white supremacy.

III.

In the face of the Communist challenge we must examine honestly the weaknesses of traditional capitalism. In all fairness, we must admit that capitalism has often left a gulf between superfluous wealth and abject poverty, has created conditions permitting necessities to be taken from the many to give luxuries to the few, and has encouraged small-hearted men to become cold and conscienceless so that, like Dives before Lazarus, they are unmoved by suffering, poverty-stricken humanity. Although through social reform American capitalism is doing much to reduce such tendencies, there is much yet to be accomplished. God intends that all of his children shall have the basic necessities for meaningful, healthful life. Surely it is unchristian and unethical for some to wallow in the soft beds of luxury while others sink in the quicksands of poverty.

The Communist Manifesto (PD).

The profit motive, when it is the sole basis of an economic system, encourages a cutthroat competition and selfish ambition that inspires men to be more concerned about making a living than making a life. It can make men so I-centered that they no longer are Thou-centered. Are we not too prone to judge success by the index of our salaries and the size of the wheel base on our automobiles, and not by the quality of our service and relationship to humanity? Capitalism may lead to a practical materialism that is as pernicious as the theoretical materialism taught by Communism.

We must honestly recognize that truth is not to be found either in traditional capitalism or in Marxism. Each represents a partial truth. Historically, capitalism failed to discern the truth in collective enterprise and Marxism failed to see the truth in individual enterprise. Nineteenth-century capitalism failed to appreciate that life is social, and Marxism failed, and still fails, to see that life is individual and social. The Kingdom of God is neither the thesis of individual enterprise nor the antithesis of collective enterprise, but a synthesis which reconciles the truth of both.

IV.

Finally, we are challenged to dedicate our lives to the cause of Christ even as the Communists dedicate theirs to Communism. We who cannot accept the creed of the Communists recognize their zeal and commitment to a cause which they believe will create a better world. They have a sense of purpose and destiny, and they work passionately and assiduously to win others to Communism. How many Christians are as concerned to win others to Christ? Often we have neither zeal for Christ nor zest for his kingdom. For so many Christians, Christianity is a Sunday activity having no relevancy for Monday and the church is little more than a secular social club having a thin veneer of religiosity. Jesus is an ancient symbol whom we do the honor of calling Christ, and yet his Lordship is neither affirmed nor acknowledged by our substanceless lives. Would that the Christian fire were burning in the hearts of all Christians with the same intensity as the Communist fire is burning in the hearts of Communists! Is Communism alive in the world today because we have not been Christian enough?

We need to pledge ourselves anew to the cause of Christ. We must recapture the spirit of the early church. Wherever the early Christians went, they made a triumphant witness for Christ. Whether on the village streets or in the city jails, they daringly proclaimed the good news of the gospel. Their reward for this audacious witness was often the excruciating agony of a lion's den or the poignant pain of a chopping block, but they continued in the faith that they had discovered a cause so great and had been

As with any political theory, communism comes in many different kinds and applications. The taking of an individual's resources like land and cattle in order to create collective farms was known as collectivization under Stalin's rule from 1928 and 1940. Peasants who refused to work or resisted these efforts were denied food rations and forced to resettle in other areas, hundreds of thousands dying along the way (PD).

transformed by a Savior so divine that even death was not too great a sacrifice. When they entered a town, the power structure became disturbed. Their new gospel brought the refreshing warmth of spring to men whose lives had been hardened by the long winter of traditionalism. They urged men to revolt against old systems of injustice and old structures of immorality. When the rulers objected, these strange people, intoxicated with the wine of God's grace, continued to proclaim the gospel until even men and women in Caesar's household were convinced, until jailers dropped their keys, and until kings trembled on their thrones. T. R. Glover has written that the early Christians "out-thought, out-lived, and out-died" everyone else. Where is that kind of fervor today?

Where is that kind of daring, revolutionary commitment to Christ today? Is it hidden behind smoke screens and altars? Is it buried in a grave called respectability? Is it inextricably bound with nameless status quos and imprisoned within cells of stagnant mores? This devotion must again be released. Christ must once more be enthroned in our lives.

This is our best defense against Communism. War is not the answer. Communism will never be defeated by the use of atomic bombs or nuclear weapons. Let us not join those who shout war and who through their misguided passions urge the United States to relinquish its participation in the United Nations. These are days when Christians must evince wise restraint and calm reasonableness. We must not call everyone a Communist or an appeaser who recognizes that hate and hysteria are not the final answers to the problems of these turbulent days. We must not engage in a negative anti-Communism, but rather in a positive thrust for democracy, realizing that our greatest defense against Communism is to take offensive action in behalf of justice and righteousness. After our condemnation of the philosophy of Communism has been eloquently expressed, we must with positive action seek to remove those conditions of poverty, insecurity, injustice, and racial discrimination which are the fertile soil in which the seed of Communism grows and develops. Communism thrives only when the doors of opportunity are closed and human aspirations are stifled. Like the early Christians, we must move into a sometimes hostile world armed with the revolutionary gospel of Jesus Christ. With this powerful gospel we shall boldly challenge the status quos and unjust mores and thereby speed the day when "every valley shall be exalted, and every mountain and hill shall be made low: and the crooked shall be made straight, and the rough places plain: and the glory of the Lord shall be revealed."

Our hard challenge and our sublime opportunity is to bear witness to the spirit of Christ in fashioning a truly Christian world. If we accept the challenge with devotion and valor, the bell of history will toll for Communism. And we shall make the world safe for democracy and secure for the people of Christ.[5]

Discussion Question

Summarize Martin Luther King Jr.'s views of communism.

---

5. Martin Luther King Jr., *Strength to Love* (Minneapolis, MN: Fortress Press, 1981), p. 97–106; http://www.redmoon-rising.com/AmericanBabylon/christandcomm.htm.

Bullet-riddled taxi and the bodies of two gangsters in a New York City street after a gun battle with police, 1931 (NARA).

Chapter 7

The Volstead Act: Legislating Morality

First Thoughts

Prohibition was a noble experiment. So convinced were Americans that alcohol was the cause of virtually all evil that on the eve of Prohibition, some towns actually sold their jails. In a PBS special on Prohibition, Ken Burns tells the following story. "When the Mayor of Berlin, Gustav Boess, visited New York City in the fall of 1929, one of the questions he had for his host, Mayor James J. Walker, was when Prohibition was to go into effect. The problem was that Prohibition has already been the law of the United States for nearly a decade. When the Prohibition era in the United States began on January 19, 1920, a few naysayers predicted it would not work. They were right. Certainly, previous attempts to outlaw the use of alcohol in American history had fared poorly. When a Massachusetts town banned the sale of alcohol in 1844, an enterprising tavern owner took to charging patrons for the price of seeing a striped pig — the drinks came free with the price of admission. . . . Now, Prohibition was being implemented on a national scale, and being enshrined in the Constitution no less. What followed was a litany of unintended consequences."[1]

Chapter Learning Objectives

Chapter 7 examines the Volstead Act and Prohibition and ancillary issues surrounding this controversial attempt to legislate morality. We will look at the Women's Christian Temperance Union and gauge its effectiveness. We will end by looking at the rise of organized crime and, in particular, we will look at the life of Al Capone.

As a result of this chapter you should be able to:

1. Compare the battle over the legalization of marijuana with the legalization of alcohol

2. Evaluate when/if it is right for Christians to violate the law

3. To discuss when/if it is right to dilute one's social cause with tangential social causes

4. Explain why organized crime prospered during Prohibition

5. Analyze why it would be impossible for a colorful crime figure like Al Capone to function in today's world

1. http://www.pbs.org/kenburns/prohibition/unintended-consequences/.

Prohibition

Orange County Sheriff's deputies dumping illegal booze, Santa Ana, 1932 (PD).

At midnight, January 16, 1920, breweries, distilleries, and saloons closed their doors. The Women's Christian Temperance Union triumphed by linking Prohibition to a variety of progressive-era social causes. Proponents of Prohibition had persuaded a majority of Americans that alcohol was linked to wife beating and child abuse. They insisted that wine, beer, and hard liquor had robbed Americans of millions of dollars in the last century.

The WCTU was not the only opponent of alcohol. Henry Ford believed that imbibing decreased labor productivity. Advocates of Prohibition argued that outlawing drinking would advance all laudable social causes.

Even before the **18th Amendment** was ratified, about 65 percent of the country had already banned alcohol. In 1916, seven states adopted anti-liquor laws, bringing the number of states that prohibited the manufacture and sale of alcoholic beverages to 19. America's entry into World War I made Prohibition seem patriotic, since many breweries were owned by German Americans. In December 1917, Congress passed the 18th Amendment. A month later, President Woodrow Wilson instituted a partial Prohibition. In September, the president issued a ban on the wartime production of beer.

National Prohibition was perceived as a patriotic act. The amendment's proponents argued that grain should be used to make bread for fighting men and not to make liquor.

The wording of the 18th Amendment banned the manufacture and sale (but not the possession, consumption, or transportation) of "intoxicating liquors." A year after the ratification, Congress enacted the Volstead Act, which defined intoxicating beverages as anything with more than 0.5 percent alcohol. This meant that beer and wine, as well as whiskey and gin, were barred from being legally sold.

No one thought it would be necessary to enforce the law. Surely Americans would willingly abstain from alcohol. Advocates did not believe it would be necessary to establish a large administrative apparatus to enforce the law. The federal government never had more than 2,500 agents enforcing the law. A few states did try to help out. Indiana banned the sale of cocktail shakers and hip flasks; Vermont required drunks to identify the source of their alcohol. The original congressional appropriation for enforcement was $5 million; several years later, the government estimated enforcement would cost $300 million.

Enforcing the law proved almost impossible. Smuggling and bootlegging were widespread. In 1930, enforcement was transferred to the Justice Department.

Prohibition failed because it was unenforceable. By 1925, half a dozen states, including New York, passed laws banning local police from investigating violations.

Nonetheless, it worked to some degree. The death rate from alcoholism was cut by 80 percent. Still, in 1927 there were an estimated 30,000 illegal speakeasies — twice the number of legal bars before Prohibition. Many people made beer and wine at home. It was relatively easy to find a doctor willing to sign a prescription for medicinal whiskey. In short, in ten years America had changed its mind about alcohol consumption. It had, in effect, had a failure of nerve.[2]

Detroit police inspecting equipment found in a clandestine underground brewery during the prohibition era (NARA).

Discussion Question

Many Americans compare present legislation about marijuana to the Volstead Act. Just as the Volstead Act could not be enforced, they claim that laws about marijuana are unenforceable, thus they should be repealed. Do you agree?

Women's Christian Temperance Union

The Woman's Christian Temperance Union (WCTU) was organized by women who were concerned about the destructive power of alcohol, especially the problems it inflicted on them and their children. In the fall of 1873, women in Ohio and New York towns who were concerned about drunkenness met in churches to pray and then marched to the saloons to ask the owners to close their establishments. Within the first five years, the WCTU established a network of over 1,000 local units. It still exists today. The WCTU defined temperance as "moderation in all things healthful; total abstinence from all things harmful."

It disagreed even with the Church. Most Christians believed that the consumption of alcohol in moderation was not sinful. The WCTU preached total abstinence. The WCTU, then, disagreed with most people in secular and religious society.

In a sense, national Prohibition was a cultural war between Protestant second- and third-century Americans and immigrant Catholic and Jewish immigrants, who typically drank alcoholic beverages as part of their cultures.

Carrie Nation, 1910 (PD).

2. http://www.digitalhistory.uh.edu/disp_textbook.cfm?smtID=2&psid=3383.

In fact, the WCTU was a **nativist** organization. This meant that the WCTU did not accept Catholic, Jewish, or African American women, or women who had not been born in North America. When the WCTU began accepting African American women, they were organized into separate chapters or unions.

Its members utilized rather extreme tactics to convince Americans to abstain from alcohol. Members picketed bars and saloons. They prayed for the souls of the bar patrons. They attacked bar stools with axes. They were nasty patrons indeed.

These tactics were tame in comparison to those of perhaps the WCTU's most notorious member, Carry A. Nation. Convinced that she was inspired by God, the six foot tall, stout woman would storm into drinking establishments dressed in her trademark black dress and bonnet with a Bible in one hand and a hatchet in the other.

A contemporary account described one of her expeditions:

> Carry took the train to Wichita and spent the first day searching for an appropriate victim. She had not intended to make herself known just yet, but lost her composure in the Hotel Carey bar room.
>
> A large, risqué painting of *Cleopatra At Her Bath* caught her eye. She marched up to the bartender and shook her quivering forefinger at him. "Young man," she thundered, "what are you doing in this hellhole?"
>
> "I'm sorry, madam," replied the bartender, "but we do not serve ladies."
>
> "Serve me?" she screamed. "Do you think I'd drink your hellish poison?" Pointing to Cleopatra, she demanded, "Take down that filthy thing, and close this murder mill."
>
> With this she snatched a bottle from the bar and smashed it to the floor. Carry marched out of the bar room amidst incredulous stares of the many imbibers.
>
> Returning to her room she withdrew a heavy wooden club and an iron bar from her suitcase and bound them into a formidable weapon.

An allegorical 1874 political cartoon print, which somewhat unusually shows temperance campaigners (alcohol prohibition advocates) as virtuous armored women warriors (riding sidesaddle), wielding axes Carrie-Nation-style to destroy barrels of beer, whisky, gin, rum, brandy, wine, and liquors. The accessibility of alchol in male-only establishments, its popularity among all social stratas, and the prevalence of drunken violence in homes all led to a desire to socially reform these bad habits. Also, women working together collectively helped to alleviate the helplessness a woman may have felt within her own marital situation (PD).

In the morning she returned to the Hotel Carey, concealing her club and a supply of stones under the black cape that became her trademark. Without a word, she began her labors by demolishing *Cleopatra At Her Bath*. "Glory to God, peace on earth and goodwill to men," she shouted as she flailed against mirrors, bottles, chairs, tables and sundry accessories. Whiskey flowed in rivers across the floor.

The hotel detective found Mrs. Nation beating furiously on the long, curving bar with a brass spittoon. "Madam," he said sternly, "I must arrest you for defacing property."

"Defacing?" she screamed. "I am destroying!"[3]

Nation was without a doubt one of the most colorful characters in American history![4]

3. Lindsey Williams, "Carry Nation Left Hatchet Home on Punta Gorda Visit," Sun Coast Media Group, January 15, 1995.
4. http://www2.potsdam.edu/hansondj/Controversies/Womans-Christian-Temperance-Union.html#.UshZHvbgVcM.

Discussion Question

All jokes aside, was it right for Mrs. Nation to violate the law to advance a righteous cause?

Speech to the Women's Christian Temperance Union

By Mary Elizabeth Lease (1890)

Madame President and Fellow Citizens:

If God were to give me my choice to live in any age of the world that has flown, or in any age of the world yet to be, I would say, O God, let me live here and now, in this day and age of the world's history.

For we are living in a grand and wonderful time — a time when old ideas, traditions and customs have broken loose from their moorings and are hopelessly adrift on the great shoreless, boundless sea of human thought — a time when the gray old world begins to dimly comprehend that there is no difference between the brain of an intelligent woman and the brain of an intelligent man; no difference between the soul-power or brainpower that nerved the arm of Charlotte Corday to deeds of heroic patriotism and the soul-power or brain-power that swayed old John Brown behind his death dealing barricade at Ossawattomie. We are living in an age of thought. The mighty dynamite of thought is upheaving the social and political structure and stirring the hearts of men from centre to circumference. Men, women and children are in commotion, discussing the mighty problems of the day. The agricultural classes, loyal and patriotic, slow to act and slow to think, are to-day thinking for themselves; and their thought has crystallized into action. Organization is the key-note to a mighty movement among the masses which is the protest of the patient burden-bearers of the nation against years of economic and political superstition. . . .

Yet, after all our years of toil and privation, dangers and hardships upon the Western frontier, monopoly is taking our homes from us by an infamous system of mortgage foreclosure, the most infamous that has ever disgraced the statutes of a civilized nation. It, takes from us at the rate of five hundred a month the homes that represent the best years of our life, our toil, our hopes, our happiness. How did it happen? The government, at the bid of Wall Street, repudiated its contracts with the people; the circulating medium was contracted in the interest of Shylock from $54 per capita to less than $8 per capita; or, as Senator [Preston] Plumb [of Kansas] tells us, "Our debts were increased, while the means to pay them was decreased"; or as grand Senator [William Morris]

Portrait of Mary Elizabeth Lease (1850–1933), American lecturer, writer, and political activist (PD).

Stewart [of Nevada] puts it, "For twenty years the market value of the dollar has gone up and the market value of labor has gone down, till to-day the American laborer, in bitterness and wrath, asks which is the worst-the black slavery that has gone or the white slavery that has come?"

Do you wonder the women are joining the Alliance? I wonder if there is a woman in all this broad land who can afford to stay out of the Alliance. Our loyal, white-ribbon women should be heart and hand in this Farmers' Alliance movement, for the men whom we have sent to represent us are the only men in the councils of this nation who have not been elected on a liquor platform; and I want to say here, with exultant pride, that the five farmer Congressmen and the United States Senator we have sent up from Kansas — the liquor traffic, Wall Street, "nor the gates of hell shall not prevail against them."

It would sound boastful were I to detail to you the active, earnest part the Kansas women took in the recent campaign. A Republican majority of 82,000 was reduced to less than 8,000 when we elected 97 representatives, 5 out of 7 Congressmen, and a United States Senator, for to the women of Kansas belongs the credit of defeating John J. Ingalls; He is feeling badly about it yet, too, for he said to-day that "women and Indians were the only class that would scalp a dead man." I rejoice that he realizes that he is politically dead.

I might weary you to tell you in detail how the Alliance women found time from cares of home and children to prepare the tempting, generous viands for the Alliance picnic dinners; where hungry thousands and tens of thousands gathered in the forests and groves to listen to the words of impassioned oratory, ofttimes from woman's lips, that nerved the men of Kansas to forget their party prejudice and vote for "Mollie and the babies." And not only did they find their way to the voters' hearts, through their stomachs, but they sang their way as well. I hold here a book of Alliance songs, composed and set to music by an Alliance woman, Mrs. Florence Olmstead of Butler County, Kan., that did much toward moulding public sentiment. Alliance Glee Clubs composed of women, gave us such stirring melodies as the nation has not heard since the Tippecanoe and Tyler campaign of 1840. And while I am individualizing, let me call your attention to a book written also by an Alliance woman. I wish a copy of it could be placed in the hands of every woman in this land. *The Fate of a Fool* is written by Mrs. Emma G. Curtis of Colorado. This book in the hands of women would teach them to be just and generous toward women, and help them to forgive and condone in each other the sins so sweetly forgiven when committed by men.

Let no one for a moment believe that this uprising and federation of the people is but a passing episode in politics. It is a religious as well as a political movement, for we seek to put into practical operation the teachings and precepts of Jesus of Nazareth. We seek to enact justice and equity between man and man. We seek to bring the nation back to the constitutional liberties guaranteed us by our forefathers. The voice that is coming up to day from the mystic chords of the American heart is the same voice that Lincoln heard blending with the guns of Fort Sumter and the Wilderness, and it is breaking into a clarion cry to-day that will be heard around the world.

Crowns will fall, thrones will tremble, kingdoms will disappear, the divine right of kings and the divine right of capital will fade away like the mists of the morning when the Angel of Liberty shall kindle the fires of justice in the hearts of men. "Exact justice to all, special privileges to none." No more millionaires, and no more paupers; no more gold kings, silver kings and oil kings, and no more little waifs of humanity starving for a crust of bread. No more gaunt faced, hollow-eyed girls in the factories, and no more little boys reared in poverty and crime for the penitentiaries and the gallows. But we shall have the golden age of which Isaiah sang and the prophets have so long foretold; when the farmers shall be prosperous and happy, dwelling under their own vine and fig tree; when the laborer shall have that for which he toils; when occupancy and use shall be the only title to land, and every one shall obey the divine injunction, "In the sweat of thy face shalt thou eat bread." When men shall be just and generous, little less than gods, and women shall be just and charitable toward each other, little less than angels; when we shall have not a government of the people by capitalists, but a government of the people, by the people.

Ladies and gentlemen, I thank you.[5]

Discussion Question

Mary Elizabeth Lease (1853–1933) was an American lecturer, writer, and political activist. She was an advocate of the suffrage movement as well as an advocate of temperance, but she was best known for her work with the Populist Party. It is instructive that temperance was connected with other social causes: populism (a sort of 19th century Tea Party Movement) and the suffrage movement. Critics of Lease argued that she diluted her temperance work with tangential politics. Some WCTU members, Carry Nation for one, saw the temperance movement as the primary and most holy calling above all other social causes. Sometimes reformers hurt their main cause by joining tangential causes. Another example was Martin Luther King Jr. King was making great strides with Civil Rights legislation when he joined the anti-Vietnam War movement. He lost many supporters who thought he should stay focused on Civil Rights. What do you think? Do you think Lease and King were wrong to support equally important, but at times contradictory social causes?

The temperance movement was a response to a growing worry of drunkenness and excess living, especially to protect women and children. At the time, women had limited educational or career options beyond marrying and having children. They relied on their husbands to make the living and provide for them and their family. Imagine a woman with hungry mouths to feed only to find out her husband drank away his entire paycheck and she has no recourse.

Remember, up until this time, family assets were owned by men, though in the 1830s, movement began to allow married women to have some control over marital assets, and after 70 years of struggle, by 1920 women finally won the right to vote (LOC).

5. http://www.historyisaweapon.org/defcon1/marylease2.html.

The Mafia

The Mafia settled in the United States in the early 20th century, where newly arrived Italian immigrants frequently knew no English and clustered in the same neighborhoods. Immigrants joined these secret societies, or gangs.

Prohibition birthed many criminal organizations in the United States.

The Mafia, also known as La Cosa Nostra or the Mob, was the umbrella name of several clandestine organizations in Sicily and the United States. It prospered during Prohibition.

"Mafia" was originally the name of a loose association of Sicilians in the Middle Ages who collaborated for protection during the Spanish occupation of the island. Local citizens believed they could not trust Spanish law enforcement officials, and so organized their own protection societies that eventually evolved into the Mafia. The confederation later engaged in organized crime.

Midway through the 20th century, Mafia influence crested in the United States. A flurry of FBI investigations in the 1970s and 1980s somewhat blunted the Mafia's power.

The Prohibition era of the 1920s prospered the Mafia and other organized crime syndicates in the United States. Federal efforts to enforce Prohibition, including raids on speakeasies, were countered by well-organized bootlegging operations with national and international connections. These were multi-million dollar operations. Bootlegging liquor across the border from Canada was relatively easy and highly profitable.

A particularly notorious gang of the times was Al Capone's mob in Chicago. There were also gangs in Detroit, New York, and other cities. Wars among gangs, producing ugly killings, frequently made headlines.

Organized crime did not go away when Prohibition ended. When the 1933 repeal of Prohibition made buying liquor legal once again, gangs found other profit-making ventures. They resorted to different sources of illegal gain, among them gambling, narcotics trafficking, and labor racketeering.

Crime leaders of the 1930s knew from experience in the previous decade that solid political connections were an advantage, and inter-gang wars benefited no one. Gang meetings were held frequently to solve problems and maintain the peace. By the 1950s, organized crime was a billion-dollar industry and involved in many diversified industries and businesses.[6]

Discussion Question

Why did the mob prosper during Prohibition?

6. http://www.u-s-history.com/pages/h1596.html.

Al Capone

Born of an immigrant family in Brooklyn, New York, in 1899, Al Capone quit school after the sixth grade and associated with a notorious street gang, eventually becoming accepted as a member. Johnny Torrio was the street gang leader and among the other members was Lucky Luciano, who would later become a mob leader. This turn-of-the-century mob would spawn some of the most notorious criminals of the 20th century.

Al Capone was one of the most notorious gangsters of the 20th century (PD).

In 1920, at Torrio's invitation, Capone joined Torrio in Chicago, where he had become an influential lieutenant in the Colosimo mob. Everyone was prospering with liquor sales, or the "growth industries." Torrio and Capone, though, were careful to invest in legitimate businesses. They were part owners of businesses in the cleaning and dyeing field. They also joined the Chamber of Commerce and were highly visible in Chicago society. Through bribes and threats, they influenced public officials and labor unions.

Torrio soon rose to full leadership of the gang with the violent demise of Big Jim Colosimo, and Capone was his strong right arm.

In 1925, Capone became boss when Torrio, seriously wounded in an assassination attempt, surrendered control and retired to Brooklyn. Capone had built a fearsome reputation in the ruthless gang rivalries of the period, struggling to acquire and retain "racketeering rights" to several areas of Chicago. That reputation grew as rival gangs were eliminated or nullified, and the suburb of Cicero became, in effect, a fiefdom of the Capone mob. Capone was cruel, brutal, and vengeful, even in a society where such characteristics were normal.

The FBI became involved when Al Capone failed to appear before a federal grand jury on March 12, 1929, in response to a subpoena. On March 11, his lawyers formally filed for postponement of his appearance, submitting a physician's affidavit dated March 5. This affidavit attested that Capone had been suffering from bronchial pneumonia in Miami and had been confined to bed from January 13 to February 23, thus it would be dangerous to Capone's health to travel to Chicago. The date of his appearance before the grand jury was re-set for March 20.

However, Capone was healthy enough to take a vacation to Bimini and a cruise to Nassau in the Bahamas.

Law enforcement officials could not convict Capone of murder, although he had committed murder several times. Thus they had to rely on more minor offenses.

Capone appeared before the federal grand jury in Chicago on March 20, 1929, and completed his testimony on March 27. As he left the courtroom, he was arrested by agents for contempt of court, an offense for which the penalty could be one year in prison and a $1,000 fine. He posted a $5,000 bond and was released.

Bonnie Parker and Clyde Barrow, pictured sometime between 1932 and 1934, when their exploits in Arkansas included murder, robbery, and kidnapping. Contrary to popular belief the two never married. (LOC).

On May 17, 1929, Al Capone and his bodyguard were arrested in Philadelphia for carrying concealed deadly weapons. Within 16 hours they had been sentenced to terms of one year each. Capone served his time and was released in nine months for good behavior on March 17, 1930.

On February 28, 1931, Capone was found guilty in federal court on the contempt of court charge and was sentenced to six months in Cook County Jail. His appeal on that charge was subsequently dismissed.

Meanwhile, the U.S. Treasury Department had been developing evidence on tax evasion charges — in addition to Al Capone, his brother Ralph "Bottles" Capone, Jake "Greasy Thumb" Guzik, Frank Nitti, and other mobsters were subjects of tax-evasion charges.

On June 16, 1931, Al Capone pled guilty to tax evasion and Prohibition charges. He then leaked to the press that he had struck a deal for a two-and-a-half year sentence, but the judge informed Capone that he, the judge, was not bound by any deal. Capone then changed his plea to not guilty.

On October 18, 1931, Capone was convicted after trial and on November 24 was sentenced to 11 years in federal prison, fined $50,000, and charged $7,692 for court costs in addition to $215,000 plus interest due on back taxes. The six-month contempt of court sentence was to be served concurrently.

While awaiting the results of appeals, Capone was confined to the Cook County Jail. Upon denial of appeals, he entered the U.S. penitentiary in Atlanta, serving his sentence there and at Alcatraz.

On November 16, 1939, Al Capone was released after having served seven years, six months and 15 days, and having paid all fines and back taxes. Capone died on January 25, 1947.[7]

Discussion Question

Why would it be impossible for a colorful crime figure like Al Capone to function in today's world?

7. http://www.fbi.gov/about-us/history/famous-cases/al-capone.

Family reading time (CCA-
SA2.0).

Chapter 8

American Education:
A Dream Deferred

First Thoughts

Of all the ideas advanced by pre-Civil War reformers, none was more radical and
controversial than the principle that all American children, regardless of social class,
should be educated to their fullest capacity at public expense. Educational reformers
left our nation with a lasting legacy: a faith that schools provide the best solution to
our nation's problems. Unfortunately, as we move forward in the 21st century, more
than ever, American public education (some call it "American government school") is a
dream deferred.

Chapter Learning Objectives

Chapter 8 examines American education, specifically American public education. First
we look at education for the first 250 years of our history. Then we listen to teacher
voices from the 19th century. Next we examine the socialization challenges that public
education has brought to American education. Finally, we look more closely at the
history of homeschooling.

As a result of this chapter you should be able to:

1. Define the moment when American education showed signs of decline

2. Pretend that you are a student in one of the early American schools

3. Evaluate Horace Mann's contribution to education

4. Analyze an essay's views of government schools

5. Discuss the impact of Moore and Holt on education

6. Research *Stobaugh v. Pittsburgh Board of Education*

CONCEPTS

Homeschooling

Horace Mann

Raymond Moore

John Holt

Public Education

From the beginning of American history, education occurred in the home or at church. Only later did it move into the public arena, and not until 200 years after the Pilgrims landed at Plymouth, Massachusetts.

As a result, during the early 19th century, the United States had the highest rate of literacy in the Western world. We were the most educated nation in the world because we taught our kids in our homes and churches. But we changed all that.

The industrial revolution took moms out of the home and, at the same time, educational theory proposed that education by the "professional" was preferable to any other option. Education thus moved into the public arena.

Schools were not originally graded or differentiated. All students of all ages and abilities were taught in these one-room school houses. Often students learned by speaking out loud. These were called "blab" schools.

By the 1830s, most American communities offered some sort of public education. It was normally funded by public monies (usually property taxes) and in some cases private donations and subscriptions. This was especially true in towns where there were large industries. Businesses would heavily subsidize the schools.

For all of the 19th century and part of the 20th, schools, North and South, were segregated. In the South, until the early 20th century, African Americans did not have a public school option. Neither did Roman Catholics. That is one reason Roman Catholic parochial schools were started.

Still, the opportunity to attend schools was limited. Formal schooling was largely restricted to those who could afford to pay. Even "free" schools often required payment of tuition, and primary schools required entering students to be literate, barring children who had not been taught to read by their parents. Even though most Americans now preferred a public or private education, very few could actually afford it. Some free public schools required parents to pay for materials and other fees, so, in actuality, free public education was anything but free.

Many schools admitted pupils regardless of age, mixing children as young as two or three with adults in their twenties or early thirties. One-room classrooms could contain as many as 80 pupils. Few textbooks were available, and most learning amounted to a monotonous repetition of facts. School buildings were generally unpainted, overcrowded, lacked blackboards and windows, and often had no more than one outdoor toilet!

The American classroom was sparsely decorated and furnished. School design was simple, expressing the frugality of a largely rural, agricultural economy. Schools usually pulled double or triple duty as a church or municipal building. Often the school would be open only for a few months of the year, usually when children were not needed to work at home or on the farm.

The sole teacher was usually an unmarried woman, and sometimes the students were older than the teacher. Using only the most basic resources — slate, chalk, and a few books — teaching and learning consisted mainly of literacy, penmanship, arithmetic, and etiquette. Recitation, drilling, and oral quizzes at the end of the day were the norm in classrooms across America.

Throughout the 17th and 18th centuries, wooden canes were used to enforce discipline in the classroom. The leather strap was introduced in the 1850s, along with the hickory switch — a narrow branch of green wood, often cut by the student in trouble. By the 1890s the paddle was introduced and usually kept within sight behind the teacher's desk. Back then, there was no afterschool detention!

Nonetheless, Americans highly valued their schools, even if they did not wish to pay for them. Parents supplied the wood or other fuel for the stove to keep the schoolroom warm in the winter. Parents built school desks and took turns cleaning and maintaining the school. Teachers often lived with local families, rotating from household to household.

Discussion Question

What was the defining moment when American education showed signs of decline?

Primary Source, 1831

Ten years ago I was called to superintend a district school . . . in Connecticut. . . .

The school had usually been under the care of a male instructor four or five months in the winter, and a female as many months in the summer, with a vacation in the spring, and another in the fall, off from one to two months each. The instructors had been changed often; few of them ever taught two seasons in succession. The school was large, and the pupils rather ungovernable. . . . No one remaining in the school more than little could be done, except assisting the pupils in recalling what they had forgotten during the previous long vacation, inculcating new laws, and perhaps introducing some new school-book. . . . School was commenced precisely at 9 a.m., and 1 p.m., throughout the year. . . . The greatest number I ever had . . . was about sixty, and this only during a very short period of the winter; the school averaged forty-four throughout the year. . . .

Many pupils had a mile to walk, and some nearly two. . . . When I entered the school, there were fifty scholars under five years of age. The greater part were under four, and several only about three. . . . I stoutly maintained, that no child ought to be sent to school under five years of age. But the parents insisted on sending them, and I was obliged to submit. To meet the exigency, means were provided at the schoolhouse for allowing them to sleep occasionally during the hot weather. . . .

Interior view of Oakdale School near Loyston, Tennessee. From 30 to 40 pupils usually attend, 1933 (NARA).

The second teacher's account:

The school house stood . . . at the junction of four roads, so near the usual track of carriages that a large stone was set up at the end of the building to defend it from injury. Except in the dry season the ground is wet, permitting small collections of water on the surface. . . . The spot is peculiarly exposed to the bleak winds of winter; nor are there at present any shade trees near, to shelter the children from the scorching rays of the summer's sun during their recreations. . . . Neither is there any such thing as an outhouse of any kind, not even a wood shed. The size of the building was twenty-two feet long, by twenty broad. . . . Around three sides of the room, were connected desks arranged so that when the pupils were sitting at them, their faces were towards the instructor and their backs towards the wall. Attached to the sides of the desks nearest the instructor, were benches for small pupils. The instructor's desk and chair occupied the centre. On this desk were stationed a rod or ferule [a cane]; sometimes both. . . .

The windows were five in number. . . . They were situated so low in the walls, as to give full opportunity to the pupils to see every traveler as he passed, and to be easily broken. . . . The school was not infrequently broken up for a day or two for want of wood in former years; but since they have used a smaller fire place, this occurrence has been more rare. The instructor or pupils were, however, sometimes compelled to cut or saw it, to prevent the closing of the school. . . . The [school]house was frequently cold and uncomfortable. . . . Frequently too, we were annoyed by smoke. . . .

The ventilation of the school room, was as much neglected as its temperature; and its cleanliness, more perhaps than either. . . . There were . . . no arrangements made for cleaning feet at the door, or for washing floors, windows. Instructors have usually boarded in the families of the pupils. The compensation has varied from seven to eleven dollars a month for males; and from sixty two and a half cents to one dollar a week for females. . . .[1]

Discussion Question

Pretend that you are a student in one of these schools. Keep a two-day diary where you describe everything that happens.

---

1. From *America Annals of Instruction*, II (August and October 1831), p. 380–383, 468–472.

Horace Mann

The nation's leading advocate of public schools was Massachusetts' **Horace Mann** (1796–1859). As a state legislator, he lobbied for the establishment of a state board of education, and then resigned his seat to become secretary of the board in 1837.

During his twelve years as board secretary, he successfully campaigned against formidable opposition for property taxes to pay for public schools. He also succeeded in keeping formal religious instruction outside of schools and confined to churches. His other achievements included establishing teacher training colleges, placing students in grades according to their age and ability, and lengthening the school year.[2]

Mann's commitment to the public education sprang from his belief that a healthy free society depended on education: a basic level of literacy and the inculcation of common public ideals. He declared, "Without undervaluing any other human agency, it may be safely affirmed that the common school . . . may become the most effective and benignant of all forces of civilization." Mann believed that public schooling was central to good citizenship. He observed, "A republican form of government, without intelligence in the people, must be, on a vast scale, what a mad-house, without superintendent or keepers, would be on a small one."

Horace Mann formed most assumptions about public schooling that still affect education policy today (PD).

Biographer Jonathan Messerli writes, "Mann was influential in the development of teacher training schools and the earliest attempts to professionalize teaching. He was not the first to propose state-sponsored teacher training institutes (James Carter had recommended them in the 1820s), but, in 1838, he was crucial to the actual establishment of the first Normal Schools in Massachusetts. Mann knew that the quality of rural schools had to be raised, and that teaching was the key to that improvement. He also recognized that the corps of teachers for the new Common Schools were most likely to be women, and he argued forcefully (if, by contemporary standards, sometimes insultingly) for the recruitment of women into the ranks of teachers, often through the Normal Schools. These developments were all part of Mann's driving determination to create a system of effective, secular, universal education in the United States."[3]

Discussion Question

Many conservative Christians, both Protestant and Roman Catholic, feel that Horace Mann did a great disservice to American education. Why?

---

2. http://www.class.uh.edu/gl/educ6.htm.
3. Jonathan Messerli, *Horace Mann, A Biography* (New York: Knopf, 1972).

Secondary Essay

Education and Socialization, **Erich Rauch**

An education is one of the few things that we can give ourselves and our children that will have lifelong effects. Although most American families send their children — as they themselves were sent by their own parents — to public schools, how often have we stopped to question the goals of the public education system? Christian parents especially should be asking this question if they are truly concerned whether their goals for educating their children are similar to the public schools'. Proverbs 1:7 tells us "the fear of the Lord is the beginning of knowledge." It should stand to reason that if "the fear of the Lord" is the beginning of knowledge, starting a quest for knowledge anywhere else will not yield true knowledge.

Revelation 21 describes the "new heaven and earth" and the New Jerusalem. In verse 23–24 we read: "And the city has no need of the sun or of the moon to shine on it, for the glory of God has illumined it, and its lamp is the Lamb. The nations will walk by its light, and the kings of the earth will bring their glory into it." Notice that the final chapters of the final book of the Bible speak of being "illumined" by the light of God. The Lord is the beginning AND end of understanding and learning. This is the goal of education for the Christian. Notice also that the "kings of the earth" have glory of their own, but they bring it into (i.e. subject it to) God's light. We must remember that our mind is a gift from God and we are to think His thoughts after Him.

The goal of education then — for the Christian at least — is not to acquire a bunch of facts and knowledge, but to glorify God. Our minds are to be sacrificed in humble dedication to the One who made thought possible. "Do not be conformed to this world, but be transformed by the renewing of your mind, so that you may prove what the will of God is, that which is good and acceptable and perfect" (Romans 12:2). Rather than viewing education as a means to an end — a better job, more money, higher social status, better at Trivial Pursuit, etc. — we must view our education as a constant renewing of our minds in order to better think God's thoughts after Him. If the educational establishment where you or your children are enrolled does not share this goal, then it should cause you to rethink sending you or your children there to be "educated." As Allan Bloom points out below (and it has only gotten worse since he wrote these words in 1987), every educational

"Snap-the-Whip" [9 boys playing in front of rural schoolhouse], first appeared in Harpers Weekly 1873 (LOC).

system has a goal. And although he is primarily referring to universities in his book, the same holds true at every level of education.

Every educational system has a moral goal that it tries to attain and that informs its curriculum. It wants to produce a certain kind of human being. This intention is more or less explicit, more or less a result of reflection; but even the neutral subjects, like reading and writing and arithmetic, take their place in a vision of the educated person. In some nations the goal was the pious person, in others the warlike, in others the industrious. Always important is the political regime, which needs citizens who are in accord with its fundamental principle. Aristocracies want gentlemen, oligarchies men who respect and pursue money, and democracies lovers of equality. Democratic education, whether it admits it or not, wants and needs to produce men and women who have the tastes, knowledge, and character supportive of a democratic regime. Over the history of our republic, there have obviously been changes of opinion as to what kind of man is best for our regime. . . . This education has evolved in the last half-century from the education of democratic man to the education of the democratic personality.

The palpable difference between these two can easily be found in the changed understanding of what it means to be an American. The old view was that, by recognizing and accepting man's natural rights, men found a fundamental basis of unity and sameness. Class, race, religion, national origin or culture all disappear or become dim when bathed in the light of natural rights, which give men common interests and make them truly brothers. The immigrant had to put behind him the claims of the Old World in favor of a new and easily acquired education. This did not necessarily mean abandoning old daily habits or religions, but it did mean subordinating them to new principles. There was a tendency, if not a necessity, to homogenize nature itself.

The recent education of openness has rejected all that. It pays no attention to natural rights or the historical origins of our regime, which are now thought to have been essentially flawed and regressive. It is progressive and forward-looking. It does not demand fundamental agreement or the abandonment of old or new beliefs in favor of the natural ones. It is open to all kinds of men, all kinds of life-styles, all ideologies. There is no enemy other than the man who is not open to everything. But when there are no shared goals or vision of the public good, is the social contract any longer possible? . . .

In 1970, Ivan Illich pointed out that we had confused "going to school" with "getting an education," and this confusion has only gotten worse in the intervening 40 years. Government education is accomplishing with amazing accuracy the very goal that it has openly stated from its beginnings: a "socialized" public.

Our culture is being manipulated to worship the state. We see the state as a god, with the right to control everything which it chooses. The state is being endowed with powers for controlling the destiny of its human resources — the power of predestination. Our culture teaches us to think of the state as having a natural right to control the education of children for the sake of society, because, after all, the democratic state is the embodiment of society. Our culture teaches us that the state has a compelling interest in its own survival and success. Hence the state must own the children, for the children are the future. Though this doctrine is rarely stated in such explicit terms, it is nevertheless the implicit declaration of virtually all state programs. The state seeks to be omniscient — to know everything about us. The state seeks to be omnipresent — to be everything in society. The state seeks to be omnipotent — to control everything in society. The state is the incarnation of the god of humanism. Man, through the state, has become the measure of all things. The promise of the tempter in the Garden of Eden is at last

"In 1970, Ivan Illich pointed out that we had confused "going to school" with "getting an education," and this confusion has only gotten worse in the intervening 40 years. Government education is accomplishing with amazing accuracy the very goal that it has openly stated from its beginnings: a "socialized" public."

fulfilled in the socialist state. Man is as a god, determining for himself what is good and evil — measuring everything by his own invented standards, apart from God's revealed standards.[4]

Discussion Question

The author is obviously opposed to "government schools." What are some of his arguments?

Lesson 5

Homeschooling: Back to the Future?

Isabel Lyman (excerpts)[5]

Homeschooling is defined simply as the education of school-aged children at home rather than at a formal school 50 percent or more of the time. Homeschools, according to those who have observed or created them, are as diverse as the individuals who choose that educational method.

> They [homeschools] range from the highly structured to the structured to the unstructured, from those which use the approaches of conventional schools to those which are repulsed by conventional practice, and from the homeschool that follows homemade materials and plans to the one that consumes hundreds of dollars worth of commercial curriculum materials per year.[6]

The seeds of what has grown into the modern-day American homeschooling movement were planted by two unrelated individuals about 30 years ago. In 1969, Raymond Moore, a former U.S. Department of Education employee, laid the groundwork that would legitimatize homeschooling as one of the great, populist educational movements of the 20th century.

Raymond Moore and his wife, Dorothy Moore, went on to write *Home Grown Kids* and *Home-Spun Schools*, which were published in the 1980s. The books, which are written from a Christian perspective but offer a universal message for all interested parties, have sold hundreds of thousands of copies and offer practical advice to parents on how to succeed as home educators. The Moores advocate a firm but gentle approach to home education that balances study, chores, and work outside the home in an atmosphere geared toward a child's particular developmental needs.

---

4. http://americanvision.org/2624/the-socialization-of-education/.
5. Isabel Lyman, "Homeschooling: Back to the Future?" http://www.cato.org/pubs/pas/pa-294.html.
6. Brian D. Ray, "A Profile of Home Education Research," Home School Legal Defense Association, Purcellville, Va., 1992, p. 6.

During the 1960s and early 1970s, another voice emerged in the public school debate, a voice for decentralizing schools and returning greater autonomy to teachers and parents. John Holt, an Ivy League graduate and a teacher in alternative schools, was decrying the lack of humanity toward schoolchildren, even in the most compassionate school settings. Holt was also a critic of the compulsory nature of schooling. He wrote,

> To return once more to compulsory school in its barest form, you will surely agree that if the government told you that on one hundred and eighty days of the year, for six or more hours a day, you had to be at a particular place, and there do whatever people told you to do, you would feel that this was a gross violation of your civil liberties.[7]

Holt, who had long advocated the reform of schools, became increasingly frustrated that so few parents were willing to work toward change within the system. Consequently, after his own years as a classroom teacher, he observed that well-meaning but over-worked teachers, who program children to recite right answers and discourage self-directed learning, often retard children's natural curiosity. He chronicled his litany of complaints in *How Children Fail.*

In summary, Holt espoused a philosophy that could be considered a laissez faire approach to home-based education or, as he called it, "learning by living." It is a philosophy that Holt's followers have come to describe as "unschooling."

> What is most important and valuable about the home as a base for children's growth into the world is not that it is a better school than the schools but that it isn't school at all. It is not an artificial place, set up to make "learning" happen and in which nothing except "learning" ever happens. It is a natural, organic, central, fundamental human institution; one might easily and rightly say the foundation of all other human institutions.[8]

---

7. John Holt, *Teach Your Own* (New York: Delacorte, 1981), p. 21.
8. Ibid., p. 346.

Discussion Question

What did Moore and Holt write that influenced education in the United States?

Current homeschooling trends:

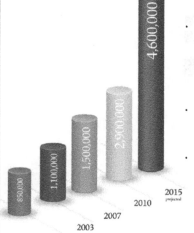

- Current estimates are that about 2.04 million students are being home-educated in the United States. Though because of lack of reporting requirements, it is felt the number is probably higher. (www.nheri.org/)

- The National Center for Education Statistics (NCES) has done two major studies—one in 2003 and in 2007. The 2007 study calculated around 3 percent of school-age children nationwide were being homeschooled, and increase of 77 percent between 1999 and 2007.

- ...and other experts have suggested that NCES estimates are too low by at least 10 percent. (http://www.wnd.com/2012/09/rural-homeschooling-on-rise/)

- The Alliance for Separation of School and State noted the number of homeschooled children in the United States is equivalent to all public schooled children in the following 13 states (and Washington, D.C.) combined: Alaska, Delaware, Hawaii, Idaho, Maine, Montana, New Hampshire, North Dakota, Rhode Island, South Dakota, Vermont, West Virginia, Wyoming, and Washington, D.C. (http://www.schoolandstate.org/stats.htm; US Dept. of Education, NCES)

Some key homeschooling facts:

- Homeschool students are statistically more successful than their public school counterparts and these students are being actively recruited by leading colleges.... homeschool students typically score higher on standardized college admissions tests.

- Homeschool freshmen have higher GPAs in their first semester at college....

- Graduation rates show a higher disparity between homeschoolers and the national average, with 66.7 percent of homeschooled students graduating, compared to 57.5 percent.

- The National Merit Scholar program is an academic competition offering prestige and scholarship money for high achieving students; in 1995, there were 21 homeschool finalists, compared with 129 in 2003, a 500 percent increase.

- Eighty percent of homeschool students were admitted to "upper levels of admission," and 67 percent were in the Honors College.

(http://www.onlinecollege.org/2011/09/13/15-key-facts-about-homeschooled-kids-in-college/)

Baptism scene from the 1913 Italian silent film *Quo Vadis?*, c1913 (LOC).

Chapter 9

Evangelicalism: Salvation and Biblical Authority

First Thoughts

Evangelicalism took America by storm in the 18th century, and its influence has not abated in 300 years. Revivalism spawned and flowed forth from a series of revivals that swept the North Atlantic Anglo-American world in the 17th, 18th, 19th, and 20th centuries. Figures associated with these revivals included the itinerant English evangelist George Whitefield (1715–1770), the founder of Methodism, John Wesley (1703–1791), and the American philosopher and theologian Jonathan Edwards (1703–1758). These revivals were particularly responsible for the rise of the Baptists and Methodists from obscure sects to their traditional position as America's two largest Protestant denominational families.

Chapter Learning Objectives

We will look closely at the development of evangelicalism from 1700 to the present. Then we will evaluate a few theories of evangelicalism and predict its future.

As a result of this chapter study you should be able to:

1. Analyze early evangelicalism

2. Review 18th and 19th-century evangelicalism

3. Choose which type of evangelical you are

4. Evaluate the veracity of Mark Noll's criticism of evangelicalism

5. Predict the future of evangelicalism

Early Evangelicalism

> Evangelicalism is a movement in the Christian Church whose members believe in the authority of the Bible and salvation through personal acceptance of Jesus Christ.

Evangelical Christianity in the 18th century represented something new. It took America by storm.

The first influence that brought evangelicalism to the forefront was the Anglican Church (the Church of England) and its emphasis on the small group, accountability meeting. These reforming societies were sponsored and defended quite strongly by John Wesley's father. Later, John and Charles Wesley formed the Methodist societies that held their members accountable to a strict ethical standard.

Next, evangelicalism emerged from Calvinistic Protestantism in the Puritan movement. This was a movement that broke with Anglicanism on questions of church order, and emphasized the sovereignty of God in salvation, as well as the comprehension of Christian assurance through the work of the Holy Spirit. The most notable proponents of this aspect of evangelicalism were Jonathan Edwards in America and George Whitefield in England.

The final distinctive of evangelicalism emerged from European pietism. The European pietists pioneered lay preaching, youth ministry, an innovative hymnology, and an emphasis on privatistic and corporate prayer. The Moravians were the most famous evangelicals of this type.

Evangelical Methodists took England and America by storm. Many new converts emerged in the southern United States. Likewise, the **Second Great Awakening** exploded in New England and became one of the most formative pre-Revolutionary events in history. Finally, the Moravians arrived in the latter part of the 18th century and were the first to be very successful in preaching to the slaves.

Discussion Question

What are the three distinctives of evangelicalism, and from which groups did they emerge?

Statue of John Wesley by Paul Raphael Montford, in Melbourne (PD).

18th- and 19th-Century Evangelicalism

London became the foremost city for the evangelical in the mid-19th century; it was the clearinghouse of people, ideas, books, and revival. Jonathan Edward's tract, *A Faithful Narrative*, which is the key early document in the evangelical movement, only had an impact when it was published in London. After that, people all over Europe and America read it.

In every major church — except the Roman Catholic Church — there existed a dissenting group. These dissenting groups, encouraged by the Moravian, Wesley, Whitfield, and Edwards' revivals, carved a new theological direction for their local churches, or abandoned their traditional churches altogether for evangelical denominations (e.g., Methodism). In general, throughout the 18th and on to the 19th century, the whole of the English-speaking world moved away from traditional religion defined by respect for authority and respect for tradition, and moved toward a more individualistic, pragmatic, and practical practice of Christianity. The clergy were either uneducated or were educated in only the most rudimentary way. In fact, higher education was more or less an impediment to career advancement in the evangelical movement!

As one historian explains, the evangelizing of religion "[was] speeded up tremendously in the United States partly because of the sparse population spread over a huge area, partly because of the American Revolution which added a kind of democratic/republican ideology to the American mix, and also because of the leadership of people like Francis Asbury among Methodists and local Baptist leaders who didn't wait for anybody to tell them what to do but just got to work."

Evangelical movements became important in Great Britain, too, but much more slowly and always in a complex connection with the Church of England. Evangelicalism remained intimately tied to the Church of England. Likewise, the burgeoning evangelical movement in Scotland was closely connected with the dominant Church of Scotland. In England and Scotland, evangelicalism formed no new denominations but remained within the traditional Protestant churches of both countries. In Great Britain, evangelicalism was more of a reform movement. In America, it was a whole new church expression or denomination.

By the 18th and 19th centuries, American evangelicalism, then, was decidedly rough and evangelistic. The emphasis on expressive evidences of faith was a trademark of American evangelicalism. The problem was, as one historian explains, "The great

Francis Asbury statue, located in the Mt. Pleasant neighborhood, on Mt. Pleasant St., NW, Washington, D.C. (LOC).

evangelical leaders are not theoreticians of institutions. Some of them are very good theologians on questions of personal salvation. They're not theologians of culture. They're not theologians of society. There are problems with the Christian outreach that is just the theology of society, but there are also problems when the individual attention is so strong that culture and society is lost sight of."[1]

Discussion Question

Compare British evangelicalism with American evangelicalism.

Lesson 3

20th Century

> The Welsh Revival (1904–1905) was the largest of the Christian revivals in Wales during the 20th century, transforming the church there for years to come.

Evangelicalism in the early part of the 20th century was dominated by the fundamentalist movement, which rejected liberal theology and focused on separation from the world. Following the Welsh Revival, the Azusa Street Revival in 1906 began the spread of Pentecostalism in North America.

In the post-World War II period, a split developed among evangelicals, as they disagreed about how a Christian ought to respond to an unbelieving world. Some evangelicals urged that Christians must engage the culture directly and constructively, and they began to express reservations about being known to the world as fundamentalists. As one theologian explains, "The name fundamentalist had become an embarrassment instead of a badge of honor."[2]

Converts' rally, Evangelistic Committee of New York City, Carnegie Hall, Sept. 14, 1908 (LOC/Geo. R. Lawrence Co.).

The term neo-evangelicalism was coined by Christian leader **Harold Ockenga** in 1947 to identify a distinct movement within self-identified fundamentalist Christianity at the time, especially in the English-speaking world. Ockenga argued that evangelicals should pursue intellectualism and accommodation when possible. He also called for an increased application of the gospel to the political world. Not all conservatives are pleased with the new direction. One author has termed it "the apostasy within evangelicalism."[3]

Fundamentalists like Bob Jones thought that Ockenga and the neo-evangelicals were too soft on modernism and liberal Christianity. The fundamentalists saw the evangelicals as often being too concerned about social acceptance and intellectual respectability, and

1. This lesson contains content from Rob Moll, "The Rise of the Evangelicals," speaking with Mark Noll, *The Rise of Evangelicalism* (Downers Grove, IL: InterVarsity Press Academic, 2004), http://www.christianitytoday.com/ch/news/2005/jun23.html?start=1
2. Kenneth Kantzer, quoted in Wendy Murray Zoba, *The Beliefnet Guide to Evangelical Christianity* (New York: Three Leaves Press, 2005); http://www.beliefnet.com/Faiths/2005/06/The-Fundamentalist-Evangelical-Split.aspx.
3. Richard Bennett, "The Alignment of New Evangelicals with Apostasy," http://www.biblebelievers.com/bennett/bennett_evangelicals-align.html.

being too accommodating to a perverse generation that needed a corrective, prophetic message of judgment. In addition, they rejected the efforts of evangelist Billy Graham, who worked with non-evangelical denominations, such as the Roman Catholics (which they claimed to be heretical).

All evangelicals, fundamentalists, Pentecostals, and neo-evangelicals held the view that the modernist and liberal parties in the Protestant churches had surrendered their heritage as evangelicals by accommodating the views and values of "the world." They charged the modernists with selling out to the world.

Contemporary evangelical leader Mark Galli says, "As part of this renewal of evangelicalism, the *new evangelicals* sought to engage the modern world and the liberal Christians in a positive way, remaining separate from worldliness but not from the world — a middle way between modernism and the separating variety of fundamentalism. They sought allies in denominational churches and liturgical traditions, disregarding views of eschatology and other 'non-essentials,' and joined also with Trinitarian varieties of Pentecostalism. They believed that in doing so, they were simply re-acquainting Protestantism with its own recent tradition. The movement's aim at the outset was to reclaim the evangelical heritage in their respective churches, not to begin something new; and for this reason, following their separation from fundamentalists, the same movement has been better known merely as 'evangelicalism.' " By the end of the 20th century, this was the most influential development in American Protestant Christianity."[4]

Discussion Question

How would you characterize yourself: Pentecostal, fundamentalist, or neo-evangelical?

The Azusa Street Revival was a historic Pentecostal revival meeting that took place in Los Angeles, California, and was led by William J. Seymour, an African American preacher. It began with a meeting on April 14, 1906, and continued until 1915. The revival was characterized by great miracles and by speaking in tongues, dramatic worship services, and interracial fellowship. This revival was the primary catalyst for the spread of Pentecostalism in the 20th century.

Baptism near Mineola, Texas, summer of 1935 (LOC).

4. http://www.theopedia.com/Neo_evangelicalism.

The Scandal of the Evangelical Mind, by Mark Noll

A Book Review by Grant Wacker

Someone has quipped that an evangelical can be defined as someone who says to a liberal, "I'll call you a Christian if you'll call me a scholar." Though Wheaton College historian Mark Noll knows all the one-liners about evangelicals, this one does not make his book. Evangelicals' anti-intellectualism is no laughing matter. "The scandal of the Evangelical mind," he laments, "is that there is not much of an Evangelical mind." Since the movement's birth in the transatlantic revivals of the early eighteenth century, it has brought millions to deep and lasting Christian faith. Even today, polls tell us, a solid majority of the folk who regularly attend and participate in the life of local churches are evangelical in belief and behavior. But in the process, Noll argues, they have paid a terrible price, for they have "abandoned the universities, the arts, and other realms of 'high' culture."

By "mind" Noll does not mean theology or biblical studies per se, where, all things considered, Evangelicals have done quite well. His target, rather, is Evangelicals' failure seriously to confront the "whole spectrum of modern learning, including economics and political science, literary criticism and imaginative writing, historical inquiry and philosophical studies, linguistics and the history of science, social theory and the arts."

The problem, in short, is evangelicals' appalling parochialism, their unwillingness to break out of the vast but all-too-comfortable ghetto of evangelical churches and colleges and publishing networks and engage an intellectual world long ago captured by Marx and Darwin and Freud.

Noll's work is a jeremiad, profound in implication but simple in form. The tragedy of evangelical's poor scholarship, he argues, is that it grew from negligence, and the roots of that negligence go way back. In his view, evangelical thought is best understood as a tissue of unexamined assumptions arising from early nineteenth century American values. Those values included revivalism, separation of church and state, political republicanism, social democracy, economic free enterprise, philosophical realism, and patriotic nationalism. Evangelical thinking suffered additional damage from the "disaster of fundamentalism." In its holiness/pentecostal form, fundamentalism encouraged morbid inwardness; in its dispensationalist form, it fostered wooden literalism and an unhealthy preoccupation with predicting the future.

According to Noll, these influences have left modern Evangelicals pathetically ill-equipped to confront the world of contemporary learning. They substitute activism for study, populism for the wisdom of the centuries, pragmatism for time-tested orthodoxy. Assuming themselves to be purely objective, disinterested readers of the biblical text, they display little concern for the staggering problems of hermeneutics. Bereft of self-criticism or subtlety, they show only grudging willingness to grapple with complexity and doubt. Evangelicals' world is a Manichean one of absolutes, affording little sense that the line between good and evil runs not between groups but (in Solzhenitsyn's terms) through every individual soul.

Things did not have to turn out this way. Medieval monastics, the reformers, the Puritans, and Jonathan Edwards himself had determined to bring every aspect of life under the guidance of Christian thinking. Noll even finds the efforts of certain late nineteenth-century giants like Charles Hodge and Augustus Strong compelling because of determined efforts to embrace the knowable world within Christian categories. If evangelicals had listened more to them, if they had been willing to draw upon the riches of other traditions like the Dutch Reformed, the Lutheran, and the Orthodox, if they had been humble enough to take a few cues from their counterparts in the British Isles, the story might have developed quite differently. But it did not because evangelicals followed the path of least resistance.

Hard words, to be sure, but they are the words of a "wounded lover," as Noll calls himself, the words of an evangelical insider calling other insiders to humility in the face of a great heritage squandered. Though the book is concisely and elegantly written, it reflects awesome erudition. The footnotes stand out as a treasure in themselves, not stacked up like index cards in a shoe box but judiciously brought forth as needed. Still more importantly, Noll shows, very much as H. Richard Niebuhr did in *The Kingdom of God in America*, how to be passionately committed to a cause without sacrificing fairness (laying one's own assumptions out on the table) or publicness (remembering that all bits of evidence and lines of argument must be open to the scrutiny of insiders and outsiders alike).

Not surprisingly, Noll (like all good historians) stirs up more questions than he answers. Some readers will feel that he errs by being too charitable toward the secular academic world. If George Marsden, Bradley Longfield, and other historians are right about the growing hegemony of secular assumptions in the modern research university, it may be difficult for orthodox voices of any kind to be heard since they are excluded from the conversation to begin with. Yet Noll seems not to think so, or at least he seems to think that evangelicals do well first to focus upon their own shortcomings rather than outsiders' prejudices.

A more troubling question is whether any religious person can expect to gain a hearing in the surging diversity of the modern academy. The only way for evangelicals and Jews and Muslims and the mass of academics who do not care very much about any faith to get along is to agree on certain rules of exchange, and those rules usually mean not talking about the issues that lie deepest in their hearts. The plain fact is that the pluralism of modern university culture makes the language of strong commitment difficult to sustain on a day to day basis. Teaching about a Maimonides or a Barth is one thing; actually working with them in a faculty meeting may be quite another.

Finally, it is not clear that evangelicals do in fact need to establish a Christian view of everything. To be sure, it is important to know that Christians in general and evangelicals in particular can engage the highest and most demanding forms of intellectual work, but it is doubtful that the adjective "evangelical" makes much difference when we are talking about the work that most scholars, especially those in the natural sciences, undertake most of the time. Even for Noll, an historian of religion, most of what he does (and he does a lot) can be assessed by technical protocols of historical scholarship that are pretty much applicable to everyone in the profession.

However we answer these questions, the largest one remains: Do resources for renewal lie within the evangelical tradition? Yes, Noll believes, but they can be salvaged only with strenuous effort. Noll thus urges evangelicals to historicize themselves, to see how their favored modes of reaction are conditioned by time and place. He calls them to develop a sense of irony, to see, in words historian Peter Brown used in a different context, that the first and final enemy of the Christian intellectual is the "patina of the obvious." It was said of Jonathan Edwards that he "smelt of the lamp"; Noll reminds Edwards' latter day heirs that there is no substitute for long grueling hours in the library, the study, the laboratory. And in an age obsessed with narrative, when everyone seems to think that his own story is as valid as anyone else's, Noll effectively says No, there really is a normative conversation out there, a conversation defined by the reality-shaping institutions of our society, and it is high time for Evangelicals to enter into it.

Thus this sermon, like all true jeremiads, ends on a note of hope. Noll urges these reforms upon evangelicals, not because they will afford them more power and prestige, but solely for the glory of God. "The search for a Christian mind is not, in the end," he tells us, "a search for mind but a search for God." Evangelicals purport to speak biblical truth, but in fact sold their soul to American culture long ago. The lips are Esau's but the voice is Jacob's. So for Noll, evangelicals must become bilingual. They must continue to address the world with the life-giving words of faith that they know so well. At the same time, they must learn to translate those words into the language of the public academic sphere.

The great and pleasant irony of this book is that as long as the evangelical subculture is able to turn out a mind as learned and as Christian as Mark Noll's, its future promises to be a lot brighter than he supposes.[5]

> Grant Wacker is Associate Professor of American Religious History at Duke Divinity School.

Discussion Question

What is the primary argument in Mark Noll's book? Do you agree?

---

5. Grant Wacker, 2008 book review of Mark Noll, *The Scandal of the Evangelical Mind* (Grand Rapids, MI: W.B. Eerdmans, 1994); www.firstthings.com.

The Author's Theological Statement

The Lord Jesus Christ has been my Savior since I invited Him into my heart in 1971 at a United Methodist Lay Witness Mission. From the beginning, God seems to have called me to a prophetic role. I felt called to the ministry several years later. I really thank God for the mistakes I've made. They help me know more about myself and to trust God more as well. At this time my wife, family, and overseer help me grow in Christ.

Dr. James Stobaugh and his wife, Karen.

I am also a classic evangelical (as defined by Mark A. Knoll, *The Scandal of the Evangelical Mind*). The key ingredients of classic evangelicalism as I see it are: conversion with an emphasis on the new birth with believer baptism; reliance on the Bible as the inspired, inerrant, and ultimate authority; activism: a clear burden to share the gospel with the unsaved and a desire to live a radical Christian life that invites others to know Him and to make Him known; and finally, crucicentrism (a focus on Christ's redeeming work on the Cross).

Understanding that we have been called as ambassadors of Jesus Christ with the ministry of reconciliation (2 Cor. 5:17–21) to a society whose culture of hopelessness no longer gives a Christian framework to sustain its members spiritually, the Church of Jesus Christ should be an intentionally interracial, covenanted body of believers who, under the Lordship of Jesus Christ, choose to be different in meaningful ways and seek to be overcomers by the blood of the Lamb, by the word of our testimony, and by not loving our lives so much as to shrink from death (Rev. 12:11). In this way, we can manifest the hope of the redemption until every knee shall bow and every tongue confess that Jesus Christ is Lord (Phil. 2:9–10).

Mainline Protestantism, of which I am a part, in the beginning of the 21st century is spinning out of control. We are stretching our wings adventurously, but drifting further away from our confessions and Scripture. We are in trouble.

As part of the Symposium at the Dedication of the Presbyterian Center, Louisville, Kentucky, October 28, 1988, the theologian Walter Brueggemann surprised the Presbyterian Church USA — as well as all white, middle class America — to repentance. "We religionists are caught in an odd endorsing and legitimating, when in our knowing, we may want to talk about the sovereign absence of God, an absence evident in the secularization of a society which seems to manage very well by itself."[6] Brueggemann further suggests that we Presbyterians are in exile and need to act accordingly.

This theme of "resident aliens" is echoed throughout America by writers like Elizabeth Achtemeir, William Willimon, Thomas Sine, and others. Increasingly, we who proclaim the Lord Jesus Christ as our Savior are finding ourselves in a minority culture.

In other books, then, Walter Brueggemann calls American believers to "nurture, nourish, and evoke a consciousness and perception alternative to the consciousness and

---

6. Walter Brueggemann, *Discipline of Readiness*, Occasional Paper No. 1 (Louisville, KY: Theology and Worship Unit, Presbyterian Church USA, 1988), p. 3.

"The Second Coming"
William Butler Yeats

Turning and turning in
    the widening gyre,
The falcon cannot hear
    the falconer.
Things fall apart; the
    centre cannot hold;
Mere anarchy is loosed
    upon the world.
The blood-dimmed
    tide is tossed, and
    everywhere
The ceremony of
    innocence is drowned;
The best lack all
    conviction, while the
    worst
Are full of passionate
    intensity.[1]

_____

1. William Butler Yeats, "The Second
Coming," in M.L. Rosenthal, ed.,
*Selected Poems and Two Plays of
William Butler Yeats* (New York:
The Macmillan Company, 1962),
p. 91.

perception of the dominant culture around us."[7] And it is not difficult to feel cut-off, alienated from this culture of which I am a part — including my own church denomination. For example, my denomination is presently embroiled in a process of self-destruction over this very issue. In fact, I am witnessing Presbyterian history unfold — I am observing the end of Presbyterian Neo-Orthodoxy as I have known it. John Mackay's lead editorial in the first issue of *Theology Today* in 1944 captures the contemporary mood: "When the earth quivers beneath the flail of total war, when battles mount in fury around the globe, when the most momentous year in modern history is running its course, why should a new journal be issued? . . . because why should extremists [fundamentalists and evangelicals] only exhibit passion?"[8] There is no moderate position anymore in the Presbyterian Church USA, and, perhaps, no middle ground in any other mainline church or in American society in general.

And good riddance. A friend tells a story (taken from Derek Prince's Foundation Series) about a young African evangelist who said to a white, American missionary: "Your churches are only storehouses, storing people for hell. . . . To some people this might appear a shocking statement . . . but the great majority of the members of those churches had never once had the basic facts of the gospel presented to them, and had never been faced with the need to make a definite, personal response to those facts. They had exchanged paganism for a form of Christianity, they had memorized a catechism . . . but of the essential facts of the gospel and of the experience of salvation, of these they had no knowledge nor understanding whatever."[9]

The great religious writer Unamuno creates a character, Augusto Perez, in his book *Mist*, who, through omniscient narration, turns to his maker (e.g., Unamuno) and cries: "Am I to die as a creature of fiction?" Such is the cry of modern humankind. The Christian author and Harvard professor Robert Coles laments that we "we have the right to think of ourselves, so rich in today's America, as in jeopardy *sub specie aeternitatis*, no matter the size and diversification of his stock portfolio."[10]

It seems, at times that we are lost. "The sense of being lost, displaced, and homeless is pervasive in contemporary culture," Walter Brueggemann writes. "The yearning to belong somewhere, to have a home, to be in a safe place, is a deep and moving pursuit."[11] In spite of our hedonistic bravado, I generally find most of my congregation — who usually are not living a life centered on Jesus Christ — to be desperately unhappy. And no wonder. This world does not provide what we need. No, no it really doesn't. It thinks that it does — my acquaintance and colleague from Harvard Divinity School, Dr. Forrest Church, now pastor in a Unitarian Church in New York City, was fond of saying, "In our faith God is not a given, God is a question. . . . God is defined by us. Our views are shaped and changed by our experiences. We create a faith which we can live — and struggle to live, up to . . . and loving a distant God has no allure."[12] Indeed. This thought has gotten us into quite a mess.

What kind of mess? While I attended seminary, I remember hurrying to the opening ceremony of the academic year held every September at Harvard Memorial Chapel

_____

7. Walter Brueggemann, *The Prophetic Imagination* (Philadelphia, PA: Fortress Press, 1978), p. 13.
8. John M. Mulder and Lee A. Wyatt, "The Predicament of Pluralism: The Study of Theology in Presbyterian Seminaries Since the 1920s," in Milton J. Coalter, John M. Mulder, Louis B. Weeks, editors, *The Pluralistic Vision: Presbyterians and Mainstream Protestant Education and Leadership* (Louisville, KY: Westminster/John Knox Press, 1992), p. 46.
9. Robert R. Kopp, "Why the Old Denominations are Going to Hell," in Ann Gillies, acting editor, *Monday Morning*, vol. 59 (March 7, 1994): p. 14–25.
10. Robert Coles, *Harvard Diary* (New York: Crossroad, 1990), p. 92.
11. Walter Brueggemann, *The Land* (Philadelphia, PA: Fortress Press, 1977), p. 1.
12. Forrest Church, *Born Again Unitarian* (Tulsa, OK: Cove Lewis Printing Co., 1986), p. 88–89.

in the Yard. Spying an impressive group of Harvard professors, decked out in all their academic robes and capes, I decided to follow them to Mem Chapel. Although I knew the way quite well, I trusted these sagacious gentlemen to show me a better way. Well, we got lost! And I was late!

One of the most disturbing essays I have ever read is an essay by Thomas Merton entitled "A Devout Meditation in Memory of Adolf Eichmann." Merton begins, "One of the most disturbing facts that came out in the Eichmann trial was that a psychiatrist examined him and pronounced him perfectly sane."[13] The fact is, given our world, we can no longer assume that because a person is "sane" or "adjusted," he/she is okay. Merton reminds us that such people can be well adjusted even in hell itself! "The whole concept of sanity in a society where spiritual values have lost their meaning is itself meaningless."

Memorial Church of Harvard University (CCA-SA3.0).

The fact is, quoting C.S. Lewis, we "are half-hearted creatures, fooling about with drink and sex and ambition when infinite joy is offered us, like an ignorant child who wants to go on making mud pies in a slum because he cannot imagine what is meant by the offer of a holiday at the sea."[14]

Jesus Christ is the way and the truth and the life. I know that this seems simplistic — some in my congregation are proponents of Ahab. King Ahab had no problem with Elijah's exuberant support of Yahweh. What bothered Ahab, and his wife Jezebel, was Elijah's darn, parochial, un-American insistence that there was only one God! Chill out, Elijah! Live and let live!

Ah, there's the rub. There is no other way to eternal life or present happiness. In the Confession of 1967, the Presbyterian Church USA affirms: "No one type of confession is exclusively valid, no one statement is irreformable. Obedience to Jesus Christ alone identifies the one universal church and supplies the continuity of its traditions." America in general, and certainly my denomination, needs to place Christ again at the center of its theology and worldview.

And certainly, as we overhaul our Christology (or lack of!) we need to remember that the central symbol for every Christian must be the Cross. At least from the second century onward, Christians used the Cross as their central symbol. I will not argue with Professor Ahlstrom who asserts that Puritanism died in the 1960 American Revolution (although I grieve with J.I. Packer at its demise!). And I do not want to see Puritanism resurrected, but I fervently hope that Jesus Christ — crucified and resurrected — will again be preached in mainline churches.

Paul had no trouble defining his Gospel and his life as "the message of the Cross." On the contrary, he boldly declared that though the Cross seemed either foolishness or a stumbling block to the self-confident (i.e., modern humankind!) it was in fact the very essence of God's wisdom and power (1 Cor. 1:18–25).[15] I yearn, as Dietrich Bonhoeffer did at the end of his life, for the crucified Lord to return again — as the rediscovered center — to the center of the Church and American society. The world does not need a new religion — it needs Jesus Christ, crucified and resurrected.[16]

13. Thomas Merton, *Raids on the Unspeakable*, "A Devout Meditation in Memory of Adolf Eichmann" (New York: New Directions, 1966), p. 45–50.
14. C.S. Lewis, *The Weight of Glory and Other Addresses* (Grand Rapids, MI: Eerdmans, 1965), p. 1–2. This quote is referenced in John Piper, *Desiring God* (Portland, OR: Multnomah Press, 1986), p. 16.
15. John R. W. Stott, *The Cross of Christ* (Downers Grove, IL: InterVarsity Press, 1986), p. 33.
16. Dietrich Bonhoeffer, *Letters and Papers from Prison* (New York: Macmillan Publishing Co., Inc., 1971), p. 362–363.

Don't get me wrong. What I am suggesting is truly revolutionary, or, as Walter Brueggemann suggests "subversive."[17] The Church — my church — must be called to a higher commitment. A radical commitment. The choice for Christ must occupy first place, above parents, children, job, and, if necessary, life itself. The gate leading to health and wholeness in our world is not a reasonable size. It is narrow. In that sense, I am calling us all to a radical faith, a prophetic faith.[18] We are called to a major reclamation project of our views of atonement so completely presented in Scripture and in our confessions.

Oh, how my heart yearns for revival! For our world to reclaim the centrality of the Cross! With John Stott, in *The Cross of Christ*, my prayer is that this new generation, haunted by so many bad memories, so bewitched by technology and social science theories, would again come to the Cross of our Lord Jesus Christ. And, at the same time, I want us to reclaim the joy of this adventure — so persuasively presented by John Piper in *Desiring God*. That we would no longer settle for the mud pies of delight our world offers us but, like the Puritans, would reclaim the delights of a life centered on the Lordship of Jesus Christ! That we would again enjoy the Lord — which is after all what worship and praise is.

Discussion Question

Write a statement of your own theological beliefs.

Andover Hall, home to the Harvard Divinity School at Harvard University in Cambridge, Massachusetts. The building was completed in 1911 and named for the Andover Theological Seminary, who financed its construction (PD).

17. Walter Brueggemann, *Hopeful Imagination and Finally Comes the Poet* (Minneapolis, MN: Fortress Press, 1989).
18. Segundo Galilea, *Following Jesus* (New York: Maryknoll, 1983), p. 76–85.

During the 1870s, a widening division occurred within the Protestant faith in regard to Charles Darwin's attempt to propose a godless creation premise that has come to be called "evolution," 1874 (PD).

Chapter 10

The Scopes Trial: The Fool, Fixed on His Folly

First Thoughts

The Scopes Trial is one of the best known in American history because it symbolized the conflict between science and theology, faith and reason, individual liberty and majority rule. But it was so much more. It was that moment when modernity went too far and decided it did not need God. It had already rejected the Word of God, but now, modern secular society decided that God Himself was old-fashioned, that He was no longer the logos. The tragedy was compounded when Clarence Darrow mocked William Jennings Bryan on national radio. Bryan was broken and would die five days after the trial. But in a sense, our world as we knew it ended. What folly. Born-again Christian T.S. Eliot, at the end of his life, wrote, "Only the fool, fixed in his folly, may think he can turn the wheel on which he turns."[1]

Chapter Learning Objectives

In chapter 10 we will look at the Scopes Trial. We will be alarmed at its implication. We will then discuss why a literal reading of the Word of God is critical. Next, we will look at Bryan's life, then predict the future culture wars that you will face!

As a result of this chapter you should be able to:

1. Explain why the Scopes Trial was so disastrous for America

2. Analyze the Scopes Trial

3. Discuss why a literal interpretation of creation is important

4. Evaluate William Jennings Bryan's impact on history

5. Predict the future culture wars (like the Scopes Trial) that are before us

---

1. T. S. Eliot, *Murder in the Cathedral* (New York: Harcourt, 1964), Act I.

Lesson 1

Early Evangelicalism

James' Island, Galapagos Archipelago from John Gould's *The Zoology of the Voyage of H.M.S. Beagle*. Part III: Birds. London: Smith, Elder & Co., 1841. (PD).

Religion has always been a central part of American history. We are, and have always been, a religious people. It was natural, then, that in the midst of a booming economy and unprecedented prosperity, Americans would fight a religious battle known as the Scopes Trial.

Many historians will ask us to see it otherwise. They will tell us it was a victory for liberty and justice. It was a landmark case emphasizing the need for separation of Church and state. But they are wrong.

It was a disaster. A sort of spiritual suicide. In the mind of the insane, but brilliant German nihilist, Frederick Nietzsche, at that time we looked into the abyss.

"When you look into the abyss, the abyss also looks into you" (Friedrich Nietzsche).[2] *On Looking into the Abyss: Untimely Thoughts on Culture and Society*[3] by Gertrude Himmelfarb argues that the abyss is the abyss of meaninglessness. In the Scopes Trial, Americans chose to write history to suit themselves and in the process chose to ignore the Word of God.

It was the most natural thing in the world. In the 1920s, Americans were dedicated to the pleasure principle. "They yearn to be considered creative and imaginative, casting off the chains of mere causal and chronological 'narrativity,' they . . . conceive of history as a form of fiction."[4]

Before the Civil War, the Protestant denominations were united in a belief that the findings of science confirmed the teachings of religion. But during the 1870s, a lasting division had occurred in American Protestantism over Charles Darwin's theory of evolution. Religious modernists argued that religion had to be accommodated to the teachings of science, while religious traditionalists sought to preserve the basic tenets of their religious faith.

The fundamentalist and Pentecostal movements arose in the early 20th century as a backlash against modernism, secularism, and scientific teachings that contradicted their religious beliefs. Early fundamentalist doctrine attacked competing religions — especially Catholicism, which it portrayed as an agent of the Antichrist — and insisted on the literal truth of the Bible, a strict return to fundamental principles, and a thorough-going rejection of modernity.

Between 1921 and 1929, fundamentalists introduced 37 anti-evolution bills into 20 state legislatures. The first law to pass was in Tennessee.

During the summer of 1925, John Scopes, a high school science teacher in Dayton, Tennessee, was tried and convicted for violating the prohibition on the teaching of evolution in public schools. The statute forbade the teaching of any scientific theory that

---

2. Frederick Nietzsche, *Beyond Good and Evil* (1886), section 146.
3. Gertrude Himmelfarb, *On Looking into the Abyss: Untimely Thoughts on Culture and Society* (New York: Knopf, 1994).
4. Ibid.

denied the literalness of the biblical account of creation. And during those eight days in July 1927, America looked into the abyss, and the abyss looked back. . . .

Discussion Question

Why was the Scopes Trial so disastrous for America?

The Scopes Trial

In March 1925, the Tennessee legislature passed a measure known as the **Butler Act**, which made it illegal for teachers in the public schools to present as factual any theory of creation other than the biblical account.

The **American Civil Liberties Union** (ACLU), an advocacy group formed in 1920 to protect the rights bestowed by the Constitution and its Bill of Rights, advertised in Tennessee newspapers to find an individual willing to challenge the Butler Act. Several civic leaders in the hamlet of Dayton found a willing participant in John T. Scopes (1900–1970), a substitute high school biology teacher. The cultural battle of the century was fought so that a town could get some publicity.

Scopes was represented by a group of ACLU lawyers headed by the famous and capable defense attorney **Clarence Darrow**. Darrow told Scopes to admit his violation of the Tennessee statute but argued that the law violated the constitutionally required separation of church and state as well as Scopes' academic freedom. The most damaging argument Darrow presented was that evolution, in the minds of many theologians, was consistent with some interpretations of Scripture. In other words, the barbarians are in the City of God and they have never left! What Darrow did is what many have attempted ever since: he presumed to make the Word of God into something it is not — secular writing.

If Darrow was a capable lawyer, but shady character, the prosecution had the gold standard — **William Jennings Bryan**, the former secretary of state and three-time presidential candidate. Near the end of his long career, Bryan was a firm religious fundamentalist, but urged the prosecution to fight its battle on constitutional grounds. Bryan believed that communities were justified in setting curriculum standards in tax-supported schools. However, his colleagues who chose to argue science and religion overruled him.

The great catastrophe was sealed on the seventh day of testimony, when Bryan blundered by allowing Darrow to call him as an expert witness on the Bible. Under relentless questioning carried live on the radio, Bryan came across to many as old, senile, and eccentric. Poor Bryan. Poor Christian America. The modernists had moved from attacking Christianity to outright mockery.

The Scopes Trial, then, was a pivotal cultural battleground during the 1920s. The roots of this religious conflict were planted in the late 19th century.

Clarence Darrow and William Jennings Bryan.

John Scopes in 1925 (PD).

Clarence Darrow, 1922 (LOC).

In the end, Bryan disappointed even his supporters by admitting that some biblical events should not be taken literally. Bryan died five days after the trial's conclusion.

Of course Bryan won the case. The outcome of the proceedings was never in doubt. The judge made clear to the jury that the law's constitutionality or efforts to support the validity of Darwin's theory were not germane; the only issue in question was whether or not Scopes had presented evolution as fact — and he said that he had. The substitute teacher was found guilty and fined $100.

Later, on appeal, the Tennessee Supreme Court upheld the constitutionality of the law but reversed Scopes' conviction on the technical point that the fine had been excessive.

Some historians argue that the Scopes Trial was the turning point in the struggle between rural fundamentalist values and those of scientifically inclined urban dwellers. I see this trial as a watershed date where secular, unsaved public officials opened hunting season on evangelical Christians and everything they believed. In the short term, the celebrated "Monkey Trial" probably inhibited the passage of laws similar to Tennessee's in other states that did not want to endure the ridicule that had been heaped on Dayton. In the long run, godless forces put other Judeo-Christian values in their gun sights. Abortion was made legal. Homosexuals may now serve openly in the military. The dastardly deed was done, the die was cast, and the case proved, as T.S. Eliot wrote, "Only the fool, fixed in his folly, may think he can turn the wheel on which he turns."[5]

Discussion Question

If you were Williams Jennings Bryan, how would you have conducted this case? The same or differently? Why?

Lesson 3

The Necessity for Believing in Six Literal Days

Ken Ham

The majority of Christians in churches probably aren't sure whether God really created everything in six literal days. Many believe it doesn't matter whether it took six days or six million years. However, it is vital to believe in six literal days for many reasons.

---

5. Eliot, *Murder in the Cathedral*.

Foremost is that allowing these days to be long periods of time undermines the foundations of the message of the Cross.

Why do people doubt the days?

The major reason why people doubt that the days of creation are 24-hour literal days usually has nothing to do with what the Bible says, but comes from outside influences. For example, many believe that because scientists have supposedly proved the earth to be billions of years old then the days of creation cannot be ordinary days.

If people use Scripture to try to justify that the days of creation are long periods of time, they usually quote passages such as 2 Peter 3:8, ". . . one day is with the Lord as a thousand years. . . ." Because of this, they think the days could be a thousand years, or perhaps even millions of years. However, if you look at the rest of the verse, it says, ". . . and a thousand years as one day." This cancels out their argument! The context of this passage concerns the Second Coming of the Lord Jesus Christ. This particular verse is telling people that with God, waiting a day is like waiting a thousand years, and waiting a thousand years is like waiting a day because God is outside of time — He is not limited by natural processes and time. This has absolutely nothing to do with defining the days of creation. Besides, the word "day" already exists and has been defined, which is why in 2 Peter it can be compared to a thousand years. There is no reference in this passage to the days of creation.

What does "day" mean?

The Hebrew word for day in Genesis chapter 1 is the word *yom*. It is important to understand that almost any word can have two or more meanings, depending on context. We need to understand the context of the usage of this word in Genesis chapter 1.

> The Hebrew word for day in Genesis chapter 1 is the word *yom*.

Respected Hebrew dictionaries, like the *Brown, Driver, Briggs Lexicon*, give a number of meanings for the word *yom* depending upon context. One of the passages they give for *yom*'s meaning an ordinary day happens to be Genesis chapter 1. The reason is obvious. Every time the word *yom* is used with a number, or with the phrase "evening and morning," anywhere in the Old Testament, it always means an ordinary day. In Genesis chapter 1, for each of the six days of creation, the Hebrew word *yom* is used with a number and the phrase, "evening and morning." There is no doubt that the writer is being emphatic that these are ordinary days.

What if the days were millions of years?

The whole of the creation restored . . . to what?

The idea of millions of years came from the belief that the fossil record was built up over a long time. As soon as people allow for millions of years, they allow for the fossil record to be millions of years old. This creates an insurmountable problem regarding the gospel. The fossil record consists of the death of billions of creatures. In fact, it is a record of death, disease, suffering, cruelty, and brutality. It is a very ugly record.

The Bible is adamant though, that death, disease, and suffering came into the world as a result of sin. God instituted death and bloodshed because of sin so man could be redeemed. As soon as Christians allow for death, suffering, and disease before sin, then the whole foundations of the message of the Cross and the Atonement have been destroyed. The doctrine of original sin, then, is totally undermined.

On February 4, 2014, leading creation apologist Ken Ham was joined at the Creation Museum by popular TV personality and evolution apologist Bill Nye. The topic was "Is creation a viable model of origins in today's modern, scientific era?" It had over 5 million viewers from 190 countries and top trending numbers on Facebook, Twitter, and YouTube, as the debate stirred up major discussion around the world. You can see more about the debate and ways to answer evolutionists at www.answersingenesis.org.

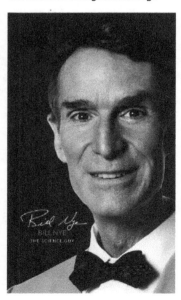

If there were death, disease, and suffering before Adam rebelled — then what did sin do to the world? What does Paul mean in Romans 8 when he says the whole of creation groans in pain because of the Curse? How can all things be restored in the future to no more death and suffering, unless the beginning was also free of death and suffering? The whole message of the gospel falls apart if one allows millions of years for the creation of the world.

How should we approach Scripture?

One of the major problems we all have (in fact, it is the same problem Adam and Eve had) is that we tend to start from outside God's Word and then go to what God has written in the Bible (or — in Adam's case — what God said directly to him) to try to interpret it on the basis of our own ideas. This is really the major reason why most people question the days of creation.

We need to realize that the Bible is God's Word. And as it is the inspired Word of the infinite Creator, God, then it must be self-authenticating and self-attesting. Thus, we should always start with what God's Word says regardless of outside ideas. Only God's Word is infallible.

If we allow our children to accept the possibility that we can doubt the days of creation when the language speaks so plainly, then we are teaching them a particular approach to all of Scripture. Why shouldn't they then start to doubt that Christ's virgin birth really means a virgin birth? Why shouldn't they start to doubt that the Resurrection really means resurrection?

In fact, there are many theologians who doubt these very things, as they have come to disbelieve the plain words of Scripture written in the foundational Book of Genesis.

Why did God take six days?

If you think about it, an infinite Creator God could have created everything in no time. Why, then, did He take as long as six days? The answer is given in Exodus 20:11. Here we find that God tells us that He deliberately took six days and rested for one as a pattern for man — this is where the seven-day week comes from. The seven-day week has no basis for existing except from Scripture. If one believes that the days of creation are long periods of time, then the week becomes meaningless.

The Bible tells us that Adam was created on the sixth day. If he lived through day six and day seven, and then died when he was 930 years old, and if each of these days was a thousand or a million years, you have major problems! On the fourth day of creation (Genesis 1:14–19), we are given the comparison of day to night, and days to years. If the word "day" doesn't mean an ordinary day, then the comparison of day to night and day to years becomes meaningless.

Were the days 24 hours? Most definitely! "Let God be true, but every man a liar" (Rom. 3:4).[6]

Discussion Question

Why is a literal interpretation of the creation story so important to Ham?

---

6. http://www.answersingenesis.org/articles/cm/v18/n1/six-days.

William Jennings Bryan

William Jennings Bryan (March 19, 1860–July 26, 1925) was a dominant force in the "liberal" wing of the Democratic Party, standing three times as its candidate for president of the United States (1896, 1900, and 1908). Of course, the meaning of liberal has changed considerably. In the late 19th century it meant "populist" or "for the people."

He served in the United States Congress briefly as a representative from Nebraska and was the 41st United States secretary of state under President Woodrow Wilson, 1913–1915. Bryan was a devout Presbyterian, born-again Christian, supporter of popular sovereignty, and enemy of the gold standard, as well as banks and railroads. He was also a prohibitionist. And with his deep, commanding voice Bryan was a very gifted orator.

William Jennings Bryan (PD).

During the intensely fought 1896 and 1900 elections, Bryan was defeated by William McKinley but remained a powerful force in the Democratic Party. With over 500 speeches in 1896, Bryan resurrected the akin to the Lincoln/Douglas debates. President Wilson appointed him secretary of state in 1913, but Wilson's strong demands on Germany after the *Lusitania* was torpedoed in 1915 caused Bryan to resign in protest. After 1920 he was a strong supporter of prohibition and energetically attacked Darwinism and evolution, most famously at the Scopes Trial in 1925. Five days after the Scopes Trial, he died in his sleep.

In his famous Chautauqua lecture, "The Prince of Peace," Bryan warned of the possibility that the theory of evolution could undermine the foundations of morality. However, at this point, he concluded, "While I do not accept the Darwinian theory, I shall not quarrel with you about it."[7] However, after witnessing the horrors of World War I, his attitude changed. Bryan was convinced that Darwinism had exceeded his previous assumption of being a potential threat and had in fact undermined morality.

Bryan was a prominent progressive Christian who was offended by the theory of evolution. Characterizing the evolutionary theory as "guesses strung together,"[8] Bryan argued that evolution was illogical and immoral and liable to encourage an ungodly belief of "survival of the fittest" found in social Darwinism. He also genuinely believed in the right of the people to determine what should be taught in their tax-supported schools. When Jennings died in 1925, much of common decency died with him, and the American political scene has not been the same since.

Discussion Question

William Jennings Bryan, for my money, was one of the greatest Americans who ever lived. He was brilliant and hard working. He had a servant's heart, and he loved the Lord. Describe at least one other great Christian American who has had a great impact on this country.

7. http://thriceholy.net/Texts/Prince.html.
8. https://biblio.ugent.be/publication/815990.

A Cultural Revolution

> Revolutions are by definition radical departures from the status quo. They are demarcations, not merely digressions. They are new beginnings in a culture or society.

What is evangelicalism? Evangelicalism is a Christian movement that began in Great Britain in the 1730s and gained popularity in the United States during the series of Great Awakenings of the 18th and 19th century. Evangelicals have two distinctive beliefs: the Word of God (Bible) is inspired and inerrant in its original form and a person must have a definable moment in his life where he confesses that Jesus Christ is Lord (called a salvation experience).

By this point you must suspect that I am an oldtimer, a crusty evangelical. That is true. My wife, Karen, committed her life to Christ when she was 5, and I committed my life to Christ when I was 17. We homeschooled our four children.

Professor John Jefferson Davis, homeschooling father of five children, quotes Dr. Robert Foote of Cornell in his book *Evangelical Ethics*. "I am reminded of a story," Dr. Robert Foote says, "where the pilot came on and said, 'This is your captain speaking. We are flying at an altitude of 35,000 feet and speed of 700 miles an hour. We have some good news and some bad news. The bad news is that we are lost. The good news is that we are making excellent time.' "[9]

Dr. Foote's characterization of the modern world, in my opinion, captures the dilemma 21st-century American families are facing: there is no doubt that we are making significant progress on all scientific fronts, but at the same time we seem to be lost. As we begin the new millennium, Robert Bork, in his prophetic book *Slouching Towards Gomorrah*,[10] warns us that the out-of-control individualism and egalitarianism of the 1960s are very much with us. He is correct. One merely has to recall the Clinton impeachment hearings in the 1990s to see evidence of the sort of morality where "if what he is doing harms no one (individualism) then it is okay to do it (egalitariansim)." We are part of a therapeutic culture, where wholeness is replaced by holiness, and sanctification is replaced by therapy. And even the most ardent pagan is getting really tired of this mess! And, as he does, he may very well choose homeschooling as an alternative to public education.

Culture is "the behavior patterns, arts, beliefs, institutions, and all other products of human work and thought, especially as expressed in a particular community or period."[11] Where do we discern culture? In the billboards that line our highways, in the songs that play on our radios, in the movies that play in our theaters. Culture is exemplified in the courses our universities teach, in the books our nation reads. Os Guinness warns us that at some point Americans will become fed up with the excess and dysfunctional aspects of our culture.

The 71st Session Illinois Conference, Evangelical Association, 1915 (LOC).

9. John Jefferson Davis, *Evangelical Ethics: Issues Facing the Church Today* (Phillipsburg, NJ: P&R Pub., 1993).
10. Robert H. Bork, *Slouching Towards Gomorrah* (New York: ReganBooks, 2003).
11. http://www.thefreedictionary.com/culture.

He says that as American mainline culture fails to sustain Americans in their hedonistic pursuit of self-interest, they will want something more.[12] It is now questionable whether America's cultural order is capable of nourishing the freedom, responsibility, and civility that Americans require to sustain democracy. Modernity (a word describing modern American culture) creates problems far deeper than drugs. It creates a crisis of cultural authority in which America's beliefs, ideals, and traditions are losing their compelling power in society. William Bennett is right to warn us that there is a "death of outrage"[13] in our country, but he might add that there is a numbness spreading across the land that offers much opportunity for Christians in general and for evangelicals in particular.

Guinness encourages Christians with the fact that in the near future Americans will be looking to places of stability and strength for direction. By default, those people whose lives are in reasonable good shape, who have some reason to live beyond the next paycheck, will have an almost inexorable appeal. That is good news for evangelicals. In fact, I calculate that somewhere around one-twelfth of the new graduates/leaders of our nation may be evangelicals. Even if I am overestimating our number, it would be hard to over-estimate our potential. Can you imagine what it will mean to a culture to suddenly have three or four million Spirit-filled, stable Christian leaders coming forth into the nation? I don't think I can recall a more potentially ameliorating cultural possibility than the time Augustine and his generation led his nation at the end of the Roman Empire.

The post-Christian age is one dominated by anxiety, irrationalism, and helplessness. In such a world, consciousness is adrift, unable to anchor itself to any universal ground of justice, truth, or reason. Consciousness itself is thus "decentered": no longer an agent of action in the world, but a function through which impersonal forces pass and intersect.[14] Let's examine some modern trends.

The first is a pervasive and abiding concern about the future. To those of us who lived through the Cold War, this seems ludicrous. But the tentativeness and fear that pervade American society are real. Witness the catastrophe at Columbine. Those two young men were angry and confused, but most of all hopeless. Likewise, we have lost our way, lost our dreams. Harvard professor Dr. Harvey Cox writes: "We once had dreams and no technology to bring them to pass. Now we have technology but no dreams!"[15]

In fact, most social critics argue persuasively that this generation is one of the most hopeless in history. Interestingly enough, this hopelessness has made us rather sentimental. We have become very sentimental about the past. Even in our most creative creations it is more of the same. For instance, even though Luke Skywalker is a loner and a womanizer, he is still a do-gooder spreading George Lucas's version of truth and justice across the land. But God is totally absent. The *Star Wars* phenomenon is so appealing because it is about the past, not about the future. Luke Skywalker is more like John Wayne than he is like Tom Cruise.

To this hopeless generation, history is not sacred; it is merely utilitarian. It is not didactic; it helps them feel better. The modern psychologist B.F. Skinner, for instance, disdains history and gives M&Ms to monkeys. We have no actions, only fate driving us. We are rudderless. However, we Christians know that God is in absolute control of history, so we need to teach our children to be tirelessly hopeful. We need to make sure that we are not mawkish! We can easily do so by speaking the truth found in the Word of God in places of deception.

12. http://www.forsuchatimeasthis.com/blog/category/college-prep/.
13. William J. Bennett, *The Death of Outrage* (New York: Free Press, 1999).
14. Patricia Waugh in Gene Edward Veith Jr., *Postmodern Times: A Christian Guide to Contemporary Thought and Culture* (Westchester, IL: Crossway, 1994), p. 45.
15. http://www.forsuchatimeasthis.com/blog/category/postmodernism/.

John Wayne (PD).

Clint Eastwood (PD).

Tom Cruise (CCA-SA2.0).

One of the greatest problems in this generation is confusion about individual responsibility. It was Freud who told us that feelings of guilt were a sign not of vice but of virtue. And it was Freud who told us that our problems stemmed from our mothers, not from our sin. Perhaps our problem began with Goethe, whose Faust escapes the consequences of his sin by sincerity and good humor. What does this say for poor theistic Gretchen? Look at the evolution of the American understanding of hero:

a. Traditional John Wayne — a moral, golden rule hero. He was never immoral. He always did the right thing.

b. Modern Clint Eastwood — Eastwood is tough. "Make my day" world. Doing something invites any appropriate response — as defined by offended person.

c. Post-Christian Tom Cruise — Cruse is selfish but moral. Commits adultery and lies for the sake of good things in *The Firm*. But there is a hint of morality.

Perhaps our movie icons best typify what America values and promotes in her culture.

If we are confused about what is right and wrong, and about individual responsibilities, we are even more confused about tolerance. S.D. Gaede, in *When Tolerance Is No Virtue*, says, "In our culture, there is considerable confusion about how we ought to live with our differences and a cacophony of contradictory justifications for one approach as opposed to another. All appeal to the need of tolerance, but there is nothing like common argument on what that means. The question our culture raises by nature and development is what is truth and what can we believe? Our culture doesn't know the answers. In fact, we have lost confidence in truth and have come to the conclusion that truth is unattainable. Thus, tolerance moves to the forefront."[16] G.K. Chesterton added: "Toleration is the virtue of the man without convictions."[17]

Finally, in the years ahead there will be real confusion about sexual roles. Based on his study of 21 civilizations, British historian Arnold Toynbee came to the following conclusions: societies in disintegration suffer a kind of "schism of the soul."[18] They are seldom simply overrun by some other civilization. Rather, they commit a sort of cultural suicide. Disintegrating societies have several characteristics, Toynbee argues. They fall into a sense of abandon as people begin to yield to their impulses — especially in the sexual area. They also succumb to truancy that is escapism, or seek to avoid their problems by retreating into their worlds of distraction and entertainment. There is a sense of drift as they realize that they have no control over their lives. Consciousness is lost, unable to anchor itself to any universal ground of justice, truth on which the ideals of modernity have been founded in the past.

Evangelicals, we are experiencing a cultural revolution, a violent one. We must not merely talk the talk, we must walk the walk. We must create an alternative community of hope. We must sabotage the conspiracy of hopelessness and self-centeredness that is so pervasive in our nation. Bring on the revolution!

Discussion Question

What advice does the author give evangelicals?

16. S.D. Gaede, *When Tolerance Is No Virtue* (Downers Grove, IL: InterVarsity Press, 1993).
17. http://www.brainyquote.com/quotes/quotes/g/gilbertkc163172.html.
18. Arnold J. Toynbee, *A Study of History* (1961), "Schism in the Soul."

In 1927, a man reads a sign advertising "Attention, Unemployed, Haircut 40 pfennigs, Shave 15 pfennigs." Pfennings were like pennies in the United States (PD).

Chapter 11

Germany 1871–1945: A Failed Democracy

First Thoughts

The failure of the Weimar Republic to solve the problems faced by Germany during the 1920s and the consequences of this failure were catastrophic. The deck was stacked against the Weimar Republic, which had a ton of problems from the outset. Democracy was a new concept within Germany, and no one knew how to do it. No one party gained hegemony, and no one was happy anyway. The republic also suffered at the hands of the Treaty of Versailles. Many groups within Germany blamed the fledgling government for the harsh terms imposed by the treaty, and opposition to the government was both open and violent, with varying amounts of success over the period of the republic's life. Finally, from 1932–33, Germans had had enough and they invited another "fuhrer" to rule them.

Chapter Learning Objectives

In chapter 11 we examine the background of German democracy and watch as it fails in the Weimar Republic. We will see that a combination of a deep depression and runaway inflation caused the collapse of democracy. Along the way, we will look at the influence of the cabaret and its impact on German history. Finally, we will compare Weimar to the United States and speculate upon whether or not a similar catastrophe could visit America.

As a result of this chapter you should be able to:

1. Explain why Germans rejected democracy

2. Understand why the Weimar Republic economy collapsed. What effect did inflation have on Weimar Germany?

3. Analyze how the cabaret became the place where government policy was established

4. Evaluate if the United States could experience the same collapse as the Weimar Republic

Concepts

Weimar Republic

German Reich

Reparation Payments

Protective Tariffs

Inflation

Cabaret

McCarthy Era

Weimar Republic

The **Weimar Republic** was the name given by historians to the federal republic and parliamentary representative democracy established in 1919 in Germany to replace the imperial form of government. It was named after Weimar, the city where the constitutional assembly took place. Its official name was German Realm (Deutsches Reich), German Empire, or, as rendered by a partial translation, **German Reich**.

But the Weimar Republic was anything but an empire. After World War I, the republic emerged from the German Revolution in November 1918. At that time, Germany was in terrible shape.

In 1919, a national assembly convened in Weimar where a new constitution for the German Reich was written. Germany's period of liberal democracy lapsed in the early 1930s, leading to the ascent of the Nazi Party and Adolf Hitler in 1932. Hitler ignored the Weimar constitution. Thus, 1932 was the end of the Weimar Republic and the beginning of Hitler's Third Reich. Why did this noble experiment fail so quickly? The answer lies in German history.

The German nation state at the end of the 19th century, which emerged under the leadership of Bismarck, had been set up with the appearance and feel of a Western parliamentary state. The problem is, Germans did not know how to do this "democratic thing." Those who wanted to couldn't because most Germans did not prefer this type of government.

Bismarck successfully protracted his German alliance between Bavaria, Prussia, Hanover, and others, during the rise of the German Empire (1871–1914) by extending significant privileges to the middle class. Empowering and enriching the middle class — average working-class people — is typically the preferred way to build a new government. In pre-modern Europe (1500–1600), when Europe was leaving the Middle Ages and moving toward industrialization and the modern era, the growth of the urban middle class ensured that feudalism was dead. Likewise, the middle class

The Schienenzeppelin or rail zeppelin was an experimental railcar that resembled a zeppelin airship in appearance. It was designed and developed by the German aircraft engineer Franz Kruckenberg in 1929. Propulsion was by means of a propeller located at the rear that accelerated the railcar to 143.0 mph setting the land speed record for a petrol-powered rail vehicle (CCA-SA3.0).

championed the nationalistic revolutions, mostly peaceful, of the middle 19th century. Now, at the end of the 19th century, Bismarck again built an empire by seducing the middle class with benefits, new trade, and secure borders — all the things the German middle class needed to prosper.

An exhibit of boxing, jiu jitsu, and other sports in the Lustgarten, 1925 (left). The Graf Zeppelin flies over the Victory Column, 1928 (CCA-SA3.0).

However, like the French middle class in the rise of absolutism in France in the 18th century, the German middle class was willing to sacrifice democracy for the security that an oligarchy brought. Adolf Hitler had over 80 percent of the German vote in 1932 when he took over. Clearly, he did not bully his way into Germany. He was invited in by the middle class!

The same thing was true of Bismarck, although Bismarck would have been horrified by the draconian methods that Hitler employed.

Since the nationalist movements of Post-Napoleonic Europe, the German middle class had sought unification, a feat almost impossible unless under strong leadership, which Bismarck finally provided. This early era of German unification created a lot of the precedents that were to follow, of anti-democratic feeling and the masses longing for strong leadership to see them through hard times. When push came to shove in the 1920s, when communism was a threat and the economy collapsed, Germans were ready to abandon the Weimar Republic and democracy in a heartbeat. Strong tertiary leadership had worked for their grandparents, so why not for them?

The reign of Bismarck, then, in many ways, set a very negative precedent for German political development, and for Germany's rise as a Great Power. One could argue that Adolf Hitler did what every German leader had done, but "better." He became a dictator for life. No German leader, other than a monarch, had done that.

During the reign of Adolf Hitler, Germany fully realized this downward spiral to a state governed more in the fashion of the age of absolutist monarchs, than an early 20th-century liberal West where France had the Republic and the United Kingdom the Parliament.

Discussion Question

Why was the rejection of the Weimar Republic, as laudable and just of a government as it might be, the most natural thing in the world for Germany to do?

The Weimar Economy

Germany was devastated after its jarring defeat in World War I. For that reason alone, the Weimar Republic had perhaps no chance to survive. Due to the Versailles Treaty, Germany was forced to pay incredibly sizeable reparations to France and Great Britain. In addition, the Versailles Treaty, which many agreed was far too harsh, forced Germany to give up 13 percent of its land. Germany was broken financially and spiritually. It was the latter problem that most probably caused the collapse of the Weimar Republic.

At first, Germany (like the United States in the 1930s) tried to recover from the war by way of social spending. Germany began creating transportation projects and modernizing municipal plants. These were all used to battle the increasing unemployment rate. It did not work in the United States, as America did not come out of the Depression until World War II. And it did not work in Germany — the economy did not improve until Adolf Hitler became chancellor and started the war material build-up.

In 1913, the government was spending approximately 20.5 marks per resident. By 1925 government spending had risen to almost 65 marks per resident and finally, in 1929, it reached over 100 marks per resident. The elevating amounts of money that were used for social spending, combined with plummeting revenues, caused continuing deficits. Eventually, the municipal finance division collapsed in 1930. The nation carried a huge deficit and city governments collapsed. Although it seemed as if the collapse was due to debt, in actuality, ordinary budgets were the initial reason for the collapse. Municipal officials and politicians were unable to restore order to the budgets. Further adding to Germany's economic problems, the revenue from income tax began to fall. In 1913, over 53 percent of all tax revenue was from income, but in 1925 this figure dropped down to 28 percent. As the returns on income taxes decreased, the government began to depend much more on state trade and property taxes. A recipe for disaster was brewing: tax revenues went down because people were out of work. The government, meanwhile, went bankrupt trying to hire workers to increase employment.

Children being fed by a soup kitchen, 1924 (left). An elderly woman gathers vegetable waste tossed from a vegetable seller's wagon for her lunch, 1923 (CCA-SA3.0).

To make things worse, the Versailles Treaty forced Germany to make **Weimar Republic (German Reich) reparation** payments for the war. It was hard enough for the struggling Weimar Republic to make reparation payments, but foreign countries made it impossible by placing **protective tariffs** on Germany's goods.

With the income Germany could have gained by selling goods in foreign countries for relatively low prices, reparation payments could have become feasible. The protective tariffs made this idea impossible and further depressed the German economy. Faced with reparation payments it could not afford, Germany began printing huge amounts of paper money. This threw Germany into a state of super inflation. Inflation eventually reached the point where millions of marks were worthless.

With Germany at its weakest and most vulnerable point, Hitler took the opportunity to begin his ascent to power. Hitler had two significant ideas that helped launch him into power. He had someone to blame for the economy, and he had a plan for a swift economic recovery. Hitler outlined a plan where in four years he would completely eliminate unemployment throughout Germany. He was able to keep his promise of economic growth and begin his climb to power.[1]

Discussion Question

Why did the Weimar Republic economy collapse?

A medal commemorating Germany's 1923 hyperinflation. The engraving reads: "On 1st November 1923 1 pound of bread cost 3 billion, 1 pound of meat: 36 billion, 1 glass of beer: 4 billion" (PD).

Impact of Inflation

In the early 1920s, Germany experienced one of the most severe **inflations** of all time. The inflation was not apparent in 1920, but began showing up in 1921. Thereafter it got steadily worse until it came to an abrupt halt at the end of 1923. At its worst in the second half of 1923, prices rose more than fivefold each week. Can you imagine? A loaf of bread cost $1 on Monday and $5 on Saturday!

From the middle of 1922 until the middle of 1923, prices increased more than a hundred-fold. Measured by the price of food, prices were 135 times higher at the end of the period than they were at the beginning. Measured by how many marks it took to buy a dollar, prices were 222 times higher. Yet even this horrid inflation was mild compared to what happened from July to November of 1923 when prices increased by somewhere between a million and a billion times their previous level.

Inflation, quite simply, was caused by spending more money than the country had. It did not raise taxes — it printed more worthless money!

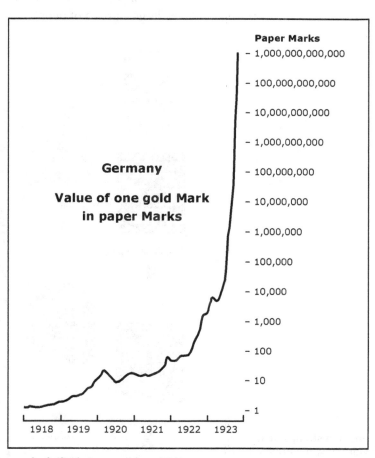

Paper Marks

Germany

Value of one gold Mark in paper Marks

- 1,000,000,000,000
- 100,000,000,000
- 10,000,000,000
- 1,000,000,000
- 100,000,000
- 10,000,000
- 1,000,000
- 100,000
- 10,000
- 1,000
- 100
- 10
- 1

1918 1919 1920 1921 1922 1923

---

1. Daniel Castillo, "German Economy in the 1920s," Dec. 2003, http://www.history.ucsb.edu/faculty/marcuse/classes/33d/ projects/1920s/Econ20s.htm.

A 50,000,000 (50 million) mark banknote from 1923.

Not everyone was hurt by inflation. Buyers, for example, were hurt by higher prices, but offsetting this was the gain that the producers get from the higher prices. People on fixed incomes suffered, as did creditors, who were owed fixed amounts of money at a future date. On the other hand, those making fixed payments, such as most debtors, would benefit. For example, the value of German mortgages in 1913 measured in U.S. dollars was about $10 billion, but in late 1923 those mortgages were worth only one U.S. penny.

By 1930, inflation had radically redistributed the wealth of Germany. The segment of society that was hit the hardest seems to have been the middle class. The poor had little wealth to lose while the rich were often able to get their wealth into forms not adversely affected by inflation. The middle class, to say the least, was ready for a change!

Getting rid of money was the key to financial survival since it lost its value so quickly. And people who borrowed heavily almost always did well.

People dislike inflation because it redistributes wealth in ways they consider unfair, because it forces them to take actions to protect themselves, and because it makes it more difficult to make decisions. Decisions to invest are based on a person's knowledge of what normal prices are and this knowledge of normal prices is based on remembering past prices. With inflation, a person must remember not only past prices, but also the dates of those past prices, and then try to compute what their present equivalents would be. As such, people like stable prices because they minimize the cost of making economic decisions. In Germany in the 1920s, the middle class — normally the largest group of people investing in any society — could not take stock of the

Postage stamps of Weimar Germany, hyperinflation of early 1920s (PD).

economy and therefore failed to invest, hurting the economy further, and in the long run hurting themselves too.

The German hyperinflation came to an abrupt end in November of 1923. The man who received credit for this achievement was named Hjalmar Schacht, the new currency commissioner of the Weimar Republic. But the damage was done. Even a slight increase in prices made the middle class flinch!

Discussion Question

What effect did inflation have on Weimar Germany?

In 1923 German banknotes had lost so much value that they were used as wallpaper. (PD).

Sociology: The Cabaret

At times in history, government policies and decisions are made in the most unlikely places. For instance, in American history, the American Revolution was planned and implemented in drab pubs up and down the East Coast. Likewise, in early Washington D.C., most politics occurred in boarding houses (sort of cheap motels that also offer provisions). Perhaps the best example of the intermixing of culture and politics is Germany's 20th-century cabarets. Cabaret in 20th-century Germany was a distinctive art form — a combination of dance, song, drama, and other random skits designed to provoke thought while maintaining the audience's amusement. It is difficult to find anything like it in American history. Perhaps the 1920 vaudeville acts would come closest.

By the late 1920s the German cabaret gradually had come to feature mildly risque musical entertainment for the middle-class man.

Historian Lisa Appignanesi[2] argues that the intermixing of food, drink, and art were a unique combination that bred a level of intimacy between performers and viewers that was previously unheard of. But what exactly was the relationship between 20th-century German cabarets and contemporary politics of the time? Cabarets served a special role as an outlet for political discourse, but in the end they catered to public tastes and had to strike an appropriate balance between mindless entertainment and engaging political commentary. Twentieth-century German **cabaret** was both. Through examining cabaret during Germany in World War I, the Weimar Republic, and Nazi Germany, it will be shown that it served as a barometer of public opinion. Political commentary within cabaret flourished during times of uncertainty and mitigated peace, while in times of war, the political content and satire within cabaret was suppressed by external factors such as the state, but also by internal factors like public taste. The level of escapism

2. Lisa Appignanesi, *The Cabaret* (New Haven, CT: Yale University Press, 2004).

versus the amount of political commentary and mockery within cabaret during a specific time period was the product of a delicate balance between public opinion and the political developments of the day. It is this delicate balance that makes 20th-century German cabaret so fascinating to explore.

The Weimar Republic was perhaps the most interesting time period for cabaret in 20th-century history. Cabarets became debate societies. One popular theory was advanced by Erich Ludendorff, the famous German general, stating that Germany was not actually defeated in battle, but rather sabotaged by mutinous sailors. This theory was a reference to members of the German Navy in Kiel who rebuffed attempts at forcing them to participate in a large battle toward the end of World War I, as well as a reference to Communists, whose strikes undermined war efforts. Over mugs of beer and salacious entertainment, these accusations made more sense than they would have in other surroundings. It is not coincidence that Adolf Hitler began his futile rebellion in a 1920s beer hall!

People could go to a cabaret, have a beer, share some laughs, and critique the state without the feeling that they were being disloyal. It was this transformation in public opinion that allowed the cabaret to go from existing only in a technical sense in World War I to the powerful cultural, intellectual, and political force it became in the Weimar Republic. To a large degree, the Nazi Party was launched in cabarets.

Discussion Question

Why was the cabaret the perfect place to dismantle a declining democracy and plan a revolution?

Oscar Straus, cover of a music sheet for Wolzogen's cabarat Überbrettl in Berlin 1902 (PD).

Cabarets were places that featured live entertainment – comedy, music, dance, drama – that often were risqué and making comments on cultural and political issues of the day; it was a form of intellectual criticism that rose in popular following World War 1. Such was the case in Germany during the Weimar Republic, but with the rise of the Nazi Party, more and more of the stars of these "kabaretts" faced discrimination, harsh restrictions, harassment, and even arrest. Some Jewish performers like the popular and talented Fritz Grünbaum, if caught, would die in concentration camps like Dachau.

Cabarat "Überbrettl" in Berlin 1901 (PD).

What We Can Learn from 1920s Germany

Brian E. Fogarty

Imagine this situation: Your country has had a military setback in a war that was supposed to be over after a few months of "shock and awe." Because of that war, it has lost the goodwill and prestige of much of the international community.

McCarthy Era:
A time of heightened fear against Communism in the U. S. A.

The national debt has grown to staggering size. Citizens complain bitterly about the government, especially the legislative branch, for being a bunch of do-nothings working solely for themselves or for special interest groups. In fact, the political scene has pretty much lost its center — moderates are attacked by all sides as the political discourse becomes a clamor of increasingly extreme positions.

It seems there are election campaigns going on all the time, and they are increasingly vicious. The politicians just want to argue about moral issues — sexuality, decadent art, the crumbling family and the like — while pragmatic matters of governance seem neglected.

Sound familiar? That society was Germany of the 1920s — the ill-fated Weimar Republic. But it also describes more and more the political climate in America today.

Germans were worried about the future of their country. They suffered from all sorts of terror, as assassinations, coup attempts, and crime pulled their society apart. The left blamed the right, the right blamed the left, and the political center simply dried up.

To get themselves out of the mess, Germans might have demanded a government that carefully mended fences with its allies and enemies; one that judiciously hammered out compromises among the various political parties and sought the middle path.

But we know that didn't happen. In Germany of the 1920s, as now in 21st-century America, appeals to reason and prudence were no way to get votes in times of crisis. Much more effective were appeals to the anger and fear of the German people. A politician could attract more votes by criticizing the government than by praising it, and a vicious negative campaign was usually more effective than a clean one. One of the problems of democracy is that voters aren't always rational, and appeals like these could be very effective.

As usually happens in times of distress, the Germans became a people for whom resolve was valued more highly than prudence, daring more than caution, and righteousness more than discretion. In many ways, they were a people not so different from today's Americans.

What was needed, the Germans thought, was a strong leader — someone who would put an end to politics as usual; most of all, someone who could unite all the divisions in Germany and dispel the clamor. They found that leader in Adolf Hitler, and for a time, most Germans were glad they did.

Of course, America is not 1920s Germany, and we are certainly not on the verge of a fascist state. But neither have we experienced the deep crises the Germans faced. The

setbacks of the Iraq/Afghan war are a far cry from the devastating loss of the First World War; we are not considered the scourge of the international community, and we don't need wheelbarrows full of money to buy a loaf of bread. But even in these relatively secure times, we have shown an alarming willingness to choose headstrong leadership over thoughtful leadership, to value security over liberty; to accept compromises to constitutional principles, and to defy the opinion of the rest of the world.

How would we react if things got worse? If we were to lose a war, leaving a fundamentalist regime in place; if we endured several more major terrorist attacks; if the economy collapsed; if fuel prices reached $7 per gallon — would we cling even more fiercely to our democratic ideals? Or would we instead demand greater surveillance, more secret prisons, more arrests for "conspiracies" that amount to little more than daydreams, and more quashing of dissent?

Our history suggests the latter. We Americans have had our flights from democracy — the internment of Japanese-Americans in World War II, the Red Scare and the **McCarthy era**, Watergate — but we have always pulled back from the brink and returned to normal.

The time is coming for us to pull back from the brink again. This must happen before the government gets so strong that it can completely demonize opposition, gain complete control of the media, and develop dossiers on all its citizens. By then it will be too late, and we'll have ourselves to blame.[3]

The ending of World War 1 brought only political and economic upheaval to Germany. Adding to the humiliation of the country was the loss of territorial right, a period of revolt and anarchy, and instability from rampant inflation. Amid the chaos and struggle, the voice of Adolf Hitler rose to promise the battered and suffering country a new period of prosperity – albeit at what would become an unimaginable cost, 1919 (PD).

Brian E. Fogarty, a sociology professor at the College of St. Catherine in St. Paul, is the author of *War, Peace, and the Social Order*.

Discussion Question

Germany in its moment of crisis turned from the best form of government to the worst because it felt threatened. What might America do if we were in a similar crisis?

3. Brian E. Fogarty, "What We Can Learn from 1920s Germany," *Minneapolis Star-Tribune*, July 26, 2006; http://www.commondreams.org/cgi-bin/print.cgi?file=/views06/0726-28.htm.

People standing in line to get their surplus commodities. The young men in the line come to get supplies for their families, 1940 (NARA).

Chapter 12

The New Deal: Failure of the Liberal State

First Thoughts

The Great Depression, 1929–1941, was the most devastating experience in American history. The Great Depression resulted from problems in the industrial economies of Europe and the United States, combined with the long-term weakness in economies like those of Latin America and Asia that depended on sales of cheap exports. The result was an unprecedented worldwide collapse. Franklin Delano Roosevelt's solution was the New Deal, a comprehensive social and economic intervention that was both thorough and revolutionary. President Roosevelt established the positive liberal state, an intervention where the state was aggressively involved in social engineering and economic revitalization, with ominous consequences. Adolf Hitler employed a similar tactic with some success, but he had to fight a war to really use what he had built. Only when America fought Hitler's war did it come out of the Great Depression. America's dance with the positive liberal state continues. . . .

Chapter Learning Objectives

In chapter 12 we examine the creation of the positive liberal state and analyze its effectiveness. After an overview of the Great Depression and resulting New Deal legislation, we evaluate the effectiveness of this legislation. Finally, we look at political cartooning and analyze its effectiveness.

As a result of this chapter you should be able to:

1. Explain how the New Dealers differed from the progressives

2. Offer evidence of the positive liberal state in Franklin Delano Roosevelt's First Inaugural Address

3. Analyze the 1935 Social Security Act and explain why it was necessary

4. Discuss the results of social welfare

5. Analyze political cartoons

CONCEPTS

Great Depression

Brain trust

The New Deal

Positive liberal state

National Recovery Administration

Public Works Administration

Herb Block

The Great Depression and New Deal

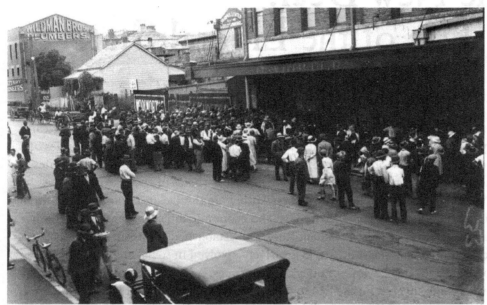

Crowd gathered for free food outside the McWhirters' building, Fortitude Valley, Brisbane, on Christmas Day 1933. Free parcels of food were handed out to over 4,500 people (PD).

The **Great Depression** formally started in October 1929, when the New York stock market crashed. Stock values tumbled as investors quickly lost confidence. A macabre domino effect resulted. United States banks, which had depended heavily on their stock investments, failed, dragging their depositors along with them.

With investment receding, industrial production quickly began to fall, beginning in the industries that produced capital goods and extending quickly to consumer products industries. Falling production — levels had dropped by as much as one-third by 1932 — meant rising unemployment and lower wages, which in turn withdrew more demand from the economy and led to further hardship.

The economic collapse of the 1930s was staggering in its dimensions. Unemployment jumped from less than 3 million in 1929 to 4 million in 1930, to 8 million in 1931, and to 12 ½ million in 1932. In that year, a quarter of the nation's families did not have a single employed wage earner. Even those fortunate enough to have jobs suffered drastic pay cuts and reductions in working hours. Only one company in ten failed to cut pay, and in 1932 three-quarters of all workers were on part-time schedules, averaging just 60 percent of the normal work week.

The economic collapse was terrifying in its scope and impact. By 1933 average family income had tumbled 40 percent, from $2,300 in 1929 to just $1,500 four years later.

A homeless family of seven, walking the highway from Phoenix, Arizona, where they picked cotton, to San Diego, where the father hoped to get on the relief because he once lived there, 1939 (USDA).

In the Pennsylvania coalfields, three or four families crowded together in one-room shacks and lived on wild weeds. In Arkansas, families were found inhabiting caves. In Oakland, California, whole families lived in sewer pipes.

Vagrancy shot up as many families were evicted from their homes for nonpayment of rent. The Southern Pacific Railroad boasted that it threw 683,000 vagrants off its trains in 1931. Free public flophouses and missions in Los Angeles provided beds for 200,000 of the uprooted.

To save money, families neglected medical and dental care. Many families sought to cope by planting gardens, canning food, buying used bread, and using cardboard and cotton for shoe soles. Despite a steep decline in food prices, many families did without milk or meat. In New York City, milk consumption declined by a million gallons a day.[1]

Americans endured 12 years of agony. Only World War II could end this catastrophe. However, President Franklin Delano Roosevelt, elected in 1932, tried to bring the Great Depression to an end.

Franklin Roosevelt brought a new breed of government officials to Washington. Previously, most government administrators were wealthy businessmen or political insiders. Roosevelt brought to Washington a team of Ivy League intellectuals and New York State social workers. Known as the "**brain trust**," these advisors provided Roosevelt with a plethora of new ideals, collectively called **The New Deal**.

Florence Thompson with several of her children in a tent shelter at Pea-Pickers Camp, Nipomo, California, 1936 (LOC).

The New Dealers were strongly influenced by the progressive reformers of the early 20th century, who believed the government had not only a right but also a duty to intervene in all aspects of the economy in order to improve the quality of American life. They were strong supporters of "big government." The New Dealers, in effect, created the **positive liberal state**.

In one significant respect, however, the New Dealers differed decisively from the progressives. Progressive reform had a strong moral dimension; many reformers wanted to curb drinking, eliminate what they considered immoral behavior, and ameliorate human character. In comparison, the New Dealers were much more pragmatic. They sought to establish social policy without any connection to Judeo-Christian morality. If a policy encouraged out-of-wedlock pregnancies, then so be it. It was no concern of the New Dealers.

In the next ten years, New Dealers transformed American society forever. All aspects of American life were touched by make-work projects, labor reform, and social security. The entire infrastructure of America was rebuilt.

Discussion Question

How did the New Dealers differ from the progressives?

Labor contractors' camp for field labor during the pea harvests of California, Washington, Idaho, Wyoming, Utah, and New Mexico. Many of these families moved from state to state at their own expense, 1940 (NARA).

1. http://www.digitalhistory.uh.edu/learning_history/children_depression/depression_children_menu.cfm.

Franklin Delano Roosevelt's First Inaugural Address, March 4, 1933

"Happiness lies not in the mere possession of money; it lies in the joy of achievement, in the thrill of creative effort."

I am certain that my fellow Americans expect that on my induction into the Presidency I will address them with a candor and a decision which the present situation of our Nation impels. This is preeminently the time to speak the truth, the whole truth, frankly and boldly. Nor need we shrink from honestly facing conditions in our country today. This great Nation will endure as it has endured, will revive and will prosper. So, first of all, let me assert my firm belief that the only thing we have to fear is fear itself — nameless, unreasoning, unjustified terror which paralyzes needed efforts to convert retreat into advance. In every dark hour of our national life a leadership of frankness and vigor has met with that understanding and support of the people themselves which is essential to victory. I am convinced that you will again give that support to leadership in these critical days.

In such a spirit on my part and on yours we face our common difficulties. They concern, thank God, only material things. Values have shrunken to fantastic levels; taxes have risen; our ability to pay has fallen; government of all kinds is faced by serious curtailment of income; the means of exchange are frozen in the currents of trade; the withered leaves of industrial enterprise lie on every side; farmers find no markets for their produce; the savings of many years in thousands of families are gone.

One of the few photographs of FDR in his wheelchair, as he generally refused to be photographed in or around it. Roosevelt, who had been crippled in 1921, went to great lengths to hide his depedence on the wheelchair, to the point of actually teaching himself to walk with iron braces on his legs so as to keep up appearences, 1941 (PD).

More important, a host of unemployed citizens face the grim problem of existence, and an equally great number toil with little return. Only a foolish optimist can deny the dark realities of the moment.

Yet our distress comes from no failure of substance. We are stricken by no plague of locusts. Compared with the perils which our forefathers conquered because they believed and were not afraid, we have still much to be thankful for. Nature still offers her bounty and human efforts have multiplied it. Plenty is at our doorstep, but a generous use of it languishes in the very sight of the supply. Primarily this is because the rulers of the exchange of mankind's goods have failed, through their own stubbornness and their own incompetence, have admitted their failure, and abdicated. Practices of the unscrupulous money changers stand indicted in the court of public opinion, rejected by the hearts and minds of men.

True they have tried, but their efforts have been cast in the pattern of an outworn tradition. Faced by failure of credit they have proposed only the lending of more money. Stripped of the lure of profit by which to induce our people to follow their false leadership, they have resorted to exhortations, pleading tearfully for restored confidence. They know only the rules of a generation of self-seekers. They have no vision, and when there is no vision the people perish.

The money changers have fled from their high seats in the temple of our civilization. We may now restore that temple to the ancient truths. The measure of the restoration lies in the extent to which we apply social values more noble than mere monetary profit.

Happiness lies not in the mere possession of money; it lies in the joy of achievement, in the thrill of creative effort. The joy and moral stimulation of work no longer must be forgotten in the mad chase of evanescent profits. These dark days will be worth all they cost us if they teach us that our true destiny is not to be ministered unto but to minister to ourselves and to our fellow men.

Recognition of the falsity of material wealth as the standard of success goes hand in hand with the abandonment of the false belief that public office and high political position are to be valued only by the standards of pride of place and personal profit; and there must be an end to a conduct in banking and in business which too often has given to a sacred trust the likeness of callous and selfish wrong-doing. Small wonder that confidence languishes, for it thrives only on honesty, on honor, on the sacredness of obligations, on faithful protection, on unselfish performance; without them it cannot live.

Restoration calls, however, not for changes in ethics alone. This Nation asks for action, and action now.

Franklin Delano Roosevelt and Herbert Hoover in convertible automobile on way to U.S. Capitol for Roosevelt's inauguration, March 4, 1933 (LOC).

Our greatest primary task is to put people to work. This is no unsolvable problem if we face it wisely and courageously. It can be accomplished in part by direct recruiting by the Government itself, treating the task as we would treat the emergency of a war, but at the same time, through this employment, accomplishing greatly needed projects to stimulate and reorganize the use of our natural resources.

Hand in hand with this we must frankly recognize the overbalance of population in our industrial centers and, by engaging on a national scale in a redistribution, endeavor to provide a better use of the land for those best fitted for the land. The task can be helped by definite efforts to raise the values of agricultural products and with this the power to purchase the output of our cities. It can be helped by preventing realistically the tragedy of the growing loss through foreclosure of our small homes and our farms. It can be helped by insistence that the Federal, State, and local governments act forthwith on the demand that their cost be drastically reduced. It can be helped by the unifying of relief activities which today are often scattered, uneconomical, and unequal. It can be helped by national planning for and supervision of all forms of transportation and of communications and other utilities which have a definitely public character. There are many ways in which it can be helped, but it can never be helped merely by talking about it. We must act and act quickly.

Finally, in our progress toward a resumption of work we require two safeguards against a return of the evils of the old order; there must be a strict supervision of all banking and credits and investments; there must be an end to speculation with other people's money, and there must be provision for an adequate but sound currency.

There are the lines of attack. I shall presently urge upon a new Congress in special session detailed measures for their fulfillment, and I shall seek the immediate assistance of the several States.

Through this program of action we address ourselves to putting our own national house in order and making income balance outgo. Our international trade relations, though

137

Churchill, FDR, and Stalin at Yalta, two months before Roosevelt's death, February 1945 (PD).

vastly important, are in point of time and necessity secondary to the establishment of a sound national economy. I favor as a practical policy the putting of first things first. I shall spare no effort to restore world trade by international economic readjustment, but the emergency at home cannot wait on that accomplishment.

The basic thought that guides these specific means of national recovery is not narrowly nationalistic. It is the insistence, as a first consideration, upon the interdependence of the various elements in all parts of the United States — a recognition of the old and permanently important manifestation of the American spirit of the pioneer. It is the way to recovery. It is the immediate way. It is the strongest assurance that the recovery will endure.

In the field of world policy I would dedicate this Nation to the policy of the good neighbor — the neighbor who resolutely respects himself and, because he does so, respects the rights of others — the neighbor who respects his obligations and respects the sanctity of his agreements in and with a world of neighbors.

If I read the temper of our people correctly, we now realize as we have never realized before our interdependence on each other; that we can not merely take but we must give as well; that if we are to go forward, we must move as a trained and loyal army willing to sacrifice for the good of a common discipline, because without such discipline no progress is made, no leadership becomes effective. We are, I know, ready and willing to submit our lives and property to such discipline, because it makes possible a leadership which aims at a larger good. This I propose to offer, pledging that the larger purposes will bind upon us all as a sacred obligation with a unity of duty hitherto evoked only in time of armed strife.

With this pledge taken, I assume unhesitatingly the leadership of this great army of our people dedicated to a disciplined attack upon our common problems.

Action in this image and to this end is feasible under the form of government which we have inherited from our ancestors. Our Constitution is so simple and practical that it is possible always to meet extraordinary needs by changes in emphasis and arrangement without loss of essential form. That is why our constitutional system has proved itself the most superbly enduring political mechanism the modern world has produced. It has met every stress of vast expansion of territory, of foreign wars, of bitter internal strife, of world relations.

It is to be hoped that the normal balance of executive and legislative authority may be wholly adequate to meet the unprecedented task before us. But it may be that an unprecedented demand and need for undelayed action may call for temporary departure from that normal balance of public procedure.

I am prepared under my constitutional duty to recommend the measures that a stricken nation in the midst of a stricken world may require. These measures, or such other measures as the Congress may build out of its experience and wisdom, I shall seek, within my constitutional authority, to bring to speedy adoption.

But in the event that the Congress shall fail to take one of these two courses, and in the event that the national emergency is still critical, I shall not evade the clear course of duty that will then confront me. I shall ask the Congress for the one remaining instrument to meet the crisis — broad Executive power to wage a war against the emergency, as great as the power that would be given to me if we were in fact invaded by a foreign foe.

For the trust reposed in me I will return the courage and the devotion that befit the time. I can do no less.

We face the arduous days that lie before us in the warm courage of the national unity; with the clear consciousness of seeking old and precious moral values; with the clean satisfaction that comes from the stern performance of duty by old and young alike. We aim at the assurance of a rounded and permanent national life.

We do not distrust the future of essential democracy. The people of the United States have not failed. In their need they have registered a mandate that they want direct, vigorous action. They have asked for discipline and direction under leadership. They have made me the present instrument of their wishes. In the spirit of the gift I take it.

In this dedication of a Nation we humbly ask the blessing of God. May He protect each and every one of us. May He guide me in the days to come.[2]

Discussion Question

Offer evidence of the positive liberal state in this speech.

Social Legislation

Congress established the **National Recovery Administration** (NRA) to make industry and labor cooperate to bring economic recovery. Representatives of business, labor, and government must establish policies of fair practices that would set polices within each industry. The NRA also supported workers' rights to join labor unions. For labor, the NRA was a mixed blessing. On the positive side, the codes abolished child labor and established the precedent of federal regulation of minimum wages and maximum hours. On the negative side, however, the NRA codes set wages in most industries well below what labor needed.

Roosevelt signs the Social Security Act, August 14, 1935 (LOC).

The first major program to attack unemployment through public works was the **Public Works Administration** (PWA). The New Deal's

2. http://www.bartleby.com/124/pres49.html.

most popular jobs program was the Civilian Conservation Corps (CCC). By mid-1933, some 300,000 jobless young men between the ages of 18 and 25 were hired to work in the nation's parks and forests. Despite its immense popularity, the CCC failed to have a serious impact on unemployment. It excluded women, imposed rigid quotas on African Americans, and offered employment to a small number of the young people who needed work.[3]

Public Works Administration Project, U.S. Army Corps of Engineers, Bonneville Power and Navigation Dam in Oregon on the Columbia River, 1936 (NARA).

Nonetheless, some government interventions were needed and have been very successful to date.

The 1935 Social Security Act was a triumph of social legislation. Financed by the federal government and the states, the act offered workers age 65 or older monthly stipends based on previous earnings, and gave the indigent elderly small relief payments. In addition, it provided assistance to handicapped Americans and to dependent children who did not have a wage-earning parent. The act also established the nation's first federally sponsored system of unemployment insurance. The program was funded by mandatory payroll deductions.

Before the 1930s, support for the elderly was a matter of family, city, and state responsibilities, rather than a federal concern. However, the widespread suffering caused by the Great Depression changed all that. On January 17, 1935, President Franklin D. Roosevelt sent a message to Congress asking for "social security" legislation. The same day, Senator Robert Wagner of New York, and Representative David Lewis of Maryland, introduced bills reflecting the administration's views. Eventually the bill passed both houses, and on August 15, 1935, President Roosevelt signed the Social Security Act into law.

The 1935 Social Security Act was good and necessary legislation. It was an example of how the federal government can handle problems that are too large for the local government. A major political victory for Roosevelt, the Social Security Act was a triumph of social legislation.

The Social Security Act introduced a new era in American history. It committed the government to a social welfare role by providing for elderly, disabled, and unemployed Americans. By doing so, the act greatly expanded the public's sense of entitlement.

Discussion Question

What was the 1935 Social Security Act and why was it necessary?

---

3. http://www.digitalhistory.uh.edu/disp_textbook.cfm?smtID=2&psid=3443.

The Failure of the Positive Liberal State

The positive liberal state has not worked.

The social welfare system is a runaway juggernaut. We have spent over $5 trillion since 1965, and we are worse off. If all this money had given us happy, healthy families, it would have been worth it. But the opposite is true. It has consigned untold millions of children to lives of bitterness and failure.[4]

In 1960, 5 of every 100 American births were illegitimate. By 1991, that figure was 30 of every 100, and the upward trend shows no sign of slowing down. Government welfare programs dealing with the problem have also increased. But the cost of illegitimacy is not measured only in dollars, as New York's Senator Daniel Patrick Moynihan once observed: "A community that allows a large number of young men to grow up in broken families, never acquiring any stable relationship to male authority, asks for and gets chaos. Crime, violence, unrest, disorder — most particularly the furious, unrestrained lashing out at the whole social structure — that is not only to be expected, it is very near to inevitable."[5]

Poor mother and children during the Great Depression in Elm Grove, Oklahoma, August 1936 (LOC).

By 1994, the number of illegitimate births grew to 40 percent and, an even more alarming figure, 27 percent of pregnancies were aborted. "Now, I don't care what your position is, whether you're pro-choice or anti — that's too many," President Clinton told the National Baptist Convention USA.[6] Having a baby out of wedlock is "simply not right," he said. "You shouldn't have a baby before you're ready, and you shouldn't have a baby when you're not married."

"Children who do not live with a mother and a father are more likely to be high school dropouts, more likely to abuse drugs and alcohol, and more likely to be dependent on welfare than children who live with both biological parents," Human Services Chief Louis Sullivan said in October 1994.[7] Psychologists point out that fathers are not simply substitute mothers. Fathers tend to be stronger disciplinarians than mothers and that's particularly true for boys. Boys are much less likely to develop good self-control when fathers are not present.[8] But, as Senator Daniel Patrick Moniyhan pointed out in 1965, a man already suffering from his failure as a provider, is further demeaned by becoming

4. Mortimer B. Zuckerman, "Fixing the Welfare Mess," in *U.S. News and World Report*, January 16, 1995, p. 68.
5. Statistical Abstract of the United States, U.S. Census Bureau; Bureau of Vital Statistics. In *Reader's Digest. Reader's Digest*'s quote of Moynihan is from *Family and Nation* (1965) and *Policy Review* (Fall 1993).
6. *Christianity Today*, October 24, 1994, p. 80.
7. Richard Whitmire, Gannett News Service, in *Tribune Democrat*, October 27, 1994, p. 1. There is abundant evidence to support my argument that the family is in decline primarily because of the absence of fathers. For example, see Glenn Stanton, "From Guffaws to Hurrahs," *Focus on the Family: Citizen*, January 16, 1995, p. 6–7. Also, see Dan Quayle, *Standing Firm* (New York: Zondervan, 1994), ch. 32: "Murphy and Me."
8. Ibid., p. 1.

Young migratory mother at Edison, California, originally from Texas. On the day before the photograph was made she and her husband traveled 35 miles each way to pick peas. They worked 5 hours each and together earned $2.25, 1940 (NARA).

dependent on the woman who gets the welfare check. As a result, many African American men have turned to violence to gain self-esteem. Roughly 40 percent of young black men ages 17 to 35 are in prison, on probation, or on the dole.[9] I blame human depravity and the social welfare system for this deplorable situation.

Of course the real victims are the children. Single households statistically are usually poorer than two-parent households. In 1993, 46.1 percent of the 8.8 million female-headed families with children lived in poverty, compared with only 9.0 percent of the 26.1 million married couple families with children. Of 1.6 million families headed by unmarried men, only 22.5 percent lived in poverty.[10] Out of 69.3 million children younger than 18, a total of 15.7 million — one in four — are poor. Most of these poor children are illegitimate, and illegitimacy is approaching an 80 percent rate in some inner cities.[11] And it is not simply an inner-city phenomenon. Twenty-three percent of American children live in families below the poverty line and 31 percent of these in suburbia.[12]

Clearly, single parenthood exacerbates poverty, but would marriage cure it? Yes. Research suggests that over 60 percent of poor children in mother-only families would be lifted out of poverty if they were in two-parent households.[13]

Would money help the problem? "Unless we slow down these social trends — out-of-wedlock births, crime, drugs, the breakdown of values — government money is not going to do much," says Gary Bauer of the Family Research Council. Bauer concludes by saying, "Kids are not in poverty because Washington is not spending more money."[14] "Programs like AFDC combined with food stamps and housing assistance, although meant for good, have broken up more families than slavery ever did. As a result of these broken families, children are being raised without fathers in the house. This single fact contributes more than anything to the chaotic atmosphere in our inner cities," writes Rev. John Perkins, a pioneer of African American self-help programs, in *Policy Review*, a publication of the Heritage Foundation.[15]

In spite of trillions of federal dollars being poured into social projects since the New Deal and war on poverty in the mid-1960s, there are more poor people today than at any other time in American history. Even in the idealistic decade of 1960–1970, when everyone thought the war on poverty would be won in a generation and in spite of the fact that the government provided unprecedented resources for children, the well being of children declined.[16]

Young persons who grow up in single-parent households are much more likely to commit crime than any other population group. Three out of four teenage suicides occur in households where a parent has been absent. Eighty percent of adolescents in psychiatric hospitals come from broken homes. Tracking studies indicate that five of

9. Zuckerman, "Fixing the Welfare Mess," p. 68.

10. Patricia Edmonds and Margaret I. Usdansky, "Children Get Poorer; Nation gets richer," in *USA Today*, November 14, 1994, p. 1.

11. Jean Bethke Elhstain, "Family Matters: The Plight of America's Children," in *Christian Century*, July 14-21, 1993, pp. 710-711.

12. Ibid., p.1.

13. Ibid., p. 2.

14. For a general work on urbanization and the growth of the social welfare state see J. John Palen's, *The Urban World* (New York: McGraw-Hill Book Company, 1987).

15. Mike Manus, "Give the Church a Role in Welfare Reform," in *Expressions*, Pittsburgh, PA, March 1995.

16. Don Browning and Ian Evison, "The Family Debate: A Middle Way," in *Christian Century*, July 14–21, 1993, p. 712–713.

six adolescents caught up in the criminal-justice system come from families in which a parent (usually the father) has been absent. In fact, in 1988 a government survey of 17,000 children found, according to one analyst, that "children living apart from a biological parent are 20 to 40 percent more vulnerable to sickness."[17] As broken homes increase, so does criminal activity. And most social scientists insist that there is a clear connection. In 1972, when about 10 percent of children were illegitimate, the federal and state prison population in the United States was 94.6 per 100,000 people. In 1982, the rate was 170 per 100,000. By 1992, when over 30 percent of American children were illegitimate, the prison rate had grown to 330 for every 100,000.[18]

Most historians — and social scientists — agree that a stable, two-parent American family is the key to a revitalization of American society. Whether it is 1850 Cincinnati described by the historian Mary Ryan, or 1995 Los Angeles, a two-parent family brings significant bonuses to American society. Its absence creates all sorts of problems.[19]

In conclusion, these are no longer right-wing, conservative Judeo-Christian organizations saying these things. According to a study by the National Commission on Children, the "Kids Count Data Book: State Profiles of Child Well-Being," published by the liberal Center for the Study of Social Policy, children growing up in single-parent households are at greater risk than those in two-parent families for substance abuse, adolescent childbearing, criminality, suicide, mental illness, and dropping out of school. It is also clear that the economic risks to children are greatest among unwed mothers. And there is no compelling evidence that a decline in government spending alone accounts for the growing risks to children. In fact, let me make myself very clear. All my research points to an unavoidable conclusion: the most important indicator of child-hood problems — from poor health to poverty to behavioral problems — is whether a child grows up in a two-parent or single-parent household. No other indicator — race, economics, ethnicity, demographics — is as important as whether or not there is a father in the house.[20] In that sense, the loss of fatherhood in our society has had a devastating effect. The single most devastating trend in American families today is the increased absence of fathers.

The problem is not simply missing fathers, but the cultural shift stripping fatherhood of its masculinity. In the movie *Mrs. Doubtfire*, Robin Williams is badly needed by his children as an androgynous parent; as a father, he is irrelevant.[21] Fathers are becoming an extinct species.

Discussion Question

What has been the result of social welfare?

---

17. "Professor's Study Sees us All Behind Bars in a Hundred Years," in *Tribune Democrat*, Johnstown, PA, January 7, 1995. Reprinted from *The Des Moines Register*. See Jean Bethke Elshtain, "Family Matters: The Plight of American's Children," in *The Christian Century*, July 14–21, 1993, p. 710–711. Barbera Vobejda, "More U.S. Children Growing Up Fatherless," in *The Charlotte Observer*, April 24, 1995, p. 3A. "In 1994, 19 million or 24% of children were living in families without fathers present. In 1950, 6% of children were living in mother-only households . . . children who grow up without fathers are five times more likely to be poor, twice as likely to drop out of high school and much more likely to end up in foster care or juvenile-justice facilities."
18. *Tribune Democrat*, January 7, 1995, p. 1.
19. Mary P. Ryan, *Cradle of the Middle Class* (Cambridge; New York: Cambridge University Press, 1981), p. 240.
20. Report: Number of Young Kids in Poverty Hits Record in U.S.," in *Tribune Democrat*, January 30, 1995, p. 1. Andrew Billingsley in his book *Black Families in White America* (Englewood Cliffs, NJ: Prentice-Hall, Inc., 1968), argues that the African American family structure is critical to the future of black society. He prophetically predicted that its collapse would doom African American culture.
21. Richard Whitmire, "Fatherless America: What can be done?" in *Tribune Democrat*, January 30, 1995, p. C1. Whitmire quotes a book by David Blankenhorn entitled *Fatherless America* (New York: BasicBooks, 1995).

Political Cartoons — Herb Block

A political cartoon commenting on national domestic policy by Herb Block. (PD).

A political cartoon is a cartoon containing a commentary that usually relates to current events or personalities. It typically combines artistic skill, exaggeration, and vitriolic humor in order to question authority and draw attention to corruption and other social ills. Cartoonist **Herb Block** published his first editorial cartoon six months before the 1929 New York Stock Exchange crash that plunged the country into the Great Depression. His concern for the national physical environment broadened into concern for the economic and international environment. He also warned throughout the decade of the danger represented by Fascist political gains in Europe and Adolf Hitler's rise to power in Germany at the head of the Nazi Party.[22]

Discussion Question

What criticism is Block speaking to?

22. http://www.loc.gov/rr/print/swann/herblock/light.html.

An ex-slave in front of his home in 1937 (LOC).

Chapter 13

Born in Slavery: Slave Narratives 1936–1938

First Thoughts

Between 1936 and 1938, the WPA Federal Writers' Project (FWP) sent writers into 17 states to interview ordinary people in order to write down their life stories. Initially, only four states focused on collecting the stories of people who had once been held in slavery.

John A. Lomax, the National Advisor on Folklore and Folkways for the FWP (and the curator of the Archive of American Folk Song at the Library of Congress), was extremely interested in the ex-slave material he received from these states. In 1937, he directed the remaining states involved in the project to carry out interviews with former slaves as well.

In 1939, the FWP lost its funding, and the states were ordered to send whatever manuscripts they had collected to Washington. What they had was extraordinary!

Chapter Learning Objectives

In chapter 13 we will examine the lives of five ex-slaves and, in the process, understand more about the African American experience before and after the American Civil War.

As a result of this chapter study you should be able to:

Understand more completely the life of antebellum slaves

CONCEPTS

Federal Writers' Project (FWP)

John A. Lomax

Mary Reynolds

Walter Calloway

Ben Horry

Mary Reynolds, Dallas, Texas

Mary Reynolds claimed to be more than a hundred years old. She was born in slavery to the Kilpatrick family, in Black River, Louisiana.

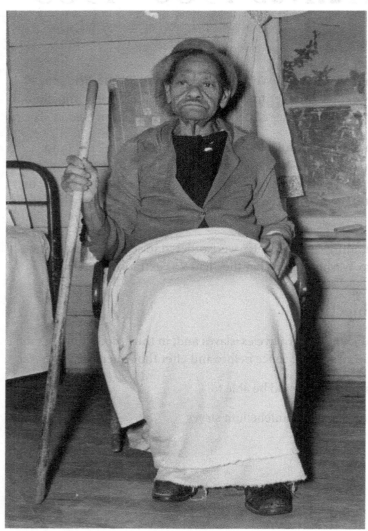

Mary Reynolds, 105 years old (PD).

My paw's name was Tom Vaughn and he was from the north, born free man and lived and died free to the end of his days. He wasn't no eddicated man, but he was what he calls himself a piano man. He told me once he lived in New York and Chicago and he built the insides of pianos and knew how to make them play in tune. He said some white folks from the south told he if he'd come with them to the south he'd find a lot of work to do with pianos in them parts, and he come off with them. . . .

I was born same time as Miss Sara Kilpatrick. Dr. Kilpatrick's first wife and my maw come to their time right together. Miss Sara's maw died and they brung Miss Sara to suck with me. It's a thing we ain't never forgot. My maw's name was Sallie and Miss Sara allus looked with kindness on my maw. . . .

I was jus' bout big nough to start playin' with a broom to go bout sweepin' up and not even half doin' it when Dr. Kilpatrick sold me. They was a old white man in Trinity and his wife died and he didn't have chick or child or slave or nothin'. That old man bought me a big doll and went off and left me all day, with the door open. I jus' sot on the floor and played with that doll. I used to cry. He'd come home and give me somethin' to eat and then go to bed, and I slep' on the foot of the bed with him. I was scart all the time in the dark. He never did close the door.

Miss Sara pined and sickened. Massa done what he could, but they wasn't no peartness in her. She got sicker and sicker, and massa brung nother doctor. He say, You li'l gal is grievin' the life out her body and she sho' gwine die iffen you don't do somethin' bout it. Miss Sara says over and over, I wants Mary. The doctor tells him he better git me back iffen he wants to save the life of his child. Dr. Kilpatrick has to give a big plenty more to git me back than what he sold me for, but Miss Sara plumps up right off and grows into fine health.

Then massa marries a rich lady from Mississippi and they has chillun for company to Miss Sara and seem like for a time she forgits me.

Massa Kilpatrick wasn't no piddlin' man. He was a man of plenty. He had a big house with no more style to it than a crib, but it could room plenty people. He was a medicine doctor and they was rooms in the second story for sick folks what come to lay in. It would take two days to go all over the land he owned. He had cattle and stock and sheep and more'n a hundred slaves and more besides. . . .

The times I hated most was pickin' cotton when the frost was on the bolls. My hands git sore and crack open and bleed. We'd have a li'l fire in the fields and iffen the ones with tender hands couldn't stand it no longer, we'd run and warm our hands a li'l bit. When I could steal a tater, I used to slip it in the ashes and when I'd run to the fire I'd take it out and eat it on the sly.

In the cabins it was nice and warm. They was built of pine boardin' and they was one long rom of them up the hill back of the big house. Near one side of the cabins was a fireplace. They'd bring in two, three big logs and put on the fire and they'd last near a week. The beds was made out of puncheons fitted on holes bored in the wall, and planks laid cross them poles. We had tickin' mattresses filled with corn shucks. Sometimes the men build chairs at night. We didn't know much bout havin' nothin', though. . . .

In them days I weared shirts, like all the young'uns. They had collars and come below the knees and was split up the sides. That's all we weared in hot weather. The men weared jeans and women gingham. Shoes was the worstes' trouble. We weared rough russets when it got cold, and it seem powerful strange they'd never git them to fit. Once when I was a young gal, they got me a new pair and all brass studs in the toes. They was too li'l for me, but I had to wear them. The trimmin's cut into my ankles and them places got mis'ble bad. I rubs tallow in them sore places and wrops rags around them and my sores got worser and worser. The scars are there to this day. . . .

Well, she didn't never leave and massa bought her a fine new span of surrey hosses. But she don't never have no more chillun and she ain't so cordial with the massa. Margaret, that yallow gal, has more white young'uns, but they don't never go down the hill no more to the big house. . . .

I didn't know bout the passin' of time, but Miss Sara come to me. Some white folks done git word to her. Mr. Kidd tries to talk hisself out of it, but Miss Sara fotches me home when I'm well enough to move. She took me in a cart and my maw takes care of me. Massa looks me over good and says I'll git well, but I'm ruint for breedin' chillun.

We jus' sot on the place doin' nothin' till the white folks comes home. Miss Sara come out to the cabin and say she wants to read a letter to my mammy. It come from Louis Carter, which is brother to my mammy, and he done follow the Fed'rals to Galveston. A white man done write the letter for him. It am tored in half and massa done that. The letter say Louis am workin' in Galveston and wants mammy to come with us, and he'll pay our way. Miss Sara say massa swear, Damn Louis Carter. I ain't gwine tell Sallie nothin', and he starts to tear the letter up. but she won't let him, and she reads it to mammy. . . .

My husband and me farmed round for times, and then I done housework and cookin' for many years. I come to Dallas and cooked seven year for one white family. My husband died years ago. I guess Miss Sara been dead these long years. I allus kep' my years by Miss Sara's years, count we is born so close.

I been blind and mos' helpless for five year. I'm gittin' might enfeeblin' and I ain't walked outside the door for a long time back. I sets and members the times in the world. I members now clear as yesterday things I forgot for a long time. I members bout the days of slavery and I don't lieve they ever gwine have slaves no more on this earth. I think Gawd done took that burden offen his black chillun and I'm aimin' to praise him for it to his face in the days of Glory what ain't so far off.[1]

Discussion Question

Recall one or two memorable events in the life of Mrs. Reynolds.

Lesson 2

Emma Crockett, Livingston, Alabama

On the old east road from Livingston to Epes, about six miles northeast of Livingston, is the double house built of widely assorted materials, where Emma Crockett lives.

Emma settled herself on the top step at the front of the hall to talk to me, after first ironing a tiny wrinkle out of her string apron with her hand.

Miss, I'm 'bout sebenty-nine or eighty year old, she told me, and I belonged to Marse Bill Hawkins end Miss Betty. I lived on deir plantation right over yander. My mammy was called Cassie Hawkins and my pappy was Alfred Jolly. I was Emma Jolly 'fore I married Old Henry Crockett. Us had five chillun and dey's two of 'em livin' in Bummingham, Fannie and Mary.

Sometimes I kain't git my min' together so as I kin tell nothin'. I fell out t'other day and had a misery in my head ever since. I wish I could read, but I wa'n't never l'arnt nothin' 'ceptin' atter Surrender Miss Sallie Cotes she showed us how to read printin'; but I kain't read no writin'. I kain't tell you so much 'bout de wah' ca'se my recollection ain't no 'count dese days. All I knowed, 'twas bad times and folks got whupped, but I kain't say who was to blame; some was good and some was bad. I seed de patterollers, and atter Surrender de Ku Kluxes dey come din, but didn't never bother me. See, I wan't so old and I minded ev'ybody, and didn't vex 'em none. Us didn't go to church none, but I goes now to de New Prophet Church and my favorite song is:

Set down, set down, set down, Set down, set down, Set down, chile, set down. Soul so happy till I kain't set down.

1. George P. Rawick, *The American Slave*, Vol. 5 (Westport, CN: Greenwood Pub. Co., 1972–79) p. 236–246; http://xroads. virginia.edu/~hyper/wpa/reynold1.html.

Move de member, move Dan-u-el, Move de member, move Dan-u-el. Dan-u-el, member, don' move so slow. Dan-u-el, member, don' move so slow. Got on my rockin' shoes, Dan-u-el. Got on my rockin' shoes, Dan-u-el.

Shoes gwine to rock me home, Shoes gwine to rock me home, Dan-u-el, Shoes gwine to rock me home, Dan-u-el, Shoes gwine to rock me home, Dan-u-el, Dan-u-el.

Shoes gwine to rock by faith, Shoes gwine to rock by faith, Dan-u-el, Shoes gwine to rock by faith, Dan-u-el.

Love de member, move Dan-u-el. Love de member, move Dan-u-el. Got on my starry crown, Dan-u-el. Got on my starry crown, Dan-u-el.

Emma Crockett (LOC).

Dat's all I kin tell you today, honey. Come back when dis misery leave my head and I gwine to think up some tales and old songs.

But I didn't never fool wid no hoodoo and no animal stories neither. I didn't have no time for no sich foolishness. And I ain't scared of nothin' neither.

I lives here wid my grandchile now on Mr. Bob Davis' place. Us gits enough to eat, I reckon, but it's tight, I tell you dat![2]

Discussion Question

The church was a central part of the lives of most Depression-era African Americans. Why?

Lesson 3

Walter Calloway, Birmingham, Alabama

Walter Calloway lives alone half a block off Avenue F, the thoroughfare on the southside of Birmingham where many of the leaders in the Negro life of the city live. For his 89 years he was apparently vigorous except for temporary illness. A glance at the interior of

2. Ibid., *Supplement Series 1*, Vol. 1: 13–16; see also Vol. 6: 92–94.

Walter Calloway (PD).

his cabin disclosed the fact that it was scrupulously neat and quite orderly in its arrangement, a characteristic of many ex-slaves.

Come in, white folks. You ain't no doctor is you? Fo' de las' past twenty-five years I been keepin' right on, wukkin' for de city in de street department. 'Bout two mont's ago dis mis'ry attackted me an' don't 'pear lak nothin' dem doctors gimme do no good. De preacher he come to see me dis mornin' an' he say he know a white gemman doctor, what he gwine to sen' him to see me. I sho' wants to get well ag'in pow'ful bad, but mebby I done live long 'nuff an' my time 'bout come.

Quizzed about his age and antecedents, he began his story:

Well, Sir, Cap'n, I was born in Richmond, Virginny, in 1848. Befo' I was ole 'nuff to 'member much, my mammy wid me an' my older brudder was sold to Marse John Calloway at Snodoun in Montgomery County, ten miles south of de town of Montgomery.

Marse John hab a big plantation an' lots of slaves. Dey treated us purty good, but we hab to wuk hard. Time I was ten years ole I was makin' a reg'lar han' 'hin de plow. Oh, yassuh, Marse John good 'nough to us an' we get plenty to eat, but he had a oberseer name Green Bush what sho' whup us iffen we don't do to suit him. Yassuh, he mighty rough wid us be he didn't do de whippin' hisse'f. He had a big black boy name Mose, mean as de debil an' strong as a ox, and de oberseer let him do all de whuppin'. An', man, he could sho' lay on dat rawhide lash. . . .

Same time Marse John buy mammy an' us boys, he buy a black man name Joe. He a preacher an' de marster let de slaves buil' a bresh arbor in de pecan grove over in de big pastor', an' when de wedder warn't too cold all de slaves was 'lowed to meet dar on Sunday fo' preachin'. . . .

Nawsuh, we didn't git no schoolin' 'cep'in' befo' we got big 'nough to wuk in de fiel' we go 'long to school wid de white chillun to take care of 'em. Dey show us pictures an' tell us all dey kin, but it didn't 'mount to much.

When de war started 'mos' all I know 'bout it was all de white mens go to Montgomery an' jine de army. My brudder, he 'bout fifteen year ole, so he go 'long wid de ration wagon to Montgomery 'mos' ebry week. One day he come back from Montgomery an' he say, "Hell done broke loose in Gawgy." He couldn't tell us much 'bout what done happen, but de slaves dey get all 'cited 'caze dey didn' know what to 'spect. Purty soon we fin' out day some of de big mens call a meetin' at de capitol on Goat Hill in Montgomery. Dey 'lected Mista Jeff Davis president an' done busted de Nunited States wide open.

Atter dat dar warn't much happen on de plantation 'cep'in' gangs of so'jers passin' th'ough gwine off to de war. Den 'bout ebry so often a squad of Confederate so'jers would come to de neighborhood gatherin' up rations for Gin'ral Lee's army dey say. Dat make it purty hard on bofe whites an' blacks, takin' off some of de bes' stock an' runnin' us low on grub.

But we wuk right on 'til one day somebody seen a runner sayin' de Yankees comin'. Ole mistis tell me to hurry ober to Mrs. Freeman's an' tell 'em Wilson's Yankee raiders was on de way an' comin' lak a harrikin. I hop on a mule an' go jes' as fas' as I can make him trabel, but befo' I git back dey done retch de plantation, smashin' things comin' an' gwine.

Dey broke in de smoke house an' tuk all de hams an' yuther rations dey fin' what dey want an' burn up de res'. Den dey ramshack de big house lookin' fo' money an' jewelry an' raise Cain wid de wimmin folks 'caze dey didn't fin' what dey wanted. Den dey leave dere ole hosses an' mules an' take de bes' we got. Atter dey don dat, dey burn de smoke house, de barns, de cribs an' some yuther prop'ty. Den dey skedaddle some place else.

I warn't up dar but I heern tell dey burn up piles an' piles of cotton an' lots of steamboats at Montgomery an' lef' de ole town jes' 'bout ruint'. Twarn't long atter dat dey tell us we'se free. But lawdy, Cap'n, we ain't nebber been what I calls free. 'Cose ole marster didn' own us no mo', an' all de folks soon scatter all ober, but iffen dey all lak me day still hafter wuk jes' as hard, an some times hab less dan we useter hab when we stay on Marster John's plantation. Well, Cap'n, dat's 'bout all I know. I feel dat misery comin' on me now. Will you please, suh, gimme a lif' back in de house. I wisht dat white gemman doctor come on iffen he comin'.[3]

Discussion Question

Why didn't Mr. Calloway show more allegiance to the Northern army that would have promised him freedom?

Richard Toler, Cincinnati, Ohio

"Ah never fit in de wah; no suh, ah couldn't. Mah belly's been broke! But ah sho' did want to, and ah went up to be examined, but they didn't receive me on account of mah broken stomach. But ah sho' tried, 'cause ah wanted to be free. Ah didn't like to be no slave. Dat wasn't good times."

3. Ibid., Vol. 6: 51–54.

Richard Toler (PD).

Ricard Toler, 515 Poplar Street, century-old former slave lifted a bony knee with one hnarled [sic] hand and crossed his legs, then smoothed his thick white beard. His rocking chair creaked, the flies droned, and through the open, unscreened door came the bawling of a calf from the building of a hide company across the street. A maltese kitten sauntered into the front room, which served as parlor and bedroom, and climbed complacently into his lap. In one corner a wooden bed was piled high with feather ticks, and bedecked with a crazy quilt and an number of small, brightly-colored pillows; a bureau opposite was laden to the edges with a collection of odds and ends — a one-legged alarm clock, a coal oil lamp, faded artificial flowers in a gaudy vase, a pile of newspapers. A trunk against the wall was littered with several large books (one of which was the family Bible), a stock of dusty lamp shades, a dingy sweater, and several bushel-basket lids. Several packing cases and crates, a lard can full of cracked ice, a small, round oil heating stove, and an assorted lot of chairs completed the furnishings. The one decorative spot in the room was on the wall over the bed, where hung a large framed picture of Christ in The Temple. The two rooms beyond exhibited various broken-down additions to the heterogeneous collection.

"Ah never had no good times till ah was free," the old man continued. "Ah was bo'n on Mastah Tolah's (Henry Toler) plantation down in ole V'ginia, near Lynchburg in Campbell County. Mah pappy was a slave befo' me, and mah mammy, too. His name was George Washington Tolah, and her'n was Lucy Tolah. We took ouah name from ouah ownah, and we lived in a cabin way back of the big house, me and mah pappy and mammy and two brothahs. . . .

"Ah never went to school. Learned to read and write my name after ah was free in night school, but they nevah allowed us to have a book in ouah hand, and we couldn't have no money neither. If we had money we had to tu'n it ovah to ouah ownah. Chu'ch was not allowed in ouah pa't neithah. Ah go to the Meth'dist Chu'ch now, everybody ought to go. I think RELIGION MUST BE FINE, 'CAUSE GOD ALMIGHTY'S AT THE HEAD OF IT."

Toler took a small piece of ice from the lard can, popped it between his toothless gum, smacking enjoyment, swished at the swarming flies with a soiled rag handkerchief, and continued.

"Ah nevah could unnerstan about ghos'es. Nevah did see one. Lots of folks tell about seein' ghos'es, but ah nevah feared 'em. Ah was nevah raised up undah such supastitious believin's.

"We was nevah allowed no pa'ties, and when they had goin' ons at the big house, we had to clear out. Ah had to wo'k hard all the time every day in the week. Had to min' the cows and calves, and when ah got older ah had to hoe in the field. Mastah Tolah had about 500 acres, so they tell me, and he had a lot of cows and ho'ses and oxens, and he was a big fa'mer. Ah've done about evahthing in mah life, blacksmith and stone mason, ca'penter, evahthing but brick-layin'. Ah was a blacksmith heah fo' 36 yea's. Learned it down at Tolah's.

"Ah stayed on the plantation during the wah, and jes' did what they tol' me. Ah was 21 then. And ah walked 50 mile to vote for Gen'l Grant at Vaughn's precinct. Ah voted fo' him in two sessions, he run twice. And ah was 21 the fust time, cause they come and got me, and say, 'Come on now. You can vote now, you is 21.' And theah now — mah age is right theah. 'Bout as close as you can git it.

"Ah was close to the battle front, and I seen all dem famous men. Seen Gen'l Lee, and Grant, and Abe Lincoln. Seen John Brown, and seen the seven men that was hung with him, but we wasn't allowed to talk to any of 'em, jes' looked on in the street. Jes' spoke, and say 'How d' do.

"But ah did talk to Lincoln, and ah tol' him ah wanted to be free, and he was a fine man, 'cause he made us all free. And ah got a ole history, it's the *Sanford American History*, and was published in 1784. But ah don't know where it is now, ah misplaced it. It is printed in the book, something ah said, now written by hand. And it says, 'Ah am a ole slave which has suvved fo' 21 yeahs, and ah would be quite pleased if you could help us to be free. We thank you very much. Ah trust that some day ah can do you the same privilege that you are doing for me. Ah have been a slave for many years. (Note discrepancy.)

"Aftah the wah, ah came to Cincinnati, and was married three times. Mah fust wife was Mannie. Then there was Mollie. They both died, and then ah was married Cora heah, and ah had six child'en, one girl and fo' boys. (Note discrepancy) They's two living yet; James is 70 and he is not married. And Bob's about thutty or fo'ty. Ah done lost all mah rememb'ance, too ole now. But Mollie died when he was bo'n, and he is crazy. He is out of Longview (Home for Mentally Infirm) now fo' a while, and he jes' wanders around, and wo'ks a little. He ha'mless, he wouldn't hurt nobody. He ain't married neithah.

"After the wah, ah bought a fiddle, and ah was a good fiddlah. Used to be a fiddlah fo' the white girls to dance. Jes' picked it up. It was a natural gif'. Ah could still play if ah had a fiddle. Ah used to play at our hoe downs, too. Played all those ole time songs — Soldier's Joy, Jimmy Long Josey, Arkansas Traveler, and Black Eye Susie. Ah remembah the wo'ds to that one."

Smiling inwardly with pleasure as he again lived the past, the old Negro swayed and recited:

"Black Eye Susie, you look so fine, Black Eye Susie, ah think youah mine. A wondahful time we're having now, Oh, Black Eye Susie, ah believe that youah mine.

"And away down we stomp aroun' the bush, We'd think that we'd get back to wheah we could push Black Eye Susie, ah think youah fine, Black Eye Susie, Ah know youah mine."

Then, he resumed his conversational tone:

"Befo' the wah we never had no good times. They took good care of us, though. As pa'taculah with slave as with the stock — that was their money, you know. And if we claimed bein' sick, they'd give us a dose of castah oil and tu'pentine. That was the principal medicine cullud folks had to take, and sometimes salts. But nevah no whiskey — that was not allowed. And if we was real sick, they had the Doctah fo' us.

"We had very bad eatin'. Bread, meat, water. And they fed it to us in a trough, jes' like the hogs. And ah went in may [sic] shirt till I was 16, nevah had no clothes. And the flo' in ouah cabin was dirt, and at night we'd jes' take a blanket and lay down on the flo'. The dog was supe'ior to us; they would take him in the house.

"I sho' is glad I ain't no slave no moah. Ah thank God that ah lived to pass the yeahs until the day of 1937. Ah'm happy and satisfied now, and ah hopes ah see a million yeahs to come."[4]

Discussion Question

If you could ask Mr. Toler one question, what would that be?

Lesson 5

Ben Horry, Murrells Inlet, South Carolina

Ben Horry, former slave on Brookgreen plantation, Georgetown County, South Carolina, 1938 (LOC).

God knows Missus, glad to yeddy dat! Picture in Washington! You mean bout my fadder? Been in duh — lemme see now kin I remember — 'casionally he would drink a little sumpting. Gone to town. Come back. Drink. Bring jug from town. Drop 'em. Broke 'em. To disencourage him from doing that again — (boss man lowing nobody to whip my fadder thout he do it!) — overseer, them men give my fadder a piece of the broke jug (every time he share out rations) to disencourage him bout drink. Thought that a great way to broke him off. And he do so. Fadder have the three brudder — Daniel, Summer, and Define.

Look on you hand! Look on mine! I know you ain't want me black man — buck up, gainst all o' you! And you had the law in you hand all dese day! You had the learning in you head! Give me that pencil to catch up dem thing. I couldn't to save my life! 'Am I my Brudder Keeper?' You'll find that stripture round somewhere bout Cain and Able!

Missus, I play "STOP" wid duh lawyer. Storm? Yes, Missus, more den one. Carry duh boat out. Carry duh seine outside. As we get the boat outside, been rough. Make the rope been taut. And dat make the breaker have the boat. And I swim till I get the rope

4. Ibid., Vol. 16: 97–101.

hold — wuz on the outside holding the top rope hold and two men on the shore have the end rope.

I turn over twice outside, When I turn over there in that ocean, been forty odd. Vettril Deas come the Captain o' the crew. September. Nobody drown them trip we didn't have nobody drown outside there. Yorrick — I miss he name by it so long — but he kin to Feenie — dem family — dem relation. Diss a young man jest growed out coming on to get married. Had boat full o' people this last go round.

Had a boat full o' people this last go round — Miss Mary, he Aunty and the lawyer and I take them out there. And I take them outside there and I come halfway to Drunken Jack. And then breaker start to lick in the boat. And I start to bail. And that been dangerous because we have all women in there — and couldn't swim like a man! And it happen by accident, when the boat swamp our FEET COULD TECH BOTTOM! Only an accident from God. When he turn over, I didn't a do nothing but SWIM FOR MYSELF for I couldn't help nobody. But our feet tech bottom!

When I swamp outside we wuz coming from South Santee to North Santee — on government work. Jest as we got 'tween Georgetown and Charleston, the boat get captied with water. Nothing to do. Try to bail. Stay outside. Swim with one hand and hold boat with other. Roughest time I ever had cause it cold wedder. First frost. Missus, I gone through some ROUGH. Old before time yawl boat. Old make-out boat — yonder 1877. Young man then! Boat carry eight oar — four on each side. We wuz there hunting fish you know. Go out-side see big school fish, put dem gang o' man to dat car and dat net get a gang o' fish! After de wedder surrender, went back in dere and get hold o' line going up and down — save net and all!

In 1893 working for Ravenel and Holmes and Company in dere steamer boat. I wuz taken up in dat storm. Went from Charleston. Start Georgetown. Ginerally start boat five o'clock; never reach Georgetown till nine! Come on breakers and front head o' boat went down. And we had to go in the hold and take all the barrel. Meet a man got his wife hug to mast. In little thing they call life boat. And I quile my line! I fly dat line! If she go round you neck and you hold that rope you safe! We save five or six different people. One man had a little corn boat. Had he wife and two little children. Had he two chillun rope rop round dat mast. Dem get his wife den gone back and save man and trunk. Quit call me Ben den; call me Rooster.

On steamer *Planter* one time. Couldn't talk bout come to no land a tall. Leave Charleston five in Morning and that storm rise on us! Rise at the bell buoy Charleston. Have a Cap'n and a mate. Cap'n Scott — dat wuz duh Cap'n. Dis here man been mate been one 'Brook' — New Jersey. Missus, people goes out dere for fish to bring in fish for breakfast, dinner, supper! In row boat. See man holding up he hand — but floating. If he catch duh line I save 'em! Miss the line — he drown man! When you come up on next wave, you way yonder! Cap'n Springs hunt dem dead body! He wuz a mighty one out dere!

After Flagg storm Colonel Ward take me and Peter Carr, give us a horse a pier take that shore to Little River. All two dem chillun find to Dick Pond. Been on Magnolia. Find them in a distant here to that house. Couldn't dentify wedder

Miss — or she dater-in-law. (Reported articles of clothing and household linen found all way to Little River.) I got on this shirt got Ben on it. Have no trouble trace when clothes got he mark. One man broke open one trunk, but I didn't care cause I had somebody to my back. Thing you put on your wrist (bracelet) comb for your hair and all in that trunk find to Myrtle Beach. Sich a thing like towel and collar, I find some; Peter find some. Something else Gracious God! Don't want to see no more sumpting like cat! White folks dem time move carry dem poetry (poultry). Dead horses, dead cow, ox, turkey, fowl everywhere! But no dead body find on us beach outside Flagg family, One Northern woman marry in Ward family. Dr. Flagg marry in Ward family. Didn't want to acknowledge this lady richer den him. Dat malice. All his family and chillun drown out. Doctor wouldn't go this lady house. Wouldn't let none rest go. He had one woman somewhere bout Lenwood — Betsy. Kit, Mom Adele drown! Tom Duncan boy, drown! Couldn't identify who loss from who save — till next morning! Kinder feet (effect) like a fog raise by storm and can't see. If you servant they can put confidence in they send you where the tornado been. My house wash down from block. Didn't broke up.

Dem time (fore freedom) most o' people treated right by owner. Diss blue drilling — yards after yards! Have a man wuz tailor. Make little pants for you. And you wuz gal, make dress out of same. Uncle Tomas make the clothes — Tomas Rutledge. Our Master didn't want to see us patchety up — nor naked! Our Master treat us right. My days they give you (you know we wuz rice-planter! You know these FINE (small) rice they save for feeding Prospect, Watsaw, Longwood, Brookgreen. Never have much grits. Have fine rice. Peck o' grits (large family) half bushel dis fine rice (week's supply family.) He got three nets running (to supply fish in plantations.) Send men woods, kill cow. Kill hog. He see that you get garden. Talk bout garden — all run here to see Brookgreen garden. Dem day you could see a garden! Right dere to Marty gate had what you call 'shrubs.' That garden been cross wid lead pipe. Dat were a garden! Orange — every fruit! We use to dig 'em up — ditch up that pipe to melt 'em for shot to shoot duck and ting![5]

Discussion Question

Based on all these accounts, how would you characterize slave-owners?

5. Ibid., Vol. 11: 194–203. For more on Ben Horry and slave life in the South Carolina low country, see Charles Joyner, *Down by the Riverside: A South Carolina Slave Community* (Urbana, IL: University of Illinois Press, 1984).

Allied Armies get lunch at the American Red Cross Canteen station in Bordeaux, France during WW 1 (NARA)

Chapter 14

World War II: Primary Sources

First Thoughts

No war to date has killed more people or destroyed more property than World War II. Seventeen million combatants — and 35 million civilians — lost their lives in the conflict. It was a citizens' war. Entire societies participated in the war either as soldiers or war workers, while others were persecuted, bombed, and murdered. In the United States, the war had vast repercussions: it ended the Great Depression and brought millions of women into the workforce. In addition, World War II marked the beginning of the nuclear age. It was a war fought by ordinary men and women, many of whom had previously been no more than 50 miles from home. Suddenly they found themselves in Alsace-Lorraine, Casablanca, Manila, and Shanghai. This chapter is their story.

Chapter Learning Objectives

In chapter 13 we will look at five American soldiers and, through their stories, discern the greatest war the world had ever fought. We will listen to an Army Air Corps nurse, a U.S. Army soldier in the European theater, a U.S. Army soldier in the Pacific theater, a U.S. Marine in the Pacific theater, and an African American in the Army Air Corps. Collectively, they tell the story of World War II better than a score of generals and presidents!

As a result of this chapter study you should be able to:

Understand the lives of five American soldiers, and through their lives, understand more about World War II

CONCEPTS

The nuclear age

Leona Cox

Andrew Melendrez

John William Manix

Carlisle Evans

Leona Cox, Red Cross Nurse

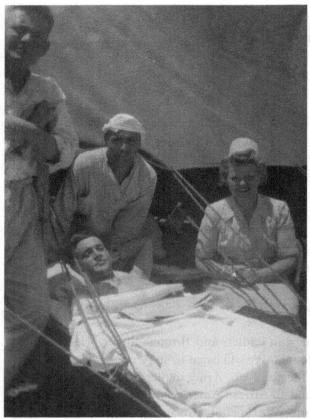

This war nurse sits with a patient in Maddaloni, Italy in 1944 (LOC).

This group of Red Cross ladies arrived in Glasgow, Scotland in 1944 (LOC).

I was an American Red Cross girl who ran an enlisted man's club in Rome and kept a distraught GI from killing our medic. We were the only two on the third floor of a big old building in Rome. When I came on duty, a distraught medic had a knife at his throat. We were the only people on the third floor, and the medic yelled at me. "Help me, Leona. He is going to kill me." I didn't know what to do, as we were the only two on that floor. I was going on duty for our Red Cross man, who was supposed to be in charge. I said a prayer: "Please God, tell me what to do. I don't know what to do." This voice came back and was very calm and said don't act afraid, and right then I found out I didn't act afraid and I asked him what was the matter and I would help. I ran the snack bar, and I invited him to come to the snack bar. He said, "You will turn me in to the police," and I said, "Trust me, I just want to help you." He said, "All right." I took him through a dark lane where we made the donuts and I treated him and talked to him very calmly and he knew he could trust me. I saved a life.

I also served in Algeria. I was a university teacher in Minnesota when someone recommended me for the Red Cross, and I got on a troop ship with no idea where I would go, for 11 days, and ended up in Algeria after having lived my whole life in Minnesota. Quite a different world. I married an Air Force officer in Rome and met the Pope twice and got permission to marry since I was not Catholic. I told the Pope that the people in Minnesota loved him so. On my wedding day the Pope was addressing the world, and they told me I could not have electricity for my wedding since it had to be saved for the Pope's address, and I told them to tell the Pope the girl from Minnesota only wanted music at her wedding. I received permission from the Pope for an organ. My wedding dress was made by [Fernanda] Gattinoni, who designed all the costumes for *War and Peace*. I had quite a wedding. My honeymoon was on the Isle of Capri at an Air Force rest camp.[1]

Discussion Question

Mrs. Cox wrote, ". . . ended up in Algeria after having lived my whole life in Minnesota." Pretend you are the air force officer that she marries. Tell your story.

1. http://lcweb2.loc.gov/diglib/vhp/story/loc.natlib.afc2001001.25043/narrative?ID=pn0001.

Andrew Melendrez Sr., Sergeant, U.S. Army, European Theater

We started in Normandy. We were surrounded by the Germans because they were trying to push us back to England. We were surrounded for seven days without food or water. They started dropping ammunition and food, but it kept dropping too far away into German territory. The glass bottles of medication would break when they dropped them from the air. Finally, the 32nd Division broke through and got us out. I wanted to get home for Christmas 1944, but we had to go down to the Bulge to help out. We didn't have any winter clothing, but we made do. A lot of the unit got frostbite, but luckily enough I didn't. In February of 1945 I was wounded and they sent me back to the hospital for three months. And then after I got out I was going back to Germany, but the war ended so I had to go back to my outfit. They pulled us out and brought us back to the States for 30 days, after which I was supposed to report to Jackson, South Carolina, (where my division is from) to go over to Japan. But they dropped the atom bomb so I was discharged.

It was always push push push forward, taking back the land the Germans had taken; the wounded and dead were left behind. We had to go forward even though Germans were firing at you and men were flying up in the air; you just had to keep going. You had to know your counter-attack. Every morning we'd attack (dawn attack) so by 3 or 4 in the afternoon we could set up for counter-attack. The squad leader in the evening would have a debriefing to get ready for the next attack. In the end there were only three guys left; I was getting scareder and scareder every day. Any guy who says he wasn't scared is lying. We weren't thinking about the job; we were thinking about staying alive. I see these movies; they don't show the push every day. We were always moving, pushing on after casualties. It brings back stuff I've kinda forgot. I used to carry a little missal in my pocket and one time a shot got caught in it, I didn't even know until later.

We never changed clothes. I don't remember going to the bathroom ever, it's funny. We'd get a change of clothes every two weeks and every two months we'd get two weeks of rest, we'd talk and write letters. After the attack, some men would find abandoned cars in the street and drive them around town while the buildings were still burning. We were scared during the attack and afterwards we would celebrate, jubilation. It

Andy Melendrez in France, July 1945 (LOC).

159

Andrew Melendrez, 30th Infantry division, 1945 (LOC).

was a cruel war, but nobody would believe the things that would happen after we took towns.

One time we were in Normandy going from hedge row to hedge row, pushing forward and then also having to retreat back. One story: I started off as a machine gunner. The plane was dropping bombs on us, and it was an Allied plane who didn't know he was dropping bombs on his own. He flew over me and was about to drop one, and crazily I got up (in plain view of the Germans) and waved my hands to get his attention and he flew away. He must have seen me. It's crazy that I survived.

I was 18 going in and 21 when I came home — I came home on my 21st birthday. Someone up there must have been watching out for me.[2]

Discussion Question

Sergeant Melendrez says, "Every morning we'd attack (dawn attack) so by 3 or 4 in the afternoon we could set up for counter-attack. The squad leader in the evening would have a debriefing to get ready for the next attack. In the end there were only three guys left; I was getting scareder and scareder every day. Any guy who says he wasn't scared is lying. We weren't thinking about the job; we were thinking about staying alive." Why did Melendrez continue fighting?

Lesson 3

John William Manix, U. S. Army, Pacific Theater

I joined the National Guard in Montana. I was stationed at Fort Lewis, Montana, on the morning of December 7, 1941. We were dispatched to the West Coast for fear that the Japanese were heading to the West Coast. We were dispatched via the Queen Elizabeth out of San Francisco en route to Australia. The trip took 23 days. We were under blackout conditions for the entire 23 days. We landed at Sydney. We trained for about a year in Australia. We were at Rockhampton, and the circus was in town. The tightrope actress was also purported to be a dancer. After her performance we tried to locate her, and we asked several of the other circus performers if they knew where she would be "performing next. We got a ride back on an elephant to our camp. The guard at the gate wouldn't let us through because we were coming in on an elephant. One of us told the guard that we knew of no regulation prohibiting entry via elephant. The first sergeant threatened to demote us to private the next day. When we were called to the captain's

2. http://lcweb2.loc.gov/diglib/vhp/story/loc.natlib.afc2001001.13862/.

quarters he told us what a ruckus we had made and that the colonel was also aware. The colonel made it a rule that from that day forward, no entry into camp via elephant. Our infantry eventually made it to New Guinea where we now understood we were in the war. We fought back the Japanese in their tracks. This was the first time the Japanese were stopped on their way to Australia. This was a major turning point in the war in the South Pacific.

We came upon a Japanese hospital, and many of their soldiers were booby-trapped. We lost two men before our command received word that from then on if we came upon a Japanese soldier we were to shoot them. The word was if they did not already have a hole in their head, to shoot them. The Chicago Sun reporter who was embedded with us gave us the nickname The Butchers. After he printed his story he understood that he might be the next guy, so he took off.

During this major series of battles, about 80 percent of us were suffering from malaria. Temperatures reached 103, and we stayed in combat. In September '43 I was sent to OCS in Australia. On my graduation day I came down with malaria again. My first assignment after OCS, I was assigned to New Guinea with the Red Arrow. They were engaged with the Japanese, pushing them back north. I was a communications officer with the Red Arrow [Division] and we were in combat. The conditions were terrible. We fought most of the time in the jungle, without much food or fresh water. We looked forward to rations being airlifted into the area. During the Battle of Aitepe [?] while walking towards another company that was without telephone service my corporal, his last name was Bunda, stepped across a booby trap and was killed instantly. The blast knocked me out. I was only about four feet from Corporal Bunda when I went down. I was hit by shrapnel in my leg, and when I woke I figured it was probably mortar fire. Later I learned the fate of Corporal Bunda.

The saddest day for me was the day we buried Corporal Bunda in a shallow grave and our bugler played Taps.

I came home before the end of the war because I had received the leg wound and had numerous bouts with malaria. Some people might think that malaria is a bad thing. For me, it got me home from the war ahead of the end and once I was well enough to go out, we were on leave in Santa Barbara at a restaurant one night where I met a beautiful girl, who later became my wife, Winnifred Ann Rudolph. I asked her if I could walk her home, and while walking I flagged down some MPs in their Jeep and they gave us a ride back to her place. She was duly impressed for it was not long after that she agreed to marry me.[3]

Discussion Question

Mr. Manix says, "This was a major turning point in the war in the South Pacific." Mr. Manix thought, or wanted to think, that his campaign in New Guinea was the turning point of the war. It was an important campaign, but the allies had stopped the Japanese previously at Guadalcanal and the real turning point was at the Battle of Midway. Yet, Mr. Manix said this. Why?

> "The blast knocked me out. I was only about four feet from Corporal Bunda when I went down. I was hit by shrapnel in my leg, and when I woke I figured it was probably mortar fire. Later I learned the fate of Corporal Bunda."

---

3. http://lcweb2.loc.gov/diglib/vhp/story/loc.natlib.afc2001001.25233/narrative?ID=pn0001.

Carlisle Evans,
U. S. Marine Corps, Pacific Theater

When I was in high school, they had one of these programs that if you were in the upper third of your class and five businessmen wrote recommendations, you could volunteer for officer training. They had the physical exam in the Moline, Illinois, Post Office. I passed everything except the dental exam; they said I didn't have enough molars. I went to the Rock Island Post Office, and they passed for the Navy Air Corps, but they told me it would be three months before they had another class starting up. I went back to the Moline Post Office the next day where I volunteered for the Marines. I told the doctor that they had kept me out because of my teeth and he said, "What did they think you were going to do, bite the enemy?"

I had seen that John Payne movie, *The Shores of Tripoli*, and I wanted to be in the Marines. I finished boot camp and went overseas with the 30th Replacement Battalion and went to Oahu, and from Oahu, over to Maui, where I joined up with the 22nd Marines, B Company, First Platoon. I became a BAR — a Browning Automatic Rifleman. The 22nd was a lone regiment for the Marshall Islands campaign. We went from Marshalls down to Guadalcanal for more training. We left Guadalcanal in the first part of May, heading up to the Marianas. The Marines invaded Saipan on the 15th of June 1944. We joined up with the Fourth Regiment and we formed the First Marine Provisional Brigade. When they hit Saipan on the 15th, we were supposed to hit Guam on the 18th. But they had so much trouble on Saipan that we laid up on ship for about sixty days from Guadalcanal. We hit Guam on the 21st of July 1944. I went in on the first wave at a village named Agat. We were just about through with capturing the Orotie [?] Peninsula, and on the afternoon of the 29th of July, two days after my 19th birthday, the tanks came up behind our front lines and the Japs started dropping mortars on them, and one of the mortars fell short and hit about five feet to my left, and I was injured. My friend called for a corpsman, and he got hit in the hand while he was working on me. My friend bandaged him up. They put me on an amphibious duck boat and took me to a Higgins boat that took me out to a hospital ship where they operated on me. They were able to get all but two pieces of shrapnel out of me. Then they took me back to Pearl Harbor to the Navy Hospital, and that's one time that the Navy is terrific for the Marines. I had a private room and a private nurse beside my bed. They told me that I'd never walk, never work, and never participate in any sports. I was walking by the time I left Pearl. I had a paralyzed left arm and they had an electrical treatment there for it. I had shrapnel in my stomach, a hole to my hipbone, a blast concussion and peritonitis in my kidneys. I spent three months in Pearl Harbor, and transferred over to Oak Knoll hospital. From there, they transferred me to San Leandro Hospital in California. While I was in the hospital there, my girlfriend from

Carlisle Evans and Barbara J. Haney on their wedding day, December 9, 1944 (LOC).

home, Barbara Haney, came to see me and we were married. It's sixty years now. I snuck out with one of my nurses and a Marine friend, who was my best man.

I went back home to Illinois and went to University of Illinois at Urbana-Champaign on Public Law 16, for disabled veterans. I graduated with a degree in architectural engineering. Back then, you had to have a degree plus three years experience working for an architect before you could take the exam, which I did. I eventually became a government architect, traveling the country working on military installations. I was traveling 25–30 weeks a year some years. I was on a national design board for the government. We did barracks, chapels, housing, industrial buildings. We did 160 installations, total. I went as far as Japan. I retired in October of 1987. I went with a contractor, doing the same thing for the government for three years. We've been fortunate; we have two boys and two girls.[4]

Discussion Question

How did the media affect the life of Mr. Evans?

Lesson 5

Robert M. Alexander,
U.S. Army Air Corps, Sergeant

When I was back in the Air Force, my first post of duty after induction in Richmond, Virginia, was on the bus ride to Fort Meade, Maryland. And in Fort Meade, Maryland, as a young Army recruit, I was served food by German prisoners of war and Italian prisoners of war. We — I was inducted with a group of young college fellows from Washington, DC, Harlem University, Morgan State University, and my school, Virginia Union University in Richmond, Virginia.

We caught a German prisoner of war spitting in our food one morning, so we took appropriate action. We did almost the same thing as the people have done to the prisoners in Iraq. It's a fact of life. War is destruction, war is cruel, war is mean, and you just lose all of your civilian attitudes and everything when you see things differently.

From Fort Meade, Maryland, I was put on a train with about 200 other black soldiers and we were sent to Sheppard Field, Texas. On our way to Sheppard Field, Texas, we passed through Charleston, West Virginia. When we got in the station there, the ladies of the Confederate were outside the station passing out magazines, fruit, and cakes and cookies to white soldiers, ignored the black troops.

4. http://lcweb2.loc.gov/diglib/vhp/story/loc.natlib.afc2001001.13282/narrative?ID=pn0001.

Sergeant Robert M. Alexander
(PD).

Fortunately, we had a commander who was black but looked like a white man. He said, Fellows, don't have a riot here, let's not mess up on our first day in the Army, sit there in your seats being quiet, I'll go outside and I'll take care of everything. And our good commander, Paul Cooke, former president of Miner's — former president of Miner's College and later president of Federal City College, Washington, DC, with his blond hair and blue eyes, went outside and collected fruit and magazines and newspapers for us, candy, cookies, and brought them to us. Avoid a riot, avoid our having been court-martialed, and my having spent many years in Leavenworth. So we avoid that crisis.

Well, in Sheppard Field, Texas, which is in the mouth of the panhandle, we took our basic training, U.S. Air Force. When we were off-duty on leave and going out into the town of Sheppard Field, of Wichita, Texas — that's what it was — we could — I went into a drugstore to get some ice cream and I say, Little girl behind the counter, give me a cone of white — of vanilla ice cream. And her father came up and said, No, we don't serve blacks, and he called me by name. He said, Give him some chocolate. I walked out.

I walked through a nice white neighborhood from the bus station through a Spanish neighborhood with no sidewalks and — but paved street to the black neighborhood, which had no paved sidewalk, no paved streets, and spent a few hours, went to a nightclub, danced, got a few beers, went back to post. I never went back in town again.[5]

Discussion Questions

Sergeant Alexander is putting his life on the line for all Americans, and he is the victim of racism. How does he feel?

5. http://lcweb2.loc.gov/diglib/vhp/story/loc.natlib.afc2001001.12854/transcript?ID=sr0001.

Child survivors of Auschwitz, wearing adult-sized prisoner jackets, standing behind a barbed wire fence, 1945 (PD).

Chapter 15

Genocide: Intention to Destroy

First Thoughts

The United States Holocaust Museum states, "Genocide is a term created during the Holocaust and declared an international crime in the 1948 United Nations Convention on the Prevention and Punishment of the Crime of Genocide. The Convention defines genocide as any of the following acts committed with the intent to destroy, in whole or in part, a national, ethnical, racial, or religious group, as such killing members of the group, causing serious bodily or mental harm to members of the group, or imposing measures intended to prevent births within the group."

The most horrific example of this genocide in world history was the Holocaust, when 80 percent of European Jewry was murdered. The story is even more tragic: over 90 percent of European Jewish children were killed. There are almost no Jewish people in Europe today between the ages of 70–75. But that is only half the story. Most of European gypsies, Pentecostal Christians, and other people groups were also murdered.

Chapter Learning Objectives

In chapter 15 we will examine the roots of anti-Semitism and the Holocaust that will follow. We will see how ingenious the Nazis were — in a macabre sort of way. They carefully defined what a Jewish person was, gathered Jews in deportation centers, and then systematically murdered them in killing centers.

As a result of this chapter you should be able to:

1. Define "Holocaust"

2. Discuss why natural rights make the Nuremberg Laws impossible

3. Describe how the Nazis placed Jewish people in communities preparing to deport them

4. Explain what problems genocide presents to the perpetrators and how are these overcome

5. Explain how civilized people act in uncivilized ways

CONCEPTS

Anti-Semitism

Holocaust

National Socialist government

Mischlinge Nuremberg Laws of 1935

Gleichschaltung

Einsatzgruppen

Ghettoization

Final Solution

Wannsee Conference

Overview

Everyone knows that **Anti-Semitism** was a strategy to build support among Germans by blaming everything on a scapegoat: the Jews. But this was not enough. Eventually the Germans went much further than any other civilization.

L a n d	Zahl
A. Altreich	131.800
Ostmark	43.700
Ostgebiete	420.000
Generalgouvernement	2.284.000
Bialystok	400.000
Protektorat Böhmen und Mähren	74.200
Estland – Judenfrei –	
Lettland	3.500
Litauen	34.000
Belgien	43.000
Dänemark	5.600
Frankreich / Besetztes Gebiet	165.000
Unbesetztes Gebiet	700.000
Griechenland	69.600
Niederlande	160.800
Norwegen	1.300
B. Bulgarien	48.000
England	330.000
Finnland	2.300
Irland	4.000
Italien einschl. Sardinien	58.000
Albanien	200
Kroatien	40.000
Portugal	3.000
Rumänien einschl. Bessarabien	342.000
Schweden	8.000
Schweiz	18.000
Serbien	10.000
Slowakei	88.000
Spanien	6.000
Türkei (europ. Teil)	55.500
Ungarn	742.800
UdSSR	5.000.000
Ukraine 2.994.684	
Weißrußland aus-	
schl. Bialystok 446.484	
Zusammen: über	11.000.000

List of Jewish populations by country used at the Wannsee Conference in 1942, (PD).

The Holocaust was the planned, systematic, bureaucratic, nation-sponsored murder of approximately six million Jews by the Nazi regime and its collaborators. The Jewish people were not the only victims. German authorities also targeted other groups because of their perceived "racial inferiority": Roma (Gypsies), the disabled, and some of the Slavic peoples (Poles, Russians, and others). Other groups were persecuted on political, ideological, and behavioral grounds, among them Communists, Socialists, Jehovah's Witnesses, Pentecostals, and homosexuals.

In 1933, the Jewish population of Europe stood at almost 9 million. By 1945, the Germans and their collaborators killed nearly two out of every three European Jews as part of the "Final Solution," the Nazi policy to murder the Jews of Europe. Although Jews, whom the Nazis deemed a priority danger to Germany, were the primary victims of Nazi racism, other victims included some 200,000 Gypsies. At least 200,000 mentally or physically disabled patients, mainly Germans, were murdered in the so-called Euthanasia Program. But German citizens protested and this last plan was stopped! It is my belief that if there had been more opposition from German citizens, the **Holocaust** could have been similarly stopped.

In the early years of the Nazi regime, the **National Socialist government** established concentration camps as maintenance centers of labor for businesses and killing centers. First, though, to concentrate and monitor the Jewish population and facilitate later deportation of the Jews, the Germans and their collaborators created ghettos. The German authorities also established numerous forced-labor camps, both in the so-called Greater German Reich and in German-occupied territory, for non-Jews whose labor the Germans sought to exploit. Porsche automobile manufacturers, for instance, used slave Jewish labor to build automobiles.[1]

Discussion Question

Define "Holocaust."

---

1. http://www.ushmm.org/wlc/en/article.php?ModuleId=10005143.

German Definition of a Jew

Judaism is a religion, not a race. Jewish people are a diverse religious and cultural group whose origins are described in the Bible. The term Jewish is not a race in any sense of the word, since there are no physical characteristics that can be defined as "Jewish." Anyone may become a Jew through study and steps leading to religious conversion.

Immediately following the Nuremberg Laws in 1935, the Nazis issued the official definition of a Jew. According to German law, anyone with three Jewish grandparents was a Jew. In addition, anyone married to a Jewish person or who had one Jewish parent was also considered a Jew in the eyes of the law.

The classifications were complicated and even silly. Those with two Jewish grandparents were to be known as **Mischlinge** of the first degree, while those with one Jewish grandparent were of the second degree. In short, Judaism for the Nazis was something racial, something people were born into and about which they could do nothing.

In order to destroy a group of people, one has to define who that group is. What if a Christian has a Jewish grandparent? Is he Jewish? What if a Jewish person converted to Christianity? What if, as was possible in 1935, that person was a veteran in the German army during World War I?

The **Nuremberg Laws of 1935** employed a pseudo-scientific system to define what "Jewish" means. People with four German grandparents were of "German blood," while people were classified as Jews if they were descended from three or more Jewish grandparents. Having one or more Jewish grandparents made someone a Mischling (of mixed blood). The Nazis used the religious observance of a person's grandparents to determine their race. So a person could be a second generation Roman Catholic and still be considered Jewish![2]

Jewish relations were tied up in the process of "**Gleichschaltung**," the policy by which the Nazis achieved complete control over German society). Jewish men were first forbidden to join the Wehrmacht (the army), and in the summer of the same year, anti-Semitic propaganda appeared in shops and restaurants. Marriage between any Jew and non-Jew was illegal. At the same time, the "Reich Citizenship Law" was passed and was reinforced in November by a decree, stating that all Jews, even quarter- and half-Jews, were no longer citizens of Germany.

In 1936, Jews were banned from all professional jobs, effectively preventing them from having any influence in education, politics, higher education, and industry. There was now nothing to stop the anti-Jewish actions that spread across the German economy.[3]

Chart to describe Nuremberg Laws, 1935. The "Nuremberg Laws" established a pseudo-scientific basis for racial identification. Only people with four German grandparents (four white circles in top row left) were of "German blood." A Jew is someone who descends from three or four Jewish grandparents (black circles in top row right). In the middle stood people of "mixed blood" of the "first or second degree" (PD).

The yellow star that Nazi Germany required all Jews over the age of six to wear is actually a continuation of other periods of history when Jews unfairly faced discrimination and violence, often being made to wear specific clothing or items to distinguish them as Jews, 1941 (CCA-SA3.0 Germany).

2. http://www.auschwitz.dk/bullseye/new_page_3.htm.
3. Khomdan Singh Lisam, *Encyclopaedia of Manipur* (New Delhi: Gyan Publishing House, 2011), p. 475.

Philosopher Hannah Arendt pointed out in her book *Origins of Totalitarianism* (1951) that Nazi Germany first deprived Jewish people of their citizenship and then was free to deprive Jewish people of their human rights. Arendt underlined that in the Declaration of the Rights of Man and of the Citizen, citizens' rights actually preceded human rights, as the latter needed the protection of a determinate state to actually be respected.[4] Why would it be legally impossible for such a thing to happen in England and the United States?

Lesson 3

Ghettoization and Resettlement

Captured Jews are searched for weapons and interrogated beside the ghetto wall before being sent to the Umschlagplatz (PD).

Suppression of Warsaw Ghetto Uprising - Captured Jews are led by German Waffen SS soldiers to the assembly point for deportation (Umschlagplatz). (PD).

On September 1, 1939, Germany invaded Poland. Two days later, Britain and France declared war on Germany, and World War II began. But within three weeks, Poland had completely succumbed to Hitler's Blitzkrieg. In 1939 there were approximately 3.3 million Jews living in Poland (10 percent of the Polish population). Hitler now had to deal with 3.3 million more Jews.

The stunning victories of the German armies in the early years of World War II brought the majority of European Jewry under Nazi control. Jewish people in the occupied territory were treated even worse than German Jews. So-called **Einsatzgruppen**, mobile killing units, were at work just behind the front lines. These special units of the German army gathered up Jewish people and shot them. Typically, Jewish people were taken outside of town, and after they dug their own graves, they were stripped of their belongings and shot. But this was causing some anxiety for the German troops assigned to do it. So German engineers designed portable vans where the carbon monoxide exhaust was pumped into the back section of the van. Vans would pull into town and load up with Jewish victims. The van would drive out to a ravine or gravesite and the dead bodies would be removed and thrown into these mass graves. Over the next 18 months, Einsatzgruppen units

---

4. Hannah Arendt, *Origins of Totalitarianism* (New York: Harcourt, Brace and Co., 1951).

killed, either by shooting or by mobile gas vans, more than 1,300,000 Jews. However, this was not good enough for the Nazis.

So what were the Germans going to do about the Jewish problem?

Despite the effectiveness of the Einsatzgruppen, there were problems with carrying out mass extermination in that manner. First, it was too public. Second, there are indications that such firing squad activities were having a demoralizing effect on those military personnel who participated — particularly the close-range shooting of women and children. Heinrich Himmler, head of the SS, suggested that a "more humane" and "rational" method of "disinfecting" the area was needed. Already, at this point, Himmler was planning the construction of special annihilation centers populated with special technology and staff specially trained for mass extermination.

Ghettoization: Placing Jews in containment areas for later deportation.

However, before that occurred, Jewish people had to be placed in holding centers or resettlement centers. These places were called "ghettos." The **ghettoization** process was merely a necessary first step in preparing Jewish people to be shipped to the concentration camp killing centers.

As a result, Jewish ghettos were set up in urban centers all over Germany. Now the Nazis were ready to carry out the final wicked step of their demonic plan.[5]

Southern side of the Jewish Lane (PD).

Discussion Question

From 1935 to 1942, European Jewry was first defined and then localized into which controlled communities?

Killing Centers

In 1942, the Nazi leadership decided to implement the "**Final Solution**," the systematic mass murder of European Jewry. The German authorities used rail systems across the continent to transport or deport Jews from their homes, to ghettos, and then to killing centers. Once they had begun to methodically kill Jews in specially constructed killing centers, German officials deported Jews to these facilities by train or, when trains were not available or the distances were short, by truck or on foot.

Schönbrunn Psychiatric Hospital, 1934 (CCA-SSA3.0 Germany).

---

5. http://www.jewishvirtuallibrary.org/jsource/Holocaust/ghet.html.

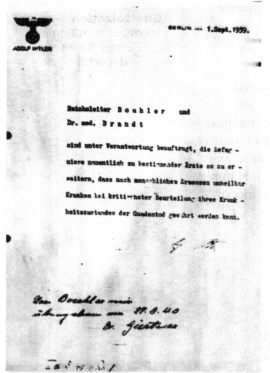

Hitler's order for the Aktion T4, which led to 70,000 people being killed (PD).

At the **Wannsee Conference** on January 20, 1942, held near Berlin, SS, Nazi Party, and German state officials met to coordinate the deportation of European Jews to killing centers (also known as "extermination camps") already in operation or under construction in German-occupied Poland. The participants of the conference estimated that the "Final Solution" would involve the deportation and murder of 11 million Jews, including Jewish residents of nations outside German control such as Ireland, Sweden, Turkey, United States, and Great Britain. Nazis were sure they would eventually conquer these places.

The Final Solution was, without a doubt, the greatest technological challenge in all of history. The world had never seen anything like it. A professor of mine at Harvard, said, "The Final Solution required more technological innovations and expertise, more coordination among government agencies, more manpower than anything mankind has ever done — including walking on the moon." Deportations of this scale required the coordination of numerous German government agencies and foreign agencies.

The Germans attempted to disguise their intentions. They sought to portray the deportations as a "resettlement" of the Jewish population in labor camps in the "East." In reality, the "resettlement" in the "East" became a euphemism for transport to the killing centers and mass murder.

German railroad officials were ingenious. They used both freight and passenger cars for the deportations. German authorities generally did not give the deportees food or water for the journey, even when they had to wait for days on railroad spurs for other trains to pass. Why bother? Most were going to die anyway.

Packed in sealed freight cars and suffering from overcrowding, the Jewish deportees endured intense heat during the summer and freezing temperatures during the winter. Aside from a bucket, there was no sanitary facility. The stench of urine and excrement was overwhelming. Local residents said that they could smell a deportation train before they saw it.

A few of the thousands of wedding rings the Germans removed from Holocaust victims to salvage the gold. The U.S. troops found rings, watches, precious stones, eyeglasses, and gold fillings, near Buchenwald concentration camp (NARA).

Between December 1941 and July 1942, the SS and police officials established five killing centers in German-occupied Poland: Chelmno, Belzec, Sobibor, Treblinka 2 (Treblinka 1 was a forced-labor camp for Jews), and Auschwitz-Birkenau.

On a good day, Auschwitz was killing 10,000 people a day. It was not the killing that was the problem. The problem was disposing of so many bodies. Human bodies do not burn well. The shrewd Nazi technicians, however, would not be deterred. They created crematoria, which burned the victims quite well. In fact, they were designed to make the most of human fat by using it as fuel for already horrendous fires.

Discussion Question

What problems did genocide present to the perpetrators of the Final Solution and how were these overcome?

A Devout Meditation in Memory of Adolf Eichmann

By Thomas Merton

Adolf Eichmann (1906–1962) was head of the "Department for Jewish Affairs" in the Gestapo from 1941 to 1945 and was chief of operations in the deportation of three million Jews to extermination camps. He was tried for his crimes against humanity in 1961. During the court proceedings, Eichmann was declared to be sane. In fact, Eichmann was well-adjusted and liked by his peers. He was a productive member of society. In short, if we did not know who Eichmann was, we would probably have wanted to be his friend!

The following is a meditation from the late Thomas Merton on the meaning of sanity in our modern world.

Adolf Eichmann, 1942 (Wikimedia-Fair Use).

One of the most disturbing facts that came out in the Eichmann trial was that a psychiatrist examined him and pronounced him perfectly sane. I do not doubt it all, and that is precisely why I find it disturbing.

If all the Nazis had been psychotics, as some of their leaders probably were, their appalling cruelty would have been in some sense easier to understand. It is much worse to consider this calm, "well-balanced," unperturbed official conscientiously going about his desk work, his administrative job which happened to be the supervision of mass murder. He was thoughtful, orderly, and unimaginative. He had a profound respect for system, for law and order. He was obedient, loyal, a faithful officer of a great state. He served his government very well.

He was not bothered much by guilt. I have not heard that he developed any psychosomatic illnesses. Apparently he slept well. He had a good appetite, or so it seems. True, when he visited Auschwitz, the Camp Commandant, Hoess, in a spirit of sly deviltry, tried to tease the big boss and scare him with some of the sight, Eichmann was disturbed, yes. He was disturbed. Even Himmler had been disturbed, and had gone weak at the knees. Perhaps, in the same way, the general manager of a big steel mill might be disturbed if an accident took place while he happened to be somewhere in the plant. But of course what happened at Auschwitz was not an accident: just the routine unpleasantness of the daily task. One must shoulder the burden of daily monotonous work for the Fatherland. Yes, one must suffer discomfort and even nausea from unpleasant sights and sounds. It all comes under the heading of duty, self-sacrifice, and obedience. Eichmann was devoted to duty and proud of his job.

Prisoners from the first transport to Auschwitz at the train station in Tarnów. The transport was composed mostly of Polish political prisoners but among them were also some Jews (PD).

The sanity of Eichmann is disturbing. We equate sanity with a sense of justice, with humaneness, with prudence, with the capacity to love and understand other people. We rely on the sane people of the world to preserve it from

Photograph of prisoners at Auschwitz-Birkenau during liberation, 1945 (PD).

barbarism, madness, destruction. And now it begins to dawn on us that it is precisely the sane ones who are the most dangerous.

It is the sane ones, the well-adapted ones, who can without qualms and without nausea aim the missile, and press the buttons that will initiate the great festival of destruction that they, the sane ones, have prepared. What makes us so sure, after all, that the danger comes from a psychotic getting into a position to fire the first shot in a nuclear war? Psychotics will be suspect. The sane ones will keep them far from the button. No one suspects the sane, and the sane ones will have perfectly good reasons, logical, well-adjusted reasons, for firing the shot. They will be obeying sane orders that have come sanely down the chain of command. And because of their sanity they will have no qualms at all. When the missiles take off, then, it will be no mistake. We can no longer assume that because a man is "sane" he is therefore in his "right mind." The whole concept of sanity in a society where spiritual values have lost their meaning is itself meaningless. A man can be "sane" in the limited sense that he is not impeded by disordered emotions from acting in a cool, orderly tier, according to the needs and dictates of the social situation in which he finds himself. He can be perfectly "adjusted." God knows, perhaps such people can be perfectly adjusted even in hell itself.

And so I ask myself: what is the meaning of a concept of sanity that excludes love, considers it irrelevant, and destroys our capacity to love other human beings, to respond to their needs and their sufferings, to recognize them also as persons, to apprehend their pain as one's own? Evidently this is not necessary for "sanity" at all. It is a religious notion, a spiritual notion, a Christian notion. What business have we to equate "sanity" with "Christianity"? None at all, obviously. The worst error is to imagine that a Christian must try to be "sane" like everybody else, that we belong in our kind of society. That we must be "realistic" about it. We must develop a sane Christianity: and there have been plenty of sane Christians in the past. Torture is nothing new, is it? We ought

Oswiecim, the former concentration camp of "Auschwitz-Birkenau"(CCA-SA3.0 Poland).

to be able to rationalize a little brainwashing and genocide, and find a place for nuclear war, or at least for napalm bombs, in our moral theology. Certainly some of us are doing our best along those lines already. There are hopes! Even Christians can shake off their sentimental prejudices about charity, and become sane like Eichmann. They can even cling to a certain set of Christian formulas, and fit them into a Totalist Ideology. Let them talk about justice, charity, love, and the rest. These words have not stopped some sane men from acting very sanely and cleverly in the past. . . . No, Eichmann

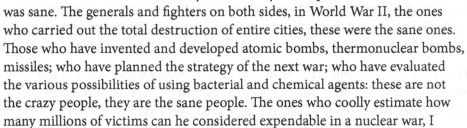

was sane. The generals and fighters on both sides, in World War II, the ones who carried out the total destruction of entire cities, these were the sane ones. Those who have invented and developed atomic bombs, thermonuclear bombs, missiles; who have planned the strategy of the next war; who have evaluated the various possibilities of using bacterial and chemical agents: these are not the crazy people, they are the sane people. The ones who coolly estimate how many millions of victims can he considered expendable in a nuclear war, I presume they do all right with the Rorschach ink blots too. On the other hand, you will probably find that the pacifists and the ban-the-bomb people are, quite seriously, just as we read in *Time*, a little crazy. I am beginning to realize that "sanity" is no longer a value or an end in itself. The "sanity" of modern man is about as useful to him as the huge bulk and muscles of the dinosaur. If he were a little less sane, a little more doubtful, a little more aware of his absurdities and contradictions, perhaps there might be a possibility of his survival. But if he is sane, too sane . . . perhaps we must say that in a society like ours the worst insanity is to be totally without anxiety, totally "sane."[6]

From *Raids on the Unspeakable* by Thomas Merton.

Discussion Questions

How can it happen? How can the world produce a sane, even loving person like Eichmann who loved his children at night but murdered millions of people in the daytime? What can we learn from this?

One final note.

The victorious Allies were first horrified, and then furious with the Third Reich for perpetrating such horrific crimes. They held the Nuremberg Trials immediately after World War II. The Nuremberg Trials were a series of military tribunals, for the prosecution of prominent members of the political, military, and economic leadership of Nazi Germany, held in the city of Nuremberg. The first, and best known of these trials was held between November 20th, 1945, and October 1, 1946. Twenty-four of the most infamous Nazi leaders were put on trial. Defendants included Abert Speer, Hermann Goring, and Rudolph Hess.

In the end, the international tribunal found all but three of the defendants guilty. Twelve were sentenced to death, and the rest were given prison sentences ranging from 10 years to life. Ten of the condemned were executed by hanging on October 16, 1946. Hermann Göring (1893-1946), Hitler's designated successor, committed suicide the night before his execution.

Above: Defendants in their dock, circa 1945-1946 (PD).

Left: Master-Sergeant John C. Woods, U.S. Army Hangman, readies the gallows at Nuremberg in 1946 (PD).

---

6. Thomas Merton, *Raids on the Unspeakable* (New York: New Directions, 1966).

Visions of Hope

"I have survived them all. If there were any left, they'd be too old and weak to stand trial today. My work is done," said legendary Nazi Hunter Simon Wiesenthal. The last Nazi he had a hand in bringing to trial was Untersturmführer Julius Viel, who was convicted in 2001 of shooting seven Jewish prisoners. Wiesenthal died on September 20, 2005, at age 96 (PD).

Secretary of Defense Chuck Hagel stands in the Hall of Names with Israeli Minister of Defense Moshe Ya'alon, Doctor Robert Ozzett, Director of Libraries at Yad Vashem, and his son, Ziller, during a tour of Yad Vashem in Jerusalem, Israel, April 21, 2013. (CCA-SA2.0).

On April 11, 2005 HKP Labor Camp survivor Pearl Good points to Karl Plagge's name on the Wall of the Righteous at Yad Vashem. Those recognized by the State of Israel as "Righteous Among the Nations" are honored in a section of Yad Vashem known as the Garden of the Righteous Among the Nations. "Righteous Among the Nations" is an honorific used by the State of Israel to describe non-Jews who risked their lives during the Holocaust to save Jews from extermination by the Nazis (CCA-SA3.0).

The inscription reads: "Oskar Schindler, the unforgettable lifesaver of 1200 persecuted Jews." The Hebrew inscription reads: "Righteous Among the Nations." The stones upon Schindler's grave are from Jewish visitors, even some who may not have known him, but know of his remarkable efforts on behalf of the Jewish people. It is a Jewish custom to leave a stone on the grave using their hand. (CCA-SA3.0).

Atomic bombing of Nagasaki
on August 9, 1945 (NARA).

Chapter 16

The Cold War:
Geopolitical Conflict

First Thoughts

In February 1945, at the end of World War II, British Prime Minister Winston Churchill discerned that world peace was closer to being reality than at any time in history. "It would be a great tragedy," he said, "if they, through inertia or carelessness, let it slip from their grasp. History would never forgive them if it did."[1] Peace did slip through their grasp. World War II was followed by a Cold War that pitted the United States and its allies against the Soviet Union and its supporters. It was called a Cold War, but it would flare into violence in Korea and Vietnam and in many smaller conflicts. The period from 1946 to 1991 was a time of turmoil and fear for the whole world as these two super-powers, Russia and the United States, positioned themselves for hegemony!

Chapter Learning Objectives

In chapter 16 we examine the Cold War, its genesis, and its resolution. We will look at the war as a geopolitical conflict. Next, we will look at the Korean and Vietnam Wars, understanding the problems with waging a limited war. We will shiver as we contemplate how close the United States and the Soviet Union were to annihilating one another during the Cuban Missile Crisis.

As a result of this chapter you should be able to:

1. Explain why Russia and her former allies become enemies even before World War II ended

2. Discuss in what way the Cold War was a geopolitical conflict

3. Analyze the problems associated with fighting a limited war

4. Discuss what would have happened if America and the Soviet Union went to war over the Cuban Nuclear Crisis

5. Evaluate why America entered the Vietnam War and why it lost the war

1. http://www.digitalhistory.uh.edu/disp_textbook.cfm?smtID=2&psid=3401.

CONCEPTS

Iron Curtain

Geopolitical conflict

Limited war

Vietnamization

The Origins of the Cold War

Iron Curtain: A metaphor for the closing of the borders between free, democratic Europe and Soviet-controlled Eastern Europe.

In May 1945, the war in Europe ended. The allies were completely victorious. Germany was prostrate. But a new, different type of war was starting.

In March 1946, Winston Churchill announced that "an **iron curtain** has descended across"[2] Europe. On one side was the Russian-led Communist bloc; on the other side were the American-led democratic nations.

One source of conflict between the United States and the Soviet Union was the fate of eastern Europe. The United States was committed to free and democratic elections in eastern Europe, while the Soviet Union had no intentions of abandoning territories it had won with so much sacrifice. Russia had to have a buffer between itself and the West.

EASTERN BLOC MEMBERS

- ■ Satellite States
- ■ USSR-aligned until 1948
- ■ USSR-aligned until 1960

SOVIET UNION

POLAND

EAST GERMANY

CZECHOSLOVAKIA

HUNGARY

ROMANIA

YUGOSLAVIA

BULGARIA

ALBANIA

The Eastern Bloc countries. (CCA-SA3.0).

Even before World War II ended, the Soviet Union had annexed — not "made treaties with" — the Baltic states of Estonia, Latvia, and Lithuania, and parts of Czechoslovakia, Finland, Poland, and Romania. Albania established a communist government in 1944, and Yugoslavia formed one in 1945. In 1946, the Soviet Union placed communist governments in Bulgaria and Romania, and in Hungary and Poland in 1947. Communists took over Czechoslovakia in 1948.

There was another unsettling event. In August, the nuclear age began and Russia had no nuclear weapons. In 1946, the Soviet Union rejected a U.S. proposal for an international agency to control nuclear energy production and research. The Soviets were convinced that the United States was trying to preserve its monopoly on nuclear weapons, and it intended to have its own. In time it did, and an unnerving arms race began.

A third source of conflict was post-war economic development assistance. While the United States generously rebuilt Western Europe with the Marshall Plan, the United States refused a Soviet request for massive reconstruction loans. In response, the Soviets called for substantial reparations from Germany and informally assumed an adversarial role with the United States.[3]

Discussion Question

Why did Russia and her former allies become enemies even before World War II ended?

---

2. Ibid.
3. Ibid.

A Geopolitical Conflict

The conflict between the democratic West and the communist East was a **geopolitical conflict**. The difference between these two former friends was about land and security, two geopolitical considerations. Geopolitical issues concern the relationships that exist between a country's politics and its geography, or the influences that geography has on political relations between countries. Following World War II, Russia wished to have a geographical buffer between itself and the West. Twice, one time very nearly fatally, Germany invaded Russia. Russia did not wish to see that happen again.

The West, on the other hand, wished for each nation to decide for itself. The West knew that, given a choice, most nations would choose self-determination and democracy. There was also great resentment that Russia had replaced one tyranny with another. America had no geopolitical interest in eastern Europe except as a shield against Communist Russia! America had heard the Communist claim that a Communist revolution was inevitable and desirable in the whole world.

So in a real way America and Russia wanted the same thing.

This was a strange war. Other wars were fought to preserve honor — like the Franco Prussian War, or to keep the balance of power — like the Napoleonic Wars. Perhaps there was a precipitating event — like World War I. Some wars were provoked by a dastardly attack — like World War II. Some wars were mistakes — like the French and Indian War. But this war, the Cold War, was the first war fought — and it was a war no doubt about it, even though it was not fought with tanks and weapons — between two victors to preserve geopolitical fault lines to maintain a safe distance from their perceived enemies.

That is not to say that one side of the conflict was wrong and one right. America stood for freedom and liberty; Russia stood for tyranny and subjugation. But they both had the same geopolitical interests in mind.

Inevitably, when two nations have the same geopolitical desires in the same region, significant conflict results.

The Cold War was a product of misconceptions and misunderstandings between Russia, the United States, and other Western powers. However, even though there were a series of misunderstandings between Russia and the West, the world essentially became a battlefield between the two superpowers of Russia and the United States. The war was not fought on the outskirts of Budapest, as everyone expected. It was fought in Korea and Southeast Asia, Africa, and the Caribbean.

The story of the Cold War, then, is the story of how two nations both felt threatened, and fought a "cold" war. It occasionally became a "hot" war, but it thankfully was never a world war. Ironically, this "peace" was made possible by the atomic and hydrogen bombs. No superpower would dare go to war for fear that the other would retaliate. An uneasy peace of sorts ensued for almost 50 years.

> Geopolitical issues concern the relationships that exist between a country's politics and its geography, or the influences that geography has on political relations between countries.

Lesson 3

Korean War: A Limited War

At the end of World War II, Korea was a free nation for the first time in its history. Would it become free or become Communist? That was the question asked and answered emphatically from 1950–1953.

General Douglas MacArthur, UN Command CiC (seated), observes the naval shelling of Incheon from the USS Mt. McKinley, September 15, 1950 (USGOV).

On June 25, 1950, Communist North Korean forces invaded South Korea, beginning a three-year war. In only three days, the South Korean capital of Seoul fell to the North Koreans. President Truman immediately ordered U.S. air and sea forces to "give the Korean government troops cover and support." No land forces were committed yet.

The conflict lasted until July 27, 1953. The United States suffered 54,246 battle deaths and 103,284 wounded.

As a sideshow of the existing Cold War, Russia supported North Korean ambitions to control the entire Korean peninsula. Tensions had festered in Korea since the Korean peninsula had been divided into a Communist North and a non-Communist South in 1945. With the partition, ten million Koreans were separated from their families. It was not a happy time in Korean history.

For three months, the United States could not stop the North Koreans. In fact, America was very close to losing everything. Troops were held at bay in the Pusan sector. Then, Douglas MacArthur successfully landed two divisions of Marines ashore at Inchon, behind enemy lines. The North Koreans fled in disarray across the 38th parallel, the pre-war border between North and South Korea. It was one of the most brilliant military victories in history.

The initial mandate that the United States had received from the United Nations called for the restoration of the original border at the 38th parallel. But the South Korean army had no intention of stopping at the pre-war border, and on September 30, 1950, they crossed into the North. In effect, South Korea wanted to restore the unity of the two Koreas — but under South Korean rule. This was a violation of an unspoken rule in the Cold War: never be greedy. Take what you need but leave the rest alone. South Korea should have left things alone.

The United States pushed an updated mandate through the United Nations, and on October 7, the Eighth Army crossed the border. They were headed to the Yellow River, to China, and to a truckload of trouble.

By November, United States Army and Marine units thought the war would end in only a few months. China's Communist leaders threatened to send combat forces into Korea, but the U.S. commander, Douglas MacArthur, thought they were bluffing. Besides, if they did that, the United States could inflict "limited tactical nuclear" strikes on the Chinese.

MacArthur did not understand, but his Commander in Chief, Harry Truman, did understand that a "limited nuclear strike" was an oxymoron. The Chinese and the Russians would be obligated to retaliate and, at the very least, America would be involved in World War III. No one wanted that. Korea was not worth it!

A 16-inch salvo from the USS Missouri at Chong Jin, Korea, in effort to cut Northern Korean communications. Chong Jin is only 39 miles from the border of China, 1950. (USNavy).

In mid-October, 300,000 Chinese soldiers quietly slipped into North Korea. When U.S. forces began what they expected to be their final assault in late November, they ran into the Chinese army. The Chinese intervention ended any hope of reunifying Korea by force of arms. The Chinese troops were not well equipped, but 300,000 of anything could overwhelm the best-equipped army in the world!

General MacArthur called for the U.S. Joint Chiefs of Staff to unleash American air and naval power against China and to bomb them back to pre-history. Chairman of the Joint Chiefs of Staff, Army General Omar Bradley, said a clash with China would be "the wrong war, in the wrong place, at the wrong time, and with the wrong enemy."[4]

By mid-January 1951, Lt. Gen. Matthew B. Ridgway, a brilliant tactician, succeeded in halting an American retreat 50 miles south of the 38th parallel. A week and a half later, he had the army attacking northward again. By March, the front settled along the 38th parallel (the border between North and South Korea) and the South Korean capital of Seoul was back in South Korean hands. American officials informed MacArthur that peace negotiations would be sought.

Meanwhile, in April, President Truman relieved MacArthur of his command after the general, in defiance of Truman's orders, commanded the bombing of Chinese military bases in Manchuria. The president feared that such actions would bring the Soviet Union into the conflict. The Soviet Union had hydrogen bombs and was itching to use them.

The Korean War ended with no clear winner, but it was filled with lessons. It demonstrated that the United States was committed to stopping the spread of communism, not only in Western Europe, but throughout the world. Next, the Korean War proved how difficult it was to achieve victory even under the best circumstances imaginable. In Korea, the United States faced a relatively weak adversary and had strong support from its allies. The United States possessed an almost total monopoly of sophisticated weaponry, yet the war dragged on for almost four years. This was a lesson forgotten in the Vietnam War but relearned with disastrous consequences. Finally, the world had come to the brink of nuclear war, and it was disorienting. It would not be the last time, and each time both the Soviet Union and the United states, like two sumo wrestlers, grew wearier. Eventually, it appeared that the nation that lasted the longest and had the most resources would win. There would be no clear-cut military victory. The victor would be the nation who would endure.

4. http://www.nytimes.com/books/first/r/record-war.html.

Furthermore, the Korean War illustrated the difficulty of fighting a **limited war**. Limited wars are, by definition, fought for limited objectives. It is difficult to win a limited war, but a nation dare not lose one. It is always unpopular because it is difficult to explain precisely what the country is fighting for and why the nation doesn't bomb the heck out of its opponents! I remember my mother was convinced, all of her life, that President Truman was wrong to keep MacArthur from blowing up the Chinese! During the Korean War, the military was also frustrated. How does one halfway fight a war?

Finally, in Korea U.S. policymakers assumed that they could make the South Korean government do what they wanted. They involved themselves in nation building in a big way with mixed results. In reality, the situation was often reversed. The South Korean government really called the shots and America was unable to save face and withdraw from the war until it was unwinnable.[5]

Discussion Question

What are the problems associated with fighting a limited war?

Lesson 4

The Cuban Missile Crisis: At the Brink

CIA reference photograph of Soviet R-12 intermediate-range nuclear ballistic missile (NATO designation SS-4) in Red Square, Moscow 1959-1962 (CIA).

The "13 days" of the Cuban Missile Crisis was the closest that the Soviet Union and the United States came to total war. It stands as the most ominous period of the Cold War conflict between the United States and the Soviet Union. The world appeared to be on the edge of a nuclear abyss that threatened to overwhelm the two superpowers. In short, the nation almost came unglued.

No exaggeration. Without the world really knowing it, American and Russia came very close to destroying each other.

The Soviet leader made it clear to Washington that Cuba would feature in Soviet foreign policy. Why not? Americans had thermo-nuclear warheads aimed toward Moscow in countries of Western Europe.

As a result, in October 1962, the Soviet Union and the United States went eyeball-to-eyeball and were on the brink of nuclear war.

Surveillance photographs taken by a U-2 spy plane over Cuba revealed that the Soviet Union was installing intermediate-range ballistic missiles. Once operational, in about ten days, the missiles would need only five minutes to reach Washington, DC.

---

5. http://www.digitalhistory.uh.edu/disp_textbook.cfm?smtID=2&psid=3406.

President Kennedy could not allow this to happen, so he imposed a naval blockade. Soviet freighters were steaming toward Cuba. The president realized that if these ships were boarded and their cargoes seized, the Soviet Union might regard this as an act of war. American nuclear forces were put on alert. The Soviets acted in kind.

Soviet Premier Khrushchev sent a signal that he might be willing to negotiate. In exchange for the Soviets agreeing to remove the missiles, the United States publicly pledged not to invade Cuba and secretly agreed to remove its missiles from Turkey.

The crisis was abated but not over. This crisis, dramatized in the movie *Fail Safe* (1965) warned America what might happen if the Soviets and Americans went too far. In the movie a series of human and computer errors sends a squadron of American "Vindicator" bombers to nuke Moscow. The president, in order to convince the Soviets that this is a mistake, orders the Strategic Air Command to help the Soviets stop them. When the United States Air Force's elaborate fail-safe systems fail, a squadron of nuclear-armed bombers crosses the Bering Strait into the USSR to attack. No one is quite sure why this has happened, but it's left to the president of the United States to try to find a solution with his Soviet counterpart. For some, like political scientist Professor Groetschele, the situation presents opportunities. He argues that they should not dwell on the morality of the attack and simply accept that it has happened. On that basis, he argues in favor of an all-out nuclear attack against the Soviet Union as the only sure way to ensure the survival of American culture and beliefs. The president sees things differently and works with the Soviets to stop the American bombers before they reach their target. However, a technical malfunction in the Pentagon's strategic control system causes an erroneous order to be sent to a B-52 squadron on a routine training mission, instructing the bombers to fly beyond their fail-safe distance. At this point, the flight crews are trained to cease communications and fulfill their objective by bombing Moscow. As the planes near their target, the crisis deepens, and together the Americans and Soviets decide on a final, desperate solution. Slowly it becomes clear to all involved that Moscow will be bombed and nothing can stop it. When the full horror of the accidental attack order becomes clear, the president must work to recall or stop the bombers, but all efforts are frustrated by the skill and working orders of the pilots involved as well as by the power of their planes, and when they penetrate Soviet airspace a running sky battle erupts. Nothing works and the president sees only one possible way to prevent global thermo-nuclear war. The movie ends with the president, knowing that his wife is in New York City, offering to bomb New York City to placate the Russians. The deal works and other than the destruction of these two cities, nuclear holocaust is averted.[6] This was the ending to the movie, but reflected true concerns at the time.

After the Cuban Missile Crisis, Cold War tensions eased. In July 1963, the United States, the Soviet Union, and Britain approved a treaty to halt the testing of nuclear weapons in the atmosphere, in outer space, and under water. The following month, the United States and the Soviet Union established a hotline providing a direct communication link between the White House and the Kremlin.[7]

Women Strike for Peace protesting during the crisis of 1962 (LOC).

Discussion Question

Discuss what would have happened if America and the Soviet Union went to war over the Cuban Nuclear Crisis.

---

6. http://www.imdb.com/title/tt0058083/plotsummary.
7. Thomas G. Paterson, *Kennedy's Quest for Victory, American Foreign Policy 1961–1963* (Oxford, UK; New York: Cambridge University Press, 1989) p. 125.

Vietnam War

Flying under radar control with a B-66 Destroyer, Air Force F-105 Thunderchief pilots bomb a military target through low clouds over the southern panhandle of North Vietnam, June 14, 1966 (PD).

The Vietnam War was a Cold War-era military conflict that occurred in Vietnam, Laos, and Cambodia from November 1, 1955, to the fall of Saigon on April 30, 1975. It was the author's war — the war that I knew intimately, a war in which my friends died.

This war followed the First Indochina War lost by France and North Vietnam. The second war was fought between North Vietnam, supported by its Communist allies and the government of South Vietnam, supported by the United States of America and other anti-Communist countries. The Viet Cong, an irregular South Vietnamese Communist-controlled militia, largely fought a guerrilla war against South Vietnam and the Americans. The Vietnam People's Army (North Vietnamese Army) engaged in a more conventional war, at times committing large units into battle. Allied forces relied on air superiority and overwhelming firepower to conduct search-and-destroy operations, involving ground forces, artillery, and airstrikes. Eventually, though, this was not enough.

The U.S. government saw itself fighting a Korean-type war, but it was not to be. It was not a war that could be won.

The North Vietnamese government and Viet Cong viewed the conflict as a colonial war, fought initially against France, backed by the United States, and later against South Vietnam, which it regarded as a U.S. puppet state. American military advisors arrived in what was then known as French Indochina beginning in 1950. U.S. involvement escalated in the early 1960s. Regular U.S. combat units were deployed beginning in 1965. Operations spanned international borders, with Laos and Cambodia heavily bombed.

Quang Tri residents fleeing 1972 Battle of Quang Tri during the Easter Offensive (USGOV).

American involvement in the war peaked in 1968, at the time of the Tet Offensive. After this, U.S. ground forces were gradually withdrawn as part of a policy known as Vietnamization. Despite the Paris Peace Accords, signed by all parties in January 1973, fighting continued.

U.S. military involvement ended in 1973 as a result of the Case-Church Amendment passed by the U.S. Congress. The capture of Saigon by the Vietnam People's Army in April 1975 marked the end of the war, and North and South Vietnam were reunified the following year. Millions of Vietnamese and 58,000 Americans died in this tragic conflict.

Technically speaking, America did not lose the war. When America left in 1973, the South Vietnamese controlled their country. However, the South Vietnamese government could not build enough popular support for its government to successfully counter the North Vietnamese assault.

Discussion Question

Why did American enter the Vietnam War, and why did it lose the war?

Publicity still for Charlie Chaplin's 1925 film *The Gold Rush* (PD).

Chapter 17

The Cinema: A Cultural Force in Society

First Thoughts

From its inception, cinema was an influential cultural force in American society. As such, films have been scrutinized by public and civic officials and endured official and unofficial censorship campaigns. Many officials have used films to generate sympathy for national causes; many others have rallied to protect alleged moral or patriotic threats. Movies created the "movie star," a cultural entertainment icon who replaced other American heroes. Movies, in short, tell Americans about their times and their worldviews. Cinema was thus an important window into the changing social landscape of the United States in the 20th and 21st centuries.

Chapter Learning Objectives

We will discuss cinema in general and how it reflects American society. Next, we will look more specifically at the technological advances that were necessary for cinema culture to evolve. We will then analyze the impact this cinema culture has had on society and finish with a closer look at one 1950s movie, *The Searchers*.

As a result of this chapter you should be able to:

1. Discuss cinema as history

2. Review the pre-history of the cinema

3. Analyze the cultural impact of cinema

4. Review the movie *The Searchers*

5. Discuss the future of technology in cinema

CONCEPTS

Thaumatrope

Phenakistiscope

Daguerreotype

Vitascope

Tom Mix

Satosphere

Hollywood as History

James Cagney and Mae Clarke in *The Public Enemy* from 1931 (Fair Use).

Perhaps nothing is more "American" than the cinema; perhaps no place exemplifies what is "American" more than Hollywood. As social historian Steve Mintz explains, "Most Americans instantly recognize images produced by the movies: Charlie Chaplin, the starving prospector in *The Gold Rush*, eating his shoe, treating the laces like spaghetti. James Cagney, the gun-toting gangster in *Public Enemy*, shoving a grapefruit into the side of Mae Clarke's face. Paul Muni, the jobless World War I veteran in *I Am a Fugitive from a Chain Gang*, who is asked how he lives and replies, "I steal." Gloria Swanson, the fading movie goddess in *Sunset Boulevard*, belittling suggestions that she is no longer a big star: "It's the pictures that got small." Even those who have never seen *Citizen Kane* or *Casablanca* or *The Treasure of the Sierra Madre* respond instantly to the advertisements, parodies, and TV skits that use these films' dialogue, images, and characters."[1]

John Wayne was a paradigm of virtue to a generation of young men. Hundreds no doubt joined the Green Berets, for instance, in response to his movie *Green Beret*. We were all delighted when David Janssen, the skeptical reporter in this movie, saw the error of his ways concerning the Vietnam War and embraced American patriotism. Janssen ended his transformation by saying, "They had to be the toughest fighting force on earth — and the men who led them had to be just a little bit tougher!" Did we not all fly with light sabers and pretend we were Luke Skywalker? Did we not all struggle with the ambivalence Spiderman felt when he realized he was part of his uncle's untimely death? All these emotional, archetypical invitations have formed the American character since the advent of movies.

Movie theaters were the cathedrals of their age. Some seated 6,500, and most Americans attended movie performances more often than churches. Cultural historians today treat movies as sociological footprints that record the narrative and mood of particular historical settings; as cultural documents that present particular images of gender, ethnicity, and class.

Beside Macy's Department Store, in Herald Square, New York City, there is a plaque commemorating the first public showing of a motion picture on a screen in the United States. It was here, on April 23, 1896, that Thomas Edison presented the first movie, which included scenes of the beach, a boxing match, and two women dancing. A review in the *New York Times*

Macy's Building & Herald Square, New York City, 1907 (LOC).

1. http://www.digitalhistory.uh.edu/topic_display.cfm?tcid=119.

described the exhibition as "all wonderfully real and singularly exhilarating."[2] That was one of the greatest understatements in history!

A new era had begun.

Discussion Question

In what way is the cinema a metaphor for what is uniquely American?

The Pre-History of Motion Pictures

The first true moving images appeared in the 1820s were really toys. The **thaumatrope**, which appeared in 1826, was a simple disk with separate images printed on each side (for example, a dog on one side and a dog house on another). When rapidly spun, the images appeared to blend together (so that the dog seemed to be inside the dog house). In 1834, Baron Franz von Uchatius, developed a more sophisticated device called the "**phenakistiscope**." It consisted of a disk with a series of slots along its edge, which was printed with a series of slightly differing pictures. When the disk was spun in front of a mirror and the viewer looked through the slots, the pictures appeared to move. A simpler way to display movement was the flipbook, which became popular by the late 1860s. Each page showed a subject in a subtly different position. When a reader flipped the book's pages, the pictures gave the illusion of movement. These are still popular today.

A 1893 phenakistoscope disc by Eadweard Muybridge. When the disc is spun, it gives the illusion of a couple dancing (LOC).

In 1826, a French inventor named Joseph Nicephore Niepce made the first true photograph. During the 1830s, another French inventor, Louis Daguerre, improved Niepce's technique and created the **daguerreotype**, the first popular form of photography. The daguerreotype led indirectly to theater movie technology, though it was not very useful overall.

The first successful photographs of motion grew out of a California railroad tycoon's $25,000 bet. In 1872, California Governor Leland Stanford hired a photographer to help settle a bet. Stanford bet that a galloping horse lifts all four hoofs off the ground simultaneously. In 1878, the English-born photographer lined up 24 cameras along the edge of a racetrack, with strings attached to the shutters. When the horse ran by, it tripped the shutters, producing 24 closely spaced pictures that proved Stanford's contention. Horses do indeed have four feet off the ground!

---

2. *New York Times*, April 24, 1896; http://query.nytimes.com/gst/abstract.
html?res=F40F13FE385515738DDDAD0A94DC405B8685F0D3.

Four years later, Etienne-Jules Marey became the first person to take pictures of motion with a single camera. Marey built his camera in the shape of a rifle. At the end of the camera, he placed a circular photographic plate. A small motor rotated the plate after Marey snapped the shutter. With his camera, Marey could take 12 pictures a second.

In 1887, Thomas Edison gave William K.L. Dickson, one of his leading inventors, the task of developing a motion picture apparatus. Edison envisioned a machine "that should do for the eye what the phonograph did for the ear."[3] Dickson initially modeled his device on Edison's phonograph, placing tiny pictures on a revolving drum. A light inside the drum was supposed to illuminate the pictures. Then he decided to use the flexible celluloid film that George Eastman had invented in 1880 and begun to use in his Kodak camera. Dickson added perforations to the edge of the filmstrip to help it feed evenly into his camera. This was arguably the first motion picture camera.

Finally recognizing the potential of the motion picture projector, Edison entered into an agreement with a Washington, DC, realtor, Thomas Armat, who had designed a workable projector. In April 1896, the two men unveiled the **Vitascope,** and presented the first motion pictures on a public screen in the United States.

During film's first decade from 1896 to 1905, movies were little more than a novelty, often used as a sideshow to signal the end of a show in live theater. Early films

Marey's photographic gun (CCA-SA3.0)

Flying pelican captured by Marey around 1882. He found a way to record several phases of movements in one photo (PD).

3. http://inventors.about.com/od/estartinventors/a/Edison_Bio_3.htm.

were utterly unlike anything seen today. They lasted just seven to ten minutes — too brief to develop a very interesting story. And there was no money in it! As late as 1908, a movie actor made no more than $8 a day and received no credit onscreen.

The first movies had no sound. Some film historians have argued that early silent films revolved around "characteristically working class settings" and expressed the interests of the poor in their struggles with the rich and powerful. Other scholars maintain that early movies drew largely upon conventions, stock characters, and routines derived from Wild West shows, comic strips, and other forms of late 19th-century popular entertainment. One film historian explains, "American films were born in an age of reform, and many early silent movies took as their subject matter the major social and moral issues of the Progressive era: birth control, child labor, divorce, immigration, political corruption, poverty, prisons, prostitution, and women's suffrage. The tone of these films varied widely — some were realistic and straightforward; others treated their subjects with sentimentality or humor; and many transformed complex social issues into personal melodramas. Yet there can be no doubt that many silent films dealt at least obliquely with the dominant issues of the time."[4]

Discussion Question

What was the subject matter of early silent movies?

1896 poster advertising the Vitascope (LOC).

Thomas Alva Edison, circa 1922 (LOC).

4. http://www.digitalhistory.uh.edu/topic_display.cfm?tcid=122; http://www.tc.umn.edu/~ryahnke/film/cinema.htm.

The Movies as a Cultural Battleground

During the 1920s, movie attendance soared. By the middle of the decade, 50 million people a week went to the movies — the equivalent of half the nation's population.

Americans have always had an ambivalent view of the movies. Some praised movies as a benign alternative to the saloon. Others, especially fundamentalist Christians, saw them as breeding grounds of crime and sexual promiscuity. The author's wife, for instance, raised in a fundamentalist church, saw no movies until she was in her teens, and then it was a Walt Disney move. She remembers sitting in the movie theater and worrying that God might strike her dead!

In the early part of the 20th century, Chicago established the nation's first censorship board to protect its population "against the evil influence of obscene and immoral representations."

A 1915 Supreme Court ruling stated that movies were not protected by the First Amendment because they "were a business pure and simple . . . not to be regarded as part of the press of the country or as organs of public opinion."[5] Eager to combat the trend toward local censorship, movie manufacturers worked with moral reformers in New York to establish the voluntary Board of Censorship of Motion Pictures in 1909, intended to review the movies' treatment of violence, drugs, prostitution, and, above all, sexual impropriety.

Postcard sent in response to mail from the Ralston-Purina sponsored Tom Mix radio program, 1941 (PD).

By the early 1920s, Hollywood had become the world's film capital. It produced virtually all films shown in the United States and received 80 percent of the revenue from films shown abroad. Hollywood had also come to symbolize "the new morality" of the 1920s — a mixture of extravagance and immorality. Where else but Hollywood would an actress like Gloria Swanson bathe in a solid gold bathtub or a screen cowboy like **Tom Mix** have his name raised atop his house in six-foot-high letters?

Perhaps no media event so mesmerized Americans as much as the movies. On a Tuesday, for instance, perhaps half of the adult population of the United States would watch a new Tom Mix movie. There were no other choices. There were no television shows to watch, very few entertainment options on the whole. Americans shared the same cultural experience — imagine! This was the first time that Americans had such a common experience. Only the Super Bowl approximates the same thing today. Perhaps Americans watch the Academy Awards, but not 50 percent of Americans! With the plethora of choices, perhaps Americans will never experience this again.

But it increased even more. The arrival of sound produced a sharp upsurge in movie attendance, which jumped from 50 million a week in the mid-1920s to 110 million in 1929. But it also produced a number of fundamental transformations in the movies themselves. One historian explains, "Sound made the movies more American. The words that Al Jolson used in *The Jazz Singer* to herald the arrival of sound in the movies

---

5. http://supreme.justia.com/cases/federal/us/236/230/case.html.

— 'You ain't heard nothing yet' — embodied the new slangy, vernacular tone of the talkies. Distinctive American accents and inflections quickly appeared on the screen, like James Cagney's New Yorkese or Gary Cooper's Western drawl. The introduction of sound also encouraged new film genres — like the musical, the gangster film, and comedies that relied on wit rather than slapstick."[6] Americans not only looked like their movie idols, they talked like them!

In addition, talking movies dramatically changed the movie-going experience. Movie-goers were now expected to remain quiet. The movie theater, then, became a place of individual, private entertainment. While the community could share the same experience, it had to share it silently until later. No longer was the movie theater a social event where everyone shared their weekly events; it was a moment to reflect and to enjoy a world becoming increasingly distant from the world of most patrons.[7]

Actor James Cagney in the early 1930s (PD).

Discussion Question

What impact did sound have on the movie-going experience?

The Searchers — A Movie Review

The Searchers, starring John Wayne and directed by John Ford, is, at its core, a movie about race. While *The Searchers* in fact belongs in the Western genre, "in its complexity and ambiguity, [it] was a product of post-World War II American culture and sparked the deconstruction of the Western film myth by looking unblinkingly at white racism and violence and suggesting its social psychological origins."[8]

Nothing has been as enduring to the American nation as racism.[9] As W.E.B. Dubois wrote at the beginning of the twentieth century, "Herein lie buried many things which if read with patience may show the strange meaning of being black here at the dawning of the twentieth century . . . for the problem of the twentieth century is the problem of the color line."[10] In a way then, *The Searchers* is the quintessential American movie. It captures the essence of the American character.

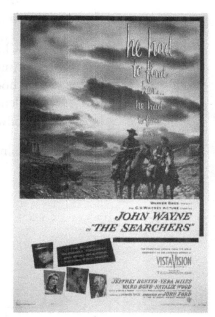

US theatrical release poster for the film *The Searchers* (1956) (PD).

6. Steven Mintz and Randy W. Roberts, *Hollywood's America: Twentieth-Century America Through Film* (Chichester, England: John Wiley & Sons, 2010), p. 16.
7. http://www.digitalhistory.uh.edu/topic_display.cfm?tcid=124.
8. Arthur M. Eckstein and Peter Lehman, eds., a review of *The Searchers: Essays and Reflections* (Detroit, MI: Wayne State University Press, 2004).
9. Studs Terkel, *Race: How Blacks and Whites Think and Feel About the American Obsession* (New York: The New Press, 1992), p. 204–205.
10. W.E.B. Dubois, *The Souls of Black Folk* (New York: Signet Classic, 1982), p. xi.

L'Idéal Cinéma in France, opened on November 23, 1905, and claims to be the oldest still-active movie theater in the world (CCA-SA3.0).

The Searchers is also a compelling story. Three years after the American Civil War ends, unrepentant Confederate Ethan Edwards (John Wayne) returns to visit his brother Aaron (Walter Coy), his sister-in-law and alleged lover/old flame Martha (Dorothy Jordan), and their family. Shortly after Edwards' arrival, a renegade party of Comanche Native Americans murders all of the Edwards' family except a daughter, Debbie (Natalie Wood). After an initial search party is turned back, Ethan, as well as Aaron's adopted son, Martin (a suspected mixed Native American), head out on a search mission. The rest of the movie is a quest whose purpose allegedly is to rescue Debbie; however, before long, it is obvious that Ethan wishes to kill Debbie. Finally, after five years, and an epic journey reminiscent of the Hebrew journey to the Promised Land, Ethan finds Debbie, scalps Debbie's Native American husband, Scar (Henry Brandon), and nearly kills Debbie. At the end, though, Ethan softens, and returns with Debbie to her home.

The Searchers is also an enigma. Perhaps, in microcosm, it represents the dilemma that racism has presented American culture since its genesis.[11] For one thing, Ethan Edwards, like most Americans, is betrayed by the myth of homogeneity. Thus, racial discussions are complicated by this myth — as if there is a pure white race. Martin, for one, is evidence that that is not true. But ironically, American racial homogeneity is an illusion. Very few Americans are 100 percent anything. But Americans normally describe their racial identity in homogeneous terms. Ethan certainly maintains that myth.

When one is classified as white, one enjoys the privileges of the dominant caste. Non-whites do not enjoy these privileges. So *The Searchers* is rendered even more complicated by the ambiguous defining apparatus of American racial language.[12] White Americans enjoy race mixing as long as it is ambiguously defined. Non-white Americans find that race mixing leads inevitably to white exploitation.[13]

Ultimately, *The Searchers*, like race relations, is a moral issue.[14] The way white Americans treat people of color is very much a moral issue. Whatever categories they choose to define their relationships affect their souls. Its manifestations are systemically demonic and individually destructive.[15] In effect, this is the demon with which Ethan Edwards journeys.

Film critic Roger Ebert, in a *Chicago Sun-Times* article cogently states the issue:

> A cover story in *New York Magazine* called it the most influential movie in American history. And yet at its center is a difficult question, because the Wayne character is racist without apology — and, so, in a less outspoken way, are the other white characters. Is the film intended to endorse their attitudes, or to dramatize and regret them?

This thematic ambivalence is perhaps director John Ford's shining moment.

11. Eckstein and Lehman, *The Searchers*, p. 197–217.
12. James P. Stobaugh, *Racial Anger*, unpublished dissertation, South Hamilton, MA, Gordon Conwell Seminary, 1996, p. 12.
13. Nicholas Lemann, *The Promised Land* (New York: Vintage Books, 1992).
14. Robert Stone, "The Search Party," in *The New York Times Magazine*, November 10, 2007, p. 3.
15. William Schweiker, "Power and the Agency of God," *Theology Today* (July 1995): p. 240.

Ironically, in spite of its racist theme, *The Searchers* is made in the waning days of the classic Western, which falters when Indians cease to be typecast as savages. As Ebert explains, "Revisionist Westerns, including Ford's own *Cheyenne Autumn* in 1964, take a more enlightened view of native Americans, but the Western audience doesn't want moral complexity; like the audience for today's violent thrillers and urban warfare pictures, it wants action with clear-cut bad guys."[16]

As one commentator, Nick Redman, observes, *The Searchers* both enthralls and frustrates. It is a cinematic masterpiece and does break new ground, but the Ethan Edwards character at times lacks credibility — especially at the end of the movie.[17] Or, as Stephen Metcalf argues, it is the "worst best movie." Metcalf calls the movie "boring," and I must confess, there are parts that are boring, and predictable. Like Metcalf, I was surprised at how "gidgeted-together this supposedly great film is, how weird its quilting is, of unregenerate violence with doltish comic set pieces, all pitched against Ford's signature backdrop, the buttes and spires of Monument Valley.[18]

I agree with Ebert who says, there are two movies in *The Searchers*. First is the internal and external development of the round protagonist Ethan Edwards who ruthlessly pursues his psychological and physical enemies. Second, and this goes to the credibility of this masterpiece, is the final scene of Debbie's salvation. Ebert says, "The shot is famous and beloved, but small counterbalance to his views throughout the film — and indeed, there is no indication he thinks differently about Indians."[19]

Discussion Question

What is the compelling theme of *The Searchers*?

The Future of Cinema?

Globe and Mail Update, clarified version, Jan. 17, 2012

By James Martin

It's cinema's great creation myth: In 1896, the projected image of a speeding train caused frightened French carnival goers to leap out of harm's way. Those early screenings are historical fact — the 50-second film, sensibly titled *L'arrivée d'un train en gare de La*

16. Roger Ebert, "The Searchers," *Chicago Sun-Times*, November 25, 2001, p. 1–2, http://www.rogerebert.com/reviews/great-movie-the-searchers-1956.

17. Nick Redman, *A Turning of the Earth: John Ford, John Wayne, and The Searchers*, Warner Brothers Special Edition Video, 1999, special feature.

18. Stephen Metcalf, "The Worst Best Movie: Why on Earth did *The Searchers* Get Canonized?" p. 1–10, www.slate.com/id/2145142.

19. Ebert, "The Searchers," p.3.

Ciotat, was made by the pioneering Lumière Brothers — but the panicked reactions may be apocryphal. Still, the story persists. It appears most recently in *Hugo*, Martin Scorsese's love letter to early cinema — because it neatly encapsulates how a passing gimmick redeemed itself through its near-magical ability to plunge us into other worlds.

Now a new technology, being developed on a sketchy block of downtown Montreal, promises viewers an immersive film experience to out-plunge the Lumières' train or Scorsese's masterful 3D. No glasses required. No chairs, either.

Eighteen metres in diameter, the three-month-old **Satosphere** is a round cinema, but — unlike similar planetarium theatres of old — it uses a hi-tech network of eight video projectors and 157 speakers to completely surround (save the floor) up to 400 people with lifelike sound and images. The effect isn't 3D in the comin'-at-ya! sense recently back in vogue. Rather, it gives viewers the sense of moving inside the images — even, during particularly kinetic sequences, verging on motion sickness.

"People have made domed theatres before," admits Mr. St-Arnault. "But, strangely enough, they still tried to make the viewer look only at the front, like in a regular cinema. We're trying to move away from that by not having fixed seating. We want people to be able to walk around, to choose their point of view, both by their body position and what captures their interest."

Two viewers standing back-to-back in the Satosphere would see, and possibly hear, completely different things, making the experience as much about what you miss as what you catch. Sound overwhelming? That's kind of the point.

"Everywhere you look in the world, there's too much information," says Mr. St-Arnault. "If I choose to look in front of me right now, then I'm missing whatever's happening behind me." He turns around. "Now I'm missing something else. Nobody in the Satosphere sees or hears exactly the same movie."[20]

Discussion Question

The cinema technology has come full circle from a silent movie with a common experience, to a talking film where each person quietly experiences the same film, to a satosphere where no one "sees or hears exactly the same movie." Predict what effect the satosphere will have on American culture.

Theater goers watching a 3D movie with the classic glasses complete the experience.

The Beatles wave to fans after arriving at Kennedy Airport in 1964 (LOC).

Chapter 18

Rock 'n' Roll: Times Were A-Changin'

First Thoughts

Viewed as an historical marker, popular music is a revealing barometer of culture. It exemplifies the diverse moods and views of the American public at different times in history. Music presents insights and multiple points of view as well as an emotional impact that other historical documents, particularly written, often lack. People listen to and enjoy music. It speaks to the heart of what is America. It shows in uninhibited fashion the hopes and dreams of a people. Through music, history comes alive and we can connect directly with people and events that may otherwise seem remote to us. As such, rock 'n' roll can be a powerful tool to introduce recent historical events and issues. It is the only indigenous American music that has been with us since the first African set foot on the North American continent.

Chapter Learning Objectives

In chapter 18 we will outline the beginnings of rock 'n' roll and show how it captured the pathos of our nation. It was a music birthed in violence and anger on the auction blocks of chattel slavery and matured into the peaceful love of waterlogged Woodstock. We will examine how it molded and created much of the culture that emerged in the latter part of the 20th century. Along the way we will also talk about how Christians should react to rock 'n' roll.

As a result of this chapter you should be able to:

1. Discuss what is unique about the origins of rock 'n' roll

2. Explain why rock 'n' roll moved from African American protest music to mainstream, mostly white, music.

3. Analyze why rock 'n' roll become the first socially relevant music in America

4. Judge whether or not Christians should listen to rock 'n' roll

5. Evaluate how Barwick and her generation were affected by Woodstock

CONCEPTS

Rock 'n' roll

Blues

Jazz

Ragtime

Dixieland

Woodstock

Origins

Rock 'n' roll was resurrected in the American folk music of Stephen Foster and Cole Porter.

Rock 'n' roll traces its origins to the African American slave community. Rock 'n' roll began in the crucible of African culture, chattel slavery, and resulting slave resistance. Thus, from the beginning, rock 'n' roll was a subversive activity, a protest movement. In a sense, it never really lost that tone.

Ironically, then, perhaps our most indigenous music was from an enslaved society. Every society has its indigenous music, which serves as entertainment and accompaniment to ritual and ceremony. Our music was rock 'n' roll.

Music historian David Townsend writes, "This last ingredient is crucial: they didn't sing the Blues back in Africa. Rock 'n' roll is an African American hybrid, but its strongest root is the very suffering, and survival, of generations of slaves, who learned how music could help a man to transcend earthly pain for awhile. The Blues sings of sadness, toil, and loss, but the reason for singing the Blues is to relieve the hurt these things cause. The Blues, with its simple, repetitive rhythms and chords and lyrical phrases, provides a comforting communal message that musician and audience can share, as long as

Bill Haley and his Comets, circa 1955 (PD).

they know where the singer is coming from. It's no wonder that Blues singers were so popular during the Depression, especially in the South, among both black and white audiences. It's also easy to understand the strong bonds between rock 'n' roll and Gospel music: from a secular point of view, singing about the Lord lifting you up and singing about the Blues fallin' down like rain are spiritually equivalent acts."

Nonetheless, rock 'n' roll emerged as a defined musical style in the United States in the early to mid 1950s. Rock 'n' roll in turn provided the main basis for the music that, since the mid 1960s, has been generally known as rock music. In 1951, Cleveland, Ohio, disc jockey Alan Freed began playing this music style while popularizing the term "rock 'n' roll" to describe it.

Because the development of rock 'n' roll was an evolutionary process, no single record can be identified as the first rock 'n' roll music. In terms of its wide cultural impact across society in the United States and elsewhere, Bill Haley's "Rock Around the Clock," recorded in April 1954 but not a commercial success until the following year, is generally recognized as the first, unadulterated rock 'n' roll of the modern era.[1]

Discussion Question

What is unique about the origins of rock 'n' roll?

---

1. David Townsend, "Changing the World: Rock 'n' Roll Culture and Ideology," Unpublished Article.

A Music Revolution

The rock 'n' roll music that emerged in the 1950s was a hybrid of several varieties of music such as the **blues, jazz, ragtime,** and **Dixieland**. Each type of music developed over time, and each one exchanged ideas and stylistic elements with all the others. The greatest contribution came from the musical traditions of America's African American population, with an ancient heritage of oral storytelling through music of African origin, usually with strong rhythmic elements and frequent use of "blue notes," and often using a "call and response" vocal pattern. This early rock 'n' roll had its fullest expression in African American churches. At this point, rock 'n' roll, which was not really rock 'n' roll until the 1950s, absorbed a Gospel music style.

There was a defiance, an anger, in rock 'n' roll that protested the unjust treatment of African Americans in American society. Rock 'n' roll was an inevitable outgrowth of the social and musical interactions between blacks and whites in the South.

By the 1930s, music genres took a sharp turn toward rock 'n' roll. African American musician Duke Ellington developed swing music, essentially jazz played for dancing, and in some areas such as New York City, processes of social integration were taking place. Everyone liked swing music, and it was in the African American swing dance halls that integration first occurred in the United States.

By the mid 1930s, rock 'n' roll was everywhere. Elements of rock 'n' roll could be found in every type of American folk and blues music. Some jazz bands, such as Count Basie's, increasingly played rhythmic music that was heavily dependent on percussion instruments and even the guitar, the two favorite instruments of rock 'n' roll. Early rock 'n' roll also experimented with the use of amplification.

Duke Ellington at his piano on November 3, 1954 (PD).

More and more music types shared styles and composition. These processes of exchange and mixing were fueled by the spread of radio, 78 rpm, and later records and jukeboxes, and the expansion of the commercial popular music business. The music also benefited from the development of new amplification and electronic recording techniques from the 1930s onward, including the invention of the electric guitar, first recorded as a virtuoso instrument by Charlie Christian.

In 1947, blues singer Roy Brown recorded "Good Rocking Tonight," a song that parodied church music. This was followed by a plethora of songs about "rocking," including "We're Gonna Rock" by Wild Bill Moore, the first commercially successful "honking" sax record, with the words "We're gonna rock, we're gonna roll" as a background chant. One of the most popular was "Rock the Joint," first recorded by Jimmy Preston in May 1949.

By the year I was born, 1953, the phrase "rock 'n' roll" was used more widely to market the music beyond its initial African American audience.

Blues: The name given to both a musical form and a music genre that originated in African American communities of primarily the "Deep South" of the United States.

Dixieland: Dixieland music, sometimes referred to as Hot Jazz, Early Jazz or New Orleans jazz, is a style of jazz music that developed in New Orleans at the start of the 20th century.

195

Fats Domino at a concert in 1992 (CCA-SA3.0).

Rock 'n' roll was not merely loud music. Vocal harmony group recordings in the style that later became known as "doo-wop" became huge commercial successes. When rock 'n' roll made a lot of money — through record sales and concerts — it became mainstream.

Some of the rhythm and blues musicians who had been successful in earlier years, such as Fats Domino who had his first hit in 1950, were able to make the transition into new markets, markets that were appealing more and more to middle class whites.

In fact, much of the initial breakthrough into the wider pop music market came from white musicians such as Elvis Presley and Jerry Lee Lewis. At the same time, younger black musicians such as Little Richard, Chuck Berry, and Bo Diddley became wildly popular and launched the rock 'n' roll era. By 1954 rock 'n' roll was the most popular music in America.

Discussion Question

Rock 'n' roll moved from African American protest music to mainstream, mostly white, music. How?

Lesson 3

The Times They Were A-Changin'

Rock 'n' roll, by its very nature, was also considered dangerous during its early days in the 1950s. And rightly so. For the first time, music crossed over racial boundaries. Integrated audiences listened to music born of the blending of black and white musical styles and performed by both black and white artists. To many, it was also irreverent and loud, expressing a spirit of nihilism that was revolutionary.

I remember Elvis Presley presenting a concert in our small town in the 1950s. He was relatively unknown. My mother forebade us from attending his concert because "his gyrations were sexually suggestive." Of course I was about seven years old and did not know what she meant!

Rock 'n' roll expressly rebelled against the status quo. And more threatening, during the 1950s, for the first time, a teenage culture emerged — one with buying power and its own tastes in music which were contrary to the pop music (Frank Sinatra, Doris Day) most adults preferred. Rock 'n' roll, with its emphasis on rhythm, provided an outlet for feelings of angst that many American teenagers were experiencing. A song like 1958's "Yakety Yak" by The Coasters is the poster boy for rock 'n' roll protest music.

It was no surprise to anyone that in the 1960s rock 'n' roll became increasingly reactionary and countercultural. As a matter of fact, rock music was the first American music genre to become socially relevant. The most important figure of the 1960s folk boom was Bob Dylan, who invented the singer-songwriter, ballad genre. Inspired by people like Woody Guthrie and Pete Seeger, Dylan wrote deeply personal but relevant songs like "Blowin' in the Wind." Additionally, in the 1960s, there was a frenzy of new rock 'n' roll songs and groups to sing them. The Mamas and the Papas, the Beatles, the Rolling Stones, the Grateful Dead, and the Beach Boys stormed American cultural walls.

At this moment and forever, rock 'n' roll was connected to the drug culture. By the mid-to-late 1960s, musicians in the San Francisco Bay area, including such bands as the Grateful Dead and Jefferson Airplane, influenced both rock music and society at large. Centered around LSD (which was legal) and tribal spirit, the hippie counter-culture challenged authority and galvanized young people already alienated from an adult world. Long hair and rock music became symbols of the struggle against social convention.

Rock 'n' roll, now called rock music, had left mild protestation and folk ballads far behind![2]

Elvis Presley in 1957 (LOC).

Discussion Question

In what way did rock 'n' roll become the first socially relevant music in America?

Lesson 4

Religion and Rock 'n' Roll

The adulation and popularity of rock 'n' roll groups reaches a certain level of religious fervor. John Lennon became infamous for a statement he made in 1966 that the Beatles were "bigger than Jesus."

There is some pretty bad stuff out there. Iron Maiden, King Diamond, Alice Cooper, Led Zeppelin, and Marilyn Manson are clearly immoral or other-wise having an "evil" influence on their listeners. Anti-religious sentiments also appear in punk and hardcore.

Christian rock, alternative rock, metal, punk, and hardcore are specific, identifiable genres of rock music with strong Christian overtones and influence. However, some secular groups and singers also seem to have religious beliefs. For example the Edge and Bono of U2 are a Methodist and an Anglican, respectively.

The Beatles in 1964 at the height of Beatlemania (CCA-SA3.0).

2. http://rockhall.com/education/resources/lesson-plans/sti-lesson-5/.

Bono and The Edge of U2 in 2009 (CCA-SA2.0).

Nonetheless, a few Christians are opposed to hip hop and rock as well as blues and jazz as inherently evil, immoral, and/or sensual.

Christian conservative author David Noebel is one of the most notable proponents of the existence of jungle beats. In his writings and speeches, Noebel argued that the use of such beats in music was a communist plot to subvert the morality of the youth of the United States. Pope Benedict XVI was quoted as saying, according to the British Broadcasting Corporation, that "Rock . . . is the expression of the elemental passions, and at rock festivals it assumes a sometimes cultic character, a form of worship, in fact, in opposition to Christian worship."[3]

Discussion Question

Should Christians listen to rock 'n' roll?

Lesson 5

"40 Years Later, Woodstock's Impact Still Being Felt"

Rosemary Ford

Forty years later, Woodstock's iconic status hasn't diminished. The name of the show — taken from a small town located about 70 miles from the venue — is synonymous with the youth movement of the 1960s. It was the culmination of the peace movement, the questioning of authority, and a generation's quest for freedom and equality.

In 1969, Beth Barwick's blonde hair was down to her waist. The 18-year-old made her own clothes and spent that August getting ready for her first year at New York University.

But earlier that summer, she'd heard about this great weekend-long concert called the Woodstock Music and Art Fair in Bethel, N.Y., featuring some of her favorite bands, like Jefferson Airplane and Joan Baez. She bought an advance ticket, paying $20 for it at a local grocery store (the equivalent of more than $70 today).

"That was a lot of money back then," Barwick said.

Her parents didn't really want her and her older brother to go to the outdoor show, but felt better about it when they heard she would be part of a group of 16 kids headed there.

The teenagers' plan was to head up to **Woodstock** and meet up at the show. Barwick road up from her home near Poughkeepsie, N.Y., with her brother and six friends in a station wagon filled with a tent, sleeping bags, and other supplies.

---

3. http://www.rtforum.org/lt/lt92.html.

Though they arrived early on Friday, traffic was already insane. They abandoned their car three miles away by the side of the road, hauled the tents and sleeping bags up to the concert, and set up shop behind the stage. Their friends never made it to the show — by the time they started driving, most of the roads had already been shut down.

At the time, Barwick remembers thinking how cool it was that so many people her age headed to this central spot. But looking back, she thinks about how her parents must have felt as they watched the news at home.

"Now I think about my poor parents. What were they thinking?" said Barwick, now the mother of a 19-year-old.

At the time, Barwick knew she was at a special event, but she had no idea that she had a front-row seat to history in the making.

Opening ceremony at Woodstock, August 1969 (PD).

"I had no inkling how legendary this would be," she said. "The love and the peace and the whole atmosphere of the '60s and early '70s — we were trying to save the country, save the world."

"I was very proud back then," Barwick said. "I really thought one person could make a difference. We did make a difference, but not the difference we thought we could."

Today, there is even a museum to commemorate the experience.

"Society changed in 1969," said Wade Lawrence, director of the Museum at Bethel Woods, which has events planned for this weekend's 40th anniversary and the rest of the year. "I think it's good to celebrate it."

University of Massachusetts associate professor Chad Montrie, who teaches a course on the '60s in the school's History Department, said few understood the importance of Woodstock at the time. It became a touchstone for social, political and musical history. The generation questioned values and how they lived their lives alongside a very politically charged type of rock 'n' roll.

"These things have an influence on how we think of ourselves today," Montrie said. "What happens today is grounded in what happened in the past."

It is, perhaps, the most legendary concert of all time, and just part of the reason is because of the assembly of acts — like Creedence Clearwater Revival, Janis Joplin, Santana, and Jimi Hendrix — that played from Friday evening, Aug. 15, to early Monday morning, Aug. 18.

Until this festival, different types of music were segregated, Boston University professor Victor Coelho said. Folk fans weren't listening to Santana, Hendrix fans weren't listening to Baez, Sha Na Na fans weren't the same as fans of The Who, and so on.

"All these genres came together with Woodstock," said Coelho, the associate provost for undergraduate education and a music professor at the university's College of Fine Arts. "It shaped music history."

Advertisement for the "Aquarian Exposition" of the "Woodstock Music & Art Fair," in Wallkill, NY, 1969 (PD).

Reunion concerts in 1994 and 1999 didn't capture the magic of that moment in time. They attracted crowds, but the feelings of peace and love were gone. The 1999 concert ended in mayhem and destruction, with concertgoers setting fires and destroying property.

Woodstock itself was somewhat accidental. It began as a profit-making venture that went awry, in what many would consider a wonderful way.

Organizers told the people of Bethel they expected 50,000 at the show. They didn't want to tell the tiny town they had in fact sold 180,000 tickets in advance.

Crowds showed up early and they showed up in force. Fences and ticket booths seemed to make no difference, as the crowd that would become nearly a half million strong began to arrive.

Food and toilets were in short supply. Unofficial vendors sold everything from T-shirts to knick-knacks for a few bucks. Rain covered everything in mud, but, according to Barwick, never really dampened anyone's spirits.

"It was a warm rain," Barwick recalled. "It was amazing. Everybody was having a good time and didn't bother anyone else."

She remembers strangers sharing whatever they had, especially when it came to food. This was a marked difference from the later Woodstock incarnations, where personal pizzas cost $12 each, and bottled water $4.

"If people had fruit and stuff, they would pass it around," Barwick said.

Lawrence said one of the legacies of Woodstock is civic engagement.

"The feeling that anything is possible if you believe in it," he said. "That we can change the world."

Woodstock was ahead of its time in many ways, including the successful movie about the show, edited by a young Martin Scorsese. The movie and albums about Woodstock that followed the festival allowed people to re-live that weekend in a way they weren't able to with most shows of the time, spreading the concert's impact beyond the thousands who attended.

"It's part of our lives. I can't imagine going back," Montrie said.

The legend of Woodstock still manages to inspire. Lawrence said many young people come to his museum and leave with a yearning for that time and its ideals of peace, love, and equality.

But so far, no one has been able to replicate either the atmosphere or the significance of that kind of concert. Many wonder if such a thing is even possible.

"That was unique," Barwick said.[4]

Discussion Question

How were Barwick and her generation affected by Woodstock?

4. Rosemary Ford, "40 Years Later, Woodstock's Impact Still Being Felt," EagleTribune.com, North Andover, MA, August 9, 2009, http://www.eagletribune.com/lifestyle/x1896344689/40-years-later-Woodstocks-impact-still-being-felt/print.

Bell's First Telephone

An example of Bell's first telephone, between 1915 and 1925. (LOC).

Chapter 19

The 20th Century: Radical Revolutions

First Thoughts

Social historians argue that the 20th century reflected all the extremes of human nature. It was the best of times and it was the worst of times. It was scarred by some of history's most horrific examples of human depravity. But it also demonstrated humanity's idealism, inventiveness, goodness, and humanitarianism. It was the most technologically advanced century, but more often than not, technology was used to kill and maim people. The 20th century was both the most ideological and most destructive in human history. More than 150 million people perished in war, in concentration camps, or in government-induced famines (e.g., Stalinist purge in 1930s). It was a century of mass production, mass consumption, mass media, and mass entertainment — but also of mass murder. It was a century of excesses and parsimony. It was a century of love children and murdered children.

Chapter Learning Objectives

We will examine the advances that were made in the 20th century and the revolutions that they precipitated. We will discern that many of these changes were quite radical and represented social rather than political revolutions. We will assess the positive and negative effects of these changes and will together look to the future.

As a result of this chapter you should be able to:

1. Discuss what it was like to live in 1900

2. Explore the impact of nationalism and advanced technology

3. Evaluate the impact of American culture

4. List four problems that could sink America

5. Analyze the progress that was made in the 20th century

A Century of Change

Steve Mintz

[In 1900] life expectancy for white Americans was just 48 years and just 33 years for African Americans — about the same as a peasant in early 19th-century India. Today, Americans' average life expectancy is 74 years for men and 79 for women. The gap in life expectancy between whites and non-whites has narrowed from 15 years to 7 years.

Man with apprentice boy making shoes, circa 1914 (LOC).

In 1900, if a mother had four children, there was a fifty-fifty chance that one would die before the age of 5. At the same time, half of all young people lost a parent before they reached the age of 21.

In 1900, the average family had an annual income of $3,000 (in today's dollars). The family had no indoor plumbing, no phone, and no car. About half of all American children lived in poverty. Most teens did not attend school; instead, they labored in factories or fields.

The nation's population shifted from the Northeast to the Sunbelt. In 1900, Toledo was bigger than Los Angeles. California's population was the size of the population in Arkansas or Alabama. Today, Sunbelt cities like Houston, Phoenix, and San Diego have replaced Boston, Cleveland, and St. Louis. In 1900, about 60 percent of the population lived on farms or in rural areas. Today, one in four lives in rural areas; more than half live in suburbs.

The top five names in 1900 for boys were John, William, James, George, and Charles; for girls they were Mary, Helen, Anna, Margaret, and Ruth — almost entirely traditional biblical and Anglo-Saxon names. The top five names today: Michael, Jacob, Matthew, Christopher, and Joshua for boys; Emily, Samantha, Madison, Ashley, and Sarah for girls. These names still reflect the strong influence of the Bible on naming patterns but also the growing influence of entertainment. Florence and Bertha no longer even make the top 10,000 list of names.

Two of America's ten biggest industries were boot making and malt liquor production. There were only 8,000 cars in the country — none west of the Mississippi River. Dot-com communication still meant the telegraph.[1]

Discussion Question

Would you want to live in 1900? Why or why not?

---

1. http://www.digitalhistory.uh.edu/disp_textbook.cfm?smtID=2&psid=3175.

20th-Century Revolutions

The 20th century was a century of revolutions. There were political revolutions: the Russian Revolution, the Chinese Revolution, and so forth. But many of the century's most lasting revolutions were **social revolutions**. There was the sexual revolution, the women's liberation movement, the business revolution, and government revolution. These revolutions transformed the way people lived.

The scientific revolution changed more lives than any other. During the 1890s, physics and medicine radically changed our view of the world. The discovery of x-rays, radio-activity, sub-atomic particles, relativity, and quantum theory produced a revolution in how scientists viewed matter and energy. That was only the beginning. Radio and television were invented. The automobile and airplane were invented. Then the computer. Technology continues profoundly to change the world — almost hourly!

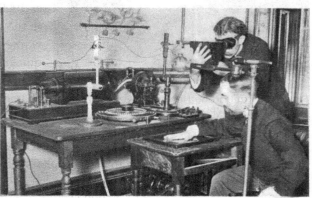

Photo of experimenters taking an X-ray with an early Crookes tube apparatus, from the late 1800s. The Crookes x-ray tube is visible suspended at center. The upper man is examining the bones of his hand with a fluoroscope screen. The lower man is taking a radiograph of his hand with a photographic plate, 1896 (PD).

We also built the atomic bomb and experimented with chemical warfare. Clearly not all science has led to progress.

The 20th century also witnessed a revolution in economic productivity. Between 1900 and 2000, the world's population roughly quadrupled from almost 1.6 billion to 6 billion people. But global production of goods and services rose 14- or 15-fold. In 1900, the Standard & Poor's 500 index stood at 6.2. In 2012, the index was 13,000+ (Stephen Mintz; Peter Stearns).

Equally important was the rise of popular use of technology. In 1900, each person made an average of 38 telephone calls. By 1997, the figure had grown to 2,325 phone calls. In 2011 the average American made or received eight mobile phone calls per day. That is roughly 2.4 billion phone calls across the 300 million cell phone users in the United States per day. The average mobile phone user in the United States makes 250 phone calls per month or 3,000 phone calls per year. There are 300 million cell phone users in the United States, so that is 900 billion cell phone calls made per year. The changes in mass communication from the turn of the 20th century until now are mind-boggling!

In 1890, there were no billboards, no trademarks, and no advertising slogans. There were no movies, no radio, no television, and few spectator sports. No magazine had a million readers. The 1890s saw the advent of the mass circulation newspaper, the national magazine, the best-selling novel, many modern spectator and team sports, and the first million-dollar nationwide advertising campaign. In 1900, some 6,000 new books were published. By the end of the 20th century, 60,000 books were published every year. Going into the next century, over 1,000,000 books (many were e-books) were published in 2011, and over 50,000 of those are published in the United States.

Life expectancy has increased by 30 years from 1900 statistics. A person born in 2012 can expect to live to at least 76 years old. Child mortality has fallen ten-fold. In 1900, families spent an average of 43 percent of their income on food; now they spend 15 percent.

Field-Marshal Horatio Herbert Kitchener, 1916 (PD).

The expansion of government was one of the 20th century's most striking developments. In 1900, the U.S. government took in just $567 million in taxes. In 1999, they took in $1.7 trillion. Government spending in the United States has steadily increased from 7 percent of GDP in 1902 to 40 percent today. President Clinton said in 1995 that the era of big government was over. But he was wrong. The post-World War II era has been a golden age of government spending, and it shows no sign of ending. Although spending dropped back to 21 percent of GDP immediately after WWII, it steadily climbed thereafter until it hit a peak of 36 percent of GDP in the bottom of the recession of 1980–82. Thereafter, government spending chugged along in the mid-30s until the mortgage meltdown of 2008. In the aftermath of bank and auto bailouts, government spending surged to wartime levels at 45 percent of GDP.

Another macabre revolution was people's ability to kill others. As early as 1900, British leader Horatio Kitchener came up with a new strategy in the Boer War in South Africa. He rounded up 75,000 people, mostly women and children, and confined them to prison camps where most quickly died. They were the first victims of one of the 20th century's most destructive inventions: the concentration camp. As we have seen in earlier chapters, it turns out that the world was pretty good at killing.

The turn of the century also introduced genocide. In 1904, in the German colony of South-West Africa, now Namibia, the Kaiser's troops systematically exterminated as many as 80,000 Herero. After poisoning the water holes, the Kaiser's troops drove the Herero into the desert, where they were bayoneted, shot, or starved. Those not killed — 20,000 Herero — were condemned to slavery on German farms and ranches.[2]

Discussion Question

The human capacity for mass killing increased exponentially as a result of improved weaponry and the increased power of the state. The marriage of nationalism and technology has been fatal for mankind. The 20th century introduced new concepts: gulags, concentration camps, secret police, terrorism, genocide, and war. Why?

Lesson 3

A Youth Revolution

In 1900, children and teenagers under the age of 16 accounted for 44 percent of the population. Today, the young make up 29 percent. However, that number, with its economic power and technological acumen, has far more clout than in any previous

---

2. http://www.usgovernmentspending.com/past_spending; http://www.digitalhistory.uh.edu/disp_textbook.cfm?smtID=2&psid=3176.

generation. In 1900, less than 2 percent of young people graduated from high school.[3] Seventy-one percent graduate from high school now.

The presence of youth culture is a relatively recent historical phenomenon. How did such a thing occur?

Sociologist James Coleman credits the emergence of **youth culture** to the beginning of compulsory schooling. He argues that age segregation is at the root of a separate youth culture. Before compulsory schooling, many children and adolescents interacted primarily with adults.[4] Public school created shared experiences and made possible a youth culture.

Modernization and universalistic norms have encouraged the growth of youth culture. The need for conformity, something that every industrial society values, has made it impractical for young people's socialization to come primarily from parents, which would lead to significant variation in the norms that are communicated. Each parental couple might teach different morals and ruin the norm. Therefore, modern America chose to educate its children by use of other children. They relied on significant professionals (adults) to train children to communicate society's norms and prepare them for adulthood. Youth culture was a byproduct of this tactic. Because children spent so much time together and learned the same things as the rest of their age group, they developed their own culture.

This process of enculturation did not happen quickly, so the youth epoch was elongated to include late puberty to almost the middle 20s. This delayed differentiation (breaking away) made inevitable the physical presence of youth in parental homes until they were married. This phenomenon had a profound effect on American society.

The growing youth culture, both in number and in influence, assured a growing influence on American life. Some scholars have studied the trends that accompany social unrest, and have suggested ties between youth and revolt. According to this theory, an especially large population of young people, especially males, is associated with social unrest, war, and terrorism. Many people are unable to find prestigious places in society, so they turn their attention to creating change in society.[5]

> Among the new words that entered the English language during the 20th century were "adolescence," "dating," and "teenager." For the first time there was a gap between puberty and incorporation into adult life. Before, there was no name for that stage of life. Someone was a child or an adult — nothing in between.

For many teens, texting has become a vital part of feeling connected to the broader world, often at the expense of those closest to them.

Discussion Question

Sociologist F. Fasick argues that youth culture is full of paradoxes. According to Fasick, adolescents face contradictory pulls from society. On the one hand, compulsory schooling keeps them socially and economically dependent on their parents. On the other hand, young people are encouraged to achieve some sort of independence in order to participate in the market economy of modern society.[6] What sorts of problems will this inevitably create?

3. http://www.digitalhistory.uh.edu/disp_textbook.cfm?smtID=2&psid=3176.
4. James Coleman, *The Adolescent Society* (Glencoe, IL: Free Press, 1961).
5. David S. Meyer, *The Politics of Protest: Social Movements in America* (New York: Oxford University Press, 2007).
6. Frank Fasick, "Parents, Peers, Youth Culture and Autonomy in Adolescence," *Adolescence* 1973 (1984): 143–157.

Prosperity

The Gross Domestic Product was almost seven times higher in 1999 than in 1900. Manufacturing wages, in today's dollars, climbed from $3.43 per hour in 1900 to $12.47 per hour in 1999. This did not include the growth in fringe benefits. Household assets — everything from the value of our homes to our personal possessions — were seven times greater. Meanwhile, home ownership increased by 43 percent. At the beginning of the century, 40 to 50 percent of all Americans had income levels that classified them as poor. At the end of the century, that figure was cut to between 10 and 15 percent. During the 20th century, household incomes of African Americans increased 1,000 percent. Although African Americans still earn less than whites today, the gap has decreased. In 1900, African Americans earned about 40 percent of what whites earn. Today, they earn roughly 80 percent of what whites earn.

The average length of the work week decreased by 30 percent, falling from 66 hours to 35 hours. With the introduction of more holidays and a shorter work week, the average number of hours worked in a year is half of what it was in the latter part of the 19th century. Meanwhile, the number of workers on the farm fell by 93 percent. Nevertheless, the percentage of holidays in 2012 barely equals the percentage of religious holidays that a medieval serf enjoyed in feudal Europe!

The percentage of households with electricity increased from 10 percent to near universal. At the same time, the average American in 1900 had to work six times as many hours to pay his electric bill as did an American a century later.[7]

Technology permeates every aspect of our lives now, often distracting us from the "real" world.

But there are storm clouds brewing. Rick Newmann, "4 Problems That Could Sink America," writes:

American innovation has solved daunting problems before and could again. But it would be a mistake to assume that American prosperity will continue on some preordained upward course. Nations rise and fall, often realizing what happened only in retrospect. Here are four problems that are undermining our future prosperity:

We don't like to work. Sure, now that jobs are scarce, everybody's willing to put in a few extra hours to stay ahead of the ax. But look around: We still expect easy money, hope to retire early. . . . Unfortunately, the rest of the world isn't sending as much money our way as it used to, which makes it harder to do less with more.

White-collar jobs are now migrating overseas just like blue-collar ones. Kids in Asia spend the summer studying math and science while American mall rats are texting each other about Britney and Miley. "We need a different mind-set," says [economist Mauro] Guillen. "People need to invest more in their own future. Instead of buying stuff at the mall, spend the money on evening classes. Learn a language or skills you don't have."

---

7. http://www.digitalhistory.uh.edu/disp_textbook.cfm?smtID=2&psid=3176.

I recently interviewed entrepreneur Gary Vaynerchuk, who transformed his father's neighborhood liquor store into a $60 million business anchored by the Web site winelibrarytv.com. An overnight success? Hardly. Vaynerchuk has big plans, and he works at least 16 hours a day to achieve them. "If you want to work eight hours a day," he says, "you're going to get eight-hour-a-day results. . . .

Nobody wants to sacrifice. Why should we? The government is standing by with stimulus money, banker bailouts, homeowner aid, cash for clunkers, expanded healthcare, and maybe more stimulus money. And most Americans will never have to pay an extra dime for any of this. Somehow, $9 trillion worth of government debt will just become somebody else's problem. . . .

We're uninformed. The healthcare smackdown — sorry, "debate" — is Exhibits A, B, and C. The soaring cost of healthcare is a problem that affects most Americans. It's shrinking paychecks, squeezing small businesses, bankrupting families and swelling the national debt. Yet outraged Americans seem most concerned about fictions like death panels and government-enforced euthanasia, while clinging to the myth that our current system of selective availability and perverse incentives somehow represents capitalist ideals. . . .

People who lack the sense to question Big Lies always end up in deep trouble. Being well informed takes work, even with the Internet. In a democracy, that's simply a civic burden. If we're too foolish or lazy to educate ourselves on healthcare, global warming, financial reform, and other complicated issues, then we're signing ourselves over to special interests who see nothing wrong with plundering our national — and personal — wealth.

i-culture. We may be chastened by the recession, but Americans still believe they deserve the best of everything — the best job, the best healthcare, the best education for our kids. And we want it at a discount — or better yet, free — which brings us back to the usual disconnect between what we want and what we're willing to pay for.

Rationing is a dirty word, so we can't have a system that officially rations something as vital as healthcare or education. Instead, we have unacknowledged, de facto rationing that directs the most resources to those with the best connections, the most money, or the savvy to game the system. What keeps the rest of us content is the illusion that we, too, will be able to game the system someday — as long as the government doesn't interfere.

Solutions that serve some public good — like Social Security and bank deposit insurance in the 1930s and Medicare in the 1960s — usually require everybody to give something to get something. If it works, the overall benefits outweigh the costs. Good programs leave individuals the option to pay more if they want more. Bad programs promise more than they can deliver. But often we don't know that until it's too late.[8]

4 Problems That Could Sink America:

1. We don't like to work

2. Nobody wants to sacrifice

3. We're uninformed

4. i-culture.

Discussion Question

What are the four problems that could sink America?

8. U.S. News and World Report, Sept. 2, 2009, http://money.usnews.com/money/blogs/
flowchart/2009/09/02/4-problems-that-could-sink-america.

Free at Last

Perhaps the greatest of all 20th-century revolutions was an expansion in human freedom and its extension to heretofore enslaved groups of people. Vast strides were made in civil rights and civil liberties.

Historian Steven Mintz writes, "European imperialism and colonial empires came to an end. In 1900, the British Empire contained roughly 400 million people, about a quarter of the world's population. Lesser empires, including the Austro-Hungarian, the Ottoman, and the French, ruled large parts of the globe. In the span of less than 20 years, Europe had partitioned nine-tenths of Africa. France ruled Southeast Asia. The Netherlands established rule in Indonesia and part of New Guinea. Japan established a colonial empire in Korea, Manchuria, Taiwan, and many Pacific Islands. Not to be left out, the United States acquired the Philippines, Guam, and Puerto Rico as a result of war with Spain, and also annexed Hawaii. At the start of the 21st century, 88 of the world's 191 countries were free. These countries are home to 2.4 billion people — about 40 percent of the total world population. These nations enjoy free elections and the rights of speech, religion, and assembly."[9]

Janitorial workers striking in front of the MTV building in Santa Monica, California. Striking in a trade union is a way of exercising freedom of assembly and freedom of association, 2008 (CCA-SA2.0).

The definition of freedom expanded in the 20th century. In the 19th century, freedom meant equal treatment before the law, freedom of worship, free elections, and economic opportunity. Twentieth-century reformers argued that freedom included government regulation, consumer protection, minimum wage, and social security — in short — the positive liberal state.

At the end of the century, a process of democratization took place on a global scale. "People power" led to the overthrow of totalitarian regimes all over the world!

There is still much work to be done in ecology. America remains a "throw-away" society that produces twice as much garbage as Europeans. With just 2 percent of the world's population, the United States uses 24 percent of the world's energy — twice as much as Japan and Western Europe. And the United States remains a growth-oriented society that continues to absorb millions of acres of cropland each year for highways, tract housing, and office buildings.[10]

Discussion Question

What evidences do historians offer that progress in human rights was made in the 20th century?

9. http://www.digitalhistory.uh.edu/disp_textbook.cfm?smtID=2&psid=3176.
10. http://www.digitalhistory.uh.edu/disp_textbook.cfm?smtID=2&psid=3350.

John Wayne & Marsha Hunt in
Born to the West, 1937 (PD).

Chapter 20

1960s:
The Death of Outrage

First Thoughts

In the sixties, the population of the United States was 177,830,000. Unemployment was 3,852,000. The national debt was $286.3 billion and the average salary was $4,743. The minimum wage was $1.00/hour. The life expectancy of males was 66.6 years, and of females 73.1 years. Auto deaths were 21.3 per 100,000. An estimated 850,000 "war baby" freshmen entered college, and emergency living quarters are set up in dorm lounges, hotels, and trailer camps.

The sixties were the age of youth, as 70 million children became teenagers. The movement away from the placid fifties resulted in real change in the cultural fabric of American life. No longer content to be mirror images of the generation ahead of them, young people wanted change. They demanded change. The changes affected education, morality, and entertainment. Many of the revolutionary ideas that began in the sixties are continuing to evolve today.[1]

Chapter Learning Objectives

The 1960s was a great time of change — but not all for the better. Not hardly! We will examine some of this change and assess its veracity and value. We will look at several reform movements and end with a discussion of the emerging hero archetype.

As a result of this chapter you should be able to:

1. Explain one sociological anomaly of the 1950s and 1960s

2. Discuss consumer protection and explain when it goes too far

3. Evaluate the reason the northern city was such a great disappointment to African Americans

4. Define "white guilt"

5. Understand the concept of "hero" and how it has changed

---

1. http://kclibrary.lonestar.edu/decade60.html.

Shadows in Paradise

During the 1950s and 1960s, America changed more than at any time in history, including the 1770–1790 (Revolution and Constitution) period. In the 1950s, Americans were in a mad rush away from the poverty of the Great Depression. They intended to enjoy to the fullest the new prosperity of modern America. Part of that enjoyment was focused on family life. World War II veterans intended to make up for lost time. Young women married earlier than had their mothers, had more children, and bore them faster. My father married my mother when he was barely 17! They had three children by the time he was 25 years old!

Democratic party poster 1952 for Adlai Stevenson (PD).

The average age of marriage for American women dropped to 20 years old, a record low. The fertility rate rose 50 percent between 1940 and 1950, producing a population growth rate approaching that of India. More babies, more money, and more products to buy, conspired to create an unprecedented social cornucopia of change.

During the sixties, college campuses became centers of debate and scenes of protest more than ever before. Course electives and massive enrollments precipitated by Pell Grants and other government financial aid gave aspiring college students impetus to take off from mediocre courses, and to express their social consciences.

In 1966, sociologist James S. Coleman published *Equality of Educational Opportunity*, a landmark study that led the way to forced integration and busing to public schools in the 1970s.[2]

Other ceilings were broken. For instance, my mother, the head of the history department at my local high school, was paid less than my father, a math teacher with less experience and responsibility, because she was a woman. In 1968, the federal government said this was illegal and my mom received equal pay. Also, in 1968, the first pregnant teacher was allowed to teach until her baby was born. However, in spite of gaining job skills and leverage in World War II, a growing number of women rejected higher education or a full-time career and instead preferred to be housewives and mothers. In many ways, the social gains women gained in the 1940s were willingly abandoned in the 1950s and 1960s.

A 1952 advertisement for Gimbel's department store expressed this prevailing point-of-view. "What's college?" the ad asked. "That's where girls who are above cooking and sewing go to meet a man so they can spend their lives cooking and sewing." According

---

2. http://kclibrary.lonestar.edu/decade60.html.

to *McCall's* magazine, young women believed that they could find their "deepest satisfaction" by "marrying at an earlier age, rearing larger families, and purchasing a house in the suburbs."

Politicians, educators, psychologists, and the mass media all echoed the view that women would find their highest fulfillment managing a house and caring for children. Adlai Stevenson, the Democratic presidential nominee in 1952 and 1956, told the graduating women at Smith College in 1955 that their role in life was to "influence us, men and boys" and "restore valid, meaningful purpose to life in [their] home." Many educators agreed with the president of Barnard College, who argued that women could not compete with men in the workplace because they "had less physical strength, a lower fatigue point, and a less stable nervous system." Women's magazines depicted housewives as happy with their tasks and career women as neurotic, unhappy, and dissatisfied.[3]

Discussion Question

What is at least one sociological anomaly of the 1950s and 1960s?

Ralph Nader and the Consumer Movement

In 1963, **Ralph Nader** hitchhiked from Hartford, Connecticut, where he had practiced law, to Washington, DC, to devote his life to consumer protection. Nader came to prominence in 1965 with his most famous book, *Unsafe at Any Speed*, a critique of the safety record of American automobile manufacturers in general, and most famously the Chevrolet Corvair. In *Unsafe at Any Speed*, a bestseller, he charged that automakers stressed styling, comfort, speed, power, and a desire to cut costs at the expense of safety. The book sold 60,000 copies in hardcover and 400,000 copies in paperback.[4]

During the 1960s and 1970s, Nader championed the passage of more than two dozen landmark consumer-protection laws, including the National Traffic and Motor Vehicle Safety Act (which set up a federal agency to establish auto-safety standards and order recalls of cars that failed to meet them), the Occupational Safety and Health Act (which established another agency to set standards for on-the-job safety), the Consumer Products Safety Act, and the Freedom of Information Act (which allows citizens to request and see government records). Perhaps no American had more impact on the future than quiet, humble Ralph Nader!

Ralph Nader, 1975 (LOC).

---

3. http://www.digitalhistory.uh.edu/disp_textbook.cfm?smtid=2&psid=3340.

4. David Bollier, *Citizen Action and Other Big Ideas, A History of Ralph Nader and the Modern Consumer Movement* (Washington, DC: Center for Study of Responsive Law, 1991).

The notion that the government should be involved in the safety of its citizens was a novel idea. Today, consumer protection consists of laws and organizations designed to ensure the rights of consumers as well as fair trade competition and the free flow of truthful information in the marketplace. Consumer protection laws are a form of government regulation aiming to protect the rights of consumers. For example, a government may require businesses to disclose detailed information about products — particularly in areas where safety or public health is an issue. Consumer protection has expanded to include many other areas, including ecological and health concerns.

Ralph Nader, and others, insisted upon a connection between consumer interests in the marketplace and increased, fair competition. To insist upon fair competition, Nader discovered, would, in the long run, benefit all Americans.

Historian David Bollier writes, "While Nader did not invent the idea of consumer advocacy, he and his associates did radically transform its meaning. Before Nader's appearance, 'consumerism' was often a trivialized concept that dealt with shopping for the best bargains and redeeming supermarket cents-off coupons; it did not put forth an analysis of corporate or governmental power. Nor did it constitute an independent 'countervailing force' to the enormous power wielded by business in the marketplace and government policymaking."[5]

Discussion Question

While consumer protection is a good idea, when could it go too far?

Lesson 3

The City: Broken Promises

Dr. Martin Luther King Jr. in 1963 (NARA).

At first, the northern city was a symbol of this hope. American northern cities stretched along a main street — there was no beginning or ending. With its myriad of possibilities, the city felt like it would be better than the rural South. The city, however, became a metaphor for what went wrong with race relations in America. In 1978, the *New York Times* stated what most African Americans already knew: "The places that experienced urban riots in the 1960s have, with a few exceptions, changed little, and the conditions of poverty have spread in most cities."[6]

African Americans moved to the urban setting only to find that the same problems existing in Mississippi existed in Detroit. This fact was not lost on African American leaders Martin Luther King Jr. and Malcolm X. They began their protest movements in the cities.

5. Ibid. chapter 1; http://www.nader.org/history/bollier_chapter_1.html.
6. John Herbers, "Decade After Kerner Report: Division of Races Persists," *New York Times*, February 26, 1978.

Slaves were brought to America primarily as agricultural workers in the country (the South) and as laborers and house servants in the cities (the North). After the American Revolution, the invention of the cotton gin increased the need for slaves. Before 1900, the African American urban population grew very slowly, if at all, as European immigrants filled the need for unskilled labor. In the urban setting, African Americans were in competition with immigrants for jobs and opportunities. This competition explained why there was often friction between African Americans and other urban immigrant groups for most of American history.

The life of antebellum African American urban freemen in the city presaged later urban experience. Unable to vote, segregated in all sectors of public life, urban African Americans had to look for their identity and well-being inside the African American community itself. Thus, vital strong communities arose in places like Harlem in New York City as a result of ghettoization.

"**Ghettoization**" was a term that arose in the 20th century to describe the systematic accumulation of poor Americans in certain sections of urban America. It normally was synonymous with poor housing and substandard living conditions. But it was much more. It was a breeding ground for crime, illegitimacy, and drug abuse. Ghettoization maintained de facto segregation in most cities. Housing in the city was centered around three issues: adequacy, distribution, and safety. On all three issues, ghetto housing came up short.

Within the ghetto some African Americans forged strong community ties and nurtured cultural specialties. But, as we shall see, ghettoization overall had a devastating effect on most black Americans.

There was no uniform way that African American ghettos grew in the North. For instance, whereas the flat terrain of most northern cities concentrated African Americans into one or two large, homogeneous communities, Pittsburgh's hilly topography isolated them into six or seven communities. In Washington, DC, the African American community concentrated in adjacent alleys. And so forth. In general, African Americans lived mainly in tenements and alley dwellings that they did not own. When they immigrated from the South, they naturally settled into neighborhoods where other African Americans lived since many family members were part of these urban communities. If they did own a home, economic circumstances normally forced them to take in boarders. They clustered, too, in the city's lowest-paying, least-skilled occupations. Unlike their immigrant counterparts, they really could not live anywhere or work anywhere they wanted. African Americans were barred from the city's economic mainstream and entered local industry only after the First World War. Many African Americans were not even allowed to vote until after the Civil War.

Race relations in the city and country were framed by white supremacy. Social relations of slavery gave way to an informal code of exclusion and discrimination, which in turn evolved into legally mandated separation and disenfranchisement. The essence of African American life was pervasive powerlessness. There was an irony of accommodative resistance — the implications of compromises necessary to build institutions and to occupy anomalous roles — that touched every African American life. They occupied a peculiar place in the South and their acceptance of that place determined their survival. Every black American knew that this was true in the white South; what they did not anticipate was that racism also had a nefarious hold over the

Roughly, it was in the period from 1870 to 1915 that most African American ghettos were formed in the United States. From 1915 to the present these ghettos were expanded. Housing patterns, like all other parts of the African American experience, were framed by racism.

Chicago ghetto on the south side. Although the percentage of Chicago blacks making $7,000 or more jumped from 26 to 58 percent between 1960 and 1970, a large percentage still remained unemployed. The black unemployment rate generally is assumed to be twice that of the national unemployment rate published monthly by the Bureau of Labor statistics (NARA).

Ku Klux Klan at a camp, 1925 (LOC).

white North. Whether in the southern countryside or the southern city — or in the northern city — racism remained an inescapable demon.

Ghettoization enhanced control. African Americans were contained and controlled in the ghetto. Control became more difficult in the northern city in the mid-20th century. As television programs like *Leave It to Beaver* and *Ozzie and Harriet* teased destitute ghetto dwellers, it became increasingly difficult for control to be maintained. Mass produced and affordable televisions made isolation virtually impossible. Television, too, contributed to increased violence in the African American ghetto.

Once they arrived in northern cities, African American newcomers reveled in newfound freedom. But they soon were absorbed into a deadly paradox: they could sit anywhere they wished on the trolley, but their children had to attend separate schools. In most cities they could vote, but there were no African American candidates. They were accepted by relatives, but often rejected by other indigenous African Americans and nearly always rejected by other immigrant groups. Education was better; housing was better; jobs were better. But the dream was compromised by hostility and prejudice. And by the middle 1960s, the dream had soured all together.

And the Klan was present in the North, too. For instance, Robert and Helen Lynd's seminal social history study of Middletown, New York, showed that with the rise of the Klan in the 1920s, with the increase of ethnic and racial migration, racism was very much present. "Negroes are allowed under protest in the schools but not in the larger motion picture houses or in Y.M.C.A. or Y.W.C.A. . . . Negro children must play in their own restricted corner of the Park."[7] In the local newspaper, Middletown black news was featured separate from Middletown white news. Clearly northern urban society saw two Americas emerging as surely as two had existed in the southern agrarian society. White privilege in the North was as strong as it was in the South.

Racism mitigated any economic gains that were available everywhere in the capitalistic society arising in most cities. If an African American migrant was fortunate enough to possess a skilled trade and could gain entrance to the union controlling the craft — which was doubtful — then he might prosper. But even the adequately compensated artisan or industrial worker had to return each night to live in the least desirable section of the city. Gains in industry by African Americans in World War I and in the twenties were substantial, but after World War I, and during the Great Depression, African Americans were the first ones to be let go.

African Americans, in another way, were out of step with other labor developments. For instance, while other northern workers were shifting from manual to non-manual employment, from blue-collar to white-collar work, African Americans did not share in much of this upward mobility. The number of African Americans in white-collar jobs was 2.8 percent in 1910, 3.8 percent in 1920, and by 1930, 4.6 percent. In fact, by 1930, over two-thirds of the African American population was still working in unskilled jobs.[8] There was no other ethnic group in such a position. As the African American community braced for the Great Depression, it found itself in a particularly vulnerable position.

---

7. Robert Staughton Lynd and Helen Merrell Lynd, *Middletown: A Study in Modern American Culture* (New York: Harcourt, Brace, and Company, 1929), p. 479.

8. www.census.gov

Did African Americans form a class identity? In other words, did African Americans grow angry with American society because they were poor or because they are black? African Americans have never formed a class identity. In the 1920s, in places like Chicago, white labor was still controlled by ethnic groups, and even though ethnicity was being challenged by mass culture, African Americans remained isolated from the normal forces of class formation — industrialization and labor — because of racism. In fact, the only institutions that thrived in the African American community were the segregated ones (like the Church).

African Americans were not just another ethnic group. No urban ethnic group experienced the frequency and severity of prejudice that African Americans knew. Ethnic groups could climb the socio-economic American ladder — not so for many African Americans, or, at least it was more difficult because of racism. For no other group in America was residential segregation increased so uniformly.

Race and racial discrimination were a ubiquitous reality for blacks throughout their American experience. Whether it was 1767 Philadelphia, 1876 Atlanta, 1890 Detroit, 1920 Chicago, or 1950 Cleveland, the urban African American experience was structured by discrimination, unequal competition, and a lack of political rights. All advances in standard of living, housing, and political power were inevitably mitigated by racism.

Empty housing in the ghetto on Chicago's south side with structures that have been systematically vacated as a result of fires, vandalism, or failure by owners to provide basic tenant services. Then the vacated buildings, often substantially salvageable, are razed and replaced with highrise apartments, which appeal to few members of the black community and almost none of the area's previous residents (NARA).

The city taught African Americans an unforgettable lesson: racial discrimination could never be escaped. This was a bitter pill for the African American community to swallow.

Human depravation experienced by African American immigrants was similar to that experienced by other immigrants. Both groups initially were at the bottom of the social, economic, and political ladder. Both experienced persecution from a dominant indigenous group. Both were exploited badly by an industrial middle class. But one key difference separated them: race. The white immigrant within one generation could lose his accent, put aside his Old World folkways, and become a white American. For African Americans, however, there was no hope that racism would ever be overcome.

The quality of life of African Americans in northern cities declined steadily from 1900 to the present. Decline was measured by increased racial violence, increased residential segregation, inevitable unemployment at the slightest rumor of a recession, and home ownership. Ethnic immigrants often owned their homes; African Americans rarely did.

Group solidarity changed from a decidedly ethnic flavor to class allegiance among most ethnic groups. No such class allegiance developed among black people. Racism was the great equalizer in the black community and forbade class formation: factory workers and medical doctors both lived in the ghetto. Blacks were unable to gain the employment and housing identities necessary for class formation. Also, in Chicago, frozen out of the trade unions until after the 1930s, African Americans generally were unwelcome in the predominantly white working class and practically totally absent from middle management. In fact, many white industrialists imported white southerners to be shop foremen in northern factories.

African Americans continued to face important legal barriers to equality: their voting rights were obstructed even after they were legally granted the right to vote! They were

215

not allowed to serve on juries until the middle of the 19th century or in state militias until the late 19th century. They were segregated in public places until civil rights legislation in the mid 1960s. In most states they were forbidden to marry whites until the early 20th century. And, finally, African Americans were targets of urban violence from the beginning of the Great Migration.

Violence, too, was once more a part of northern urban life. The first examples of racial urban violence were inflicted by whites against blacks — not blacks against white. Competition between African Americans and whites often erupted into deadly violence. Large-scale riots occurred in Chicago, Washington, DC, Omaha, and other cities from 1919 to 1920. Housing and job shortages in the post-war North sparked several riots. A wave of labor strikes also fueled racial antagonisms. African Americans found themselves in the middle between labor and management. Thus, many African Americans crossed the picket lines in a 1919 labor strike at great peril. Courted by employers and at the same time intimidated by unions who had never treated them well, African Americans were in an increasingly isolated position.

For the first time, in the wake of civil rights legislation in the 1970s, the number of African Americans residing in the suburbs increased by another 43 percent. At the same time the proportion of whites living in the suburbs rose by 13 percent. Approximately 23.3 percent of the suburban population in 1980 was black. It must, however, be emphasized that while some blacks were living in the middle-class integrated suburbs, twice as many blacks as whites lived in the low-income inner suburbs close to central cities. This did not in itself represent the opening of white suburbs to African American families. More typically, it represented African American families moving from the central cities into outlying areas, which already contained small African American enclaves. And, in any event, a 1990 poll revealed that two-thirds of upper-middle class, primarily suburban blacks interviewed complained of persistent discrimination.

A scene from the play *A Raisin in the Sun*, 1959 (PD).

Lorraine Hansberry's play *A Raisin in the Sun* (1959) addresses the complex issues of segregated housing, work opportunities, and education for blacks. It is a play about a black family living in post-World War II south-side Chicago struggling with day-to-day survival. But they are sustained by a dream: moving to the suburbs. The family inherits $10,000 from an insurance policy and it appears that their dreams will come true. But a visit from a representative of a white homeowners' association bursts their bubble. To keep this black family from moving into his predominantly white neighborhood, the white owner offers to buy them out. While the family ultimately rejects the offer, this play illustrates the pressure and disappointments that urban African Americans face as they pursue the American dream.

What black Americans learned again was that resistance — not paternalism, not accommodation, not compromise — worked in American society.

Black authors of the period knew that the dream was souring. Jean Toomer's novel *Cane* explored the ugliness of race relations in the South as well as the impact of the city on African American lives. Toomer rejected any concept of a "promised land." Langston Hughes's poetry reflected the ambivalence African Americans felt toward the Great Migration. In "Elevator Boy" he wrote:

I got a job now
Running an elevator
In the Dennison Hotel in Jersey,
Job ain't no good though,
No money around.[9]

William Attaway's novel *Blood on the Forge* (1941) criticized those who see factory work as glamorous. On the contrary, he argued, black migrants were exchanging familiar southern violence for the strange and savage violence of the northern factories. But the most critical examination of migration is Richard Wright's *Native Son* (1941). The tragedy that befell the protagonist, Bigger Thomas, has much to do with his disappointment with the fact that northern urban life was no better than southern agricultural life.

The northern, white-dominated city has not been kind to African Americans. This fact was not lost on their children — the generation who marched in Selma and burned the Watts section of Los Angeles. They formed the black nationalist movement — characterized by an emphasis on separatism and cultural exclusivity. What black Americans learned again was that resistance — not paternalism, not accommodation, not compromise — worked in American society. Black author Ralph Ellison's grandfather, on his death bed, admonished young Ralph: "Our life is a war . . . we are spies in the enemy's camp . . . learn it to the younguns."[10]

By the mid 1960s, black nationalism, a primarily urban phenomenon, had captured much of the African American agenda. In fact, **black nationalism** — a celebration of African American culture as a separate entity — remains a powerful force in American culture.

Discussion Question

In spite of great economic opportunity, why was the northern city a great disappointment to African Americans?

A Book Review

Shelby Steele, *White Guilt*

Reviewed by Harper Collins Press

In 1955, the murderers of Emmett Till, a black Mississippi youth, were acquitted of their crime, undoubtedly because they were white. Forty years later, O.J. Simpson, whom

9. http://prezi.com/n0moq85n4zax/elevator-boy-by-langston-hughes/.
10. Ralph Ellison, *Invisible Man*, "Battle Royal" (New York: Random House, 1952).

Little Rock, 1959. Rally at state capitol, protesting the integration of Central High School. Protesters carry US flags and signs reading "Race Mixing is Communism" and "Stop the Race Mixing March of the Anti-Christ" (LOC).

many thought would be charged with murder by virtue of the DNA evidence against him, went free after his attorney portrayed him as a victim of racism. Clearly, a sea change had taken place in American culture, but how had it happened? In this important new work, distinguished race relations scholar Shelby Steele argues that the age of white supremacy has given way to an age of white guilt — and neither has been good for African Americans.

As the civil rights victories of the 1960s dealt a blow to racial discrimination, American institutions started acknowledging their injustices, and white Americans — who held the power in those institutions — began to lose their moral authority. Since then, our governments and universities, eager to reclaim legitimacy and avoid charges of racism, have made a show of taking responsibility for the problems of black Americans. In doing so, Steele asserts, they have only further exploited blacks, viewing them always as victims, never as equals. This phenomenon, which he calls white guilt, is a way for whites to keep up appearances, to feel righteous, and to acquire an easy moral authority — all without addressing the real underlying problems of African Americans. Steele argues that calls for diversity and programs of affirmative action serve only to stigmatize minorities, portraying them not as capable individuals but as people defined by their membership in a group for which exceptions must be made.

Through his articulate analysis and engrossing recollections of the last half-century of American race relations, Steele calls for a new culture of personal responsibility, a commitment to principles that can fill the moral void created by white guilt. White leaders must stop using minorities as a means to establish their moral authority — and black leaders must stop indulging them. As White Guilt eloquently concludes, the alternative is a dangerous ethical relativism that extends beyond race relations into all parts of American life.[11]

Discussion Question

How does Shelby Steele define "white guilt"?

Lesson 5

The Death of the Heroes

The relatively young medium, Saturday-morning television, maintained 1940s heroes through the 1960s.

The 1960s had strange heroes, ranging from Marx, Lenin, Ho, and Mao to Fidel, Che, and other revolutionaries. It also had its own uniforms, rituals, and music. Faded-blue work shirts and jeans, wire-rimmed glasses, and Converse tennis shoes were the required wardrobe of the counterculture.

11. A review of *White Guilt: How Blacks and Whites Together Destroyed the Promise of the Civil Rights Era* (New York: HarperCollins Publishers, 2006); http://books.google.com/books/about/White_guilt.html?id=KUDIisq-KksC.

For years, the American notion of a hero has been accosted, compromised, and generally diluted. Gone were the days when John Wayne rode into town and took care of business. Americans knew he was good — really good — and we were comforted by the fact that he would kill no one who did not deserve to die. "A man's got to do what a man's got to do," is a quote attributed to Wayne. "Women have the right to work wherever they want, as long as they have the dinner ready when you get home." Oops! I guess he said that, too, but never mind. . . .

Not so today. Heroes exude empathy, not goodness. Witness Robert Downey's flawed, self-centered Ironman. Or Hugh Jackson's moody Wolverine. And who can forget the poor, pathetic Hulk? Everyone wants to forget the shady, morally dubious Christian Bale's Batman! But my personal favorite for sissy of the year is the 1960s creation Spiderman. One Freudian self-identity crisis after another. He whines all the time. Can you imagine John Wayne whining?

Clayton Moore as the Lone Ranger, and Silver, his horse 1965 (PD).

Still, there were exceptions in the 1960s, like Captain America. Captain America was a different kind of hero. In 1940s America, ordinary, unspectacular, five-feet-something Steve Rogers inadvertently receives an injection that turns him into a superhero. But not a run-of-the-mill hero, he is a genuine hero. As one reviewer explains, "He's got a lot of ailments, but it hasn't made him bitter or jaded in anything. Even after he has been given his great gift, he still continues to do the right thing."[12] Now that is a novel idea — doing the right thing. Take that, Will Smith and your character Hancock!

Yes, a new hero has arrived — a hero who does the right thing without equivocation or self-interest. Captain America. Or is he that new after all?

Sounds to me like Moses, who left the courts of Egypt to obey God. Or Joshua, who conquered the Promised Land. Or Peter, who, even after much failure, found that even hell itself could not prevail against the Church he founded.

Saturday-morning television in the 1960s was full of benefice and omnificence. My brothers Bill and John Hugh and I looked forward to it all week. First came *My Friend Flicka*, snickering and shaking his head on the screen. What a great horse! They don't make them like that anymore. This was not an anthropomorphic George Lucas War Horse or a choleric Black Beauty. No, this was intrepid but loyal Flicka. What a sensitive horse. He really took care of his boy. We wanted a horse like that. Craig Towles had a horse of sorts — Potato — but he was mean and ugly. Little Ken McLaughlin loved Flicka, and Flicka loved Ken. And we loved them both. And they lived happily on Goose Bar Ranch — not a lot like 407 Pine Street but, hey, one can pretend! Remember? And then Roy Rogers. Man I'm still looking for those pants he wore. Sears and Roebuck and Ross has nothing like those things. I think they would look good on my 58-year-old body. Might help a little. Divert attention from the tummy shelf I so carefully placed above my belt buckle. Next, Hi-yo, Silver, away the adventures of the masked hero and his Indian — ugh, excuse me — his Native American sidekick. With his faithful Indian (Native American) companion, Tonto, the daring and resourceful masked rider of the plains led the fight for law and order in the early West. Return with us now to those thrilling days of yesteryear. The Lone Ranger rides again! After the Lone Ranger it was time for a little serious drama — Johnny Quest. *The Adventures of Johnny Quest* featured

---

12. http://usatoday30.usatoday.com/LIFE/usaedition/2011-03-25-captain25_ST_U.htm.

Pal, the original "Lassie" in 1942 (PD).

teenage adventurers Jonny Quest, Hadji Singh, and Jessie Bannon as they accompanied Dr. Benton Quest and bodyguard Race Bannon to investigate strange things, legends, and mysteries in exotic locales. We could only imagine that the Johnny Quest world was somewhere beyond Texarkana, Arkansas — this was as far as we had ever been in our young lives. We hoped to go there someday with a friend as good as Hadji. Johnny had a dog (aka Bandit), too. Even before the '60s began, we were captivated by Flash Gordon — Luke Skywalker could learn a little bit about courage and fortitude from Flash. No whining on his show. And Flash Gordon never had an identity crisis like wimpy Luke.

Finally, we would end our rich repertoire with Lassie. What a dog! No matter what dog we owned, we all pretended we had a female Collie named Lassie. Didn't we? The Lassie classic echoed each Saturday morning through my sizzling, flickering, black and white 22-inch Philco:

> I learned a secret that I will share with you.
> In the hush, I heard the whippoorwills reveal
> The Secret of the Silent Hills.
> Not a secret men scheme and plot for,
> Only true words, we should not forget.
> "Love can cure the world of all its ills."
> And that's the Secret of the Silent Hills.[13]

And for about half a day we would sit in front of our Philco, eat our Frosty Flakes, Little Bill, and John Hugh, and I, and enjoy the safe, child-friendly, media world of Saturday-morning television. We were not too young to know that the Russians might blow us up next Monday morning or that Ricky Mays might fall asleep in church tomorrow, but today, well, today was Saturday morning. And all was right with the world. It didn't get much better than that. Happy Saturday morning!

Family watching television, 1958 (NARA).

Theologian Walter Brueggemann, in his seminal work called *The Land*, argues that, like the wandering Israelites of old, Americans are searching for a "Promised Land."[14] A place of succor, of safety, of love, and of life. Saturday morning, in a caricatured way, in a small way, made the same promises to John Hugh, to Little Bill, and to me. We found, on the little black and white, a place of hope, of continuity, of wholesomeness.

Hi-yo, Silver, away!

Discussion Question

Why did Saturday-morning television maintain heroes who were different from those in theaters?

---

13. http://www.allthelyrics.com/lyrics/televisiontv_theme_lyrics_kids_shows_soundtrack/lassie_the_secret_of_the_silent_hills-lyrics.

14. Walter Brueggemann, *The Land: Place as Gift, Promise, and Challenge in Biblical Faith* (Minneapolis, MN: Fortress Press, 2002).

President Barack Obama signs legislation in the Oval Office, Dec. 22, 2010 (PD).

Chapter 21

American Government: A Balance of Power

First Thoughts

"Government is not reason, nor eloquence. It is force. And like fire, it is a dangerous servant and a fearsome master."[1] — George Washington. The federal government of the United States is the government of the constitutional republic of 50 states and one district that is the United States of America. The federal government comprises three distinct branches of government: a legislative, an executive, and a judiciary branch. These branches and their various powers are delineated in the U.S. Constitution. Perhaps no government created by man is better than the United States government.

Chapter Learning Objectives

We will examine the United States government in greater depth. We will see how the executive, legislative, and judicial branches, applying balance-of-power principles, move the governing process of our government forward.

As a result of this chapter you should be able to:

1. Comprehend the difference between the state and the state's government

2. Identify the types of governments in several nations

3. Understand different principles of government

4. Analyze the legislative branch

5. Evaluate the judiciary

CONCEPTS

Executive Branch

Legislative Branch

Judicial Branch

1. http://usgovinfo.about.com/blquotes2.htm.

General Government

Government refers to the way people arbitrate, control, and live their lives. Government is the way that policy is created and then enforced.

A form of government, or form of state governance, refers to the set of political institutions by which a government of a state is organized. For instance, a totalitarian regime (regime is a word for government) will rule by one tertiary, single leader. A representative democracy rules through elected officials. A monarchy rules through a king or queen.

Each government has a ritual or system to make decisions. In the United States, we rule at the federal, state, and local level. Each, more or less, has an executive, legislative, or judicial branch. In parliamentary systems, the word "government" is used to refer to what in presidential systems would be the executive branch. In parliamentary systems, the government is composed of the prime minister and the cabinet. In other cases, "government" refers to executive, legislative, judicial, bureaucratic, and possibly also devolved powers. All governments rule, legislate, and arbitrate.

In most Western societies, there is a clear distinction between a government and the state. Public disapproval of a particular government (expressed, for example, by not re-electing an incumbent) does not necessarily represent disapproval of the state itself (i.e., of the particular framework of government). When Americans did not re-elect Jimmy Carter, they did not necessarily reject the American government or state. Often the state is sustained by a written constitution or common law. However, in some totalitarian regimes, there is not a clear distinction between the regime and the state. In fact, dictators Adolf Hitler, Benito Mussolini, and Josef Stalin deliberately blurred the lines between the two in order to connect their interests with those of the state. Thus, German, Italian, and Soviet citizens were made to understand that if they rejected Hitler, Mussolini, or Stalin, they were rejecting the state itself.

Benito Mussolini and Adolf Hitler stand together during Mussolini's official visit in Munich in 1937 (PD).

Another complication is that a huge number of political systems originate as socio-economic movements (e.g., communism, socialists) and are then carried into governments by specific parties naming those movements after themselves. Experience with those movements in power, and the strong ties they may have to particular forms of government, can cause them to be considered forms of government in themselves. Inevitably, as is the case with communism, these socio-economic movements evolve into totalitarian regimes.

Discussion Question

Why in certain governments do the definitions of government and state become blurred?

Terms — Forms of Government

Authoritarian — Characterized by an emphasis on the authority of the state in a republic or union. It is a political system controlled by unelected rulers who usually permit some degree of individual freedom.

Anarchy — Sometimes said to be non-governance; it is a structure that strives for non-hierarchical voluntary associations among agents.

Chiefdom — Government based on small complex society of varying degrees of centralization that is led by an individual known as a chief.

Constitutional monarchy — Government that has a monarch, but one whose powers are limited by law or by a formal constitution, such as Great Britain.

Constitutional republic — Government whose powers are limited by law or a formal constitution, and chosen by a vote among at least some sections of the populace. (Ancient Sparta was in its own terms a republic, though most inhabitants were disenfranchised. The early United States was a republic, but large numbers of African Americans and women did not have the vote.) Republics which exclude sections of the populace from participation will typically claim to represent all citizens (by defining people without the vote as "non-citizens").

Democracy — Rule by a government chosen by election where most of the populace are enfranchised. The key distinction between a democracy and other forms of constitutional government is that the right to vote is not limited by a person's wealth or race (the main qualification for enfranchisement is generally having reached a certain age). A Democratic government is, therefore, one supported (at least at the time of the election) by a majority of the populace (provided the election was held fairly). A "majority" may be defined in different ways. There are many "power-sharing" (usually in countries where people mainly identify themselves by race or religion) or "electoral-college" or "constituency" systems where the government is not chosen by a simple one-vote-per-person headcount.

Dictatorship — Rule by an individual who has full power over the country. The term may refer to a system where the dictator came to power, and holds it, purely by force — but it also includes systems where the dictator first came to power legitimately but then was able to amend the constitution so as to, in effect, gather all power for themself.

Emirate — Similar to a monarchy or sultanate, but a government in which the supreme power is in the hands of an emir (the ruler of a Muslim state); the emir may be an absolute overlord or a sovereign with constitutionally limited authority.

Oligarchy — Rule by a small group of people who share similar interests or family relations. Sparta was ruled by an oligarchy.

Republic — A form of government in which the people, or some significant portion of them, have supreme control over the government and where offices of state are elected or chosen by elected people.

Theocracy — Rule by a religious elite or by God Himself. Israel in its early history was a theocracy.

Tribe — Government based on a small (usually family) unit with a semi-informal hierarchy, with strongest (either physical strength or strength of character) as leader. Very much like a pack seen in other animals, such as wolves.[2]

Discussion Question

Identify the types of governments of these nations:

    China
    Russia
    USA
    Vatican
    England
    France

Lesson 3

Executive Branch

The power of the executive branch is vested in the president of the United States, who also acts as head of state and commander-in-chief of the armed forces. This is important. No matter what his original vocation, the president of the United States is a civilian. A civilian — not a military man — controls the military.

The president is responsible for implementing and enforcing the laws written by Congress and, to that end, appoints the heads of the federal agencies, including the cabinet. The vice president is also part of the executive branch, ready to assume the presidency should the president become incapacitated.

The executive branch does not make the laws; it enforces the laws. This is part of the balance of power principle. The balance of power principle, in our Constitution, makes sure that power is spread between several entities so that no one entity will becomes too powerful. The cabinet and independent federal agencies are responsible for the day-to-day enforcement and administration of federal laws.

Seal of the President of the United States (PD).

Including members of the armed forces, the executive branch employs more than four million Americans.

2. *Oxford English Dictionary*, Oxford University Press, online edition, November 2010; Frank Bealey, ed., "Government," *The Blackwell Dictionary of Political Science: A User's Guide to Its Terms* (Cambridge, UK; Malden, MA: Wiley-Blackwell, 1999), p. 147; Peter Flint et al., *Political Geography: World Economy, Nation-State, and Locality*, 5th ed. (Harlow, England; New York: Pearson/Prentice Hall, 1999), p. 137.

Under Article II of the Constitution, the president is responsible for the implementation and enforcement of the laws created by Congress. Fifteen executive departments — each led by an appointed member of the president's Cabinet — carry out the daily work of the federal government.

The president has the power either to sign legislation into law or to veto bills enacted by Congress, although Congress may override a veto with a two-thirds vote of both houses. The president may not introduce legislation or laws. He/she can only enforce them.

The executive branch conducts diplomacy with other nations, and the president has the power to negotiate and sign treaties, which also must be ratified by two-thirds of the Senate. The president can issue executive orders, which direct executive officers or clarify and further existing laws. The president also has unlimited power to extend pardons and clemencies for federal crimes, except in cases of impeachment.

The Oval Office in 1981, during the first year of Ronald Reagan's Presidency. The seat is the one that Reagan used as governor of California. The desk is the Resolute Desk (PD).

The Constitution lists only three qualifications for the presidency — the president must be 35 years of age, must be a natural-born citizen, and must have lived in the United States for at least 14 years. And though millions of Americans vote in a presidential election every four years, the president is not, in fact, directly elected by the people. Instead, on the first Tuesday in November of every fourth year, the people elect the members of the Electoral College. Apportioned by population to the 50 states — one for each member of their congressional delegation (with the District of Columbia receiving 3 votes) — these electors then cast the votes for president. There are currently 538 electors in the Electoral College.[3]

Discussion Question

Federal and state officials combine efforts to fund education. Which of these statements is supported by this information?

    A. Education is mainly a responsibility of private organizations
    B. Education by the state takes priority over federal regulations
    C. The federal government shares responsibility with the states for education

South façade of the White House, the executive mansion of the President of the United States, located at 1600 Pennsylvania Avenue in Washington, D.C. (CCA-SA3.0).

The Legislative Branch

Established by Article I of the Constitution, the legislative branch consists of the House of Representatives and the Senate, which together form the United States Congress. The Constitution grants Congress the sole authority to enact laws and declare war, and the right to confirm or reject many presidential appointments. It is the president's job to carry out the laws; it is the job of Congress to write the laws.

President Barack Obama speaks to a joint session of Congress 2009 (PD).

The House of Representatives is made up of 435 elected members, divided among the 50 states in proportion to their total population. In addition, there are six non-voting members, representing the District of Columbia, Puerto Rico, and four other territories (not states) of the United States. The presiding officer of the chamber is the Speaker of the House, elected by the representatives. He/she is third in the line of succession to the presidency.

Members of the House are elected every two years and must be 25 years of age, a U.S. citizen for at least seven years, and a resident of the state (but not necessarily the district) they represent.

The House initiates revenue bills, impeaches federal officials, and elects the president in the case of an Electoral College tie.

The Senate is composed of 100 senators, two for each state. Until the ratification of the 17th Amendment in 1913, senators were chosen by state legislatures, not by popular vote. Since then, they have been elected to six-year terms by the people of each state. Senators' terms are staggered so that about one-third of the Senate is up for reelection every two years. That leaves two-thirds veteran senators. Senators must be 30 years of age, U.S. citizens for at least nine years, and residents of the state they represent.

The Senate has the sole power to confirm the president's appointments that require consent, and the Senate ratifies treaties. There are, however, two exceptions to this rule: the House must also approve appointments to the vice presidency and any treaty that involves foreign trade. The Senate also tries impeachment cases for federal officials referred to it by the House. For example, the House of Representatives voted to impeach President Clinton. It was sent to the Senate, but President Clinton was not convicted.

A class photo of the 111th United States Senate, 2010 (PD).

In order to pass legislation and send it to the president for his signature, both the House and the Senate must pass the same bill by majority vote. If the president vetoes a bill, they may override his veto by passing the bill again in each chamber with at least two-thirds of each body voting in favor.

In summary, Congress, as one of the three coequal branches of government, is granted significant powers by the Constitution. All legislative power in the government is vested in Congress, meaning that it is the only part of the government that can make new laws or change existing laws. Executive branch agencies issue regulations with the full force of law, but these are only under the authority of laws enacted by Congress. The president may veto bills Congress passes, but Congress may also override a veto by a two-thirds vote in both the Senate and the House of Representatives.[4]

Discussion Question

President Nixon wanted to continue the war in Vietnam but Congress stopped him. How?

Lesson 5

The Judiciary

The Supreme Court is appointed, not elected. Where the executive and legislative branches are elected by the people, members of the judicial branch are appointed by the president and confirmed by the Senate.

Article III of the Constitution, which establishes the judicial branch, leaves Congress significant discretion to determine the shape and structure of the federal judiciary. Even the number of Supreme Court justices is left to Congress — at times there have been as few as six, while the current number (nine, with one chief justice and eight associate justices) has only been in place since 1869. The Constitution also grants Congress the power to establish courts inferior to the Supreme Court, and to that end Congress has established the United States district courts, which try most federal cases, and 13 United States courts of appeals, which review appealed district court cases. So, indirectly, Congress has immense power over the judiciary.

But so does the president. Only the president can nominate federal judges. They have to be approved by the Congress and often are not. Federal judges can only be removed through impeachment by the House of Representatives and conviction in the Senate. Judges and justices serve no fixed term — they serve until their death, retirement, or conviction by the Senate. By design, this insulates them from politics, and allows them to apply the law with only justice in mind, and not electoral or political concerns.

The courts only try actual cases and controversies — a party must show that it has been harmed in order to bring suit in court. This means that the courts do not issue advisory opinions on the constitutionality of laws or the legality of actions if the ruling would have no practical effect. Cases brought before the judiciary typically proceed from

SCOTUS building as seen from the west side of 1st St NE. (CCA-SA3.0).

4. http://www.whitehouse.gov/our-government/legislative-branch.

The United States Supreme Court, the highest court in the United States, in 2010 (PD).

district court to appellate court and may even end at the Supreme Court, although the Supreme Court hears comparatively few cases each year.

Using judicial review, federal courts enjoy the sole power to interpret the law, determine the constitutionality of the law, and apply it to individual cases. For instance, the Supreme Court, in *Roe vs. Wade*, ruled that anti-abortion legislation was unconstitutional.

The courts, like Congress, can compel the production of evidence and testimony through the use of a subpoena. The inferior courts are constrained by the decisions of the Supreme Court — once the Supreme Court interprets a law, inferior courts must apply the Supreme Court's interpretation to the facts of a particular case. Although the Supreme Court may hear an appeal on any question of law, provided it has jurisdiction, it usually does not hold trials. Instead, the Court's task is to interpret the meaning of a law to decide whether (or not) a law is relevant to a particular set of facts, or to rule on how a law should be applied. Lower courts are obligated to follow the precedent set by the Supreme Court when rendering decisions.

Article III of the Constitution of the United States guarantees that every person accused of wrongdoing has the right to a fair trial before a competent judge and a jury of one's peers. The Fourth, Fifth, and Sixth Amendments to the Constitution provide additional protections. These include:

- A guarantee that no person shall be deprived of life, liberty, or property without the due process of law

- Protection against being tried for the same crime twice ("double jeopardy")

- Protection from excessive bail, excessive fines, and cruel and unusual punishments

- The right to a speedy trial by an impartial jury

- The right to cross-examine witnesses, and to call witnesses to support their case

- The right to legal representation

- The right to avoid self-incrimination

After a criminal or civil case is tried, it may be appealed to a higher court, all the way to the Supreme Court.[5]

Discussion Question

The Supreme Court ruled that the Virginia Military Institute (VMI), an all-male college, had to admit women who meet their admission requirements. How did this ruling show that a public institution had discriminated against American citizens?

---

5. http://www.whitehouse.gov/our-government/judicial-branch.

Buzz Aldrin walks on the moon, July 20, 1969 (NASA).

Chapter 22

Space Program: One Giant Leap for Mankind

First Thoughts

The space race was a mid-to-late 20th-century competition between Communist Soviet Union and the democratic United States for supremacy in outer space exploration. It was part of the larger Cold War. The race was both ideological and technological, and it involved pioneering efforts to launch satellites, ballistic missiles, human spaceflight around the earth, and piloted voyages to the moon. The space race sparked unprecedented advances in science. An unintended consequence was that the space race became partially responsible for the birth of the environmental movement. For the first time, access to space enabled humans to see their home-world as it really is.

Chapter Learning Objectives

We will examine the space program and space race between the United States and Russia. We will understand why America won the space race. Next, we will examine the life of Werhner von Braun and contemplate his crimes and contributions to world history. Then we will analyze several space exploration disasters and predict the future of space travel. Finally, we will finish by speculating on whether or not there are extraterrestrial aliens.

As a result of this chapter you should be able to:

1. Explain why America won the space race

2. Review the life of Werhner von Braun

3. Analyze several space exploration disasters

4. Predict the future of space travel

5. Speculate on whether or not there are extraterrestrial aliens

CONCEPTS

Project Mercury

Sputnik

Gemini

Apollo

Wernher Von Braun

Space shuttle *Columbia* disaster

UFOs

Overview of Space Travel

Space travel began on October 4, 1957, when the Soviet Union successfully launched **Sputnik I**. The world's first artificial satellite was about the size of a beach ball and took about slightly over one and one-half hours to orbit the earth on its elliptical path. It was the orbit that changed the course of history. That launch initiated a whole new technological age — it ushered in new political, military, technological, and scientific developments.[1]

I can remember my parents being frightened that the Russians had gone into space and next would bomb us! That fear, of course, was unfounded, but Americans experienced a wake-up call that they were behind in the space race, and things had not really begun.

The United States finally managed to launch its first satellite, *Explorer I*, in 1958. Then the Soviets placed the first man in orbit in 1961. John Glenn orbited the globe three times in 1962. I can remember the euphoria and relief I felt as I sat in the hallway at Queens Road Elementary School, Pasadena, California. We might actually beat the Russians after all!

President Kennedy committed the United States to landing a man on the moon and bringing him back "before this decade is out."

President John F. Kennedy in his historic message to a joint session of the Congress, on May 25, 1961: "...I believe this nation should commit itself to achieving the goal, before this decade is out, of landing a man on the Moon and returning him safely to the Earth." This goal was achieved when astronaut Neil A. Armstrong became the first human to set foot upon the Moon at 10:56 p.m. EDT, July 20, 1969 (NASA).

It was an exciting time! I grew up with words I had never heard, like Mercury, Gemini, and Apollo. We dreamed of space stations and aliens. To us, Buck Roger's world was appearing before our very eyes!

With **Project Mercury**, in August 1962, John H. Glenn Jr. became the first U.S. astronaut to orbit the earth. In the mid-1960s, U.S. scientists used the **Gemini** program to examine the effects of prolonged space flight on man. Mankind could apparently live for months in outer space! Gemini carried two astronauts, one more than the earlier Mercury series and one less than the subsequent Apollo spacecraft. Gemini achieved several firsts including an eight-day mission in August 1965 — the longest space flight at that time — and in November 1966, the first computer-controlled re-entry into the earth's atmosphere. This was a great breakthrough and tested technology that would be critical to later landings on the moon. Gemini also accomplished the first manned linkup of two spacecraft in flight as well as the first U.S. walks in space. America was surging ahead!

Finally, in July 1969, with hundreds of millions of television viewers watching, Neil A. Armstrong became the first human to walk on the moon.

Other **Apollo** flights followed, but many Americans began to question the value of manned space flight. The space race was won. In the early 1970s, as other priorities became more pressing, the United States scaled down the space program. Some Apollo missions were scrapped. Only one of two proposed Skylab space stations was built.

---

1. http://history.nasa.gov/sputnik/.

NASA then embarked on the space shuttle missions which, with two major mishaps, determined the future of American space travel for five decades.

Will America return to the moon? Visit Mars? These questions are yet to be answered.

Discussion Question

Why, in your opinion, did America win the space race?

Gemini spacecraft diagram, 1965 (NASA).

The Apollo 11 Saturn V space vehicle lifted off, 1969 (NASA).

Technicians working in the McDonnell White Room on the Mercury spacecraft, 1960 (NASA).

Astronauts in simulated weightless flight in C-131 aircraft flying "zero-g" trajectory at Wright Air Development Center. These flights were nicknamed the "vomit comet" because of the nausea that was often induced. 1959 (NASA).

Wernher von Braun

Von Braun (1912–1977) was one of the masterminds behind America's space program (NASA).

To my father, a math and science teacher, **Wernher Von Braun** was the greatest man who ever lived! Von Braun was to save America from the Russian Communist hordes who were threatening to overrun us technologically and militarily!

Von Braun is well known as the Nazi scientist who developed the V-2 ballistic (an unmanned) missile for the Nazis during World War II. The V-2s were manufactured at a forced labor factory underground. It was one of the most inhuman and notoriously cruel camps in the German Reich. And that is with competition the likes of which were Treblinka and Auschwitz! It truly was a horrible place.

Clearly von Braun knew about the cruel treatment of slaves, foreign workers, and Jewish people, and no doubt approved the use of slave labor to advance his purposes.

What he was doing was completely innovative. A new liquid propellant was used to drive the missile. The V-2 flew at speeds in excess of 3,500 miles per hour (propeller planes flew at 450 miles per hour) and delivered a 2,200-pound warhead to a target 500 miles away. That was an unprecedented development.

First flown in October 1942, the V-2 was employed against targets in Europe beginning in September 1944. The V-1 was developed first, then the V-2. Because neither the V-1 nor the V-2 could be produced in any significant quantity, and it could not be aimed accurately, rocket warfare had no strategic value.

By the beginning of 1945, it was obvious to von Braun that Germany would not achieve victory against the Allies, and von Braun surrendered 500 of his top rocket scientists, along with plans and test vehicles, to the Americans. It was understood that neither von Braun, nor his engineers, would be prosecuted. For 15 years after World War II, von Braun worked with the U.S. Army in the development of ballistic missiles. His genius was no doubt critical to the success of the United States space program.[2]

Discussion Question

No one can deny that von Braun was critical to the American space efforts. Indeed, the Russians would probably have beaten the Americans to the moon without von Braun. Yet at the same time, no one can deny that von Braun was a war criminal. However, given the perceived crisis that existed in the Cold War, American officials chose to ignore von Braun's participation in the murder of thousands of Jewish and Russian slave laborers. Did the United States make the right choice?

---

2. http://history.msfc.nasa.gov/vonbraun/bio.html.

Space Disasters

Not everything went smoothly. No discussion of the United States' space efforts would be complete without looking at the mistakes that cost several American lives.

The first tragedy to strike the young space endeavor occurred on the ground. The Apollo/Saturn mission was performing tests on the launch pad when a fire broke out, killing all three crewmembers. There were no other catastrophes until the space shuttle was launched in the 1980s. After several delays, *Challenger* lifted off on January 28, 1986. Seventy-three seconds into the mission, the *Challenger* exploded, killing the entire crew.

The **space shuttle *Columbia* disaster** occurred on February 1, 2003, when the space shuttle *Columbia* disintegrated over Texas and into parts of Louisiana during re-entry into the earth's atmosphere, resulting in the deaths of all seven crew members. The accident was a result of damage sustained during launch when a piece of foam insulation the size of a small briefcase broke off of the space shuttle's external tank during launch. The debris struck the left wing, damaging the shuttle's heat protection system. While *Columbia* was still in orbit, some engineers suspected damage, but NASA managers limited the investigation on the grounds that little could be done even if problems were found.

The following is a chronology of astronauts and cosmonauts killed in the history of space exploration:

- Jan. 27, 1967: Astronauts Gus Grissom, Edward H. White, and Roger B. Chaffee died when a fire swept their command module during a ground test at Kennedy Space Center.

On January 28, 1986, the space shuttle Challenger and her seven-member crew were lost when a ruptured O-ring in the right solid rocket booster caused an explosion soon after launch. This photograph, taken a few seconds after the accident, shows the space shuttle main engines and solid rocket booster exhaust plumes entwined around a ball of gas from the external tank (NASA).

Space Shuttle Columbia landed at Edwards Air Force Base. The ill-fated orbiter completed 20 more flights, which culminated in her destruction on February 1st, 2003, during the landing phase, killing her brave crew of seven (NASA).

Soviet postal stamp commemorating the crew of Soyuz 11 spaceship who died in a spaceflight accident. The line says: "The deed of the heroes will live forever. Dobrovolsky, Volkov, Patsayev," 1971 (PD).

- April 24, 1967: Soviet cosmonaut Vladimir Komarov became the first person to die in a space mission when his *Soyuz I* spacecraft crashed upon return to earth.

- June 29, 1971: Soviet cosmonauts Georgy Dobrovolsky, Vladislav Volkov, and Viktor Patsayev died during re-entry of their *Soyuz II* spacecraft after 24 days in an orbiting space laboratory.

- Jan. 28, 1986: The space shuttle *Challenger* exploded 73 seconds after launch, killing all seven astronauts aboard, including Christa McAuliffe, intended to be the first teacher in space.

- Feb. 1, 2003: Space shuttle *Columbia* broke apart in flames about 203,000 feet over Texas, 16 minutes before it was supposed to touch down in Florida. All seven aboard were killed. They were William McCool, Rick Husband, Michael Anderson, Kalpana Chawla, David Brown, Laurel Clark, and Ilan Ramon, Israel's first astronaut.[3]

In short, while the world grieved these fallen heroes, and those before them, the space program remains one of the great success stories of the 20th century.

Discussion Questions

Ask your parents or grandparents what they were doing when the *Challenger* and the *Columbia* exploded.

Lesson 4

The Future of Space Travel

Space exploration is not over. The evolution of the space program continues to be dramatic. America has come a long way from the three-orbit Gemini flight of John Glenn!

Former President George W. Bush directed NASA to plan a human landing on Mars by the year 2020. The space exploration Initiative that resulted was soon abandoned though. It was too costly to be sustained in the recession that began in 2008.

NASA turned in another direction. The current NASA manned space programs (space shuttle, joint operations with the Russians on Mir, and the new international space station) are not explicitly directed toward putting humans on Mars. Walking and

---

3. http://usatoday30.usatoday.com/news/nation/2003-02-01-accident-timeline_x.htm.

exploring on Mars, of course, would be the public choice, but there are a number of very serious challenges that would require solutions to make such a journey possible, not the least of which is the tremendous cost involved. In 2012, that particular project was curtailed. We will see if it is continued later.

Among the problems that would need to be solved before a human trip to Mars could take place would be that it is a two-year round trip to Mars by a direct minimum energy orbit each direction, with a few months' wait at Mars as well. The current world record for the longest duration in space is about half that time, and the Russian cosmonauts have encountered serious medical problems upon their return to earth. In short, there are real concerns that astronauts could survive a Mars landing and exploration.

Next, to send people to Mars, the mission will need to take everything it needs to get there, and live in space for two years. The problem is not packing supplies; the problem is what to do with the waste products.

A direct approach like that used for the Apollo missions to get to the moon (e.g., take all the fuel needed) won't work for Mars: the fuel required to get to Mars and back is well beyond the capability of even the most powerful rockets ever made.

Therefore, clearly, a space station would have to be established in space beyond the earth's orbit (perhaps the moon?) to refuel and perhaps refit a Mars rocket system.

Finally, there is the hostile Martian environment. Before putting astronauts on the moon, NASA explored the moon in great detail with probes sent to the moon to image it, map its gravitational field, study its surface, etc. NASA and the Russian Space Agency are both sending a number of probes to Mars in the coming years to explore the planet. *Mars Pathfinder* and *Mars Global Surveyor* are only the first in a fleet of probes heading to Mars in the next decade. Many of you will grow old with information returning from these probes! (Information supplied by NASA.)

Lander image of rover near "The Dice" (three small rocks behind the rover). Color image shows dark rocks, bright red dust, dark red soil exposed in rover tracks, and dark (black) soil. Sojourner spent 83 days of a planned seven-day mission exploring the Martian terrain, acquiring images, and taking chemical, atmospheric and other measurements. The final data transmission received from Pathfinder was at 10:23 UTC on September 27, 1997 (NASA/ JPL).

Discussion Question

What challenges must be overcome before America can land a man on Mars?

Panoramic image from Mars Pathfinder mission, 2004 (NASA).

Lesson 5

While technically a UFO refers to any unidentified flying object, in modern popular culture the term UFO has generally become synonymous with alien spacecraft.

Unidentified flying objects,[4] UFOs, have appeared with increased frequency over the last 50 years. Or so it seems.

Proponents argue that because these UFOs appear to be technological phenomena and display flight characteristics, or have shapes seemingly unknown to conventional technology — like flying saucers — then they must not be from earth. Though UFO sightings have occurred throughout recorded history, modern interest in them dates from World War I, further fueled in the late 1940s by Kenneth Arnold's coining of the term "flying saucer" and the Roswell UFO Incident.

Since then, governments have investigated UFO reports, often as a military threat. The former Soviet republics and Chinese authorities have taken UFO research more seriously than Americans. Several aircraft have been destroyed, and at least four pilots have been killed chasing UFOs.

In November 2011, the White House released an official response to two petitions asking the U.S. government to acknowledge formally that aliens have visited earth and to disclose any intentional withholding of government interactions with extraterrestrial beings. According to the response, "The U.S. government has no evidence that any life exists outside our planet, or that an extraterrestrial presence has contacted or engaged any member of the human race." Also, according to the response, there is "no credible information to suggest that any evidence is being hidden from the public's eye." The response further noted that efforts, like SETI, the Kepler space telescope, and the NASA Mars rover, continue looking for signs of life. The response noted "odds are pretty high" that there may be life on other planets but "the odds of us making contact with any of them — especially any intelligent ones — are extremely small, given the distances involved."[5]

Photograph of an alleged UFO in New Jersey, taken on July 31, 1952 (PD).

There has been little mainstream scientific study of UFOs, and the topic has received little serious attention. Official studies ended in the U.S. in December 1969, subsequent to the statement by Edward Condon that the study of UFOs probably could not be justified in the expectation that science would be advanced. The Condon report and these conclusions were endorsed by the National Academy of Scientists, of which Condon was a member. However, a scientific review by the UFO subcommittee of the AIAA disagreed with Condon's conclusion, noting that at least 30 percent of the cases studied remained unexplained, and that scientific benefit might be gained by continued study.

It has been claimed that all UFO cases are anecdotal and that all can be explained as prosaic natural phenomena. On the other hand, it has been argued that there is limited awareness among scientists of observational data, other than what is reported in the popular press.[6]

Discussion Question

Is there alien life away from earth? Why? Why not?

4. Jacques Vallée, *Revelations: Alien Contact by Human Deception* (New York: Anomalist Books, 1990).
5. Jerome Clark, *The UFO Book: Encyclopedia of the Extraterrestrial* (Detroit, MI: Visible Ink Press, 1998).
6. http://astronomyplus.weebly.com/what-are-ufos.html.

The Adventures of Ozzie and Harriet no longer reflects the American family, circa 1952. (PD).

Chapter 23

Profound Changes: The Modern Family

First Thoughts

Claude Fischer writes, "The former drover George C. Duffield, whose memoir of a cattle drive inspired the television series *Rawhide*, recalled his mother's life on the Iowa frontier in the 1820s and 1830s. She cared for the babies, cleaned the floors, made the beds, cultivated a garden, dressed turkeys, cured meat, made candles, preserved fruit, spun and knitted to make clothing, cut the children's hair, taught them to spell, and 'did the thousand things for us a mother only finds to do.' Hall of Fame ballplayer Cal Ripken Jr., whose Iron Man career inspired thousands of little leaguers, recalled his mother's life during the 1960s and '70s. Because his father was also a ballplayer, she did some of both parents' duties. She kept score at his games, coached his hitting, and bucked him up when he lost. When Cal Sr. was home, she joined in family basketball games (she 'had a really good two-handed set shot'). On the road, she packed and unpacked, set up housekeeping, did the laundry, handled the family budget, and settled the children's quarrels. . . . Such contrasting memoirs illustrate how greatly Americans' everyday lives changed over a century and a half — both in the mundane details of life and in their personal nature. This book asks how Americans' culture and character developed over the nation's history."[1]

Chapter Learning Objectives

We will examine the modern family, analyze a theory about modern American fatherhood, and then discuss the impact of feminism on the modern family. Finally, we will study the biblical view of women and the family.

As a result of this chapter you should be able to:

1. Analyze the modern family

2. Evaluate Blankenhorn's views about modern fatherhood

3. Discuss the impact of feminism on the modern family

4. Study the biblical view of women and the family

CONCEPTS

Leave It to Beaver

Feminism

Fatherhood

---

1. Claude S. Fischer, *Made in America: A Social History of American Culture and Character* (Chicago, IL: University of Chicago Press, 2010); http://press.uchicago.edu/Misc/Chicago/251431.html.

The Modern Family

Leave It to Beaver:
A successful sitcom television show in the 1950s.

The Cleaver family from the television program *Leave It to Beaver* in 1960 (PD).

Can an expectant mother obtain an abortion without her husband's permission? Who gets custody in a divorce battle? Should same-sex marriage partners be allowed to adopt? Does a father have the right to give his children his last name even if his wife objects? Should a teenager, unhappy with her parents' restrictions on her smoking, dating, and choice of friends, be allowed to have herself placed in a foster home? Should a childless couple be permitted to hire a "surrogate mother" who will be artificially inseminated and carry a child to delivery?

These are among the questions that the nation's courts have had to wrestle with as the nature of American family life has, over the course of a generation, been revolutionized.

Social historians point out that during the 1950s, the television show *Leave It to Beaver* characterized the American family. In 1960, over 70 percent of all American households were like the Cleavers: made up of a breadwinner father, a homemaker mother, and their two kids. Today, "traditional" families with a working husband, an unemployed wife, and one or more children make up less than 15 percent of the nation's households. As America's families have changed, the image of the family portrayed on television has changed accordingly. Today's television families run the gamut from two-career families to two single mothers and their children and unmarried couples who cohabitate in the same house.

Profound changes have reshaped American family life in recent years. For instance, in a decade, divorce rates have doubled. The number of divorces today is twice as high as in 1966 and three times as high as in 1950. The rapid upsurge in the divorce rate contributed to a dramatic increase in the number of single-parent households or what used to be known as broken homes. The number of households consisting of a single woman and her children has tripled since 1960. A sharp increase in female-headed homes has been accompanied by a startling increase in the number of couples cohabitating outside of marriage. The number of unmarried couples living together has quadrupled since 1970.[2]

According to Tom W. Smith of the National Opinion Research Center, while marriage is still a central institution in American society, it plays a less-dominant role than it once did. The proportion of adults who have never been married rose from 15 percent to 23 percent between 1972 and 1998. When the divorced, separated, and widowed are added in, three-quarters of adults were married in the early 1970s but only 56 percent were married by the late-1990s. According to social historians, the decline in marriage comes from four main sources.

First, people are delaying marriage. Between 1960 and 1997, the median age at first marriage rose from 22.8 to 26.8 years for men and from 20.3 to 25.0 years for women.

Second, the number of divorces has increased. The divorce rate more than doubled from 9.2 divorces per year per 1,000 married women in 1960 to a divorce rate of 22.6 in 1980. This rise was at least in part caused by increases in female labor-force participation and decreases in fertility. The divorce rate then slowly declined to 19.8 in 1995. The drop in the divorce rate in the 1980s and 1990s has been much slower than the rapid rise from

---

2. Steven Mintz, "The Modern Family," http://www.digitalhistory.uh.edu/historyonline/modernfamily.cfm.

the 1960s to the early 1980s, and as a result, the divorce rate in the 1990s is still more than twice as high as it was in 1960. Even with the slight, recent moderation in the divorce rate, the proportion of ever-married adults who have been divorced doubled from 17 percent in 1972 to 33–34 percent in 1996/1998. In some areas of the country (e.g., Southern California) the divorce rate is over 50 percent. This means that over half of American children are being raised in single parent or blended family homes.

Third, people are slower to remarry now than previously. While most people divorced or widowed before the age of 50 remarry, the length of time between marriages has grown.

Fourth, both the delay in age at first marriage and in remarriage is facilitated by an increase in cohabitation. Cohabitation represented only 1.1 percent of couples in 1960 and 7.0 percent in 1997. The cohabitation rate is still fairly low overall because most cohabitation arrangements are short term, typically leading to either a marriage or a break-up within a year. But cohabitation has become the norm for men and women both as their first form of union and as their form of union after divorce. For women born in 1933–1942, only 7 percent first lived with someone in a cohabitation arrangement rather than in a marriage. However, for women born in 1963-1974, 64 percent started off cohabiting rather than marrying. The trend for men is similar. Among the currently divorced, 16 percent are cohabiting and of those who have remarried, 50 percent report cohabiting with their new spouse before their remarriage.

Divorce rates are not significantly different between churched and unchurched families.

Along with the decline of marriage has come a decline in childbearing. The fertility rate peaked at 3.65 children per woman at the height of the Baby Boom in 1957 and then declined rapidly to a rate of 1.75 children in 1975. This is below the "replacement level" of about 2.11 children that is needed for a population to hold its own through natural increase. The rate then slowly gained ground at 2.0–2.1 children in the early 1990s. In 1972 the average adult had had 2.4 children and this number slipped to a low of 1.8 children in the mid-1990s. Likewise, while only 45 percent of households had no children under 18 living at home in 1972, this climbed to 62 percent in 1998. Thus the typical American household currently has no minor children living in it. Accompanying this decline in childbearing and childrearing was a decline in preference for larger families. In 1972, 56 percent thought that the ideal number of children was three or more. By 1996–1998 only 39 percent thought that three or more represented the ideal number of children. However, there was also little or no increase in preference for small families. Over the last three decades just 3–5 percent have favored families with 0–1 children.

Moreover, during the last generation, childbearing increasingly became disconnected from marriage. In 1960 only 5.3 percent of births were to unmarried mothers, while by 1996 over 32 percent of all births were outside of marriage. The rate of increase has been much greater for whites than for blacks. For whites, the percentage of unmarried births has expanded more than ten-fold from 2.3 percent of all births in 1960 to 25.7 percent in 1996, while the African American level grew more than three-fold from 21.6 percent in 1960 to 70.4 percent in 1994. While in 1972, 73 percent of children were being reared by two parents in an uninterrupted marriage, this proportion fell to 49 percent in 1996 and was at 52 percent in 1998. Thus, the norm of the stable, two-parent family was close to becoming the exception for American children rather than the rule.[3]

Discussion Question

Identify trends that are occurring in the modern family.

3. http://www.ropercenter.uconn.edu/public-perspective/ppscan/121/121034.pdf.

Fatherless America: Confronting Our Most Urgent Social Problem

By David Blankenhorn Jr.

David Blankenhorn, in his revolutionary work of cultural criticism, asks an anti-modern, almost heretical question: "So the question is not, What do men want? but rather, What do men do?" Blankenhorn goes where very few social historians dare to go before: he argues that men should be, very simply, good fathers — no matter how hard it is, or how foolish it may seem. "In a larger sense, the fatherhood story is the irreplaceable basis of a culture's most urgent imperative: the social-ization of males."[4] American children need fathers, American society needs fathers.

Blankenhorn begins his discussion arguing that having a father is very good for children. In the scheme of things, ironically, the notion that children have intrinsic rights and value is a relatively late-developing phenomenon among social welfare discussions. In fact, not until America developed a social welfare profession corps in the middle 1920s were children's rights seriously considered on any level. Now, Blankenhorn argues, children are more important than any other priority. So why are children so often sacrificed for individual rights? Because of individualism. Blankenhorn attacks this insidious individualism rampant in American society. No one disagrees that fathers are absent from many American families — 80 percent of urban American families have no father — but what concerns Blankenhorn even more is the fact that we no longer think fathers are important.[5] Blankenhorn says that we no longer have a distinctive "cultural script" for fatherhood. In American social welfare policy (mothers receive money — not fathers), in the popular media (e.g., *Mrs. Doubtfire*), and even in family therapy theory (e.g., only a mom is necessary for a healthy family system) fathers are seen as superfluous.

Blankenhorn's insightful analysis of the state of American fathers in modern America is disarmingly simple: the Unnecessary Father (ch. 4), the Old Father (ch. 5), the New Father (ch. 6), the Deadbeat Dad (ch. 7), the Visiting Father (ch. 8), the Sperm Father (ch. 9), the Stepfather and the Nearby Guy (ch. 10), and, our hero, the Good Family Man (ch. 11). One of the reasons this book is destined to influence social welfare policy as well as social mores is that its structure is so inescapably simple and right. The Unnecessary Father (typical notion that dads are not necessary), the Old Father (the macho, mean, domineering father), and the New Father (the sensitive, liberated, androgynous dad) are the most common, garden-variety dads we will meet in today's society. The other five roles are minor but insightful. The Deadbeat Dad is the bad guy, the guy who does not pay child support. The Visiting Father is a victim, a

---

4. David Blankenhorn Jr., *Fatherless America: Confronting Our Most Urgent Social Problem* (New York: Harper Row, 1995), p. 65.
5. Ibid., p. 67.

pathetic example of what fathering has become, proof positive that fathers are not important. The Sperm Father is a minimalist, basically just fathering the child, but doing nothing else to be a part of the child's life.[6] The Stepfather and the Nearby Guy are surrogate dads, magnanimously assuming the role of father for Deadbeat dads/jerks who have abandoned their kids. Again, though, the Nearby Guy/Stepfather is a rather innocuous version of what fathers should be. Blankenhorn uses the example of the Disney movie *The Incredible Journey* (1993) where a poor example of a father slowly earns the right to be a dad by sheepishly giving into his stepchildren's wants.

But by far, the strength of Blankenhorn's book is Part III entitled "Fatherhood." We meet finally the Good Family Man: the quintessential hope of all America. I mean it — this is the answer. This paradigm of Judeo-Christian virtue is the "father without portfolio."[7]

It would never occur to him — or to his children or wife — to make distinctions between "biological" and "social" fathering. For him, these two identities are tightly fused. Nor would it ever occur to him to suspect that the "male income" is more important for children than the "male image." For him, the two fit together. Consequently, he seldom ponders issues such as child support, visitation, paternity identification, fathers' rights, better divorce, joint custody, dating, or blended families. His priorities lie elsewhere.

Blankenhorn's image is powerful and so very true. We all thank him for pointing out to us fathers what we may have forgotten: that there is nothing wrong with putting our family first, with being a good and steady provider, and setting a good example by high moral character.[8] Yes, we all have much for which to thank David G. Blankenhorn.

The pastoral application of this book seems obvious. Finally, the pastor has a well-respected scholarly book on fathering, devoid of antiquated archetypes, to which he/she can point as a resource offering an efficacious model of fathering for his parishioners. The cultural impact is equally obvious: twelve proposals of social imperatives (found in ch. 12) will no doubt keep us all thinking for many years to come. Bravo! This book is destined to become one of the most important cultural offerings in modern America.

Discussion Question

Describe Blankenhorn's different types of fathers.

6. Ibid., p. 171.
7. Ibid., p. 201.
8. Ibid., p. 205.

Feminism

Feminism has been another major force that has transformed modern American family life.

> The women's liberation movement attacked the societal expectation. . . . Militant feminist activists . . . denounced marriage as "slavery" and "legalized rape." The larger mainstream of the women's movement articulated a powerful critique of the idea that childcare and housework were the apex of a woman's accomplishments or her sole means of fulfillment.
>
> The feminist movement awakened American women to what many viewed as one of the worst forms of social and political oppression: sexism. The introduction of this awareness would go far beyond the feminists themselves. Although only a small minority of American women openly declared themselves to be feminists, the arguments of the women's movement drastically altered women's attitudes toward family roles, child care, and housework. As a result of feminism, a substantial majority of women now believe that both husband and wife should have jobs, do housework, and take care of children.[9]

Feminism: An assertive women's rights movement.

The changes that have taken place in family life have been disruptive and troubling and have transformed the family into a major political battleground, with James Dobson and Focus on the Family being in the forefront.

Both liberals and conservatives have offered their own proposals about how the American family can best be strengthened. Conservative activists — many evangelical Christians — launched a politically influential "pro-family movement" during the 1970s. They sought to restrict access to abortion, reduce explicit sexual content on television, and limit teenagers' access to contraceptive information. Liberals are more willing to use government social policies to strengthen family life. Some of the proposals the government has made to strengthen families include expanded nutritional and health programs for pregnant women, federal subsidies for daycare services for low-income families, uniform national standards for child care centers, and a requirement that employers give parents unpaid leave to take care of a newborn or seriously ill child.[10] Most social liberals are reticent to deal with moral, ethical issues, because, in their minds, these are private, not public, concerns.

Discussion Question

What were the two emerging sides in the culture war surrounding American family life over the past few years?

---

9. Steven Mintz, "The Modern Family," http://www.digitalhistory.uh.edu/historyonline/modernfamily.cfm.
10. Ibid.

A Study of Galatians 3:28, The Role of Men and Women in the Church and the Home

By Pastor Joel Stephen Williams

What is the egalitarian interpretation of Galatians 3:28? Their understanding is that in Christ all distinctions based on race, economic status, and sex are abolished. First, there should be no distinctions based on Jew versus Gentile in the church or in the home. Second, no role distinctions in the church or the home should be based on whether or not one is a slave or free. They point out that in time the church opposed slavery and worked toward abolishing it. They then apply the same to men and women and urge Christians to adopt feminism and erase role distinctions in the church and, to one extent or another, in the home. In Christ, they claim, all of these distinctions have been reversed and social relationships are now on a plane of total equality. Richard and Joyce Boldrey write: "Galatians 3:28 does not say 'God loves each of you, but stay in your places'; it says that there are no longer places, no longer categories, no longer differences in rights and privileges, codes and values." Virginia Mollenkott says Galatians 3:28 expresses Paul's vision "of a classless, non-racist, non-sexist society."

How do evangelical and religious feminists handle Galatians 3:28? Their methodology is to use it as an interpretive center. This is a common method which everyone uses at one point or another. There are statements in the Bible which state a theological truth with such clarity or which have loomed large in forming the Christian conscience over the centuries. These "plain" statements are often taken as a starting point from which we go to other passages which may not be as clear. Evangelical feminists take Galatians 3:28 in this way as a universal principle. Limitations placed on the role of women in the church by other passages such as 1 Corinthians 14:33–35 and 1 Timothy 2:1–15 are seen as exceptions to the rule, applicable only in a limited way to a specific situation where mitigating factors are involved.

Some feminists contend that Paul's concern in the passages limiting women was missionary. While Galatians 3:28 expresses his universal teaching for all the church, the image of the church in certain local situations could affect the church's ability to evangelize. In those specific situations, in order to avoid offending local custom, Paul placed a restriction on the role of women. They would quickly argue that those same problems are not present in our modern world, so we should not follow those limitations on the role of women any longer. We should follow the universal principle of Galatians 3:28. Other feminists simply say that Paul was inconsistent. The passages which contain limitations on women supposedly reflect the Paul of rabbinic Judaism while Galatians 3:28 reflects the Paul of an enlightened Christian conscience. These latter approaches do not take the authority of the apostle Paul seriously enough, so we will not focus on them in this study.

What are the problems with this feminist view of Galatians 3:28? It is an example of hyperexegesis, that is, drawing more out of a passage than is in it. Lewis Johnson Jr. refers to "the human tendency to forget sound hermeneutics and find things that are

not really in the text."[11] Johnson did a survey of the use of Galatians 3:28 in Christian writings from the second century until the Reformation movement. He studied how this passage was used by Ignatius (c. 115), Justin Martyr (c. 155), Clement of Alexandria (c. 200), Hippolytus (c. 225), Gregory of Nyssa (c. 380), John Chrysostom (c. 390), Augustine (c. 420), Martin Luther (c. 1525), and John Calvin (c. 1555). He found that Galatians 3:28 was not looked upon as being the text that settled the issue of the role of women in the church and the home: "None of the major teachers in the history of the church thought Galatians 3:28 abolished the male-female role distinctions in marriage or the church."[12]

The traditional approach can best be explained by putting Galatians 3:28 in its context. In Galatians 3:2 Paul asks if we receive the Spirit "by doing the works of the law" or by faith? A descendant of Abraham is defined as one who believes (3:7), thus Gentiles could be blessed by means of faith (3:8). Relying on works of the law leads only to being cursed (3:10). We are not justified by the law (3:11). "In Christ Jesus" the "blessing of Abraham" comes "to the Gentiles." They can "receive the promise through faith" (3:14). The promise was made to Abraham and his offspring (3:16). The law of Moses did not deliver the promise. The law was a temporary measure until Christ came (3:17–26). It is "in Christ Jesus" that we are all children of God "through faith" (3:26). By baptism we get "into Christ" (3:27). "There is neither Jew nor Greek, slave nor free, male nor female, for you are all one in Christ Jesus" (3:28). If we are in Christ, then we are Abraham's offspring and "heirs according to the promise" (3:29). A child is no better off than a slave as an heir until the child comes of age. The Jews were in the child stage, thus they did not receive a full inheritance. In Christ "full rights of sons" are attained (4:1–7). "So you are no longer a slave, but a son; and since you are a son, God has made you also an heir" (4:7).

The chief aim of the whole passage is clear, even if some details of interpretation are difficult. Paul is explaining the relationship between the law of Moses and salvation by faith. The problem in the background was Judaizing teachers who wanted to require circumcision of Gentile converts to Christianity. Paul shows that salvation is by faith, not by law. He shows that the "promise" comes by faith, not by law. To become a Christian, one does not have to obey the law of Moses, and in particular, one does not have to be circumcised. What holds the three sub-groups (Jew/Gentile, bond/free, male/female) of Galatians 3:28 together? It is not that God established all three relationships at creation. At creation there was no Jew and Gentile. At creation there was no slave versus free. But there was male and female. What holds these three groups together is inheritance rights. As a rule, under the law of Moses only Jewish men could inherit property. Sons inherited. Gentiles, slaves, and women ordinarily did not inherit property. Drawing an analogy to Christianity, inheritance is different. One does not have to be Jewish, free, or a male to inherit. One can be Gentile, a slave, or female and inherit eternal life.

The point of Galatians 3:28 is one's status before God. Salvation, justification, and receiving the Spirit are the focus (3:2, 5, 8, 11, 24, 26, 27). The promise is given in Christ (3:16). If one can be united with Christ, if one can be "in Christ," if one can merge one's identity with Christ, then one receives the promise that is Christ's. The focus in Galatians is on the Gentile problem. It does not matter if one is slave or free, one could become a

11. S. Lewis Johnson, "Role Distinctions in the Church: Galatians 3:28," in *Recovering Biblical Manhood and Womanhood: A Response to Evangelical Feminism*, edited by John Piper and Wayne Grudem (Wheaton, IL: Crossway Books, 1991), p. 154.
12. Ibid., p. 156.

Christian (1 Cor. 7:22). Likewise, women could become Christians. The bond/free and male/female analogies simply give extra proof for Paul's point concerning the Gentiles. Salvation in Christ is available to all. This is what Galatians 3:28 is trying to teach.

What is not the aim of Galatians 3:28? It is not explaining the existence or non-existence of roles for people in the church or the home. Nothing in the context speaks of these matters. Paul is simply saying that salvation in Christ is open to all. Let me illustrate. If I say that I am starting a soccer team and membership on the team is open to anyone, young or old, male or female, white or black, rich or poor, this does not mean that the team will not have starters and bench-warmers, goalies and fullbacks. It does not mean that the team will not have a team captain. If the army announces that it has an open acceptance policy for applicants of any race or sex, that does not mean that there will be no generals versus privates. It does not mean that some will not drive tanks, while others cook, while others shuffle papers. If you started a chorus which accepted any applicant, male or female, white or black, that does not mean that you will not have sopranos, altos, tenors, and basses. . . .

By trying to make Galatians 3:28 apply to role relationships of men and women in the church and the home, feminism has not handled Scripture correctly. While we cannot know the exact dates of New Testament documents, we can know their dates approximately. Galatians is usually dated A.D. 48 by conservatives. Another theory would date it from Rome around A.D. 60. First Corinthians is dated A.D. 55 and 1 Timothy is dated A.D. 65. If Galatians 3:28 erased all role distinctions based on gender, then why did Paul later write statements which recognized some limitations based on gender? One or, more likely, both of Paul's key limiting passages were written after Galatians 3:28. Did Paul forget or did he change his mind? The answer, of course, is "Neither." Galatians 3:28 does not contradict 1 Corinthians 14:33–35 or 1 Timothy 2:1–15, because it is not erasing all role distinctions based on gender. Furthermore, the feminists are inconsistent in their handling of Scripture. Since Galatians 3:28 mentions male and female, they make it the linchpin for interpreting the rest of the New Testament in social ethics. Why do they not use Colossians 3:11 for that purpose? "Here there is no Greek or Jew, circumcised or uncircumcised, barbarian, Scythian, slave or free, but Christ is all, and is in all." It is curious that Colossians 3:11 is not the "golden text" or the "Magna Carta of humanity" since it does not mention male and female.

In conclusion, Galatians 3:28 is speaking of the accessibility of salvation to all people without regard to gender. It is not discussing role distinctions in the home or in the church, so other passages which define limitations in roles because of gender are not to be disregarded. While limitations undoubtedly were given in response to a specific problem situation, as the occasion demanded, there is no need to consider the limiting passages as contradictions of a general rule found in Galatians 3:28. Since Paul is the author of all of them, there is no reason to conclude that he saw a contradiction or that 1 Corinthians 14:33–35 and 1 Timothy 2:1–15 were temporary exceptions based on mitigating circumstances. There is no reason for us not to interpret all three passages as a harmonious whole. Therefore, Galatians 3:28 does not overrule Paul's instruction in 1 Corinthians 14:33–35 or 1 Timothy 2:1–15.[13]

Discussion Question

Summarize Pastor Williams' exegesis of Galatians 3:28.

---

13. Joel Stephen Williams, "A Study of Galatians 3:28, The Role of Men and Women in the Church and the Home," http://www.afn.org/~afn52344/longer1.html#text3.

A Modern Family in Literature

"Home Burial," Robert Frost

He saw her from the bottom of the stairs
Before she saw him. She was starting down,
Looking back over her shoulder at some fear.
She took a doubtful step and then undid it
To raise herself and look again. He spoke
Advancing toward her: "What is it you see
From up there always — for I want to know."
She turned and sank upon her skirts at that,
And her face changed from terrified to dull.
He said to gain time: "What is it you see,"
Mounting until she cowered under him.
"I will find out now — you must tell me, dear."
She, in her place, refused him any help
With the least stiffening of her neck and silence.
She let him look, sure that he wouldn't see,
Blind creature; and awhile he didn't see.
But at last he murmured, "Oh," and again, "Oh."

"What is it — what?" she said.

"Just that I see."

"You don't," she challenged. "Tell me what it is."

"The wonder is I didn't see at once.
I never noticed it from here before.
I must be wonted to it — that's the reason.
The little graveyard where my people are!
So small the window frames the whole of it.
Not so much larger than a bedroom, is it?
There are three stones of slate and one of marble,
Broad-shouldered little slabs there in the sunlight
On the sidehill. We haven't to mind those.
But I understand: it is not the stones,
But the child's mound —"

"Don't, don't, don't, don't," she cried.

She withdrew shrinking from beneath his arm
That rested on the bannister, and slid downstairs;
And turned on him with such a daunting look,
He said twice over before he knew himself:
"Can't a man speak of his own child he's lost?"

"Not you! Oh, where's my hat? Oh, I don't need it!
I must get out of here. I must get air.
I don't know rightly whether any man can."

"Amy! Don't go to someone else this time.
Listen to me. I won't come down the stairs."
He sat and fixed his chin between his fists.
"There's something I should like to ask you, dear."

"You don't know how to ask it."

"Help me, then."
Her fingers moved the latch for all reply.

"My words are nearly always an offense.
I don't know how to speak of anything
So as to please you. But I might be taught
I should suppose. I can't say I see how.
A man must partly give up being a man
With women-folk. We could have some arrangement
By which I'd bind myself to keep hands off
Anything special you're a-mind to name.
Though I don't like such things 'twixt those that love.
Two that don't love can't live together without them.
But two that do can't live together with them."
She moved the latch a little. "Don't — don't go.
Don't carry it to someone else this time.
Tell me about it if it's something human.
Let me into your grief. I'm not so much
Unlike other folks as your standing there
Apart would make me out. Give me my chance.
I do think, though, you overdo it a little.
What was it brought you up to think it the thing
To take your mother — loss of a first child
So inconsolably — in the face of love.
You'd think his memory might be satisfied —"

"There you go sneering now!"

"I'm not, I'm not!
You make me angry. I'll come down to you.
God, what a woman! And it's come to this,
A man can't speak of his own child that's dead."

"You can't because you don't know how to speak.
If you had any feelings, you that dug
With your own hand — how could you? — his little grave;
I saw you from that very window there,
Making the gravel leap and leap in air,
Leap up, like that, like that, and land so lightly
And roll back down the mound beside the hole.
I thought, Who is that man? I didn't know you.
And I crept down the stairs and up the stairs

To look again, and still your spade kept lifting.
Then you came in. I heard your rumbling voice

Out in the kitchen, and I don't know why,
But I went near to see with my own eyes.
You could sit there with the stains on your shoes
Of the fresh earth from your own baby's grave
And talk about your everyday concerns.
You had stood the spade up against the wall
Outside there in the entry, for I saw it."

"I shall laugh the worst laugh I ever laughed.
I'm cursed. God, if I don't believe I'm cursed."

"I can repeat the very words you were saying.
'Three foggy mornings and one rainy day
Will rot the best birch fence a man can build.'
Think of it, talk like that at such a time!
What had how long it takes a birch to rot
To do with what was in the darkened parlor.
You *couldn't* care! The nearest friends can go
With anyone to death, comes so far short
They might as well not try to go at all.
No, from the time when one is sick to death,
One is alone, and he dies more alone.

Friends make pretense of following to the grave,
But before one is in it, their minds are turned
And making the best of their way back to life
And living people, and things they understand.
But the world's evil. I won't have grief so
If I can change it. Oh, I won't, I won't!"

"There, you have said it all and you feel better.
You won't go now. You're crying. Close the door.
The heart's gone out of it: why keep it up.
Amy! There's someone coming down the road!"

"*You* — oh, you think the talk is all. I must go —
Somewhere out of this house. How can I make you —"

"If — you — do!" She was opening the door wider.
"Where do you mean to go? First tell me that.
I'll follow and bring you back by force. I *will*! —"[14]

Discussion Questions

What three modern questions does the mother ask that the man cannot answer?

14. http://www.bartleby.com/118/6.html

Chapter 24

A City Church: The City of God

First Thoughts

In the 40 years after the Civil War, over 24 million people flocked to American cities. They came from rural areas in the United States but also across oceans from farming areas and industrial cities in Europe. While the United States' rural population doubled during these years, the urban population increased more than seven-fold. In 1860, 16 cities had a population over 50,000 and only 9 had a population over 100,000. By 1900, 38 cities had more than 100,000 inhabitants.

Manufacturing and commerce crowded into city centers. Meanwhile, the development of steam railroad lines in the 1860s, electric-powered streetcars and elevated railways in the 1880s, and electric trolleys in the 1890s allowed the wealthy and the middle class to move along newly constructed trolley and rail lines to the country's first suburbs. At the same time, the urban poor were concentrated in newly constructed tenements, few of which had outside windows. Less than 10 percent had indoor plumbing or running water.[1]

In the midst of the growing city, the Church was challenged to minister despite growing and increasingly complicated problems. Was the Church up to the task then? Will it be able to minister to future generations?

Chapter Learning Objectives

We will examine the emerging city at the end of the 19th century. Next, we will examine the urban church and speculate on ways that it can be more effective.

As a result of this chapter you should be able to:

1. Analyze the impact of evangelicalism on the city

2. Explore the modern city and the urban church

3. List three kinds of urban churches

4. Define what a history maker is

5. Discuss how a city church can be more effective in the years ahead

CONCEPTS

City of God, City of Satan

Urbanization

History maker

Antioch Church

---

1. http://www.digitalhistory.uh.edu/disp_textbook.cfm?smtID=2&psid=3049.

"Our City: God's Creation"

He has set his foundation on the holy mountain; the LORD loves the gates of Zion more than all the dwellings of Jacob.

Glorious things are said of you, 0 city of God: "I will record [Egypt] and Babylon among those who acknowledge me — Philistia too, and Tyre, along with Cush — and will say, 'This one was born in Zion.'"

Indeed, of Zion it will be said, "This one and that one were born in her, and the Most High himself will establish her."

The LORD will write in the register of the peoples: "This one was born in Zion."

As they make music they will sing, "All my fountains are in you" (Psalm 87).

In about 19 years, the world will undergo a momentous change: for the first time in recorded history a majority of the world's people will live in cities — primarily the cities of Asia, Africa, and Latin America. These cities will be of enormous size and will be plagued by unemployment, overcrowding and disease, where services such as power, water, sanitation, or refuse disposal will be strained to the breaking point.

So said Rafael Salas, the late executive director of the United Nations Fund for Population Activities, when he spoke in Madras in 1986.

Cities all over the world are facing an unprecedented growth explosion. As Salas has indicated, sometime close to the turn of the century there will be more people living in cities than will be living in towns or villages, on farms, in tribes, or in any other human habitation. For the first time in its history, the world will be more urban than rural. Countries in the northern hemisphere will appear more urbanized than southern countries. By A.D. 2000, 94 percent of the population of Canada and the United States lived in cities, as will 82 percent of all Europeans and 80 percent of all Russians. In contrast, only 36 percent of all Asians and 45 percent of all Africans will live in cities (Latin America provides the one third-world exception — 73 percent of its people will live in its cities).

Such statistics are misleading, however. They do not reflect the tremendous number of people already concentrated in southern hemisphere cities or the tremendous growth occurring in those cities. The 36 percent of the population gathered in Asia's cities, for example, is numerically greater than the entire combined urban population of the developed countries.

Cities in the third world are not the only ones growing. Although the cities in the developed world are growing more slowly than in the third world, their metropolitan areas continue to expand. The greater Los Angeles metropolis, for example, numbered 4,000,000 in 1950 and is now 9,500,000. By the turn of the century, its population will be nearly 14,000,000. Paris, at 5,500,000 in 1950, is projected to reach 10,000,000 by the year 2000. Although economically it appears a part of the first world, Tokyo's growth compares with any third world metropolis. In 1950 the population was 6,700,000; by 2000 it will grow to be 23,800,000.

We can best see the growth in the world's cities in this simple fact. In 1950 only seven cities in the world had a population of more than 5,000,000. Thirty-five years later, the number of such giant cities had swollen to thirty-four. In another thirty-five years, there will be ninety-three cities on our globe with populations in excess of 5,000,000.

Even more obvious is the growth in third-world giant cities. Of the seven cities in 1950 with populations exceeding 5,000,000, only two were located in Asia, Africa, or Latin America. By 1985, twenty-two of the thirty-four giant cities were in the third world. By 2020 it is projected that the third world will be home to eighty of the ninety-three cities.

But what's wrong with growth? People who have lived their lives in the first world have grown up believing in growth. But in the third world — and among the first world's poor — growth is terrible news. Even a healthy city's infrastructure cannot cope with a significant increase in population. And when a city like Mexico City receives more than half a million new people each year (as it presently does), its sanitation system, refuse disposal, provision of power and water, and capacity to house, feed, and employ these people is overwhelmed.

View of the Santa Fe District in Mexico City, Mexico (CCA-SA3.0).

The results of such rapid and worldwide growth are evident everywhere. Fifty thousand homeless people live on New York City streets. Another 27,000 people live in temporary shelters, and an estimated 100,000 households are doubled up in apartments of friends and relatives. Sixty percent of the entire population of Guayaquil, Ecuador, lives in shantytowns amid garbage-strewn mud flats and polluted water. In Bombay, India, 1,000,000 people live in a slum built on a giant garbage dump.

In Detroit, 72 percent of all the young employable adults in that city's poorest census tract can't find work — and will probably never find it. Seventy-five percent of the families who live in Lagos, Nigeria, live in one-room shacks. Half a million people will live their entire lives on the streets of Calcutta and will never have a roof over their heads. In Sao Paulo, Brazil, 700,000 children have been abandoned by their parents to live by their wits on its streets.

This is the city — for God's sake! This is the city God loves and for which Christ died. And this is the city where Christ's church is and where it is called to minister.

It is incumbent upon Christians today to recognize and enthusiastically enter into the challenge of the new, emerging world. God is calling the Church into the city. Our world is becoming an urban world — and this is an inevitable and irreversible trend. Only our Lord's return or humanity's destruction of itself in a mushroom cloud will prevent the urbanization of the world. But we are not only faced with the mind-boggling growth of the world's existing cities — even the most rural and isolated areas of the world will be exposed to urbanization. It was apparent that a new age had dawned when, for two weeks in 1988, the entire world could "sit" in the stadiums and "walk" the streets of Seoul, Korea, because television brought the city into the home during live telecasts of the Olympics. There is no doubt that this is an increasingly urban world.

No previous generation has had to face human problems of this magnitude or had to wield urban power on this scale. This means that the Church has unprecedented potential for ministry and world evangelization. The world is coming to the city — and we can be there to greet it in Christ's name.

The most insightful of the Church's prophetic thinkers recognize the potential of the "open door that no one can shut" (Rev. 3:8). The Church is rediscovering the city — in both the developed and the developing worlds. Emerging from that rediscovery is a profoundly new methodology for doing urban ministry — a collective wisdom evolving from theologians and urban ministry practitioners alike. New words are entering the ministry vocabulary —words like networking, urban exegesis, community organization — all symbolic of the changing style of ministry adapted to an urban world.

While we are rediscovering the city's mission field and introducing an urban method-ology, our biblical and theological reflection is limited. We enter the city equipped with an urban sociology and urban tools for ministry, but we carry with us the baggage of a theology designed in rural Europe. Even the very way we formulate theological ques-tions and the frameworks we use to construct our theological thought have been forged from our rural past. What we are in need of is a theology as urban as our sociology and missiology— a theology, as Ray Bakke puts it, "as big as the city itself"![2]

Discussion Question

What theological challenges does the urban church face in the modern city?

Lesson 2

Problems of Urbanization

Until comparatively recently, people lived in village communities and their culture, mode of living, food, and social organization were adjusted to their surroundings. Modern urbanized life has produced a new environment, creating new problems of adaptation. It is one thing for 4,000 people in the steppes of Mongolia to adjust to their new surroundings; it is quite another for 15 million people to do the same in Mexico City.

Urbanization is a problem that has assumed gigantic proportions. There are too many people in too small an area; this leads to huge problems.

Due to the paucity of housing of any type, once-beautiful cities are being reduced to slums. This pressure of population has led to the construction of vertical skyscrapers to accommodate the maximum number within the minimum space. Skyscrapers have put incredible pressure on urban amenities like parks, playgrounds, and parking space. When I lived outside of Washington DC, my commute was, on average, four hours! On a Friday evening it could extend to eight hours!

---

2. Robert C. Linthicum, *City of God, City of Satan: A Biblical Theology of the Urban City* (Grand Rapids, MI: Zondervan Publishing House, 1991), chapter 1; books.google.com/books?isbn=0310877350.

Urbanization disturbs the equilibrium between demand and supply in the economic market, resulting in greater demand and lesser supply. It is very difficult to obtain affordable, pure food, milk, and other commodities, even pure drinking water.

Sociologically, urbanization has led to the breaking of joint (extended) families and the establishment of "nucleus" (untraditional, non-biological) families. Illegitimate births have reached an 80 percent level in Washington, DC.

Some social historians are suggesting that the most effective way to tackle the problem of urbanization is to make the economy of the villages and small cities fully viable and try to keep people there. However, Orlando, Florida, where an estimated 30 new people a day move, is the location of Walt Disney World. That fact will not change. Thus, Orlando will continue to grow. Likewise, other cities, with their attractions, will continue to draw the majority of people to them.

During the 19th and early 20th centuries, urbanization resulted from and contributed to industrialization. That is not necessarily true now. Many urban dwellers, perhaps the majority, work in service industries — maintenance workers, maids, house cleaners, and fast-food workers. This reality has severely eroded the urban tax base.

In the United States, poorly planned urban development is threatening our environment, our health, and our quality of life. In communities across the United States, sprawl is taking a serious toll.

What is the solution? The city church must return to its rightful place in the center of the city. The Church helped solve 19th-century urban problems. It needs to do the same in the 21st century.[3]

Discussion Question

Urbanization has been very disorienting in the 20th century. Why?

Image of the massive city of Guayaquil, Ecuador (CCA-SA3.0).

3. "International Migration: A Global Challenge," Population Bulletin, Population Reference Bureau, Inc., vol. 51, no. 1, 1996; www.prb.org, "Human Population: Fundamentals of Growth Patterns of World Urbanization"; http://www. globalchange.umich.edu/globalchange2/current/lectures/urban_gc/.

The Urban Church, Part I

It was Maundy Thursday. For 135 years, First Downtown Church had proudly proclaimed the gospel to its downtown community.

Rosamund, a 75-year-old lady who had a passion for impressionistic paintings, flamboyant hats, and First Downtown Church, carefully filled the communion chalice with Welch's Grape Juice. She was proud of the fact that she had never spilled a drop — except the time when Sally, reaching for a discarded napkin, rudely bumped Rosamund's right elbow. A dark purple stain spread like a terrible disease on the Women's Association's white communion cloth. The stain remained, and Rosamund had never quite been able to forgive Sally for her sin.

Wearing an auburn-brown wig over her snow-white hair, Rosamund refused to surrender her hair color — one slender vestige of youth — to old age. Her brown hair only made her look like what she really was — a well-intentioned elderly lady who tried to look 20 years younger. This brazen and futile attempt by Rosamund to hide the truth was a telling testimony of a central truth about Rosamund and many of her friends: they valiantly tried to hide the truth that their old downtown church was surely dying. Rosamund and First Church were deeply committed to unreality.

As the paraments reflected a purple hue onto the inscription on a silver chalice, Rosamund remembered. "In memory of Mr. Elias Brown and to the glory of God," Rosamund quietly read.

Rosamund knew Elias. She was a member of his 39er Sunday school class (a Sunday school class founded in 1939 for newlyweds).

She chuckled to herself, "It was a young married class — until we all died!"

Elias Brown's Sunday school class once boasted 75 couples — 150 members! Week after week, Elias laboriously read the International Bible Lesson to his bored but nonetheless loyal class.

What great times they had! They had a party to celebrate Lindbergh's crossing the Atlantic — old Betty Smith drank too much spiked apple cider and tried to fly across Saw Mill Creek (the closest facsimile to the Atlantic Ocean that Old Miss Smith could find)!

As Rosamund secretly lit a Camel Light, she remembered. No one but her closest friends knew she smoked — so she thought — in fact, everyone in First Church knew since she smelled like an ashtray. But no one told her. This was one of those polite games everyone played. They were committed to keeping the lid on the truth if it was too painful. But now Rosamund remembered and it was painful to remember.

The years had been hard on First Church. Too many unexpected expenses. Too few people to pay them. At first no one worried when the Joneses and Smiths moved. But then the Millers died and the Taylors joined a church nearer to their home. And the children stopped coming! Out of Rosamund's own six children, only one attended church, and it was at a church in the suburbs.

One funeral after another. Rosamund sighed. Now the whole church had fewer members than Rosamund's old Sunday School class!

The city is in trouble. The city church is in trouble.

City churches of all denominations and races are dying. They are being resurrected as condominiums and restaurants. In Pittsburgh, for instance, 13 Presbyterian Churches closed in the last 20 years of the century.

Cities are anomalies. Anyone who drives through a city knows that the actual edge of a city is very hard to locate. The same holds true for downtown churches. Where does the city begin? Where does it end? Where is the geographical area from which a downtown church pulls its congregation? Where is its spiritual center? To whom is it called to minister?

Some areas of the country, like New Jersey and Southern California, have become in essence one giant metropolitan area. Ninety percent of New Jerseyans live in a city. This statistic points to a new reality — for the first time in our history, most Americans live in a metropolitan area.

The city is here, alive and well, but apparently dying in some places. Where does that leave the downtown church?

From the beginning, Americans have retained rural values while living in an urban setting. As long as Americans found a "rural" environment in a downtown setting, they came to church. But with all the obstacles arising in the last few years — parking, crime, and sheer distance — Americans have increasingly decided to pursue the American dream and to attend church outside of the city.

To keep the American dream intact, Americans have moved into the suburbs with an ever-increasing frequency. Robert Gallagher's recent paper "Stay in the City" reminds us that an average of one church every year had closed up and moved out of Philadelphia.

I identify three types of metropolitan churches: the downtown church, the residential urban church, and the suburban church. The urban residential church, as contrasted with the downtown cathedral church, draws an indigenous congregation who lives around the church. Its future is tied to the economy and disposition of its local community. If the community prospers, the church also prospers — unless God intervenes!

20th-century stained glass window. Postmodernist symbolism, Tree of Life at Christinae church, Alingsås, Sweden (CCA-SA3.0).

In fact, before I accepted my present ministerial position, I served a residential urban church. This is, in my opinion, one of the most difficult ministries. Normally burdened with a huge, inefficient physical plant and a declining congregation, the residential and downtown churches share common problems. However, the residential congregant cannot escape the increasing crime rate around the church — because he lives there. The downtown church congregant can at least escape to the suburbs.

The First Mainline Denomination Downtown Church is normally a cathedral church. It may be the oldest church in the community and the parent church for most, if not all, of the nearby churches in its congregation. It normally has no or very few congregants who live nearby because it is in a commercial urban district. And of the people who do live nearby, most are poor and either do not go to churches, or attend Pentecostal churches.

With some exceptions, the years after the Civil War were very good to cities and city churches. Property values increased and transportation improved (which made it easier to go downtown on Sunday morning). To the arcane, urban elite, the downtown church was the church of choice. During this period, downtown churches amassed huge endowments: usually the equivalent of two years' budgets.

But this time of prosperity, which lasted into the late '50s, and in some cases into the '70s, created false security. Typically, downtown churches created large staffs and bureaucracies. For a voluntary organization, downtown churches had inordinately large and expensive bureaucracies and physical plants.

Clearly, this was a great time in the life of city churches! It was a time of fiscal surpluses, full pews, and expanding programs. Large, extravagant building programs were undertaken. Bowling alleys, gymnasiums, and huge pastor studies can be found in these cathedrals. Many of these buildings were built in the early 20th century and, if they are Protestant, reflect strong nativistic evidences. Coal heat was the fuel of

Brighton Evangelical Congregational Church, Boston, MA (CCA-SA3.0).

choice and was generally abundant and inexpensive. Therefore, large, inefficient physical plants were no problem for the magnificent city cathedral. Typically, beautiful (if terribly inefficient) domes adorn ornate sanctuaries. Expensive stained glass windows — some of which cost more than the whole small-town church from which many of the city congregants had come — decorate the worthy witness to God's presence in the city.

Discussion Questions

What challenges do modern cities face?

The Urban Church, Part II

Through the pulpit urban pastors directly influenced urban policy makers. On V-E Day at the end of World War II, for instance, politicians and other policymakers gathered outside First Presbyterian Church to hear a victory sermon. Symbolically and literally, the secular world gathered at the door of the church. The church, as a systemic presence, had a major impact on the urban world. As the urban historian Eric Monkkonen writes, cities were "persons — endowed by legislation with the power to act."[4] They were more economic corporations than government entities. They were, in effect, perceived as "persons" by the legal and governmental community. The church, therefore, with its affective agenda, was well suited to thrive in this milieu. And it did!

This was also the time of great urban preaching! Among the great preachers were Harry Emerson Fosdick, Alexander MaClaren, and others. At the end of World War II, Pittsburgh came to hear Dr. MaClaren at his outside pulpit. It was as if the war was not over until Dr. MaClaren declared it so.

Downtown preachers, Protestant and Catholic alike, were invited into the highest circles of urban policymaking. They were read in the newspapers, listened to on the radio, and generally well respected in the urban community.

On the other hand, noticeably absent from the urban church were well-equipped education wings and nurseries. Following the practices of early Sunday school pedagogy, the urban church built large, open education areas that doubled as a chapel. After long and elaborate opening exercises during the Sunday school hour, boys and girls were escorted to their classes, which were usually held in areas of a big room. Nurseries were not necessary because most downtown congregants employed domestic help to assist in childrearing. Normally, these nannies lived in the home on the third floor and came with their employer to church, taking care of the child throughout the worship event — even, at times, sitting in the balcony with the children away from their parents.

As intimated above, early downtown Protestant Church congregants were wealthy. At least in Pittsburgh, many of the elites were Presbyterian. Therefore, early in its history, the city church began to rely on "blue blooded, wealthy types" for leadership and financial support. This pool was at first quite large, but as we shall see, it rapidly declined in the late 1970s and 1980s. Typically, in the '40s and '50s, and especially in the '60s and '70s, the positive return on endowment investments gave downtown churches a false sense of economic stability. When this situation changed in the middle and late '80s, the downtown church found itself living beyond its means. Finally, the presence of a large and well-performing endowment gave the congregation the sense that they did not have to give. Thus, normally, 20 percent of the congregation gave 80 percent of the income. The church budget included very generous mission items — including, ironically, the founding of many suburban churches — and continuing education scholarships for its congregants (e.g., summer camp or synod school). When expenses increased, investment income declined, giving units died or moved, and the urban church found itself in crisis.

---

4. Eric H. Monkkonen, *America Becomes Urban* (University of California Press, 1988), p. xii.

Ergo, the very strength of the downtown congregation became its weakness. The wealthy elite that frequented the early American urban church gave the late-1970 church a false sense of security. At the same time, this wealthy elite and its offspring normally handled urban social problems by moving. Why not? They had no theological reason to stay, and they certainly had the financial means to move.

In addition, the large, beautiful downtown cathedral became a heating nightmare. With the advent of the energy crisis, the cost of church utilities doubled and then tripled. Denominations, feeling the same pressures, increased their demands. This was manifested most often in salary and benefit expectations among its ordained clergy.

To make matters worse, buildings that were built from 1900–1920 suddenly, in the 1970s and 1980s, required major capital improvements. Roofs needed repairing, sidewalks replaced, cracked stained glass windows replaced. And, what would be modest jobs in other churches (with 14-foot ceilings) were huge financial burdens to downtown churches. For example, my church recently paid $48,000 alone to have the scaffolding assembled in our sanctuary to paint the walls! Energy conservation measures were huge financial undertakings that downtown churches could ill-afford to assume.

And there were other obstacles that could not be changed — parking, for instance, was an increasingly difficult and expensive experience.

At the same time, the affluent city dweller was moving farther and farther from downtown. It was more and more difficult to fight traffic all week and come to work downtown, and then the following Sunday, return to the city and hope to find somewhere to park. This was especially difficult when one considers that a modern, well-equipped suburban church of the same denomination was within a few blocks for the suburbanite.

Kenneth T. Jackson, in his book *Crabgrass Frontier* reminds us that the first suburbs were on the edge of Babylon. "Our property seems to me," a man writes to the king of Persia in 539 B.C., "the most beautiful in the world. It is so close to Babylon that we enjoy all the advantages of the city, and yet when we come home we are away from all the noise and dust." Of the 86.4 million houses in the United States in 1980, about two-thirds, or 57.3 million, consisted of a single family living in a single dwelling surrounded by an ornamental yard. Most of these houses were in the suburbs. Indeed, the allure of suburban living is so intense that every downtown urban congregation has experienced urban flight. This urge to move away from the city and its institutions — including the church — has imperiled the urban church's future more than any other phenomenon.

At the same time, as the pool of available clergy increased in the 1960s, seminaries generally de-emphasized the pulpit ministry — the lifeblood of a downtown church. Many promising new pastors were more interested in a social agenda than in good preaching.

Gone, too, were the Chaucerian-type parsons, the generalists, who functioned so well in the urban residential church. They were replaced by therapists and counselors.

In Jeremiah 29:4–9, Jeremiah warns his nation that they must settle down in Babylon and get used to exile. The displacement is real and serious and will last. They are to entertain no wishful thinking about its quick end and a return to normalcy. But invest in the dream and buy the land that you may never live to enjoy — the field at Anatoth — because you believe in the dream. And some day, Jeremiah insists, God will bring us home. "I will restore your fortunes and will gather you from all the nations and from all the places where I have driven you . . . and I will bring you back to the place from where I sent you into exile!" (Jer. 29:14; NASB).

The urban congregation must be challenged to have a greater dream than the dream of a 50- by 100-foot manicured lawn in the suburbs. We must challenge ourselves to be history makers. And the city offers a place for history to be made.

Nonetheless, history makers, too, need training. And before the last ten years there was almost no urban pastoral preparation in the seminaries. This left many downtown churches with inexperienced young pastors or relatively unsuccessful late-middle-age pastors. Rather than hiring professors whose backgrounds reflected spiritual formation or community development — two critical elements for successful urban ministry — seminaries hired minority professors with backgrounds in liberation theology and called it urban ministry.

For instance, Third Presbyterian Church in Pittsburgh, once one of the major destinations of Pittsburgh's urban elites in earlier days, suddenly saw its pastor walking in civil rights marches. As laudatory as this may have been, and as necessary as it may have been, it did not substitute for the good preaching that was necessary to draw people into the life of Third Church. In most downtown churches, famous choirs and great preachers were disappearing. And with them, some of the greatest assets of city churches.

Front of Third Presbyterian Church at the intersection of Fifth and Negley Avenues on the east side of Pittsburgh, Pennsylvania (PD).

Today, the downtown church finds its income decreasing on all fronts — investment income is declining, membership is decreasing. At the same time, expenses are significantly increasing — utility bills and repair bills are skyrocketing. And, as the downtown church struggles, suburban churches, unencumbered by antiquated physical plants, are springing up everywhere. Ignoring the fact that fewer Americans attend church than any time in our history, the downtown church is attracting fewer participants, having to spend more money with less income.

The city needs the Church to reclaim its systemic importance. Early in its history, the Church was the major conduit of social welfare. Several historians have emphasized how critical the Church was to the social welfare of the city. In circa 1830 Utica, New York, after a Charles Finney revival, the women's welfare society at the local downtown church was the strongest extent social welfare system in the city. And it was extremely effective! Its budget surpassed the city's social welfare budget — an impressive $3,000. With no cost to the city and in the name of Jesus Christ, before the New Deal, the downtown church was taking care of the poor and the needy in churches all over the country.

With the collapse of the positive liberal state, the city needs its churches again. We who seek to serve God in the city must do social work without being social workers. As the urban pastor and writer Walt Wagnerian is fond of saying, we must "name" city people.

Panorama of Utica, N.Y. in 1909 (LOC).

We must give them a name, destiny, a reason to live. That is, we need to remind city folk that they are children of God.

We must remain the Body of Jesus Christ but we must not flinch in the face of social problems.

William Julius Wilson, in *The Truly Disadvantaged: The Inner City, the Underclass, and Public Policy*,[5] argues that Roosevelt's New Deal, and Johnson's Great Society failed because they ignored the most fundamental need of all disadvantaged people: employment. The downtown church is in a strategic place to affect this problem. With our often under-utilized church bureaucracy — secretaries, office managers, and their equipment — we are able to stimulate and create many small businesses. For example, in my former church, we started a small business that employed 40 seasonal employees. Furthermore, we were able to do this business/ministry with no cost to the local church. It is through these creative ventures/ministries that the Church will reclaim its proper place in the community.

I am not naive. I know that the women's association, as laudatory and important their work may be, will not end homelessness in the South Bronx. But working with the government, the Church can help.

As Robert Linthicum writes, God deeply loves the city. Many Scriptures evidence this fact (e.g., Ezekiel 16:1–14; Psalm 48). Linthicum and other Christian writers remind us that our battle is not against flesh and blood, but against powers and principalities. In that sense, the Church is an important system, or organization, in the city and it needs to act like it.

When a business is failing, one has two alternatives: cut back or find new markets.

As the downtown church faces adversity after adversity, it needs to change its image to attract new congregants. The key to these strategies is bold creativity. The downtown church has no choice but to seek new, imaginative solutions to problems.

For instance, since parking is a problem for city dwellers, why not rent a local parking garage for Sunday morning? Or why not hold meetings out of the city — in suburban homes?

The above mentioned social welfare programs might also attract a new congregant pool. My present church has defined itself in a way that attracts a new theological group previously ignored. In our case, we have become the "Bible-centered, denominational, socially active" church in the city. We have found that this combination — conservative evangelicalism and social activism — has opened a whole new market for us. Many

---

5. William J. Wilson, *Truly Disadvantaged: The Inner City, the Underclass, and Public Policy* (Chicago, IL: University of Chicago Pressm 1987).

people in our city are growing tired of the non-denominational scene and are looking for an "old-fashioned" First Church in which to raise their families. We want to be that church. We cannot be everyone's church, but we plan to be a different church that is not trying to duplicate the suburban experience. We are overtly proud of the fact that God has called us to this place in this time.

In that vein, we have emphasized that we are a cathedral. We are not trying to duplicate the suburban church. True, we do not have a spacious, modern educational wing. True, parking is a problem. But our worship experience, our choirs, and our education programs are second to none. We are growing because people are yearning for something done well and something that is familiar.

Along those lines, it seems to me that an endowment is critical to the life of a downtown church. Exorbitant heating bills, unforeseen building repairs, and shortfalls in the summer offerings can all be mitigated by the existence of an endowment. However, I challenge downtown churches to keep no more than 2.5 budget years of endowment. In other words, if a downtown church's budget is $250,000, no more than one million should be invested. The rest — if any is left! — should be used to improve the programming, building, and staff of the church. Central to programming (hopefully) is mission giving.

But good programming will still not be enough unless the downtown urban church can attract a diverse population. Notwithstanding studies to the contrary, heterogeneity can be an asset to the downtown church. It has to be, because without a definable neighborhood, a downtown church must attract a variety of different people with different backgrounds, socio-economic standing, and theological emphases. It is the job of the senior pastor and the church board to define the limits of this pluralism — a church does not want to move to the lowest common denominator — but at the same time openness must be the modus operandi of the Church's life.

As incredible as it may seem, the liberal is attracted to our social agenda. The conservative evangelical likes our Bible-centered preaching. The charismatic Christian is attracted to our praise service on Sunday night. African Americans feel welcome because my family is an interracial family and we have intentionally welcomed minorities. Families with children are attracted to our mid-week youth club. And so on. "First Church" must be a church that attracts diversity. The maintenance of diversity is critical to the success of any pluralistic venture. And, believe me, a downtown church is a pluralistic venture.

Finally, more than anything else, the city church must project hope — hope when there is no hope. Hope that comes from the knowledge that God is in control — not the president, not Congress, not the economy. God is in control. Period. We need to stand with the city, pray for the city, love the city, and do the calling God has called us to do.

Discussion Question

What is a history maker?

From Antioch to Vancouver

Ken Shigematsu

Building a church isn't like starting a McDonalds' franchise. With McDonald's you achieve success by replicating the same taste all over the world. Whether you're in Boston, Budapest, or Beijing, a Big Mac should taste pretty much the same. If it tastes different, look around you — you may be in Burger King!

When it comes to building a church, however, we can't simply download the franchise game plan for the "perfect" church. We can, however, learn from other models. Evangelicals often look to large contemporary suburban churches as model churches. City pastors, however, may be better off looking back at ancient urban models. Our post-modern cities, as scholars have noted, have many similarities to the first century cities featured in the New Testament.

Antioch, for example, was a city much like Vancouver. It had people from all over the world: Europe, East Asia, India, the Middle East, and Africa. The city's slogan was "Antioch the beautiful." It was a port city and a center for trade and commerce. Antioch also housed a great library. The city was religiously pluralistic and pleasure seeking. Like Vancouver, Antioch was even situated on an earthquake fault line.

Given Antioch's urban ethos and the Holy Spirit's transforming work there through the people of God, the church at Antioch serves as a powerful model for those of us who are called to urban ministry.

Up until the Antioch era of the early church, the Gospel of Jesus Christ had been communicated almost exclusively to Jewish people. In Acts 11:19 we read that followers of Jesus who had been scattered throughout Asia Minor had been telling the message of Jesus only to Jews. But in Acts 11:20 we read that some people from Cyprus and Cyrene went to Antioch and began communicating the news of Jesus with Greeks also.

A theological cornerstone for those of us involved in urban ministry is the conviction that the Gospel of Jesus Christ is for all people. This may sound obvious, but it is significant for us in a time when persuasive voices in the church growth movement have emphasized the need to target homogenous units of people, often people just like the leaders. The reasoning goes that people will be more receptive to the Gospel if they don't have to cross ethnic or economic lines to come to Christ. So, in this view, a church should target a specific ethnic group or socio-economic group like young professionals or a specific generational group, like Gen X or Y, so people won't have to cross social barriers to come to Jesus. But a church that focuses on a razor-thin demographic slice may expedite numerical growth, but also contradicts the reconciling power of the Gospel.

Statue of Julian the Apostate, created in Italy between 361 - 400. In the Cluny Museum collection since 1859.

The church at Antioch was passionate about reaching people of different ethnic backgrounds with the Gospel and, as a result, people were not only reconciled to God but with each other. Urban missiologist Ray Bakke points out that Antioch was a city which had both an exterior wall and interior walls which separated the various ethnic groups: Greeks, Syrians, Jewish, Latin, and African. As people were reconciled to God, they began to cross the interior walls of the city and experienced reconciliation with people who had been their cultural enemies.

Following the lead of the church in Antioch, part of my vision as a pastor of a local church in Vancouver is to serve as a community where people of all backgrounds (racial, cultural, socio-economical, and religious) can discover a relationship with God through Jesus Christ. As people experience reconciliation with God, we see them connect with people very different from themselves.

Urban churches that follow Antioch's lead will be passionate about a Gospel for all, leading to reconciliation with God and others.

We also see that the church at Antioch met both the spiritual and social needs of people.

The Emperor Julian in the first century wrote to a pagan priest asking him to explain why the Christian way was growing so quickly given that they had no political clout and little money. The priest explained Greeks helped Greeks, Romans helped Romans, Africans helped Africans, but Christians helped everyone.

Philip Jenkins, author of *The Next Christendom*, points out that the reason churches in the two-thirds world are growing is because the churches are preaching the Gospel and feeding people, providing health care, and teaching people the skills they need to survive in a rapidly developing society.

The conservative branch of the Protestant church has typically been committed to helping people make sure that their sins have been forgiven and that they are leading morally upright lives. The liberal wing of the church has often been committed to justice for the poor and social issues. Like the church of Antioch, urban ministry leaders won't want to wear either a conservative or liberal straight-jacket. We will be committed to offering a Gospel that faithfully integrates both the spiritual and social sides of the Gospel.

A church does not need to be large by North American standards to be involved in evangelism and feeding the hungry, housing the poor, helping to provide a safe house for recovering addicts, and deploying resources to Asia and other disaster stricken areas of the world.

The **church of Antioch** was prepared to not only send financial resources, but also human resources. In Acts 13 we read that as the church was worshiping the Lord, praying and fasting, the Holy Spirit said, "Set apart Saul and Barnabas . . . for the work I have for them."

Like the church at Antioch, God calls us to come to attention before him in worship, prayer, and fasting, ready to hear God's voice and prepared to be sent by the Holy Spirit.

Planning and strategy are important, but we must always be open to altering our course in response to the movements of the Holy Spirit.

Several years ago, Cathy, a member of our church, began to ask herself, "Is it just a coincidence that I am physiotherapist, or does God have some larger purpose for me?" She began to pray for guidance and sometime later she had a dream of Sudan. She didn't know where Sudan was on a map, but looked it up in an atlas. She went to Missions Fest and picked up information on Leprosy Mission International. She applied and went to England for an interview. At the end of her interview Cathy asked her interviewer, "Where might you send me?" "To Sudan," the interviewer said. Cathy told me she

The church at Antioch (Acts 11: 27–30) was a place where a hunger offering was taken to bring relief for people who had been victims of a famine in Judea. This may have been the first disaster relief offering in the history of the Christian Church. Each member of the church gave according to his or her ability. This love offering was then hand-delivered by Barnabas and Paul to those in need (vs. 29).

would be glad to stay in Vancouver, but was ready to go Africa if God made it clear she was to go. After more prayer and confirmation, Cathy ended up serving as a medical missionary to the lepers of Sudan.

The term "Christian" was first used to describe the followers of Jesus in Antioch. It was a word that described followers of Jesus who were part of a multi-ethnic community, reaching out to the spiritually and socially needy, and a church ready to send out its members in response to the Holy Spirit. That definition of Christian — as an international, holistic, Spirit-led movement — also serves as a worthy vision for our urban churches.[6]

Discussion Question

Why was the New Testament Antioch Church so special?

Ancient Roman road near Tall Aqibrin in Syria. This road connected Antioch and Chalcis (CCA-SA3.0).

6. Ken Shigematsu, "From Antioch to Vancouver," http://www.missionsfestvancouver.ca/wp-content/uploads/2012/10/2012MissionsFestMag1.pdf.

Petronas Twin Tower in Kuala Lumpur, Malaysia (CCA-SA3.0).

Chapter 25

Post-Modernism: Miserable but Enjoying It

First Thoughts

While speaking at a homeschool convention in Hawaii, I saw this statement on a t-shirt: "I am miserable but enjoying it!" This is a summary of post-modernism. In his book *Reality Isn't What It Used To Be*, Walter Truett Anderson argues that there are six competing stories in the post-modern era: 1) Western myth of progress; 2) Marxism and revolution; 3) Christian fundamentalism; 4) Islamic fundamentalism; 5) Green; and 6) New Age.[1]

Chapter Learning Objectives

This chapter examines several stories in the context of post-modernism and offers ways that Christians can minister to this post-modern generation.

As a result of this chapter you should be able to:

1. Analyze the causes and impact of post-modernism.

2. Review the impact of post-modernism on architecture.

3. Offer strategies that can be used to share the gospel with post-modern Americans.

4. Discuss why Christians have every right to be optimistic in this post-modern era.

1. Walter Truett Anderson, *Reality Isn't What It Used to Be* (San Francisco, CA: Harper & Row, 1990).

Definition and Origin

Post-modernism is a tendency in contemporary culture characterized by the rejection of objective truth and a common cultural narrative. In other words, in post-modernism, every sacrosanct ethic is in question. Before post-modernism, the Golden Rule, for instance, was universally accepted as a desirable moral trait. Not in post-modernism — everything is on the chopping block.

A few years ago on CNN, President Obama told John King, host of "State of the Union": "I think it's important for the media — you know, not to do any media-bashing here — to recognize that right now, in this 24-hour news cycle, the easiest way to get on CNN or FOX or any of the other stations — MSNBC — is to say something rude and outrageous. If you're civil and polite and you're sensible, and you don't exaggerate the bad things about your opponent, you know, you might get on one of the Sunday shows — but you're not going to be on the loop. And, you know, part of what I'd like to see is all of us reward decency and civility in our political discourse."[2]

Because of a fervent dedication to open-mindedness and subjectivity — no opinion is unimportant — post-moderns are generally intolerant of what they call "close-mindedness" or "intolerance," but what we would call principled. President Obama called this "closed-mindedness" rudeness.

President Barack Obama giving a speech, 2013 (PD).

The fight against rudeness is very serious. To be treated rudely is to be denigrated, and when done regularly it can destroy people. Being constantly put down and mistreated can have tremendous psychological effects. These effects are only exacerbated by having everyone else around you reinforce the idea that you deserve the mistreatment by letting it pass as acceptable behavior. In time, the mistreated may even come to believe that they are worthless or deserving of abuse.

In particular, President Obama wanted pro-lifers to be less "rude." If we — I am definitely pro-life — would be more "civil" we could have more productive discussions with our pro-choice president.

But to principled people, it is hard to be civil when 3,700 babies are aborted every day — 3,700! My hometown in Arkansas has a population of 4,020. That means that every day, the entire population of my hometown is murdered. It is hard to have a cup of tea and politely discuss this problem. I mean, if our tea time takes one hour, that is equivalent to over 100 dead children. If rudeness doesn't help, I am sorry, but I can't be civil.

Most scholars agree that post-modernism began in the 1990s after the end of the Cold War. Post-modernist thought is an intentional departure from modernist approaches that embraced empiricism and science. The term "post-modernism" comes from its critique of the "modernist" scientific mentality of objectivity and progress associated with the Enlightenment.

---

2. http://newsbusters.org/blogs/jeff-poor/2009/09/20/sunday-obamathon-turns-media-critique-says-press-perpetuating-rude-behavi.

Discussion Question

In post-modernism there is no right or wrong, no doctrine. What implications can this have for a church?

Post-Modern Architecture

Post-modern architecture responded to the perceived blandness, hostility, and utopianism of modernism by creating new designs and new visions in buildings.

Post-modernism thus had overlapping lines, and symmetry was not important. Modern architecture was focused on the pursuit of a perceived ideal perfection, and attempted harmony of form and function, as well as dismissal of "frivolous ornament." Post-modern critics of modernism argued that the attributes of perfection and minimalism themselves were subjective, and pointed out anachronisms in modern thought. They also questioned the benefits of modern abstract art. In short, post-modernism argued that modernism, in its pursuit of novelty, had embraced a sort of conformity.

Sydney Opera House viewed from the side, designed to look like the sails of ships (CCA-SA3.0).

To post-modern architects there was no "pure" form or "perfect" architectonic detail. Post-modernism drew from all available architectural methods, materials, forms, colors, and motifs — Victorian, Georgian, modern, etc. — and in the process created a new architectural form altogether.

Post-modernist architecture was one of the first aesthetic movements to openly challenge modernism as antiquated and "totalitarian," favoring personal preferences and variety over objective, ultimate truths or principles. It is this atmosphere of criticism, skepticism, and emphasis on difference over and against unity that distinguishes many post-moderns.

One building form that typifies post-modernism is the traditional gable roof in place of the iconic flat roof of modernism. Shedding water away from the center of the building, such a roof form always served a functional purpose in climates with rain and snow, and was a logical way to achieve larger spans with shorter structural member. Nevertheless, it was relatively rare in modern houses. However, post-modernism reclaimed the roof.

Discussion Question

What are the distinctives that exist in post-modern architecture?

Post-Modern Justice

I regularly receive a copy of the *Harvard Divinity School Bulletin*, a publication for alumni of Harvard Divinity School. The covers of the other seminary magazines I receive, from Princeton Seminary and Gordon Conwell, always sport a famous theologian or a biblical figure, or at least an innocuous oak tree. But, no, not my *Harvard Divinity School Bulletin*. It always has a picture of a bright red Hindu god or the like. Or even worse, this last quarter the front featured the picture of post-modern Richard Rorty.

Immanuel Kant: A philosopher who saw experience as the primary core reality.

I must tell you that there is nothing "divine" about Mr. Rorty. Rorty developed a novel form of pragmatism sometimes called neo-pragmatism, in which scientific and philosophical methods are merely contingent "vocabularies" which are abandoned or adopted over time according to social conventions and usefulness. In other words, "It ain't so if you don't say it." What is justice to a post-modern? Post-modernism combines the model of Rorty language games with philosopher **Immanuel Kant**'s division of the faculties (understanding, imagination, reason) and types of judgment (theoretical, practical, aesthetic) in order to explore the problem of justice. Kant was a post-modern in the 18th century before the word even existed! Kant put his money on experience, which to him was way more important than rationalism (the stuff that scientists like to bank on).

With Kantian views of subjectivity and feelings, the faculties were set free to run wild. Where Kant insists that reason must assign domains and limits to the other faculties, its dependence upon the unity of the subject for the identity of concepts as laws or rules de-legitimizes its juridical authority in the post-modern age. Instead, because we are faced with an irreducible plurality of judgments and "phrase regimes," the faculty of judgment itself is brought to the fore.

The "just decision" then, to Kant and to the post-moderns, is "What is just to me is justice."

In other words, justice is impossible.

Post-moderns, in short, are presented a plurality of realities and rules without a concept under which to unify them. Judgment must therefore be reflective rather than determining. It is a preference, not a choice. The just solution is what I choose it to be.

Reality is therapeutic and prescriptive. If it suits me, it is real. It is does not, it is illusionary.

Where Kant emphasizes the feeling of the beautiful as a harmonious interaction between imagination and understanding, post-modernism argues that beauty is the feeling of the sublime. For Kant, the sublime occurs when our faculties of sensible presentation are overwhelmed by impressions of absolute power and magnitude, and reason is thrown back upon its own power to conceive ideas (such as the moral law) that surpass the sensible world. To the post-modern, however, the sublime occurs when we are affected by a multitude of unpresentables without reference to reason as their unifying origin. Justice, then, cannot be definable, but is the ability to move and to judge among realities in their heterogeneity and multiplicity.

Post-moderns and Kant, of course, both have it wrong. Justice is acting in a fashion that is in line with the will of God. Beauty is anything that manifests the character of our most beautiful, awesome God whose Word is immutable, objective, inerrant, and inspired. Take that, Mr. Kant!

Discussion Question

What are the problems with post-modern views of justice?

Christian Voices

Several Christian teachers have offered ways to deal with post-modernism. E.R. Dodds, in his book *Pagan and Christian in an Age of Anxiety*,[3] uses the 4th century as a way to deal with hostile post-modernism. Fourth-century Christianity triumphed over paganism because Christianity rejected all gods but the one God, and at the same time accepted all people. The Church promised eternal life in heaven yet showed love to all persons. Post-modernism has no answer to the inevitability of death. Christianity has an answer that needs to be shared freely and often.

Language is at the heart of post-modernism. Grant Wacker's "Uneasy in Zion: Evangelicals in Post-Modern Society"[4] argues that evangelicals must use the media to speak forth the gospel but they must do so with fear and trembling. To understand the growth of evangelicalism one must look at the big picture as seen in the social transformations brought about by mass communication and high technology (particularly since WWII). Evangelicalism as we know it today is a cultural form that grew out of a developing America, not out of hostility to any worldview. Wacker insists that the growth that the Church has, and must, experience should employ whatever tools God provides — including the media.

Unfortunately, one casualty of post-modernism is the mainline church. By and large, mainline churches have declined significantly in the last 30 years. *The Modernization of Protestant Religion in America* by Leonard I. Sweet argues that the decline of mainline churches is tied to post-modernism: the growth of individualism, high criticism of the professionalization of the clergy, unwise and unpopular decisions made by denominational bureaucrats, ecumenism, actionism, and pluralism. The end result of all of this has been the decline of the mainline churches — both numerically and

---

3. E.R. Dodds, *Pagan and Christian in an Age of Anxiety* (Cambridge; New York: Cambridge University Press, 1990).
4. In George Marsden, *Evangelicalism and Modern America* (Grand Rapids, MI: Eerdmans Pub. Co., 1984).

spiritually. Evangelicals, fundamentalists, and Pentecostals have moved to center stage as modernism has been forced into retreat. In characterizing the mainline denominations during these five decades, Sweet notes: "With everything gone, there was little reason for people to stay." Sweet gives much attention to the increasingly distant relationship between the denominational leaders and the church members. This distance led to the leadership taking stands without considering the beliefs and feelings of the people in the pews, which then resulted in an ever-growing distrust by the members of their leaders. Sweet describes these developments as a loss of mastery and mandate — that is, the loss of mastery of the common touch and mandate of the common faith, all of which are post-modern tendencies.[5]

Thomas C. Oden in his *Agenda for Theology: After Modernity . . . What?* references the bankruptcy of modern liberalism and calls for a return to classical forms and symbols for the post-modern church. He issues a call to students and others to return to tradition and orthodoxy. Post-modernism shows an unrestrained, individual freedom, the goal of which is to liberate one from all restrictions, constraints, traditions, and all social patenting — all of which are self-evidently presumed to be humanizing.[6]

Discussion Question

Pretend that you are the youth director of your church. You must design an outreach to your post-modern world. What programs and interventions will you offer?

Lesson 5

Ministry to the Post-Modern Generation

This is a graduate speech the author presented to a homeschool graduation class in Maine several years ago. It is *apropos* to all evangelicals, homeschooled or not!

This generation is the first homeschooling generation to graduate from high school in such large numbers and ability. You are the first — the first of many to follow. You are our hope. We parents have struggled, suffered, but, most of all, enjoyed every minute with you. You are our joy; our hope. You are the reason that we are full of joy today. Let me explain.

Admittedly, you are the first generation who grew up when murder was legal; the first generation to access 130 channels and at the same time access almost nothing of value; the first generation to see a nation and Congress accept a U.S. president for lying, infidelity, and perversion with no perceivable outrage. That is the challenge, the bad news, as it were.

The good news is that, at the end of this century, to a large degree, the homeschooling movement has arrived. That is good news indeed to a nation that needs desperately what you offer.

5. Leonard Sweet, "The Modernization of Protestant Religion in America," in *Altered Landscapes: Christianity in America, 1935–1985*, David W. Lotz, Donald W. Shriver Jr., and John F. Wilson, eds. (Grand Rapids, MI: Eerdmans, 1989).
6. Thomas C. Oden, *Agenda for Theology: After Modernity . . . What?* (Grand Rapids, MI: Academie Books, 1990), p. 47.

Two and one-half million strong, homeschoolers are in almost every county in America. You will, without a doubt, be the next successful business people, craftsmen, and professionals. Within a few years you will, I believe, become leaders in our society. Besides the fact that homeschoolers are scoring higher on almost all standardized tests, you are also better adjusted emotionally and spiritually than the general population. I believe that most of you will move to the head of graduating classes of the most prestigious Christian and secular universities in America. You will become leaders in government and industry. The Christian community has not had such an opportunity to influence civil society since the time of Constantine. This is a great opportunity and challenge!

Never has America needed homeschoolers more! At the same time that Christians are beginning to take their place in society, American culture has never needed them more. The Christian teacher Os Guinness argues that American culture is no longer sustaining Americans. In our homes, in our workplaces, in our places of play — the stadium — we are struck by the facileness, superficiality, and subterfuge that permeate all parts of American society. Mediocrity has replaced meritocracy. We as a culture have dumbed down, as it were. We do not know how to think; we do not know how to analyze knowledge. We are lost. . . .

Culture has to do with making sense out of life and formulating strategies for action; and the ideas and symbols that people draw on in these fundamental undertakings are no longer working. Marriage is no longer working — over 1/2 of American marriages are failing. Fatherhood is not working — 4/5 poor American urban families are single-family homes. Many of the things that we took for granted are no longer working, and no longer have meaning.

That is the bad news.

The good news is that I think that homeschoolers will be different. [Homeschooling] families are stronger, our children are more productive. There is no magic here — my wife and I have sacrificed so much for our children. But it is working and I believe that I will live to see one of the greatest revivals in human history! This generation is, I believe, one of the most strategic generations in history. How can we prepare them?

We must prepare this generation to be different in meaningful ways. We must prepare this generation — like no other — to be in the world but not of the world. As Josh Harris loves to say, "America cannot take another Christian generation that just fits in." The post-Christian age is one dominated by anxiety, irrationalism, and helplessness. In such a world, consciousness is adrift, unable to anchor itself to any universal ground of justice, truth, or reason. Consciousness itself is thus "decentered," no longer an agent of action in the world, but a function through which impersonal forces pass and intersect.[7]

Let's examine some modern trends. The first is a pervasive and abiding concern about the future. To those of us who lived through the Cold War this seems ludicrous. But it is real and this generation is one of the most hopeless in history. Interestingly enough, this hopelessness has made us rather sentimental. We have become very sentimental about the past. We have lost our way, lost our dreams.

Even in our most creative creations it is more of the same: *Star Wars* is going after the same thing we want and still not finding it. Notice bar scene. The *Star Wars* phenomenon is so appealing because it is about the past, not about the future. Luke

"You will become leaders in government and industry. The Christian community has not had such an opportunity to influence civil society since the time of Constantine."

Rosa Parks became an icon of the civil rights movement in 1955 after her refusal to give up her seat on a bus in Montgomery, AL to a white passenger. In 1999, a controversial hip-hop song was released titled with her name, using vulgar lyrics that hinted at moving to the back of a bus and to be silent. A series of court cases followed, and a settlement was finally reached in 2005. (NARA).

7. Patricia Waugh in Gene Edward Veith Jr., *Post-Modern Times: A Christian Guide to Contemporary Thought and Culture* (Westchester, IL: Crossway Books, 1994), p. 45.

Equal rights issues are not always focused on race or gender. The 26th Amendment to the US Constitution grew out of a 30-year effort to lower the voting age to 18 across the United States. American soldiers in World War II, Korea, and Vietnam had fought and died for their country, yet many were too young to even vote at the time. (NARA).

Skywalker is more like John Wayne than he is like Tom Cruise. To this hopeless generation history is not sacred; it is merely utilitarian. It is not didactic; it helps them feel better. The Modern psychologist B.F. Skinner, for instance, disdains history and gives M&M's to monkeys. We have no actions, only fate driving us. We are rudderless. However, we Christians know that God is in absolute control of history. Thus we need to teach our children to be tirelessly hopeful. We need to make sure that we are not mawkish! We can easily do so by speaking the Truth found in the Word of God in places of deception.

Next, there is a serious breakdown of community. One of the greatest problems in this generation is confusion about individual responsibility. Perhaps the problem began with Freud who told us that feelings of guilt were a sign, not of vice, but of virtue, and that our problems stemmed from our mothers, not from our sin. Perhaps our problem began with Goethe whose Faust escapes the consequences of his sin by sincerity and good naturedness, poor Gretchen aside. The Christian homeschooler must be responsible before God. Everything must be done to His glory.

Confusion about responsibility is only one type of confusion. Confusion about the meaning of tolerance is also everywhere. S.D. Gaede, *When Tolerance Is No Virtue*,[8] says . . . "In our culture, there is considerable confusion about how we ought to live with our differences and a cacophony of contradictory justifications for one approach as opposed to another." All appeal to the need of tolerance, but there is nothing like common agreement on what that means. The question our culture raises by nature and development is, what is truth and what can we believe? Our culture doesn't know the answers. In fact, we have lost confidence in truth and have come to the conclusion that truth is unattainable. Thus, tolerance moves to the forefront. G.K. Chesterton wrote: "Toleration is the virtue of the man without convictions."[9]

We need to understand the culture in which we live — one in which relativism, which leads to injustice, is growing. We must know what is right and do it. We must seek justice — we cannot turn a blind eye to the injustices related to multi-culturalism. We must affirm truth and not tolerate relativism. The Church must be who it is — it must express its convictions about truth, justice, and practice, while expressing tolerance (i.e., love) to the multi-cultural Body of Christ.

In summary, this generation will quite literally have to create a new world. How to create a new society? These are the new Pilgrims, the new Puritans. In Joseph Conrad's *Lord Jim* (1899), Jim is instructing a young person steering a ship on how to handle a storm. "Steer neither to the right [nor] to the left of it," Lord Jim says. "Steer right into it." Christian homeschoolers, we need to steer right into the storm. We can be, and will be, more than conquerors in Christ Jesus!

Discussion Question

What hopeful message does this author offer?

---

8. S.D. Gaede, *When Tolerance is No Virtue* (Downers Grove, IL: InterVarsity Press, 1993).
9. http://www.brainyquote.com/quotes/quotes/g/gilbertkc163172.html.

A Tea Party Protest,
Pennsylvania Avenue,
Washington, D.C., in 2009
(PD).

Chapter 26

Politics and More: The State of America

First Thoughts

Each generation writes its own history — a history that reflects its own concerns and challenges. During the hedonistic 1980s, for instance, historians focused on Wall Street excesses and social conscience. The 21st century is an age preoccupied with issues of identity and intimacy. Therefore, the study of private lives and private concerns may very well be the most important history of all.

Chapter Learning Objectives

We will examine the food habits of Americans. Then, we will examine Chuck Colson's views of American courtship and marriage. Next, we will discuss the Tea Party movement, and finally, we will end with an evaluation of the 2008 recession.

As a result of this chapter you should be able to:

1. Analyze food consumption over the last three centuries

2. Review Christian views of courtship and marriage

3. Discuss the Tea Party movement

4. Evaluate the causes of the recession of 2008

5. Test your historical skills

Food in America

Steve Mintz

In Europe in the 17th and 18th centuries, food served as a class marker. A distinctive court tradition of haute cuisine and elaborate table manners arose, distinguishing the social elite from the hoi polloi. During the 19th centuries, food became a defining symbol of national identity. It is a remarkable fact that many dishes that we associate with particular countries — such as the tomato-based Italian spaghetti sauce or the American hamburger — are 19th- or even 20th-century inventions.

The European discovery of the New World represented a momentous turning point in the history of food. Foods previously unknown in Europe and Africa, such as tomatoes, potatoes, corn, yams, cassava, manioc, and a vast variety of beans, migrated eastward, while other sources of food, unknown in the Americas — including pigs, sheep, and cattle — moved westward. Sugar, coffee, and chocolate grown in the New World became the basis for the world's first truly multinational consumer-oriented industries.

> Food is much more than a mere means of subsistence. It is filled with cultural, psychological, emotional, and even religious significance. It defines shared identities and embodies religious and group traditions.

Until the late 19th century, the history of food in America was a story of fairly distinct regional traditions that stemmed largely from England. The country's earliest English, Scottish, and Irish Protestant migrants tended to cling strongly to older food traditions. Yet the presence of new ingredients, and especially contact among diverse ethnic groups, would eventually encourage experimentation and innovation. Nevertheless, for more than two centuries, English food traditions dominated American cuisine.

Before the Civil War, there were four major food traditions in the United States, each with English roots. These included a New England tradition that associated plain cooking with religious piety. Hostile toward fancy or highly seasoned foods, which they regarded as a form of sensual indulgence, New Englanders adopted an austere diet stressing boiled and baked meats, boiled vegetables, and baked breads and pies. A Southern tradition, with its high seasonings and emphasis on frying and simmering, was an amalgam of African, English, French, Spanish, and Indian foodways. In the middle Atlantic areas influenced by Quakerism, the diet tended to be plain and simple and emphasized boiling, including boiled puddings and dumplings. In frontier areas of the backcountry, the diet included many ingredients that other English used as animal feed, including potatoes, corn, and various greens. The backcountry diet stressed griddle cakes, grits, greens, and pork.

One unique feature of the American diet from an early period was the abundance of meat — and distilled liquor. Abundant and fertile lands allowed settlers to raise corn and feed it to livestock as fodder, and convert much of the rest into whiskey. By the early 19th century, adult men were drinking more than 7 gallons of pure alcohol a year.

One of the first major forces for dietary change came from German immigrants, whose distinctive emphasis on beer, marinated meats, sour flavors, wursts, and pastries was gradually assimilated into the mainstream American diet in the form of barbeque, cole slaw, hot dogs, donuts, and hamburger. The German association of food with celebrations also encouraged other Americans to make meals the centerpiece of holiday festivities.

An even greater engine of change came from industrialization. Beginning in the late 19th century, food began to be mass produced, mass marketed, and standardized. Factories processed, preserved, canned, and packaged a wide variety of foods. Processed cereals, which were originally promoted as one of the first health foods, quickly became a defining feature of the American breakfast. During the 1920s, a new industrial technique — freezing — emerged, as did some of the earliest cafeterias and chains of lunch counters and fast-food establishments. Increasingly processed and nationally distributed foods began to dominate the nation's diet. Nevertheless, distinct regional and ethnic cuisines persisted.

During the early 20th century, food became a major cultural battleground. The influx of large numbers of immigrants from southern and eastern Europe progressive era brought new foods to the United States. Settlement house workers, food nutritionists, domestic scientists tried to "Americanize" immigrant diets and teach immigrant wives and mothers "American" ways of cooking and shopping. Meanwhile, muckraking journalists and reformers raised questions about the health, purity, and wholesomeness of food, leading to the passage of the first federal laws banning unsafe food additives and mandating meat inspection.

During the 19th and early 20th centuries, change in American foodways took place slowly, despite a steady influx of immigrants. Since World War II, and especially since the 1970s, shifts in eating patterns have greatly accelerated. World War II played a key role in making the American diet more cosmopolitan. Overseas service introduced soldiers to a variety of foreign cuisines, while population movements at home exposed people to a wider variety of American foodways. The post-war expansion of international trade also made American diets more diverse, making fresh fruits and vegetables available year round.

Today, food tends to play a less distinctive role in defining ethnic or religious identity. Americans, regardless of religion or region, eat bagels, curry, egg rolls, and salsa — and a Thanksgiving turkey. Still, food has become — as it was for European aristocrats — a class marker. For the wealthier segments of the population, dining often involves fine wines and artistically prepared foods made up of expensive ingredients. Expensive dining has been very subject to fads and shifts in taste. Less likely to eat German or even French cuisine, wealthier Americans have become more likely to dine on foods influenced by Asian or Latin American cooking.

Food also has assumed a heightened political significance. The decision to adopt a vegetarian diet or to eat only natural foods has become a conscious way to express resistance to corporate foods. At the same time, the decision to eat particular foods has become a conscious way to assert one's ethnic identity.[1]

Discussion Question

Out of the four main food traditions in the United States, in which tradition does your family lie?

1. http://www.digitalhistory.uh.edu/historyonline/food.cfm.

Obvious but False:
Common Views of Love and Courtship

Chuck Colson

Ask the typical college student, What's love? That's a no-brainer — love is a romantic feeling, right? And what's the purpose of sex? Pleasure, of course. What else could it be?

In his new book *Ask Me Anything: Provocative Answers for College Students*, University of Texas professor J. Budziszewski tells students that both of these "obvious" answers are dead wrong. Take the idea that love is a feeling. If that were really true, then how could people getting married promise to love each other until they are parted by death? Feelings come and go; you can't promise a feeling. What you can promise is a commitment of the will to the good of the other person. And that's what love is.

Or take that other "obvious" but wrong answer that the purpose of sex is pleasure. "False," says Budziszewski. Of course, sex is pleasurable, but that doesn't make pleasure its purpose. The exercise of every natural power is pleasurable. Eating is pleasurable; taking a deep breath is pleasurable; flexing a muscle is pleasurable. Is the purpose of all those things also pleasure? Think what that would imply. If the purpose of eating was pleasure, then if it gave you more pleasure to eat, purge, and eat some more, you ought to do it. The reason you shouldn't is that the purpose of eating isn't pleasure, but nutrition. In the same way, says Budziszewski, the purpose of our sexual powers isn't pleasure, but procreation — in other words, making families.

In a snappy dialogue format, Budziszewski takes up these and lots of similar questions. The first part of the book is what he calls "girl and guy stuff." What are "the moves" of courtship, and why are they so hard to figure out? Is "missionary dating" a good idea or a bad one? Does it matter whom you live with? Why do so many people seem to be afraid of growing up?

My favorite question is why "sowing your wild oats" never works out the way it's supposed to. Sexuality, he says, is like duct tape. The first time you use it, it sticks you to whomever it touches. But just like that duct tape, if you rip it off and then touch it to someone else, it isn't as sticky as it was before. So what happens when you pull it loose from one partner after another? Budziszewski explains: You just don't stick anymore, your sexual partners seem like strangers, and you stop feeling anything.

I like that answer. Not only is it thoroughly biblical, but it honors the fact of our natural design — the way we are actually made to fit the way the world really is.

If you want to learn more about how to explain the creational plan for love and courtship to the young people in your life, check out this wonderful new book — *Ask Me Anything: Provocative Answers for College Students*.

Don't forget: if we go against the way God designed us to live, it is like cutting across the grain of the universe, and we're asking for trouble. All we have to do to live right is to get with the plan — His plan, that is.[2]

Discussion Question

How would you paraphrase what Chuck Colson is saying to contemporary Americans about love and pre-marital sex?

The Tea Party Movement

The **Tea Party movement** is a populist (or grassroots) movement in the United States that grew into a series of locally and nationally coordinated protests throughout 2009. The protests were partially in response to several federal laws: the Emergency Economic Stabilization Act of 2008, the American Recovery and Reinvestment Act of 2009, and a series of healthcare reform bills. The primary instigating agent was the Emergency Economic Stabilization Act, especially the bailout of the banks.

"The Destruction of Tea at Boston Harbor," lithograph depicting the 1773 Boston Tea Party Some colonist diguised themselves as Native Americans, 1846 (PD).

The name "Tea Party" refers to the Boston Tea Party, a 1774 incident where colonists destroyed British tea rather than paying what they considered a tax that violated their right to "No Taxation without Representation." It is not a national political party, and its name has not appeared on any ballots. The movement has no central leadership but is a loose affiliation of small local groups. The movement's primary concerns include, but are not limited to, cutting back the size of the government and reducing the national debt and federal budget deficit. Tea Party participants are strict constructionists of the U.S. Constitution.

Discussion Question

What do you know about the Tea Party movement?

2. http://fbwitness.serveronline.net/News.asp?ID=3601.

The Recession of 2008

The **recession of 2008** was a major worldwide economic downturn that began in 2008 and continued into 2012. It was by far the worst recession since the Great Depression of the 1930s. It appears that the worldwide recession hit bottom around September 2009; however, there are few signs that the American or world economies have started to move upward again. Britain, Spain, and Ireland remain in serious trouble, while China and Brazil have rebounded and are growing rapidly.

The Member's Gallery inside the New York Stock Exchange (PD).

There are many theories about why the recession occurred. Concerning the United States economy, proponents of free market capitalism declare that Federal Reserve Chairman Ben Bernanke should not have bailed out failing firms, and instead should have allowed free-market capitalism to recover quickly, as it did in the depression of 1920 without government intervention (free-market capitalists assert that government intervention merely drags out recessions and depressions). A 2005 study found that government corporate bailouts are often done for mere political considerations, and the economic resources allocated exhibit significantly worse economic performance than resources allocated using purely business considerations. However, the spectacular rebound of General Motors in 2010 (after its bailout) may belie those concerns.

Likewise, in the United States the economy stabilized in 2010–2011 but has not shown signs of recovery apart from the stock market rising. Serious weaknesses continue in most economic sectors, and unemployment continues to worsen.

The crisis is worldwide. Global trade declined sharply — by 13 percent from August 2008 to August 2009, hurting exporters such as Germany and Japan. China, however, continues to grow at a phenomenal rate (e.g., 8.9 percent annual rate in 2008–2009).[3]

Discussion Question

What were the causes of the 2008 recession?

---

3. http://conservapedia.com/Recession_of_2008.

The Future of America:
Elisha's Tears, 2 Kings 8:7–29

"I weep because I see what you will do to Israel. . . ."

At times we are called on to deliver messages we do not want to deliver. When Elisha was sent to Syria by God, he met Hazael. As he looked into the face of this future ruler of Syria, Elisha saw how much Israel would suffer at Hazael's hand in the future. No wonder the prophet, who loved his people, wept. It is always good news to hear that a sick man will be well . . . unless the man who gets well will kill your children.

Elisha wept. . . .

After September 11, 2001, we in America are especially somber. I am not in any way mitigating the horrendous crime that was committed on September 11, 2001. It was a great disaster. However, may I suggest that we have looked into the face of Hazael? After all, we are both the perpetrator and the victim in our present situation.

In our own country at the beginning of the millennium, in spite of unprecedented prosperity, we see the seeds of our destruction everywhere. Increased crime, poverty, and unemployment. Hopelessness and domestic violence. Some of us wonder whether our American covenant is being recklessly compromised by leaders who are choosing to condone practices that we see as immoral. We see Hazael. He will survive . . . but will we? Will the American dream survive?

Median before-tax family income by percentiles of net worth in the USA from 1989-2004 (PD).

Edward Gibbon, in his seminal work *The Decline and Fall of the Roman Empire*,[4] says that the following five attributes marked Rome at its end. First, a mounting love of affluence. Second, a widening gap between the very rich and the very poor. Third, an obsession with sex. Fourth, freakishness in the arts, masquerading as originality, and enthusiasms pretending to be creativity. Fifth, an increased desire to live on welfare. Sound familiar? Are we looking at Hazael?

That must have been how the disciples felt. Only three years with Him. Three short years. And while His work seemed to fall on deaf ears, the evil Romans prospered. Caiphas prospered. Herod prospered. Evil would win after all . . . and Elisha wept.

Jesus wept, too. In the Garden of Gethsemane, Jesus spent the last night of His life. Alone. He had to die. He knew it. And He was so afraid that He wept blood. Sometimes I think we make the Cross into something less than it was. It was a horrible death. In Jesus' day, wearing a cross around one's neck would have been like wearing an electric chair around our neck today. No, Hazael will live. Jesus will die. And Elisha wept. . . .

Elisha began his ministry during the last half of the ninth century B.C. Leaving his parents' farm in the Upper Jordan Valley, he trained under Elijah for several years, and then served in the northern kingdom for over 50 years.

---

4. Edward Gibbon, *The Decline and Fall of the Roman Empire*, published in six volumes between 1776 and 1788.

Elisha was not isolated and unpredictable, as Elijah often was. Instead, he spent time with people, sharing meals and staying in their homes. He traveled throughout the kingdom on a donkey, visiting the villages and communities. Elisha's miracles among these people reflected a deep compassion for the poor and needy.

Despite his loyalty to Israel, Elisha relentlessly fought against the idol worship of her kings. Obedience to God's instructions took him as far north as Damascus, where he appointed the Syrian king who would eventually oppress Israel. A similar mission in Israel brought the downfall of her evil kings and a massacre of the prophets.

But Elisha knew all too well that Hazael would live and someday he would destroy his nation. The rich and the poor alike would suffer. They would suffer because the nation was evil . . . was unfaithful to God. And Elisha wept.

To a large degree, we are to do nothing. We are to wait. The Hebrew understanding of "waiting" is "to stand firmly and actively watch God's will be revealed." The Greeks and the Romans, like some of us today, tried to build society upon their gods. But these gods will never be big enough because they are finite, limited. Even mighty Rome, with all its power, did not have satisfactory answers to the questions plaguing humankind. So they fell. They are finished. They were Hazael.

But we serve a God who never slumbers or sleeps. A God who, in a blink of an eye, created the universe. A God who has no beginning or ending. A God who loved us enough to send His only begotten Son to die for us . . . that is one response to Hazael — embrace the Son of God as our Savior. Do not rewrite the rules of the game — play another game!

When the three young students refused to worship mighty Babylonian King Nebuchadnezzar they were thrown into the fiery furnace (see the Book of Daniel). "We believe God will deliver us," they said. "But even if we die, we shall not worship you" (Dan. 3:17–18, paraphrased).

Believers, are we willing to stand firm in our faith no matter what the cost? If we are, then Hazael shall not have our souls . . . even if someday he takes our lives.

Will we stand with Joshua on the edge of the Promised Land and proclaim: "You may follow whom you will but as for me and my house, we shall serve the Lord!"

As Elisha weeps, he stands with saints of all ages — he stands on Carmel with Elijah, with Moses on Horeb, with Abraham on Moriah — and he asks us again, "If Baal is god then worship him; if God is God worship Him! But choose ye this day . . ." (see Josh. 24:14–15).

I know that it seems that we are looking into the face of Hazael . . . and we are. But let us stand as countless saints before us stood. Let us stand firm and choose life this year — eternal life! If the present homeschool movement does nothing else let us call our nation to be hopeful in the face of Hazael because . . . our Redeemer liveth!

Discussion Question

Why is the author of this series cautiously optimistic about the future?

Mother Teresa of Calcutta in 1980 (PD).

Chapter 27

20th-Century Saints: Culture Warriors

First Thoughts

At the beginning of the 20th century, there was a culture war brewing. Many liberal theologians rejected the claims of the Scripture and embraced the ambiguity of higher criticism. Evangelicalism was caricatured and belittled by a secular press and arrogant liberalism. The cultural defeats during the Scopes Trial in Dayton, Tennessee, and the failure of Prohibition flamed the cultural war of the 20th century. Thankfully, God raised up the saints to do battle for the truth of the gospel! This chapter will examine five of them.

Chapter Learning Objectives

We will examine the state of 20th-century evangelicalism by examining the lives of five inspiring saints: Oswald Chambers, C.S. Lewis, Thomas Merton, Francis Shaeffer, and Mother Teresa.

As a result of this chapter you should be able to:

1. Review the importance of Oswald Chambers in world history

2. Evaluate the effect of C.S. Lewis on 20th-century society

3. Review the life of Thomas Merton

4. Analyze the apologetic writings of Francis Shaeffer

5. Explore the impact of 20th-century evangelicalism on world society

CONCEPTS

Oswald Chambers

C. S. Lewis

Thomas Merton

Francis Schaefer

Mother Teresa

Lesson 1

Oswald Chambers (1874–1917)

This chapter is devoted to the lives and writings of several modern saints: Oswald Chambers, C. S. Lewis, Thomas Merton, Francis Shaeffer, and Mother Teresa.

All these saints were part of the great 20th-century cultural war that erupted between evangelicalism and liberalism. Evangelicalism emphasized a personal relationship with Jesus Christ and the inerrancy of Scripture. Liberals believed there were many paths to heaven; furthermore, the most important thing to them was social praxis — reaching out to the poor and to the infirm.

The first notable evangelical of the 20th century was Oswald Chambers. When World War I broke out, Oswald Chambers prayed: "Lord, I praise You for this place I am in, but the wonder has begun to stir in me — is this Your place for me? Hold me steady doing Your will. It may be only restlessness; if so, calm me to strength that I sin not against You by doubting."[1] Such was the man who devoted his whole life to serving God. He died in 1917 while serving in the British army. After he died, his wife gathered his material into the most famous devotions in the world: *My Utmost for His Highest* (1924).

Oswald Chambers: Early 20th century saint who wrote a very popular devotional *My Utmost for His Highest.*

Passage

"The Missionary's Master and Teacher," in *My Utmost for His Highest*, for September 22:

> To have a master and teacher is not the same thing as being mastered and taught. Having a master and teacher means that there is someone who knows me better than I know myself, who is closer than a friend, and who understands the remotest depths of my heart and is able to satisfy them fully. It means having someone who has made me secure in the knowledge that he has met and solved all the doubts, uncertainties, and problems in my mind. To have a master and teacher is this and nothing less ". . . For One is your Teacher, the Christ . . ." (Matthew 23:8).
>
> Our Lord never takes measures to make me do what He wants. Sometimes I wish God would master and control me to make me do what He wants, but He will not. And at other times I wish He would leave me alone, and He does not.
>
> "You call Me Teacher and Lord . . ." — but is He? *Teacher, Master*, and *Lord* have little place in our vocabulary. We prefer the words *Savior, Sanctifier*, and *Healer*. The only word that truly describes the experience of being mastered is love, and we know little about love as God reveals it in His Word. The way we use the word obey is proof of this. In the Bible, obedience is based on a relationship between equals; for example, that of a son with his father. Our Lord was not simply God's servant — He was His Son. ". . . *Though He was a Son*, yet He learned obedience . . ." (Hebrews 5:8). If we are consciously aware that we are being mastered, that idea itself is proof that we have no master. If that is our attitude toward Jesus, we are far away from having the relationship He wants with us. He wants us in a relationship where He is so easily our Master and

---

1. http://www.oswaldchambers.co.uk/bio/.

Teacher that we have no conscious awareness of it — a relationship where all we know is that we are His to obey.

Discussion Question

What does Chambers mean in this statement? "Our Lord never takes measures to make me do what He wants."

C.S. Lewis (1898–1963), Twentieth Century Apologist

Clive Staples Lewis (C.S. Lewis, or "Jack" to his friends) was Professor of Medieval and Renaissance English Literature at Cambridge University. Loved by adults and children alike, Lewis was the greatest defender of the Christian faith writing in English in the 20th century. He tried to make a point of avoiding disputes on matters where Christians disagree, and of defending the beliefs they hold in common.

Passage

C.S. Lewis, letter of December 23, 1950, in "Encounter with Light," by Sheldon Vanauken.

Dear Mr. Vanauken:

The contradiction "we must have faith to believe and must believe to have faith" belongs to the same class as those by which the Eleatic philosophers proved that all motion is impossible. And there are many others. You can't swim unless you can support yourself in water, and you can't support yourself in water unless you can swim. Or again, in an act of volition (e.g., getting up in the morning) is the very beginning of the act itself voluntary or involuntary? If voluntary, then you must have willed it . . . you were willing it already . . . it was not really the beginning. If involuntary, then the continuation of the act (being determined by the first movement) is involuntary too. But in spite of this we do swim, and we do get out of bed.

I do not think there is a *demonstrative proof* (like Euclid) of Christianity, nor of the existence of matter, nor of the good will and honesty of my best and oldest friends. I think all three (except perhaps the second) far more probable than the alternatives. The case for Christianity in general is well given by Chesterton; and I tried to do something in my *Broadcast Talks*. As to why God doesn't make it demonstrably clear, are we sure that He is even interested in the kind of

Prince Caspian, in *The Chronicles of Narnia* [series]: "You come of the Lord Adam and the Lady Eve," said Aslan. "And that is both honour enough to erect the head of the poorest beggar, and shame enough to bow the shoulders of the greatest emperor in earth."[1]

1. http://www.quotedb.com/ quotes/601.

Theism which would be a compelled logical assent to a conclusive argument? Are we interested in it in personal matters? I demand from my friend a trust in my good faith which is certain without demonstrative proof. It wouldn't be confidence at all if he waited for rigorous proof. Hang it all, the very fairy tales embody the truth. Othello believed in Desdemona's innocence when it was proved: but that was too late. "His praise is lost who stays till all commend." The magnanimity, the generosity which will trust on a reasonable probability, is required of us. But supposing one believed and was wrong after all? Why, then you would have paid the universe a compliment it doesn't deserve. Your error would even so be more interesting and important than the reality. And yet how could that be? How could an idiotic universe have produced creatures whose mere dreams are so much stronger, better, [and] subtler than itself?

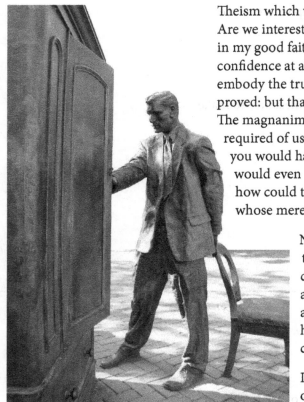

Statue of C.S. Lewis looking into a wardrobe (CCA-SA2.0).

Note that life after death, which still seems to you the essential thing, was itself a late revelation. God trained the Hebrews for centuries to believe in Him without promising them an afterlife, and, blessings on Him, He trained me in the same way for about a year. It is like the disguised prince in a fairy tale who wins the heroine's love *before* she knows he is anything more than a wood-cutter. What would be a bribe if it came first had better come last.

It is quite clear from what you say that you have conscious wishes on both sides. And now, another point about *wishes*. A wish may lead to false beliefs, granted. But what does the existence of the wish suggest? At one time I was much impressed by Arnold's line: "Nor does the being hungry prove that we have bread." But surely tho' it doesn't prove that one particular man will get food; it does prove that there is such a thing as food! i.e., if we were a species that didn't normally eat, weren't designed to eat, would we feel hungry? You say the materialist universe is "ugly." I wonder how you discovered that! If you are really a product of a materialistic universe, how is it you don't feel at home there? Do fish complain of the sea for being wet? Or if they did, would that fact itself not strongly suggest that they had not always, or would not always be, purely aquatic creatures? Notice how we are perpetually surprised at Time. ("How time flies! Fancy John being grown-up and married! I can hardly believe it!") In heaven's name, why? Unless, indeed, there is something about us that is *not* temporal.

Total humility is not in the Tao because the Tao (as such) says nothing about the Object to which it would be the right response: just as there is no law about railways in the acts of Q. Elizabeth. But from the degree of respect which the Tao demands for ancestors, parents, elders, and teachers, it is quite clear what the Tao would prescribe towards an object such as God.

But I think you are already in the meshes of the net! The Holy Spirit is after you. I doubt if you'll get away!

Yours,
C.S. Lewis[2]

---

2. http://www.discovery.org/cslewis/articles/writingspblcdmn/letters.php.

Discussion Question

Lewis is writing to an unsaved friend. What arguments does he offer to persuade his friend to commit his life to Christ?

Thomas Merton (1915–1968)

Thomas Merton was one of the most influential American spiritual writers of the 20th century. His autobiography, *The Seven Storey Mountain*, has sold over one million copies and has been translated into 28 languages. Merton wrote over 60 other books and hundreds of poems and articles on topics ranging from monastic spirituality to the nuclear arms race.

> Thomas Merton: One of the most influential American spiritual writers of the 20th century.

Passage

"To Know the Cross," in *No Man Is an Island*

> The Christian must not only accept suffering: he must make it holy. Nothing so easily becomes unholy as suffering.
>
> Merely accepted, suffering does nothing for our souls except, perhaps, to harden them. Endurance alone is no consecration. True asceticism is not a mere cult of fortitude. We can deny ourselves rigorously for the wrong reason and end up by pleasing ourselves mightily with our self-denial.
>
> Suffering is consecrated to God by faith — not by faith in suffering, but by faith in God. Some of us believe in the power and the value of suffering. But such a belief is an illusion. Suffering has no power and no value of its own.
>
> It is valuable only as a test of faith. What if our faith fails the test? Is it good to suffer, then? What if we enter into suffering with a strong faith in suffering, and then discover that suffering destroys us?
>
> To believe in suffering is pride: but to suffer, believing in God, is humility. For pride may tell us that we are strong enough to suffer, that suffering is good for us because we are good. Humility tells us that suffering is an evil which we must always expect to find in our lives because of the evil that is in ourselves. But faith also knows that the mercy of God is given to those who seek him in suffering, and that by his grace we can overcome evil with good. Suffering, then, becomes good by accident, by the good that it enables us to receive more abundantly from the mercy of God. It does not make us good by itself, but it enables us to make ourselves better than we are. Thus, what we consecrate to God in suffering is not our suffering but our selves.

"Christ on the Cross," by Carl Heinrich Bloch, 1870 (PD).

Only the sufferings of Christ are valuable in the sight of God, who hates evil, and to him they are valuable chiefly as a sign. The death of Jesus on the cross has an infinite meaning and value not because it is a death, but because it is the death of the Son of God. The cross of Christ says nothing of the power of suffering or of death. It speaks only of the power of him who overcame both suffering and death by rising from the grave.

The wounds that evil stamped upon the flesh of Christ are to be worshiped as holy not because they are wounds, but because they are his wounds. Nor would we worship them if he had merely died of them, without rising again. For Jesus is not merely someone who once loved us enough to die for us. His love for us is the infinite love of God, which is stronger than all evil and cannot be touched by death.

Suffering, therefore, can only be consecrated to God by one who believes that Jesus is not dead. And it is of the very essence of Christianity to face suffering and death not because they are good, not because they have meaning, but because the resurrection of Jesus has robbed them of their meaning.

To know the cross is not merely to know our own sufferings. For the cross is the sign of salvation, and no one is saved by his own sufferings. To know the cross is to know that we are saved by the sufferings of Christ; more, it is to know the love of Christ who underwent suffering and death in order to save us. It is, then, to know Christ. For to know his love is not merely to know the story of his love, but to experience in our spirit that we are loved by him, and that in his love the Father manifests his own love for us, through his Spirit poured forth into our hearts.[3]

Discussion Question

What does Merton mean in this statement? "The Christian must not only accept suffering: he must make it holy."

---

3. http://www.plough.com/en/articles/2011/april/to-know-the-cross.

Francis Schaeffer (1912–1984)

Francis Schaeffer became a household word among late 20th-century evangelicals. He was born in Philadelphia, moved to Switzerland in 1948 as a missionary, and in 1955, with his wife Edith, founded L'Abri (the Shelter) Fellowship, which grew to be international. Both to the uninformed enthusiast and the pedantic academic, Schaeffer spoke challenging truths. Francis Schaeffer was a pastor with a rare and deep sensitivity to the spiritual plight of the 1960s Jesus Revolution. Schaeffer genuinely loved those whom he confronted. He championed an apologetic approach. As he often said, he gave honest answers to honest questions. His style was a folksy, almost thinking-out-loud style, yet it was this quality at the personal level that proved to be so winsomely effective.

> Francis Schaeffer: Moved to Switzerland in 1948 as a missionary, and founded L'Abri (the Shelter) Fellowship with his wife, Edith.

Passage

Letter of October 26, 1951, "The Reawakening of Spiritual Reality"

> As I have thought perhaps more quietly than in previous days, it has seemed to me that in the past there has been a fallacy in my thinking. That fallacy is simply this: that insofar as we are so abundantly right (as we are concerning the Biblical position), therefore it would certainly follow of a necessity that God's rich blessing would rest upon us as individuals and as a movement. I no longer believe this is so. For increasingly the realization has welled up in my own soul that although this principle of separation is of tremendous importance, nevertheless there are other principles in the Word of God which must be kept with equal fidelity if God's full blessing is to be upon us. . . .

> What does all this mean to me? I am not sure, except that it brings me increasingly to my knees — to ask that the Holy Spirit may have His way in my life; that I may not think just of justification and then the glories of Heaven (with merely a battle for separation between). [But that I may also think of] all the wonders of the *present aspect* of my salvation, and that they may be real to me in my life and ministry. What a wonderful Lord we have, and how glorious it is to indeed have God as our Father, and to be united with Christ, and to be indwelt by the Holy Spirit. Oh, would to God that our ministry could be under His full direction, and in His power without reservation.

Letter of November 8, 1951, "Gradually My Thinking Has Changed"

> Tonight it is rainy outside, but a little higher in the mountains the snow is falling again. The wood fire is crackling with a rich personality. The children are sleeping, and Edith is typing some things which she feels she must do. In short, it is quiet here — the quiet that only the mountains can give.

> As I was walking home from the post office today, where I had gone to send off a great pile of letters and some packages, I was thinking of my answer to you. And as I walked I looked up at the Dents with their swirling mists so high above me. I thought how our dear Lord comes into more proper perspective in our thinking in such a place as this — for the higher the mountains, the more understandable is the glory of Him who made them and who holds them in His hand. But the

Francis Schaeffer

other side is also true: man also comes into his proper place. As the Lord gains in greatness, in comparison to the mountains, so man diminishes.

As it is with space, it is also true of time. My letters from here go to so many countries, and in these last few years I have found friends in many of them. As I have learned the history of these lands, from those who tell the history from their hearts, time has come to mean something different to me than it ever did before, when time was measured only by the short scope of the hurrying clock or cold dates on a page of the history book. But as time falls into its proper place, again God seems to grow greater by comparison, and again it has the opposite effect on man. As the mountains shrink him down to size, so also does time. . . .

The three and a half years since I came to Europe have been the most profitable in my life, with only one possible competitor, my three years in seminary. But certainly (with that one possible exception) no period even three times as long has marked me so.

First, the things of which I spoke above — the rectifying process of space and time — have caused my view of the Lord to grow greater, and my view of man and his works and judgments to grow proportionately smaller.

When I first found Christ through my Bible reading, he was very real to me, and I yet remember the loving wonder of His closeness. . . . Do not misunderstand me: my experiences here have convinced me more than ever that each of these struggles was needed and right; but the correct perspective got mislaid in the process. And I tell you frankly, that though I realize I may be wrong, it seems to me that I was not alone in my mistake — that many are as deeply involved, or even more, than I have been. The "movement" grew in our thinking like the great bay tree until for me that wonderful closeness which I have felt to Him in previous days was lost. I wonder if that is not what happened to the Church of Ephesus in Revelation 2?

God willing, I will push and politick no more. The mountains are too high, history is too long, and eternity is longer. God is too great, man is too small, there are many of God's dear children, and all around there are men going to Hell. And if one man and a small group of men do not approve of where I am and what I do, does it prove I've missed success? No; only one thing will determine that — whether this day I'm where the Lord of lords and King of kings wants me to be. To win as many as I can, to help strengthen the hands of those who fight unbelief in the historical setting in which they are placed, to know the reality of "the Lord is my song," and to be committed to the Holy Spirit — that is what I wish I could know to be the reality of each day as it closes.

Have I learned all this? No, but I would not exchange that portion of it which I have, by God's grace, for all the hand-clapping I have had when I have been on the top of the pile. I have been a poor learner, but I'm further on than I was three years ago and I like it.

I know I've made mistakes and I know I've sinned. And where I know it, I have tried to make it right with those I have hurt, to confess it to the Lord and try to follow His way. . . . My inclination is to think that Christ meant it in a very literal way when He said to seek the lower seats. That does not mean, as I see it, that we should refuse the higher if the Lord takes us there, but He should do the taking. I regret the times in my life when this has not been the case. . . .

Through the recent difficulties I have faced, the Lord taught me more than I ever knew of the greatness of the Lord and the smallness of any man — and the corresponding importance of pleasing the Lord, and the lack of importance of pleasing any particular man. . . . In spite of all that has happened there is no question of personal discouragement, for I am probably less discouraged than I have ever been since those bright days when I first saw the face of the Lord, and before my feet got stuck in the problems of the prestige of man. . . .[4]

Discussion Question

In what ways has Schaeffer's thinking changed?

Mother Teresa (1910–1997), Sister of Mercy

In 1952, the first Home for the Dying was opened in Calcutta, India. Over the next 30 years, Mother Teresa's Missionaries of Charity grew from 12 to thousands serving the "poorest of the poor" in 450 centers around the world. For more than 45 years, Mother Teresa comforted the poor, the dying, and the unwanted around the world. Mother Teresa gained worldwide acclaim with her tireless efforts on behalf of world peace. Her work brought her numerous accolades, including the Pope John XXIII Peace Prize in 1971 and the Nobel Peace Prize in 1979. In receiving this award, Mother Teresa insisted on a departure from the ceremonial banquet and asked that the funds be donated to the poor in Calcutta. This money would permit her to feed hundreds for a year.

"Yesterday is gone. Tomorrow has not yet come. We have only today. Let us begin." — Mother Teresa

Passage

An address at the National Prayer Breakfast, Sponsored by the US Senate and House of Representatives, February 3, 1994

On the last day, Jesus will say to those on His right hand, "Come, enter the Kingdom. For I was hungry and you gave me food, I was thirsty and you gave

4. http://www.thewords.com/articles/schaeffer1.htm.

Mother Teresa, 1988 (CCA-SA2.5).

me drink, I was sick and you visited me." Then Jesus will turn to those on His left hand and say, "Depart from me because I was hungry and you did not feed me, I was thirsty and you did not give me to drink, I was sick and you did not visit me." These will ask Him, "When did we see You hungry, or thirsty or sick and did not come to Your help?" And Jesus will answer them, "Whatever you neglected to do unto one of these least of these, you neglected to do unto Me!"

As we have gathered here to pray together, I think it will be beautiful if we begin with a prayer that expresses very well what Jesus wants us to do for the least. St. Francis of Assisi understood very well these words of Jesus and His life is very well expressed by a prayer. And this prayer, which we say every day after Holy Communion, always surprises me very much, because it is very fitting for each one of us. And I always wonder whether 800 years ago when St. Francis lived, they had the same difficulties that we have today. I think that some of you already have this prayer of peace — so we will pray it together.

Let us thank God for the opportunity He has given us today to have come here to pray together. We have come here especially to pray for peace, joy, and love. We are reminded that Jesus came to bring the good news to the poor. He had told us what that good news is when He said: "My peace I leave with you, My peace I give unto you." He came not to give the peace of the world which is only that we don't bother each other. He came to give the peace of heart which comes from loving — from doing good to others.

And God loved the world so much that He gave His son — it was a giving. God gave His son to the Virgin Mary, and what did she do with Him? As soon as Jesus came into Mary's life, immediately she went in haste to give that good news. And as she came into the house of her cousin, Elizabeth, Scripture tells us that the unborn child — the child in the womb of Elizabeth — leapt with joy. While still in the womb of Mary — Jesus brought peace to John the Baptist, who leapt for joy in the womb of Elizabeth. The unborn was the first one to proclaim the coming of Christ.

And as if that were not enough, as if it were not enough that God the Son should become one of us and bring peace and joy while still in the womb of Mary, Jesus also died on the Cross to show that greater love. He died for you and for me, and for the leper and for that man dying of hunger and that naked person lying in the street, not only of Calcutta, but of Africa, and everywhere. Our Sisters serve these poor people in 105 countries throughout the world. Jesus insisted that we love one another as He loves each one of us. Jesus gave His life to love us, and He tells us that we also have to give whatever it takes to do good to one another. And in the Gospel Jesus says very clearly: "Love as I have loved you."

Jesus died on the Cross because that is what it took for Him to do good to us — to save us from our selfishness in sin. He gave up everything to do the Father's will — to show us that we too must be willing to give up everything to do God's will — to love one another as He loves each of us. If we are not willing to give whatever it takes to do good to one another, sin is still in us. That is why we too must give to each other until it hurts.

It is not enough for us to say: "I love God," but I also have to love my neighbor. St. John says that you are a liar if you say you love God and you don't love your neighbor. How can you love God whom you do not see, if you do not love your neighbor whom you see, whom you touch, with whom you live? And so it is very important for us to realize that love, to be true, has to hurt. I must be willing to give whatever it takes not to harm other people and, in fact, to do good to them. This requires that I be willing to give until it hurts. Otherwise, there is not true love in me, and I bring injustice, not peace, to those around me.

It hurt Jesus to love us. We have been created in His image for greater things, to love and to be loved. We must "put on Christ" as Scripture tells us. And so, we have been created to love as He loves us. Jesus makes Himself the hungry one, the naked one, the homeless one, the unwanted one, and He says, "You did it to Me." On the last day He will say to those on His right, "Whatever you did to the least of these, you did to Me," and He will also say to those on His left, "Whatever you neglected to do for the least of these, you neglected to do it for Me."

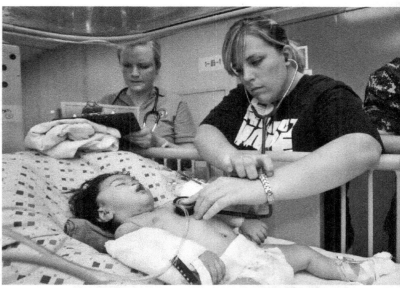

A volunteer with Project HOPE checks the vitals of a 4-month-old Indonesian girl who had surgery to fix her cleft lip aboard Military Sealift Command hospital ship USNS *Mercy* (T-AH 19) in North Sulawesi, Indonesia, June 2, 2012, during Pacific Partnership 2012. Pacific Partnership is an annual deployment of forces designed to strengthen maritime and humanitarian partnerships during disaster relief operations, while providing humanitarian, medical, dental, and engineering assistance to nations of the Pacific (PD-DOD).

When He was dying on the Cross, Jesus said, "I thirst." Jesus is thirsting for our love, and this is the thirst of everyone, poor and rich alike. We all thirst for the love of others, that they go out of their way to avoid harming us and to do good to us. This is the meaning of true love, to give until it hurts.

I can never forget the experience I had in visiting a home where they kept all these old parents of sons and daughters who had just put them into an institution and forgotten them — maybe. I saw that in that home these old people had everything — good food, comfortable place, television, everything, but everyone was looking toward the door. And I did not see a single one with a smile on the face. I turned to Sister and I asked: "Why do these people who have every comfort here, why are they all looking toward the door? Why are they not smiling?"

I am so used to seeing the smiles on our people, even the dying ones smile. And Sister said: "This is the way it is nearly every day. They are expecting, they are hoping that a son or daughter will come to visit them. They are hurt because they are forgotten." And see, this neglect to love brings spiritual poverty. Maybe in our own family we have somebody who is feeling lonely, who is feeling sick, who is feeling worried. Are we there? Are we willing to give until it hurts in order to be with our families, or do we put our own interests first? These are the questions we must ask ourselves, especially as we begin this year of the family. We must remember that love begins at home, and we must also remember that "the future of humanity passes through the family."

I was surprised in the West to see so many young boys and girls given to drugs. And I tried to find out why. Why is it like that, when those in the West have so many more things than those in the East? And the answer was: "Because there is no one in the family to receive them." Our children depend on us for every-thing — their health, their nutrition, their security, their coming to know and

Missionaries of Charity with the traditional sari (PD).

love God. For all of this, they look to us with trust, hope, and expectation. But often father and mother are so busy they have no time for their children, or perhaps they are not even married or have given up on their marriage. So their children go to the streets and get involved in drugs or other things. We are talking of love of the child, which is where love and peace must begin. These are the things that break peace.

But I feel that the greatest destroyer of peace today is abortion, because it is a war against the child, a direct killing of the innocent child, murder by the mother herself. And if we accept that a mother can kill even her own child, how can we tell other people not to kill one another? How do we persuade a woman not to have an abortion? As always, we must persuade her with love, and we remind ourselves that love means to be willing to give until it hurts. Jesus gave even His life to love us. So, the mother who is thinking of abortion should be helped to love, that is, to give until it hurts her plans, or her free time, to respect the life of her child. The father of that child, whoever he is, must also give until it hurts.

By abortion, the mother does not learn to love, but kills even her own child to solve her problems. And, by abortion, that father is told that he does not have to take any responsibility at all for the child he has brought into the world. The father is likely to put other women into the same trouble. So abortion just leads to more abortion. Any country that accepts abortion is not teaching its people to love, but to use any violence to get what they want. This is why the greatest destroyer of love and peace is abortion.

Many people are very, very concerned with the children of India, with the children of Africa where quite a few die of hunger, and so on. Many people are also concerned about all the violence in this great country of the United States. These concerns are very good. But often these same people are not concerned with the millions who are being killed by the deliberate decision of their own mothers. And this is what is the greatest destroyer of peace today — abortion which brings people to such blindness.

And for this I appeal in India and I appeal everywhere — "Let us bring the child back." The child is God's gift to the family. Each child is created in the special image and likeness of God for greater things — to love and to be loved. In this year of the family we must bring the child back to the center of our care and concern. This is the only way that our world can survive because our children are the only hope for the future. As older people are called to God, only their children can take their places.

But what does God say to us? He says: "Even if a mother could forget her child, I will not forget you. I have carved you in the palm of my hand." We are carved in the palm of His hand; that unborn child has been carved in the hand of God from conception and is called by God to love and be loved, not only now in this life, but forever. God can never forget us.

The beautiful gift God has given our congregation is to fight abortion by adoption. We have already, from our house in Calcutta, over 3,000 children in adoption. And I can't tell you what joy, what love, what peace those children have brought into those families. It has been a real gift of God for them and for us. I remember one of the little ones was very sick, so I sent for the father and the mother and I asked them: "Please give me back the sick child. I will give you a healthy one." And the father looked at me and said, "Mother Teresa, take my life first [rather] than take the child." So beautiful to see it — so much love, so much joy that little one has brought into that family. So pray for us that we continue this beautiful gift. And also I offer you — our Sisters are here — anybody who doesn't want the child, please give it to me. I want the child.

I will tell you something beautiful. We are fighting abortion by adoption — by care of the mother and adoption for her baby. We have saved thousands of lives. We have sent word to the clinics, to the hospitals and police stations: "Please don't destroy the child; we will take the child." So we always have someone tell the mothers in trouble: "Come, we will take care of you, we will get a home for your child." And we have a tremendous demand from couples who cannot have a child — but I never give a child to a couple who have done something not to have a child. Jesus said, "Anyone who receives a child in my name receives me." By adopting a child, these couples receive Jesus but, by aborting a child, a couple refuses to receive Jesus.

Please don't kill the child. I want the child. Please give me the child. I am willing to accept any child who would be aborted and to give that child to a married couple who will love the child and be loved by the child. From our children's home in Calcutta alone, we have saved over 3,000 children from abortion. These children have brought such love and joy to their adopting parents and have grown up so full of love and joy.

I know that couples have to plan their family, and for that there is natural family planning. The way to plan the family is natural family planning, not contraception. In destroying the power of giving life, through contraception, a husband or wife is doing something to self. This turns the attention to self and so it destroys the gifts of love in him or her. In loving, the husband and wife must turn the attention to each other as happens in natural family planning, and not to self, as happens in contraception. Once that living love is destroyed by contraception, abortion follows very easily.

I also know that there are great problems in the world — that many spouses do not love each other enough to practice natural family planning. We cannot solve all the problems in the world, but let us never bring in the worst problem of all, and that is to destroy love. And this is what happens when we tell people to practice contraception and abortion.

The poor are very great people. They can teach us so many beautiful things. Once one of them came to thank us for teaching her natural family planning and said: "You people who have practiced chastity; you are the best people to teach us natural family planning because it is nothing more than self-control out of love for each other." And what this poor person said is very true. These poor people maybe have nothing to eat, maybe they have not a home to live in, but they can still be great people when they are spiritually rich.

When I pick up a person from the street, hungry, I give him a plate of rice, a piece of bread. But a person who is shut out, who feels unwanted, unloved,

The Home of the Pure Heart (Nirmal Hriday) (formerly Kalighat Home for the Dying) is a hospice for the sick, destitute and the dying in Kalighat, Kolkata (Calcutta), India, established by Mother Teresa (CCA-sa3.0).

terrified, the person who has been thrown out of society — that spiritual poverty is much harder to overcome. And abortion, which often follows from contraception, brings a people to be spiritually poor, and that is the worst poverty and the most difficult to overcome.

Those who are materially poor can be very wonderful people. One evening we went out and we picked up four people from the street. And one of them was in a most terrible condition. I told the Sisters: "You take care of the other three; I will take care of the one who looks worse." So I did for her all that my love can do. I put her in bed, and there was such a beautiful smile on her face. She took hold of my hand, as she said one word only: "Thank you" — and she died.

I could not help but examine my conscience before her. And I asked: "What would I say if I were in her place?" And my answer was very simple. I would have tried to draw a little attention to myself. I would have said: "I am hungry, I am dying, I am cold, I am in pain," or something. But she gave me much more — she gave me her grateful love. And she died with a smile on her face. Then there was the man we picked up from the drain, half eaten by worms and, after we had brought him to the home, he only said, "I have lived like an animal in the street, but I am going to die as an angel, loved and cared for." Then, after we had removed all the worms from his body, all he said, with a big smile, was: "Sister, I am going home to God" — and he died. It was so wonderful to see the greatness of that man who could speak like that without blaming anybody, without comparing anything. Like an angel — this is the greatness of people who are spiritually rich even when they are materially poor.

We are not social workers. We may be doing social work in the eyes of some people, but we must be contemplatives in the heart of the world. For we must bring that presence of God into your family, for the family that prays together, stays together. There is so much hatred, so much misery, and we with our prayer, with our sacrifice, are beginning at home. Love begins at home, and it is not how much we do, but how much love we put into what we do.

If we are contemplatives in the heart of the world with all its problems, these problems can never discourage us. We must always remember what God tells us in Scripture: "Even if a mother could forget the child in her womb" — something impossible, but even if she could forget — "I will never forget you."

And so here I am talking with you. I want you to find the poor here, right in your own home first. And begin love there. Be that good news to your own people first. And find out about your next-door neighbors. Do you know who they are?

I had the most extraordinary experience of love of neighbor with a Hindu family. A gentleman came to our house and said: "Mother Teresa, there is a family who have not eaten for so long. Do something." So I took some rice and went there immediately. And I saw the children — their eyes shining with hunger. I don't know if you have ever seen hunger. But I have seen it very often. And the mother of the family took the rice I gave her and went out. When she came back, I asked her: "Where did you go? What did you do?" And she gave me a very simple answer: "They are hungry also." What struck me was that she knew — and who are they? A Muslim family — and she knew. I didn't bring any more rice that evening because I wanted them, Hindus and Muslims, to enjoy the joy of sharing.

But there were those children, radiating joy, sharing the joy and peace with their mother because she had the love to give until it hurts. And you see this is where love begins — at home in the family.

So, as the example of this family shows, God will never forget us, and there is something you and I can always do. We can keep the joy of loving Jesus in our hearts, and share that joy with all we come in contact with. Let us make that one point — that no child will be unwanted, unloved, uncared for, or killed and thrown away. And give until it hurts — with a smile.

As you know, we have a number of homes here in the United States, where people need tender love and care. This is the joy of sharing. Come and share.

The Reagans presenting Mother Teresa with the Medal of Freedom at a White House Ceremony, 1985 (NARA).

We have the young people suffering with AIDS. They need that tender love and care. But such beautiful — I've never yet seen a young man or anybody displeased or angry or frightened, really going home to God. Such a beautiful smile, always. So let us pray that we have the gift of sharing the joy with others and giving until it hurts.

Because I talk so much of giving with a smile, once a professor from the United States asked me: "Are you married?" And I said: "Yes, and I find it sometimes very difficult to smile at my spouse, Jesus, because He can be very demanding — sometimes." This is really something true. And this is where love comes in — when it is demanding, and yet we can give it with joy.

One of the most demanding things for me is traveling everywhere — and with publicity. I have said to Jesus that if I don't go to heaven for anything else, I will be going to heaven for all the traveling with all the publicity, because it has purified me and sacrificed me and made me really ready to go home to God.

If we remember that God loves us, and that we can love others as He loves us, then America can become a sign of peace for the world. From here, a sign of care for the weakest of the weak — the unborn child — must go out to the world. If you become a burning light of justice and peace in the world, then really you will be true to what the founders of this country stood for.

Let us love one another as God loves each one of us. And where does this love begin? In our own home. How does it begin? By praying together. Pray for us that we continue God's work with great love. The sisters, the brothers, and the fathers and the lay missionaries of Charity and co-workers: we are all one heart full of love, that we may bring that joy of love everywhere we go. And my prayer for you is that through this love for one another, for this peace and joy in the family, that you may grow in holiness. Holiness is not the luxury of the few; it is a simply duty, for you and for me, because Jesus has very clearly stated, "Be ye holy as my father in heaven is holy." So let us pray for each other that we grow in love for each other, and through this love become holy as Jesus wants us to be, for he died out of love for us.

One day I met a lady who was dying of cancer in a most terrible condition. And I told her, I say, "You know, this terrible pain is only the kiss of Jesus — a sign that you have come so close to Jesus on the cross that he can kiss you." And she joined her hands together and said, "Mother Teresa, please tell Jesus to stop kissing me."

So pray for us that we continue God's work with great love, and I will pray for you, for all your families. And also I want to thank the families who have been so generous in giving their daughters to us to consecrate their life to Jesus by the vow of poverty, chastity, obedience, and by giving wholehearted free service to the poorest of the poor. This is our fourth vow in our congregation. And we have a novitiate in San Francisco where we have many beautiful vocations who are wanting to give their whole life to Jesus in the service of the poorest of the poor.

So once more I thank you for giving your children to God. And pray for us that we continue God's work with great love.[5]

Discussion Question

What does Mother Teresa mean in saying, "We are not social workers"?

Poverty in India

---

5. http://www.ewtn.com/New_library/breakfast.htm.

The University of Salamanca, in Spain. (CCA-SA2.0).

Chapter 28

The University: Belshazzar's Feast

First Thoughts

Yale Professor George Marsden argues:

> Only a century ago, almost all state universities held compulsory chapel services and some required Sunday church attendance as well. In fact, state-sponsored chapel services were commonplace until the World War II era, and as late as the 1950s it was not unusual for the best universities to refer to themselves as "Christian" institutions. Today, the once pervasive influence of religion on the intellectual and cultural life of America's preeminent colleges and universities has all but vanished.[1]

How did that happen, and what are Christians to do? Do we attend secular or Christian universities, or does it matter?

Chapter Learning Objectives

We will examine the origin of the American secular university. Next, we will assess this origin and its impact on the country. Then, we will assess how Christians can prosper in a secular university, and, finally, we will look at one particular historian's view of the issue.

As a result of this chapter you should be able to:

1. Examine the origin of the university

2. Review the Church's loss of the university

3. Analyze what Christians can do to prosper in a secular university

4. Evaluate Pelikan's analysis of the university

CONCEPTS

University of Bologna

King Belshazzar's feast

Harvard University Charter

---

1. From the book description for George Marsden, *The Soul of the American University* (New York: Oxford University Press, 1994).

The Origin of the University

All major university charters contained language that specifically stated that these institutions were established for the support of the Church, and for the expressed purpose of preparing men to share the gospel.

A university, by definition, is an institution of advanced education and research that grants academic degrees. The original Latin word *universitas* was used at the time of the origin of urban town life and medieval guilds. The original Latin word referred to degree-granting institutions of learning in western Europe, where this form of organization was prevalent.

The first universities were founded to increase the effectiveness of the Church. Without exception, prior to their formal establishment, many medieval secular universities were run for hundreds of years as Christian cathedral schools or monastic schools in which monks and nuns taught classes and priests prepared for the ministry. The earliest universities were developed under the aegis of the Western church, and subject, like all ecclesiological institutions, to the authority of the local bishop.

Area above Bologna's old city center (CCA-SA2.0).

The first universities in Europe were the **University of Bologna** (1088), the University of Paris (1150, later associated with the Sorbonne), the University of Oxford (1167), the University of Palencia (1208), the University of Cambridge (1209), the University of Salamanca (1218), the University of Montpellier (1220), the University of Padua (1222), the University of Naples Federico II (1224), and the University of Toulouse (1229). The Church was responsible for the development of all of these western European medieval universities.

In the university, young men completed their study of the trivium — the preparatory arts of grammar, rhetoric, and dialectic or logic — and arithmetic, geometry, music, and astronomy.

The end of the medieval period marked the beginning of the transformation of universities that would eventually result in the modern research university. Many external forces were exerted on the university at the end of the Middle Ages and the beginning of the Renaissance — humanism for one. The Christian university, then, was replaced by a research, secular facility. This was not to be the case in America, however, until much later.

Discussion Question

Discuss the origin of the university.

Prospering in the Secular University

Who could imagine that a movement that began so quietly in the 1970s and 1980s would someday generate such a vital and anointed generation as the one that is emerging at the beginning of this century? It is a time to celebrate and to reflect.

In the 21st century it is an uncontested fact: evangelicals are dominating college admission test scores, and it is growing more evident each day that they are highly qualified and successful college students once they are admitted. When I was growing up, eons ago, elite prep schools dominated the college admission classes. Today, the new "elite" are homeschooled graduates. They are the most highly recruited, most highly valued freshmen at secular and Christian schools alike. I am privy to a Harvard University online chat room, _____ atly I saw this statement posted: "If Harvard wants to be the best, th___st rel_____ m__on in the years ahead, it must recruit and admit homeschool___ (are _____ evangelicals)." Indeed.

It is not t___ ___ pu__ of this essay to lobby for any particular post-graduate choice, although ___ound my wife at Harvard — and Inter-Varsity Fellowship on Thursday night in Cambridge is larger than the entire student body at Gordon College, a Christian College in South Hamilton. Mostly for fiscal reasons, the majority of Christian home-schoolers go to secular colleges. That is an uncontested fact.

Therefore, this article is about the secular colleges we will attend — how they got to be the way they are and how we can prosper in such places.

First, to most evangelical Christians, the modern, secular university is a hostile place. It was not always so.

In fact, the American university was built solidly on evangelical principles. There were not so-called official "secular" colleges until the rise of the land grant colleges in the middle of the 19th century. An early brochure, published in 1643, stated that the purpose of Harvard University (the oldest American university) was "To advance learning and perpetuate it to posterity; dreading to leave an illiterate ministry to the churches."[2] Harvard's motto for 300 years was *Christo et Ecclesiae* (for Christ and church). In fact, most of the U.S. universities founded before the 20th century had a strongly religious, usually Protestant evangelical Christian character. Yale, Princeton, Chicago, Stanford, Duke, William and Mary, Boston University, Michigan, and the University of California all had a decidedly evangelical Christian character in the early years of their existence but had abandoned it by the 20th century. By the 1920s, the American university had stepped back completely from its evangelical roots. This was true of almost every American university founded in the first 200 years of our nation's existence.

Readers would be surprised to see how evangelical and Christ-centered early universities were. They had pastors as presidents. These men closely tied the identity of their university to a strong Christian worldview. The core curriculum included Bible courses and Christian theology. These were mandatory Bible courses. All American universities insisted on doctrinally sound content for sensitive courses and often

> I spoke to a Yale recruiter and she told me that while Yale wants homeschoolers, homeschoolers do not seem to want Yale. They are not applying to Yale. Likewise, I have two distance-learning students who were heavily recruited by Ivy League schools. They both chose local alternatives.

"A View of the Buildings of Yale College at New Haven," lithograph, published by A. Doolittle & Son, New Haven, 1807 (PD).

2. http://www.hds.harvard.edu/about/history-and-mission.

The west end of King's College Chapel seen from The Backs. Clare College Old Court is on the left. A group of people punting along the River Cam can be seen in the foreground. (CCA-SA2.0).

required that faculty be born-again Christians! Imagine this: the famous historian Frederick Jackson Turner was refused a professorship at Princeton because he was a Unitarian! Chapel attendance was required at Harvard and Yale! It is more than coincidental that the architects who designed early universities designed them to look like churches. At the University of Pittsburgh, for instance, the most prominent building on campus is the Cathedral of Learning.

Discussion Question

On what grounds can a Christian argue that the American university was founded on Christian principles?

Lesson 3

Harvard and Heaven — How Christians Can Prosper in a Secular University

To a large degree the American university abandoned the evangelical, and the evangelical abandoned the American university.

Universities were founded because early Americans earnestly believed that American society should be governed by evangelical Christian people. They believed that American industry should be run by evangelical Christian entrepreneurs. They also believed that American culture should be created by evangelical artists. The early American university was committed to making sure that this happened.

The marriage of spiritual maturity and elite education is a potent combination that, to a large degree, assured the success of the American experiment. Its divorce may presage its demise.

Today the university is not even loosely a Christian institution. Religion in the university and in public life is relegated to the private experience. So-called "academic freedom" has become a sacrosanct concept and precludes anything that smacks of religiosity — especially the orthodoxy that evangelicals so enthusiastically embrace. Religion is represented on campus in sanitary denominational ministries and token chapel ministries (that are hardly more than counseling centers).

To a large degree, then, the American university abandoned the evangelical, and the evangelical abandoned the American university.

This created a crisis in the American university and in the evangelical community. The secular American university compromised its "soul" for naturalism; evangelicalism compromised its epistemological hegemony for ontological supremacy. In other words, the secular university became a sort of academic hothouse for pompous rationalism. Evangelicals abandoned the secular university, and, until recently, more or less compromised their academic base. Evangelicals even founded their own universities but they were poor academic substitutes for secular offerings; however, even as I write this article, this is changing.

The university, if it has any value, must be involved in the communication of immutable, metaphysical truth. The American secular university is not about to accept such limits. It recognizes no citadel of orthodoxy, no limits to its knowledge. But like Jesus reminds Thomas in John 14, our hope lies not in what we know, but most assuredly in Whom we know.

Most secular universities have concluded that abstract concepts like grace, hope, and especially faith are indefinable, immeasurable, and above all unreasonable. Not that God or the uniqueness of Jesus Christ can be proved or disproved. There are certain issues that the order of the intellect simply cannot address, so we must rise above that to the order of the heart. Faith is our consent to receive the good that God would have for us. Evangelicals believe God can and does act in our world and in our lives. Human needs are greater than this world can satisfy, so therefore it is reasonable to look elsewhere. The university has forgotten or ignores this fact.

That is all changing — and partly due to the popularity of the American homeschooling movement. In massive numbers, the American homeschool movement — initially and at present primarily an evangelical Christian movement — is depositing some of the brightest, most capable students in our country into the old, august institutions like Harvard. And what is more exciting, the flashpoint of cultural change is shifting from Harvard, Princeton, Dartmouth, and Stanford to Wheaton, Grove City, Calvin, and Liberty (all evangelical universities). Before long the new wave of elite culture creators will be graduating from American secular universities and Christian universities, and they shall be a great deal different from the elite of which I was a part in the mid 1970s. I am not saying the secular university will change quickly — intellectual naturalistic reductionism makes that extremely difficult. However, I do see the whole complexion of university graduates changing significantly in the next 20 years. Never in the history of the world has such a thing happened.

Divinity Hall (1826) is the oldest building in the Harvard Divinity School at Harvard University. (CCA-SA3.0).

Young people, make sure you know who you are and Who your God is. "By faith, Moses, when he had grown up, refused to be known as the son of Pharaoh's daughter" (Heb. 11:24). Theologian Walter Brueggemann calls American believers to "nurture, nourish, and evoke a consciousness and perception alternative to the consciousness and perception of the dominant culture around us."[3]

Refuse to be absorbed into the world but choose to be a part of God's Kingdom. There is no moderate position anymore in American society — either we are taking a stand for Christ in this inhospitable culture or we are not.

You are a special and peculiar generation. Much loved. But you live among a people who do not know who they are. A people without hope. You need to know who you are — children of the Living God — and then you must live a hopeful life. Quoting C.S. Lewis,

3. Walter Brueggemann, *The Prophetic Imagination* (Minneapolis, MN: Augsburg Fortress Press, 2001), p. 13.

we "are half-hearted creatures, fooling about with drink and sex and ambition when infinite joy is offered us, like an ignorant child who wants to go on making mud pies in a slum because he cannot imagine what is meant by the offer of a holiday at the sea."[4]

Take responsibility for your life. Moses accepted responsibility for his life. "He chose to be mistreated along with the people of God rather than to enjoy the pleasures of sin" (Heb. 11:25). If you don't make decisions for your life, someone else will.

Get a cause worth dying for. Moses accepted necessary suffering even unto death. You need a cause worth dying for (as well as living for). "He [Moses] regarded disgrace for the sake of Christ as of greater value than the treasures of Egypt, because he was looking ahead to his reward" (Heb. 11:26). "I have been crucified with Christ and I no longer live, but Christ lives in me" (Gal. 2:20).

Finally, never take your eyes off the goal. "By faith he left Egypt, not fearing the king's anger; he persevered because he saw him who is invisible" (Heb. 11:27). What is your threshold of obedience?

Young people, if you are part of the new evangelical elite. You have immense opportunities ahead of you. A new godly generation is arising. You will be called to guide this nation into another unprecedented revival. We shall see.

Discussion Question

What advice does the author have for Christians attending secular colleges?

Lesson 4

A Book Review

Jaroslav Pelikan (PD).

The Idea of the University: A Reexamination by Jaroslave Pelikan[5]

The main argument of Pelikan's book is that the true crisis of the university lies not in financial exigencies, political assaults from the left or right, or the myopia of modern life; it lies in the crisis of confidence within the university itself about its abiding nature/purpose.[6] The university, as it were, is having an Ericksonian self-identity crisis. Yale Professor George Marsden would entirely agree; however, he knows exactly where the trouble lies — in the loss of the "soul of the American university."[7] Pelikan is sure that the university has lost something, but like the main character in Kafka's *The Stranger*, it (he) has lost its way, lost its identity, does not quite know from where it has come, how it got to where it is, or where it is to go from here. In any event, it is a quest for an

4. C.S. Lewis, "Weight of Glory," in *Weight of Glory and Other Addresses* (New York: Touchstone, 1996), p. 1–2.
5. Jaroslave Pelikan, *The Idea of the University: A Reexamination* (New Haven, CT: Yale University Press, 1992).
6. Book Review by Alvin Neiman, *Review of Politics* (Winter 1994).
7. George M. Marsden, *The Soul of the American University* (Oxford, UK; New York: Oxford University Press, 1996).

existential goal — not a Judeo-Christian one. Pelikan insists that intelligent discussion of the university requires an analysis of its most basic nature and a discussion of the role it can and should play among other institutions and communities within the local, national, and international community.

Pelikan's book has three parts: Section I deals with Newman's first principles — the bedrock of university education. Section II deals with the business of a university. And the last section deals with a university's duties to a free society.

Central to Pelikan's thesis is an ongoing dialogue with John Henry Newman's *The Idea of a University Defined and Illustrated* (1852).[8] Newman's Idea of a university grew out of Newman's struggle with the rise of scientific learning — a struggle that continues today. Newman, it seems to me, is a 19th-century evangelical trying to come to grips with his culture. Pelikan is a 20th-century intellectual coming to grips with his Christianity. "A university," Newman wrote, "is not a birthplace of poets or of immortal authors, or founders of schools, leaders of colonies, or conquerors of nations. It does promise a generation of Aristotles or Newtons . . . a university training is the great ordinary means to a great but ordinary end; it aims at raising the intellectual tone of society."[9] In other words, the purpose of an education is to enable a person to live a life rather than to earn a living. Pelikan adds his own interpretation: The view taken of a university

Belshazzar's Feast., circa 1635-1638 (PD).

in these discourses is the following: that it is a place of teaching universal knowledge, but also of advancing knowledge through research and of diffusing knowledge through publication, as well as of relating such advancement, teaching, and diffusion to the training of professionals.[10]

Pelikan examines Newman's thesis and agrees. There must be in a university, Pelikan argues, freedom of inquiry, intellectual honesty, civility in discourse, toleration and trust in rationality. To that end, therefore, the university is concerned with intellectual rather than moral ends. Knowledge must lead to "moral" virtues.[11] But these moral virtues, it seems to me, are separated from their Judeo-Christian moorings. They are simply part of "Golden Rule" sort of morality — akin to Lawrence Kohlberg's Level Six morality.

I find this portion of Pelikan's book to be most disturbing. First, I am disturbed by his lack of humility. As if the university and humankind can know so much truth! Pelikan's university is **King Belshazzar's feast** (Daniel 7). My understanding of a university, and I think Newman would agree, is a time on Mt. Horeb, humbly bowing before Almighty God, freely admitting our own limits and extolling His omnipotence (Exodus 3). Pelikan's lack of appreciation of God's wisdom, whose humble acceptance is the beginning of human wisdom, is evident. While I am shocked that American students would read John Milton's *Paradise Lost* without knowing the outcome before they read it, Pelikan suggests that the excitement of discovery mitigates the sting of American spiritual paupery.[12] And, in spite of himself, Dr. Pelikan is indeed showing us the problem of the American secular university. Pelikan's suggestions are merely another

8. John Henry Newman, *The Idea of a University Defined and Illustrated* (1852), p. x.
9. John Henry Newman, "Essay on Educated Man"; http://www.newmanreader.org/works/idea/discourse7.html, p. 10.
10. Pelikan, *The Idea of the University*, p. 88.
11. Ibid., p. 44.
12. Ibid., p. 41.

form of veiled Gnosticism dressed up in pretty language. Knowledge — its acquisition, its dissemination — even in a gentleman's way — is the god of the modern American university. As the cognitive-moral formation specialist, psychologist Lawrence Kohlberg, Ed Fenton, and others have so convincingly shown us, there is no value in free education. And we better be careful if we claim otherwise.

Let me readily admit that I do not presume to know John Henry Newman better than Professor Pelikan. But let me offer a few conjectures. Ultimately, I believe, Pelikan disagrees with Newman, as I knew he would. Because Newman, a committed Christian, never embraced Hegelian notions of the dialectic. Truth to the born-again, Catholic priest Newman is not in the search. Jesus Christ is the way, the truth, and the life. Pelikan, on the other hand, deifies the "search." Both teachers and students are on the "hunt" because Truth is yet to be fully understood.[13] He celebrates the modern research university, or, as he says in Section III, "duties to society." Of course, a modern dialectic deifies the utilitarian notion of the greatest good for the most people. And, again, while the Christian theistic Newman is willing to see the university as a site solely for the communication of truth, Pelikan is not about to accept such limits. Pelikan recognizes no citidel of orthodoxy, no limits to his knowledge. Newman is the champion of orthodoxy. It was his whole life! Faith is Newman's ultimate destination of knowledge. In "An Essay in Aid of a Grammar of Assent," Newman is comfortable having faith rise out of an epistemological base. But, like Jesus reminds Thomas in John 14, our hope lies not in what we know, but most assuredly in Whom we know.

Pelikan's university exists for the advancement of knowledge. Pelikan is uncomfortable with theological terms — terms like "original sin" that are so central to the American university (according to Dr. George Marsden).[14] Pelikan is comfortable with theology as a profession,[15] but not as a calling. Pelikan is more comfortable with a university that espouses pedagogy that emphasizes service and character building (a la the "gentleman" described by Newman in an essay) over revelation. Again, the Truth is not yet discovered, it is being revealed day by day. Newman's university humbly admits that the Truth is already known; the only quest we have is to humbly accept it. It is the job of humankind to be a good citizen by reflecting the glory of God. Pelikan sees the university as a place for the advancement of knowledge; Newman sees the university as a place for the communication of knowledge.[16]

Discussion Question

What is Pelikan's central thesis?

---

13. Ibid., p. 89.
14. Marsden, *The Soul of the American University*.
15. Pelikan, *The Idea of the University*, Section II, beginning at page 71.
16. Joraslav Pelikan is Sterling Professor of History at Yale University and president of the American Academy of Arts and Sciences. He is also the author of, among other books, *The Christian Tradition, Jesus Through the Centuries*, and *Christianity and Classical Culture*.

Harvard University Charter

WHEREAS, through the good hand of God, many well devoted persons have been, and daily are moved, and stirred up, to give and bestow, sundry gifts, legacies, lands, and revenues for the advancement of all good literature, arts, and sciences in Harvard College, in Cambridge in the County of Middlesex, and to the maintenance of the President and Fellows, and for all accommodations of buildings, and all other necessary provisions, that may conduce to the education of the English and Indian youth of this country, in knowledge and godliness: It is therefore ordered, and enacted by this Court, and the authority thereof, that for the furthering of so good a work and for the purposes aforesaid, from henceforth that the said College, in Cambridge in Middlesex, in New England, shall be a Corporation, consisting of seven persons, to wit, a President, five Fellows, and a Treasurer or Bursar: and that Henry Dunster shall be the first President, Samuel Mather, Samuel Danforth, Masters of Arts, Jonathan Mitchell, Comfort Starr, and Samuel Eaton, Bachelors of Arts, shall be the five Fellows, and Thomas Danforth to be present Treasurer, all of them being inhabitants in the Bay, and shall be the first seven persons of which the said Corporation shall consist: and that the said seven persons, or the greater number of them, procuring the presence of the Overseers of the College, and by their counsel and consent, shall have power, and are hereby authorized, at any time or times, to elect a new President, Fellows, or Treasurer, so oft, and from time to time, as any of the said person or persons shall die, or be removed, which said President and Fellows, for the time being, shall for ever hereafter, in name and fact, be one body politic and corporate in law, to all intents and purposes; and shall have perpetual succession;

and shall be called by the name of President and Fellows of Harvard College, and shall, from time to time, be eligible as aforesaid. And by that name they, and their successors, shall and may purchase and acquire to themselves, or take and receive upon free-gift and donation, any lands, tenements, or hereditaments, within this jurisdiction of the Massachusetts, not exceeding the value of five hundred pounds per annum, and any goods and sums of money whatsoever, to the use and behoof of the said President, Fellows, and scholars of the said College: and also may sue and plead, or be sued and impleaded by the name aforesaid, in all Courts and places of judicature, within the jurisdiction aforesaid.

> **Christo et Ecclesiae:** Harvard's motto for 300 years, which meant "for Christ and church."

"A Westerly View of the Colledges in Cambridge New England," line engraving by the American engraver and silversmith Paul Revere, 1767 (PD).

And that the said President, with any three of the Fellows, shall have power, and are hereby authorized, when they shall think fit, to make and appoint a common seal, for the use of the said Corporation.

And the President and Fellows, or the major part of them, from time to time, may meet and choose such officers and servants for the College, and make such allowance to them, and them also to remove, and after death, or removal, to choose such others, and to make, from time to time, such orders and by-laws, for the better ordering, and carrying on the work of the College, as they shall think fit: Provided, the said orders be allowed by the Overseers. And also, that the President and Fellows, or major part of them with the Treasurer, shall have power to make conclusive bargains for lands and tenements, to be purchased by the said Corporation, for valuable considerations. And for the better ordering of the government of the said College and Corporation, Be it enacted by the authority aforesaid, that the President, and three more of the Fellows, shall and may, from time to time, upon due warning or notice given by the President to the rest, hold a meeting, for the debating and concluding of affairs concerning the profits and revenues of any lands and disposing of their goods, (provided that all the said disposings be according to the will of the donors:) and for direction in all emergent occasions; execution of all orders and by-laws; and for the procuring of a general meeting of all the Overseers and Society, in great and difficult cases; and in cases of non-agreement; in all which cases aforesaid, the conclusion shall be made by the major part, the said President having a casting voice, the Overseers consenting thereunto. And that all the aforesaid transactions shall tend to, and for the use and behoof of the President, Fellows, scholars, and officers of the said College, and for all accommodations of buildings, books, and all other necessary provisions, and furnitures, as may be for the advancement and education of youth, in all manner of good literature, arts, and sciences. And further be it ordered by this Court, and the authority thereof, that all the lands, tenements, or hereditaments, houses, or revenues, within this jurisdiction, to the aforesaid President or College appertaining, not exceeding the value of five hundred pounds per annum, shall, from henceforth, be freed from all civil impositions, taxes, and rates; all goods to the said Corporation, or to any scholars thereof appertaining, shall be exempted from all manner of toll, customs, and excise whatsoever. And that the said President, Fellows, and scholars, together with the servants, and other necessary officers to the said President, or College appertaining, not exceeding ten, viz. three to the President, and seven to the College belonging, shall be exempted from all personal civil ofices, military exercises, or services, watchings, and wardings: and such of their estates, not exceeding one hundred pounds a man, shall be free from all country taxes, or rates whatsoever, and none others.

In witness whereof, the Court hath caused the seal of the colony to be hereunto affixed. Dated the one and thirtieth day of the third month, called May, anno 1650.

THOMAS DUDLEY, Governor.

Discussion Question

What was the purpose of Harvard University in 1650?

Man heckles Iranians demonstrating for Khomeini at police line in Washington, D.C., 1980 (LOC).

Chapter 29

Shadow History: Second-Page Stories

First Thoughts

In the last century, we developed air transport, discovered antibiotics, invented computing, and split the atom. Further, communication technology was revolutionized with the telephone, the radio, and the Internet. Medicine, too, underwent a radical transformation. The rapid spread of the automobile also modernized transportation technology. All of these are headlines. This chapter is devoted to those topics behind the headlines, the second-page stories.

Chapter Learning Objectives

We will examine the great American fear: hostage taking. Then we will review the origination of the oil industry and predict new directions that energy policy will take. Next we will examine assassination and its impact on American history.

As a result of this chapter you should be able to:

1. Examine the hostage crisis that has faced each generation since the American Revolution

2. Review the oil industry and its impact on America

3. Analyze the energy predictions of Yergin and Stobaugh

4. Evaluate the American penchant to violence and assassination

5. Relate a story behind a headline

CONCEPTS

Iranian hostage crisis

Oil crisis

Robert Stobaugh

Assassination

T.S. Eliot

Hostages

In 1979, Iranian students invaded the American embassy in Tehran and held Americans hostage for 444 days; this precipitated the **Iranian hostage crisis**. To secure their freedom, President Jimmy Carter agreed to release $8 billion in frozen Iranian assets. The Americans were finally released, but after this incident President Carter failed to gain re-election.

In Lebanon, during the mid 1980s, pro-Iranian extremists kidnapped and held hostage two dozen Americans. In one incident, militants abducted a U.S. soldier, hanged him, and broadcast videotaped pictures of his lifeless body on television.

Few political issues in the last 50 years have inflamed Americans more than the taking of hostages. Should the United States negotiate with kidnappers? Should the United States pay ransom and make political concessions to secure the hostages' freedom? Or should the country refuse to deal with kidnappers?

Hostage taking has been a favorite past time of America's enemies. Even before George Washington became president, the United States was confronted with a hostage crisis. In 1785, an American ship was captured by Algerian pirates. Its captain and five crew members were held hostage. Then a second American ship was captured, and its 15-member crew was taken to Algiers. These Americans were treated horribly.

"USS Philadelphia," a 38-gun frigate, commissioned in 1800. Stranding and capture on Oct. 31, 1803 (NARA).

During the late 18th century, three small North African states — Algiers, Tripoli, and Tunis — preyed on merchant ships sailing in the Mediterranean, seizing their crews and cargoes, and holding both for ransom. Over the next eight years, Algerian pirates

seized more than 100 hostages from a dozen captured American ships.

Finally, in 1795, the government had had enough. Thomas Jefferson, the State Department head, successfully negotiated the release of the captives. This was done without bloodshed.

Hostage taking continued after Thomas Jefferson was elected in 1800. This time, President Thomas Jefferson responded by imposing a naval blockade of Tripoli. In 1803, however, the U.S. frigate *Philadelphia* ran aground off the coast of Tripoli and its 307-member crew was captured. In a daring raid on February 16, 1804, Lieutenant Stephen Decatur Jr. and a small band of sailors boarded the *Philadelphia* and set the ship afire. But the *Philadelphia*'s crew remained imprisoned, and Tripoli's leader demanded $200,000 ransom for their release.

Iran Hostage Crisis student demonstration, Washington, D.C., 1979 (LOC).

The stage was now set for one of the most colorful hostage rescues in American history. In 1805, William Eaton, the American diplomat to Tunis, led a makeshift "seal team" consisting of 8 marines, 2 navy midshipmen, and some 300 hired mercenaries on a 50-day, 520-mile march from Egypt, and successfully stormed the Tripolitan city of Derna. Eaton's stunning victory led Tripoli to sign a peace treaty with the United States. In return, the United States agreed to pay $60,000 for the release of the *Philadelphia*'s crew.

It was not until 1815 that the United States successfully ended North African piracy. In that year, a fleet of ten American ships under the command of Stephen Decatur threatened to bombard Algiers. The threat worked. The North African states agreed to release American prisoners without ransom and to cease all interference with American shipping.

Hostage taking continues to be a major threat to American interests.[1]

Discussion Question

Based upon the above discussion, why is hostage taking such an effective tactic against American interests?

A 48th Tactical Fighter Wing F-111F aircraft retracts its landing gear as it takes off from RAF Lakenheath, East Anglia England, to participate in a retaliatory air strike on Libya. 1986 (PD-USAF)

1. www.historyguy.com/iran-us_hostage_crisis.html; http://www.digitalhistory.uh.edu/topic_display.cfm?tcid=95.

The Politics of Oil

Kerosene lamp (CCA-SA2.5Australia)

Oil was discovered on August 27, 1859, when Edwin L. Drake drilled the first successful oil well 69 feet deep near unpretentious Titusville, Pennsylvania. Just five years earlier, the invention of the kerosene lamp had ignited intense demand for oil. Before that, whale oil fueled American lights. Whale oil was expensive and dirty.

Drake's success inspired hundreds of small companies to explore for oil. In 1860, world oil production reached 500,000 barrels; by the 1870s, production soared to 20 million barrels annually. In 1879, the first oil well was drilled in California, and in 1887, in Texas. But this put small companies out of business.

Up until the 1910s, the United States produced between 60 and 70 percent of the world's oil supply. As fear grew that American oil reserves were dangerously depleted, the search for oil turned worldwide. Oil was discovered in Mexico at the beginning of the 20th century, in Iran in 1908, in Venezuela during World War I, and in Iraq in 1927. Many of the new oil discoveries occurred in areas dominated by Britain and the Netherlands: in the Dutch East Indies, Iran, and British mandates in the Middle East. By 1919, Britain controlled 50 percent of the world's proven oil reserves.

The fear that American oil reserves were nearly exhausted ended abruptly in 1924, with the discovery of enormous new oil fields in Texas, Oklahoma, and California. These discoveries, along with production from new fields in offshore areas, Europe, and Russia depressed oil prices. During World War II, the oil surpluses of the 1930s quickly disappeared. With the loss of Asian oil to the Japanese, and European oil to the Germans, six billion of the seven billion barrels of petroleum used by the Allies during the war came from the United States. Public officials again began to worry that the United States was running out of oil.

It seemed imperative that the United States secure access to foreign oil reserves. The United States discovered oil reserves in Kuwait and Saudi Arabia. Middle Eastern oil production surged upward. It was very cheap to pump, distill, and transport. Gradually, American dependence on Middle Eastern oil increased.

Automobiles lining up for fuel at a service station in the U.S. state of Maryland in the United States, in June 1979. (LOC).

During the 1950s, consumption skyrocketed. With only 6 percent of the world's population, the United States accounted for one-third of global oil consumption. World oil prices were so low that Iran, Venezuela, and Arab oil producers banded together to form OPEC, the Organization of Petroleum Producing States, a producers' cartel, to negotiate for higher oil prices.

By the early 1970s, the United States depended on the Middle East for a third of its oil. Foreign oil producers were finally in a position to raise world oil prices. The oil embargo of 1973 and 1974, during which oil prices quadrupled, and the oil crisis of 1978 and 1979, when oil prices doubled, graphically illustrated how vulnerable the nation had become to foreign producers. In the 21st century we are facing the same crisis.

Today, oil exploration and production is a major American anxiety and industry.[2]

Discussion Question

Why, in spite of an oil glut, have oil prices increased?

In 1882, John D. Rockefeller gained control of American oil production with his founding of Standard Oil. By 1920, oil production reached 450 million barrels and government officials predicted that the nation's oil reserves would last just ten years.

Energy Future, Report of the Energy Project at the Harvard Business School

Edited by Robert Stobaugh and Daniel Yergin
Reviewed by William A. Mogel

The energy crisis, which was identified in 1972 by the United States Supreme Court, is rightly the subject of much concern, analysis, and writing. The current and future social and economic problems arising from this country's heavy reliance on non-renewable sources of energy, such as domestic and imported oil, natural gas and coal, require meaningful examination and recommended solutions.

One attempt to examine the complex energy problem is set forth in *Energy Future: The Report of the Energy Project at the Harvard Business School*, which is edited by Robert Stobaugh and Daniel Yergin. The major conclusion reached by the report is that production from the four conventional sources of domestic energy — oil, gas, coal, and nuclear power — will not be as great as predicted, and, at best, will produce only one-third to one-half of the additional energy the United States will need over the next decade. As a solution, *Energy Future* advocates that conservation and various non-conventional sources of energy, including solar, can fill the gap.

Its recommendation is based on three premises. First, the energy crises and price rises of 1973–74 and 1978–79 were not isolated instances but were part of a "major transition." Second, the best way to achieve economic growth is through reliance on the free market. Third, attempts must be made to deal with the questions of who is to pay for energy development and who is to profit. However, according to *Energy Future* the long-term outlook for coal may be better. While coal production cannot replace imported oil, it will grow steadily primarily because of the entry of the large oil companies into the production of coal. The entry of these large companies adds new and large-scale bases of corporate, managerial, and technical resources to the coal industry.

---

2. http://www.digitalhistory.uh.edu/topic_display.cfm?tcid=96; www.pbs.org/now/politics/oil.html.

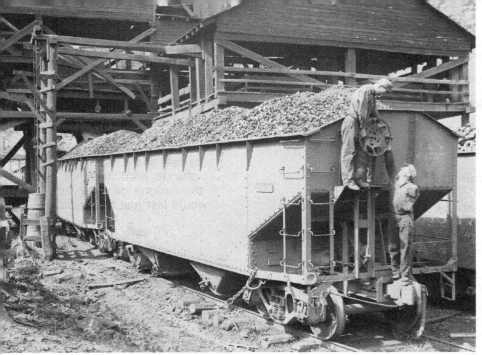

Carload of coal at the tipple in Kentucky, 1946 (NARA).

The second reason that coal will have a significant future role is that new technologies are emerging. These focus on making the direct combustion of coal more efficient and on using coal to make methane and oil. Energy Future's chapter on nuclear power is interesting. Federal government plans once called for nuclear power to provide approximately 30 to 40 percent of American electricity by the end of the 1980s. Today these prospects are much lower. This is due in part to the decrease in growth of demand for electricity. One of the biggest problems confronting the industry is how to dispose of the spent fuel from nuclear power plants. In the 1960s it was assumed that this issue would be taken care of through reprocessing. However, in the 1970s it was argued that since the plutonium produced could be used to make nuclear explosives, reprocessing posed the threat of the proliferation of nuclear weapons. In October 1976, the nuclear industry was warned by the Ford administration that fuel reprocessing might become unacceptable and six months later the Carter administration imposed an outright prohibition, thus transforming "a relatively minor technical problem, the choice of specific methods to dispose of radioactive waste materials, into an acute operational problem — what to do with spent fuel." Even if reprocessing was allowed, the problem of how to isolate radioactive wastes from the environment would remain. The government approach has been to focus on one large-scale repository. Energy Future suggests that a policy of encouraging the simultaneous development of several smaller repositories in different geologic media should be followed.

Interestingly, the United States has approximately 25 percent of the world's known reserves of coal. Energy Future does not suggest how state and local opposition to coal mining will be overcome. However, during the balance of this, conservation should not be viewed as "the product of an anti-growth crusade led by the granola-chomping children of the affluent." There are, however, four obstacles to productive conservation. The first is that conservation efforts are fragmented, decentralized, and difficult to organize and control. Second is that energy experts are used to giving advice based upon future production in contrast to reduced demand. The third obstacle is the view that the rise of energy prices will automatically result in an appropriate amount of conservation activity without any government action or change of policy.

Three areas in which conservation can be achieved are examined by Energy Future. First, increasing the automobile's efficiency is advocated as opposed to attempting to reduce dependence upon it. Second, in the manufacturing industry, conservation can be achieved by "improved housekeeping," recovery of waste (heat and other materials) and greater reliance on cogeneration. Cogeneration and other conservation methods could cut industrial energy use by one-third with a total capital investment of approximately 40 billion dollars less than that required for investment in conventional energy sources. The third area for conservation is in retrofitting existing structures, and in designing and constructing new buildings. A study done for the American Physical Society showed that in the year 1973 the same standard of living could have been achieved with 40 percent less energy. Chapter 7 is entitled "Solar America." Solar energy, the use of thermal (heating and cooling) applications, fuels from biomass, and solar electric methods, could (eventually) produce one-fifth to one-fourth of America's energy needs. According to *Energy Future*, the barriers to utilization of solar energy are institutional and economic rather than technical. It is concluded that no drastic change in lifestyles would be required from greater reliance on solar energy.[3]

Discussion Question

What energy alternatives to oil consumption do Stobaugh and Yergin suggest?

Assassination

The United States is a country prone to political violence and **assassination**. Nine American Presidents — Andrew Jackson in 1835, Abraham Lincoln in 1865, James Garfield in 1881, William McKinley in 1901, Harry S. Truman in 1950, John F. Kennedy in 1963, Richard Nixon in 1974, Gerald Ford (twice) in 1975, and Ronald Reagan in 1981 — have been the targets of assassination. Attempts have also been made on the lives of 1 president-elect (Franklin D. Roosevelt in 1933) and 3 presidential candidates (Theodore Roosevelt in 1912, Robert F. Kennedy in 1968, and George Wallace in 1972). In addition, 8 governors, 7 U.S. Senators, 9 U.S. Congressmen, 11 mayors, 17 state legislators, and 11 judges have been violently attacked. No other country with a population of over 50 million has had as high a number of political assassinations or attempted assassinations.

Lithograph of the Assassination of Abraham Lincoln. From left to right: Henry Rathbone, Clara Harris, Mary Todd Lincoln, Abraham Lincoln, and John Wilkes Booth. Rathbone is depicted as spotting Booth before he shot Lincoln and trying to stop him as Booth fired his weapon. Rathbone actually was unaware of Booth's approach, and reacted after the shot was fired. While Lincoln is depicted clutching the flag after being shot, it is also possible that he just simply pushed the flag aside to watch the performance. 1865 (LOC).

As one historian asks:

> The nation's voluminous record of political violence and assassination raises many difficult and disturbing questions. Why has the United States, with its commitment to rule of law and due process, been so susceptible to assassination? Has the U.S. always faced the horror of assassination or has the crime's frequency increased in recent years? The most troubling issue raised by political assassinations is whether they alter the course of history.[4]

3. Robert Stobaugh and Daniel Yergin, *Energy Future: Report of the Energy Project at the Harvard Business School* (New York: Vintage Books, 1983).

4. http://www.digitalhistory.uh.edu/topic_display.cfm?tcid=98.

A montage of the Reagan assassination attempt, 1981 (PD-Ronald Reagan Library).

Political assassination was a post-18th-century phenomenon. Prior to the American Revolution, there was not a single instance in which a public official was assassinated. There was political violence in early America, but it tended to take the form of mob action.

Political assassinations in the United States have tended to occur during periods of civil strife. A new wave of political violence and murder swept the nation during the decade and a half following Abraham Lincoln's assassination on Good Friday of 1865. Between 1865 and 1877, 34 political officials were attacked, 24 of them fatally. This wave of political violence ended in 1881, when President James A. Garfield was assassinated by a frustrated office seeker, four months after his inauguration.

Who are the individuals who have attempted to murder our national leaders? Have they tended to be alienated, psychotic misfits, living on the margins of society and craving publicity? Or have they tended to be rational individuals with clearly defined political goals? Historian Steven Mintz writes, "In general, Presidential assailants have tended to be outsiders, unusually sensitive to the political cults or sensations of the time. Few have had steady employment (only two of eleven worked regularly in the year leading up to the assassination attempt). Only one was married with children. A large number were immigrants or children of immigrants (seven of eleven). Few carefully planned their assault (all but two fired pistols, which are only effective at close range)."[5]

Discussion Question

When does political violence in the United States increase and who commits this violence?

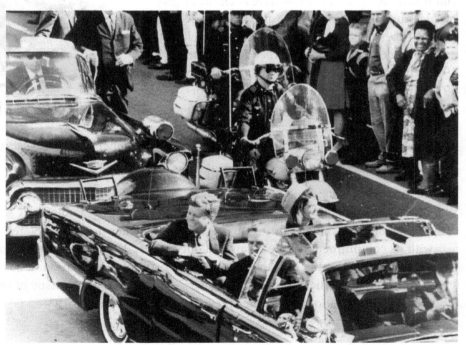

President Kennedy in the limousine in Dallas, Texas, on Main Street, minutes before the assassination. 1963 (PD).

---

5. Ibid.

Pervading Hopelessness

By T.S. Eliot

Destiny waits in the hands of God, not in the hands of statesmen.

Murder in the Cathedral (1935) by **T.S. Eliot**, American and then British modernist poet, is my personal favorite 20th-century play and is full of encouraging truths for the growing Christian believer. It is a diatribe against the excesses of modernism and a lamentation of the state of Western culture.

T. S. Eliot: Perhaps the best poet and dramatist of the 20th century.

Eliot's play concerns the assassination of Archbishop Samuel Becket by Henry II. The play begins with a chorus singing, foreshadowing the coming violence. The rest of the play concerns four temptations (roughly paralleling the temptation of Christ).

Every tempter offers Becket something that he desires. But he will have to disobey the Lord and his own conscience to attain it.

The first tempter offers long life. He makes an existential appeal that is quite persuasive.

> Take a friend's advice. Leave well alone,
> Or your goose may be cooked and eaten to the bone.

The second offers power, riches and fame.

> To set down the great, protect the poor,
> Beneath the throne of God can man do more?

The third tempter suggests a coalition with the barons and a chance to resist the king. This temptation is very appealing. He even uses biblical language!

> For us, Church favour would be an advantage,
> Blessing of Pope powerful protection
> In the fight for liberty. You, my Lord,
> In being with us, would fight a good stroke

Finally, he is urged to seek martyrdom! The very thing that he may do is thrown in his face as a selfish act!

> You hold the keys of heaven and hell.
> Power to bind and loose: bind, Thomas, bind,
> King and bishop under your heel.
> King, emperor, bishop, baron, king:

Becket responds to all of the tempters and specifically addresses the immoral suggestions of the fourth tempter at the end of the first act:

> Now is my way clear, now is the meaning plain:
> Temptation shall not come in this kind again.
> The last temptation is the greatest treason:
> To do the right deed for the wrong reason.

A martyrdom is never the design of man; for the true martyr is he who has become the instrument of God, who has lost his will in the will of God, not lost it but found it, for he has found freedom in submission to God.

Becket continues.

> The church lies bereft,
> Alone,
> Desecrated, desolated.
> And the heathen shall build
> On the ruins

Becket will die, but not for any nostalgic reason. Not for any sentimental purpose. He will die in obedience to our Lord God. He defies hyperbole.

In these Post-modern times, as we struggle to make sense of all the hard time we face, of all the good things we can do. let us choose the obedient thing to do, not the thing that may seem right in our own eyes.

There is a crisis of ethics in our time.

> Only the fool, fixed in his folly, may think he
> can turn the wheel on which he turns.

To do the right deed for the wrong reason . . . in this age of compromises, of good intentions, it is critical that we follow Becket's example. Thy will be done on earth as it is in heaven.

> Human kind cannot bear very much reality.
> The church shall be open, even to our enemies.
> We are not here to triumph by fighting, by stratagem, or by resistance,
> Not to fight with beasts as men. We have fought the beast
> And have conquered. We have only to conquer
> Now, by suffering. This is the easier victory.
> For every life and every act
> Consequence of good and evil can be shown.
> And as in time results of many deeds are blended
> So good and evil in the end become confounded.
> In life there is not time to grieve long.
> O father, father
> Gone from us, lost to us,
> The church lies bereft,
> Alone,
> Desecrated, desolated.
> And the heathen shall build
> On the ruins
> Their world without God.
> I see it.
> I see it.

Discussion Question

What are the four temptations that mankind faces? What is the Christian response?

European flag outside the Commission (CCA-SA2.0).

Chapter 30

United Europe: Foundational Changes Across the Sea

First Thoughts

Rick Steves, a travel agent (of all people), states:

> In his book *The European Dream*, Jeremy Rifkin writes that in medieval times, faith was the glue that kept society together. In the modern age, it was reason. Europe has concluded that in the global future, it must be empathy.
>
> Today 450 million people have EU citizenship. . . . The EU's power grows not by expanding sovereignty but by broadening cooperation. America still has the "hard power" (economic and military muscle), but its "soft power" — the cultural and moral inspiration, optimism, and ingenuity that so many emulated for so long — may be ebbing.[1]

Rifkin, at least, thinks the cultural baton is being passed back, after 250 years, to Europe. Rifkin warns that American must not ignore the events "unfolding across the Atlantic — much as Europe underestimated the emergence of America after 1789. America's biggest error may be in not taking Europe seriously."[2]

Chapter Learning Objectives

We will look more closely at the history and ultimate development of the European Union (EU). We will then evaluate its effectiveness and compare it to America.

As a result of this chapter you should be able to:

1. Explain why European unity has been so difficult

2. Compare the genesis of the United States of America with the genesis of the EU

3. Compare and contrast the American and European views of work

4. Assess the value of living in the United States vs. Europe

5. Criticize Jeremy Rifkin's article

1. http://www.ricksteves.com/about/pressroom/activism/eurodream.htm.
2. Ibid.

United States of Europe

A united Europe was the dream of Charlemagne, Napoleon, and Hitler. It did not happen until recently. Or at least most of Europe is trying!

The term "United States of Europe" was used by Victor Hugo, including during a speech at the International Peace Congress held in Paris in 1849. Hugo favored the creation of what he termed "a supreme senate which will be to Europe what parliament is to England."[3]

Following the catastrophe of the First World War, some thinkers and visionaries again began to float the idea of a politically unified Europe. During the World War II victories of Nazi Germany in 1940, Kaiser Wilhelm II stated that: "The hand of God is creating a new world and working miracles. . . . We are becoming the United States of Europe under German leadership, a united European Continent."[4]

Winston Churchill had a similar vision, but with a more cautious approach called the unionist position rather than the continental approach known as the federalist position. The federalists advocated full integration with a constitution, while the Unionist United Europe Movement advocated a consultative body. The federalists prevailed at the Congress of Europe. With the collapse of the Iron Curtain in 1990, the **European Union** (EU) was born.

The young EU has faced many problems. Recently, the economic collapse in Greece has torn the union apart. The EU is based on the principle of an ever-closer union, but a union of nations with widely divergent values. These divisions can be at the deepest philosophical level. Compare French romanticism and German nationalism with British pragmatism, and one can see why the UK has never felt at home in a political construct built on Franco-German foundations.

These problems remain, but the union has begun. . . .

Discussion Question

Why has European unity been so difficult?

Victor Hugo planted a tree in the grounds of his residence on the Island of Guernsey. He was noted for saying that when that tree matured, the United States of Europe would have come into being. That tree is still growing to this day.

---

3. http://www.gavroche.org/vhugo/peacecongress.shtml.
4. Jonathan Petropoulos, *Royals and the Reich* (Oxford, UK; New York: Oxford University Press, 2006), p. 170.

The EU

A frustrated Secretary of State Henry Kissinger famously asked in 1977, "What telephone number do you dial to reach Europe?" Today Europe can be reached easily, and the phone number starts with 011-32-2 — that's the European Union.

The European Union, comprised of 25 nations with 450 million people, makes up 7 percent of the world's population. The United States has 300 million people, or 5 percent. Europe now has the world's largest economy, with a GDP of $11 trillion. Now the third-largest government on earth, after China and India, the EU is unique in that it has no claim to territory.

> **European Union:** The union of continental Europe after the Iron Curtain fell in 1990.

The European Union was birthed in fear — fear that another World War II might happen. There were other attractions though. The nations of Europe are sacrificing national autonomy for the security of peace and the efficiency of a big free-trade zone.

In 1951, France, Germany, Belgium, Luxemburg, the Netherlands, and Italy created the European Coal and Steel Community. This union overcame the biggest obstacle to maintaining peace in Europe — the economic rivalry between France and Germany. In 1957, union members created a "Common Market," trading some economic independence for free trade and uniform standards. Initially sold as an economic coalition, the EEC was always designed to progress step by step toward greater unity.

In 1987, the **European Parliament** was created — a giant step. The EU was coming.

European Parliament 2014, Strasbourg, France (CCA-SA3.0).

With the collapse of the Iron Curtain in 1990, the EU gained new power. Before 1989, the EEC's mission was to not be swallowed up by the competing super powers (the US and the USSR). Now unity was necessary to ensure that other European countries wouldn't be overwhelmed by a strong, reunited Germany. The threats felt by the emergence of a united Germany trumped the reluctance to trade away sovereignty. Germany, then, was the impetus to create a unified Europe.

With the 1992 Treaty of Maastricht, the EEC became the European Union (EU). The EU developed a common currency (the euro, 2002), a common defense and foreign policy, and a common social policy. In 2004, 10 new nations joined the EU, bringing total membership to 25.

Today, the European Union has a president and a military. The EU parliament can make laws that supersede the laws of its member states. Its court has jurisdiction over EU citizens. It has a uniform currency, the euro. It legislates and regulates on matters such as commerce, trade, education, and the environment. Its citizens have a common passport.[5]

Discussion Question

The term "United States of Europe," as a direct comparison with the United States of America, would imply that the existing nations of Europe would be reduced to a status equivalent to that of a U.S. state, losing their national sovereignty in the process and becoming constituent parts of a European federation. Just as the United States of America has evolved from a confederation (under the 1777 Articles of Confederation) into a federation, the term "the United States of Europe" implies that European countries will evolve into a federal republic. Do you think that this will occur? Is the comparison between the evolution of the United States of America and the European Union an accurate one?

Lesson 3

Free Trade

The potential for trade advantages has driven European nation building for centuries. In the Middle Ages, it cost merchants half the value of their goods to simply ship their wares a few hundred miles down a river (paying tolls to those "robber baron" castles as they crossed the borders of little states). The "farmer's market" transformed the nature of medieval business. The farmer, now, could obtain specie, and the urban dweller could be fed!

With the first established single internal market, Britain emerged as Europe's first big economic power, in part because of the flow of trade without tariffs and customs. In 1600, Europe had 500 separate states. In 1900, 25 states governed most of Europe. The EU made that 1. Now there would be no trading obstacles.

Today, the United States and Great Britain maintain a solo approach and belief in the wisdom of unbridled competition. The EU has embraced economic cooperation that admittedly has emerged as a form of socialism.

The EU has had a great impact on the heretofore economically resistant regions of Europe. One historian explains:

> The EU is vigorously pursuing a vision of complete integration into one vast trans-European network. Powered by an initial investment of $500 billion, a futuristic grid of transport, energy, and telecommunications is making Europe one super-efficient playing field for commerce and communication. The EU is funding programs for over a million European students to go to high school in

5. http://www.ricksteves.com/about/pressroom/activism/eurodream.htm.

other member countries, and get job training or do volunteer service in another nation. Weak links in the giant free-trade zone — like Portugal and Ireland — are identified and brought up to par with EU money. Today Portugal is laced by new freeways, and Ireland has a higher per capita income than England for the first time in history. Workers in poor regions are getting aid for education and to learn job skills.[6]

A farmer marking prices on melons at a Lansing Farmers Market in Michigan (CCA-SA3.0).

Ironically, even though England was reluctant to join the EU, English is becoming Europe's preferred language.

The euro currency experienced significant problems in the wake of the 2008 recession. However, monetary discipline is built into the euro system — member nations do not have the option of stoking their economies with big deficit spending. This discipline, coupled with America's huge and growing deficit, has allowed the euro to challenge the U.S. dollar as the leading global currency. The EU hopes that oil-producing countries will be selling their oil in euros, not dollars. Europe is already the biggest importer of Middle Eastern oil, and Norway and Britain are big oil producers.

Jeremy Rifkin writes:

> The problem with the American Dream is the growing gap between rich and poor, making success a distant dream for those outside the bubble of wealth. Europeans produce virtually the same per worker hour as Americans, even though their per capita income is about a third less. Why? They work fewer hours. Europeans prefer to work less, earn less, live more simply, and play more. When the French government instituted the 35-hour workweek in 1998, it correctly figured that with each worker working fewer hours, there would be a need for more workers, which would in turn alleviate unemployment. The government subsidized companies to pay workers the same for 35 hours as for the previous 39-hour workweek. (This subsidy was funded by savings the government enjoyed in unemployment payments.) Employers were skeptical at first about the new seven-hour workday, but they found that happier, more rested workers accomplished virtually as much as they used to in more time. Employers were rewarded with more flexibility to assign workers for weekends or evenings, or to limit vacations to more efficient times. The result is a more relaxed populace. European wives don't need to constantly remind their work-aholic husbands, "Nobody ever went to their grave wishing they'd spent more time working."[7]

Sociologists explain that America and Europe approach work differently. Edward Crane and David Boaz, in what is now a fairly dated understanding of European politics, *An American Vision: Policies for the '90s*, explained how America embraced the Protestant work ethic (especially the English version) with enthusiasm. For an American, time is money. For a European, time is something one enjoys.[8]

Discussion Question

Compare and contrast the American and European views of work.

6. Ibid.

7. Rick Steves quoting Jeremy Rifkin, *The European Dream: How Europe's Vision of the Future Is Quietly Eclipsing the American Dream* (2005), www.ricksteves.com/about/pressroom/activism/eurodream.htm -

8. Edward Crane and David Boaz, *An American Vision: Policies for the '90s* (Washington, DC: Cato Institute, 1989).

America vs EU

Gross Domestic Product (GDP) is ...

Even though the United States and Europe have comparable economic systems, the United States spends half a trillion dollars ($500 billion) each year on its military (not counting the Afghanistan War), while Europe spends only $150 billion. Because there are more lawsuits, the United States also spends more on legal services. Moreover, the United States, with a smaller population, consumes a third more energy. Healthcare is better in Europe — Europe has more doctors per thousand people (3.22 vs. 2.79), whereas the United States has a higher infant mortality and shorter life span. While the United States spends more per capita than any other nation on health care (over $5,000 per person), we're one of only two developed nations (with South Africa) that don't provide health insurance for their citizens.

We are a more violent nation. Compared to Europe, the United States has four times the murders per capita. With more than two million Americans in prison (a quarter of the world's prison population), we have over seven times as many people in prison per capita than Europe.

This is not to say that Europeans are happier or more fulfilled than Americans! Americans are more committed churchgoers and are generally more satisfied with their lives. Europeans may think they are happier but Americans are, in fact, happier!

While America spends only 11 percent of its GDP on social services, Europe spends a whopping 26 percent. Americans are far more generous in their contributions to benevolent causes. European socialism has eroded initiative and quality of services and some critics worry about the future of European services. A pejorative comment in the United States is, "If we are not careful we will be like Europe!"

The EU has a military, but it is nothing like the American military. Of course, if it wasn't for the American military, it is doubtful that the EU could even exist! America has protected Europe for 60 years.

War is scary to Europe. France (with a quarter of our population) lost as many people in a single day during World War I as the United States did in the entire Vietnam War. It's hard to imagine the depth of the scars of war Europe lives with. This makes the unity and peace that EU offers especially appealing.

Discussion Question

Would you rather live in Europe or America? Why?

An Apache helicopter provides protection from the air while paratroopers from Company A, 1st Battalion, 325th Airborne Infantry Regiment, move into position shortly after air assaulting into Lwar Kowndalan, Afghanistan, Oct. 1 to start a five-day mission (PD).

"Worlds Apart on the Vision Thing"

Jeremy Rifkin

In a partisan America, where virtually every value has become fair game for criticism and controversy, there is one value that remains sacrosanct: the American Dream — the idea that anyone, regardless of the circumstances to which they're born, can make of their lives as they choose by dint of diligence, determination, and hard work. The American Dream unites Americans across ethnic and class divides, and gives shared purpose and direction to the American way of life.

The problem is, one-third of all Americans, according to a recent U.S. national survey, no longer believe in the American Dream. Some have lost faith because they worked hard all their lives only to find hardship and despair at the end of the line. Others question the very dream itself, arguing that its underlying tenets have become less relevant in an increasingly interconnected and interdependent world. For the first time, the American Dream no longer serves as the rallying point for everyone in America.

A new European Dream, meanwhile, is beginning to capture the world's imagination. That dream has now been codified in the form of a draft European constitution, and Europeans are currently debating whether to ratify its contents and accept its underlying values as the core values of a new Europe. Europe's vision of the future may have greater resonance — a kind of grand reversal, if you will, of what occurred 200 years ago when millions of Europeans looked to America in search of a new vision.

Twenty-five nations, representing 455 million people, have joined together to create a "United States" of Europe. Like the United States of America, this vast political entity has its own empowering myth. Although still in its adolescence, the European Dream is the first transnational vision, one far better suited to the next stage in the human journey. Europeans are beginning to adopt a new global consciousness that extends beyond, and below, the borders of their nation-states, deeply embedding them in an increasingly interconnected world.

Americans are used to thinking of their country as the most successful on earth. That's no longer the case: the European Union has grown to become the third-largest governing institution in the world. Though its land mass is half the size of the continental United States, its $10.5-trillion (U.S.) gross domestic product now eclipses the U.S. GDP, making it the world's largest economy. The EU is already the world's leading exporter and largest internal trading market. Sixty-one of the 140 biggest companies on the Global Fortune 500 rankings are European; only 50 are U.S. companies. . . .

Nowhere is the contrast between the European Dream and the American Dream sharper than when it comes to the definition of personal freedom.

For Americans, freedom has long been associated with autonomy; the more wealth one amasses, the more independent one is in the world. One is free by becoming self-reliant and an island onto oneself. With wealth comes exclusivity, and with exclusivity comes security.

Jeremy Rifkin, founder and president of the Washington-based Foundation on Economic Trends, is the author of 14 books, including his latest, *The European Dream*.

The juxtaposition of the homeless and well-to-do is common in New York. (CCA-SA3.0).

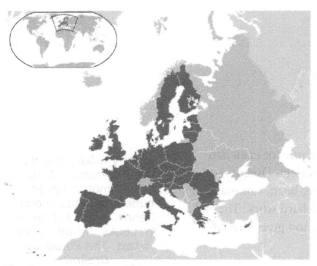

The European Union within Europe, 2009 (CCA-SA3.0).

For Europeans, freedom is not found in autonomy but in community. It's about belonging, not belongings.

The American Dream puts an emphasis on economic growth, personal wealth, and independence. The new European Dream focuses more on sustainable development, quality of life, and interdependence. The American Dream pays homage to the work ethic and religious heritage. The European Dream, more attuned to leisure, is secular to the core. The American Dream depends on assimilation. The European Dream, by contrast, is based on preserving one's cultural identity in a multicultural world.

Americans are more willing to use military force to protect what we perceive to be our vital self-interests. Europeans favor diplomacy, economic assistance to avert conflict, and peace-keeping operations to maintain order. The American Dream is deeply personal and little concerned with the rest of humanity. The European Dream is more systemic in nature and, therefore, more bound to the welfare of the planet.

That isn't to say that Europe is a utopia. Europeans have become increasingly hostile toward newly arrived immigrants and asylum-seekers. Anti-Semitism is on the rise again, as is discrimination against Muslims and religious minorities. While Europeans berate America for having a trigger-happy foreign policy, they are more than willing, on occasion, to let the U.S. armed forces safeguard European security interests. And even its supporters say the Brussels-based EU's governing machinery is a maze of bureaucratic red tape, aloof from the European citizens they supposedly serve.

The point, however, is not whether the Europeans are living up to their dream. We Americans have never fully lived up to our own dream. What's important is that a new generation of Europeans is creating a radical new vision for the future — one better suited to meet the challenges of an increasingly globalizing world in the 21st century.

Canada finds itself caught between these two 21st-century superpowers. Sharing a common border with the most powerful economy in the world makes Canada more vulnerable to U.S. economic and political influence, and some observers even suggest that Canada might be forced eventually to become part of a greater American transnational space. The North American free-trade agreement may be the first step down that road.

On the other hand, Canadians' own deeply felt values are more closely attuned to the emerging European Dream. Could Canada lobby to become part of the European Union? In a world of instant communications, fast transportation and global economic integration, the prospect of Canada's enjoying at least a special associational partnership with the EU is not inconceivable. The EU and Canada laid the foundation for such a possibility in their 1996 joint political declaration on EU-Canada relations, designed to focus on economic, trade, security, and other transnational issues. Canada could edge ever closer to its European soulmate in the decades to come.[9]

Discussion Question

How is Rifkin's article clearly anti-American?

---

9. Jeremy Rifkin, "Worlds Apart on the Vision Thing," *Globe and Mail / Canada*, August 17, 2004; http://www.common-dreams.org/views04/0817-08.htm.

Tiananmen Square-Monument in front of Maos Mausoleum. (CCA-SA2.0).

Chapter 31

A Transforming Revolution: The Chinese Century

First Thoughts

China has become a leading industrial power. However, predictions that China will become the world's largest economy by the year 2020 are based on unsustainable growth projections. And if the last 150 years of Chinese history tell us anything, it is that the only predictable thing is unpredictability. We will see how China emerges in the years ahead.

Chapter Learning Objectives

From the beginning, China has been ambivalent about its relationship with the West. Regardless, the West has sought to exploit this huge market, with some success. We will see the rise of the Chinese Republic and then its collapse in one generation. We will watch the Chinese Communist revolution go haywire in the 1960s only to emerge as a gentler, kinder China with a hunger for a juggernaut economy. Along the way, we will be amazed at what God is doing in China!

As a result of this chapter you should be able to:

1. Explain the role of the West with China

2. Evaluate the wisdom of supporting one adversary to beat another, more formidable one

3. Discuss why liberal revolutions inevitably evolve into totalitarian nightmares

4. Analyze Chinese revivalism

5. State your views on China's new era of prosperity

CONCEPTS

Manchus

Tiananmen Square

Chiang Kaishek

Mao Zedong

Great Leap Forward

And There was China

Manchus: Late 19th century ruling Chinese family.

In 1644, the **Manchus** took over China and founded the Qing Dynasty. Like the Mongols, they attempted to copy Chinese institutions and philosophy. However, in their attempt to emulate the Chinese, they became quite conservative and inflexible. It is a lesson of history that people groups that conquer and emulate the culture they conquer often become more intransigent in their cultural preferences than the ones they have conquered. That was the case when the Romans conquered the Greeks and when the Manchus conquered the Chinese. This sort of parochialism might fly in the 4th century, but in the 17th century it caused all sorts of problems with Western powers who wanted to trade with the Chinese. Quite literally, Western traders found it difficult to trade anything that the chauvinistic Chinese wanted! But they tried. And they annexed Hong Kong and Shanghai.

The Manchu Chinese never saw themselves as equal with anyone, much less the uncouth European traders who sought to do commerce with the great China. This sort of haughtiness remains in China even today. How ironic that English traders, in particular, saw themselves as superior to the Chinese who considered themselves superior to the pallid, wrinkled Westerners! One historian explained, "There was the rest of the world, and there was China. It wasn't that they rejected the idea of a community of nations; it's that they couldn't conceive of it. It would be like trying to teach a Buddhist monk about the Father, Son, and the Holy Ghost. This viewpoint was so pervasive that Chinese reformers who advocated more flexibility in China's dealings with the West were often accused of being Westerners with Chinese faces."[1]

Chinese forces in 1899–1901. Left: two infantrymen of the New Imperial Army. Front: drum major of the regular army. Seated on the trunk: field artilleryman. Right: Boxers. (PD).

The truth is, virtually no one was in control of China. It was always a difficult place to govern. Like Russia, it was huge! Frederic Wakeman Jr.'s *The Fall of Imperial China* states, "Rebellions sprouted like mushrooms after a rain; apocalyptic cults undermined what little official authority remained. Several of the rebellions, such as the Taiping Rebellion, very nearly succeeded. Compounding the problems was squabbling between various reformers who disagreed on how to best combat the chaos and the West (not necessarily in that order); in hindsight, it is clear that the entire system was slowly collapsing."[2]

The Western world did not know how to make heads or tails of China's collapsing system. On the one hand, they did their best to create open trade. On the other hand, they wanted to control that trade.

The Westerners needed a stable regime and did everything they could to make that happen. It was good for business. They did do their best to prop up the ailing Qing, the most notable example being the crushing of the Boxer Rebellion in 1900. What the Western powers were interested in was the carving up of China for their own purposes, and that, paradoxically, required keeping China together. Therein lies the problem of the West and the East trying to work together.

Two things made peace impossible. First, in 1911, the Qing Dynasty collapsed. Second, in 1914, World War I began.

Discussion Question

Since the middle of the 17th century, China has perceived itself as being in an adversarial role with the West. Why?

A French political cartoon depicting China as a pie about to be carved up by Queen Victoria (Britain), Kaiser Wilhelm II (Germany), Tsar Nicholas II (Russia), Marianne (France) and a samurai (Japan), while a Chinese mandarin helplessly looks on.

---

2. Frederic Wakeman Jr., *The Fall of Imperial China* (New York: Free Press, 1975).

Republican China (1911–1949)

During World War I, China joined the Allies. In return, they were promised that the German possessions in Shangdong province would be returned to the Chinese government at the end of the war. They weren't, and to add insult to injury, the Treaty of Versailles handed them over to Japan.

On May 4, 1919, about 3,000 students from various Beijing universities got together in **Tiananmen Square** (a favorite protest location) and held a mass rally. The movement that was born at that rally (called, not unsurprisingly, the May Fourth Movement) was the first true nationalist movement in China and has consequently served as an inspiration for Chinese patriots. The students of the "Beijing Spring" of 1989 intentionally drew parallels with the May Fourth Movement.

In the early 1920s, Dr. Sun Yatsen accepted Soviet aid. With Communist help, Sun Yatsen was able to forge an alliance with the fledgling Chinese Communist Party (CCP) and start the task of re-unifying China. Sun died in 1925 and **Chiang Kaishek** became president.

Chiang unwisely massacred as many Communists as he could. Among those who managed to escape was a young Communist named **Mao Zedong**.

In 1934, the Nationalists were closing in on the Communist positions when the Communists escaped. They didn't stop for a year. This was the Long March. When the Communists started, they had 100,000 people. A year later, when they finally stopped, they had traveled 6,000 miles, and were down to 4,000 people.

Mao's official portrait at Tiananmen gate, 1923 (PD).

Students gather for a demonstration in Tiananmen Square, ca. 1917–1919 (PD).

Meanwhile, the Japanese occupied Manchuria. In 1937, the Japanese invaded China from their bases in Manchuria. It didn't take the Japanese long to occupy the major coastal cities. The Japanese created unthinkable atrocities. By 1945, 20 million Chinese had died at the hands of the Japanese. The Nationalist Government fled up the Yangzi River to Chongqing from Nanjing.

In 1939, World War II started. After the Americans entered the war, the Communists started to consolidate their control over North China in preparation for the resumption of the civil war that would occur after the Japanese had been defeated.

The Nationalists, in contrast to the Communists, were disorganized and corrupt, problems that would only intensify after the war. Moreover, their attempts to fight the Japanese were ineffective at best.

At the end of World War II, the war between the Nationalists and the Communists started up again. The Communists were hampered by the fact that the Japanese were under orders to surrender only to the Nationalists, not the Communists. By 1949 it was all over. By that October, the Nationalists had fled to Taiwan and Mao Zedong had proclaimed the creation of the People's Republic of China.[3]

Discussion Question

In World War II, General Stillwell, in charge of American forces in China, lobbied Washington to channel some aid to the Communists. This was not because Stillwell was sympathetic to their cause but because the Communists were simply doing a better job fighting the Japanese than the Nationalists. Do you think war is a time to suspend political ambitions and to support anyone, even an enemy, to defeat a greater enemy? Why or why not?

---

3. http://condensedchina.com/china4.html.

The People's Republic of China (1949–)

With the collapse of communism in Eastern Europe, Chinese reformers demanded political reforms. This came to a head in Tiananmen Square in May 1989. The leaders of the Communist Party killed several hundred protesters.

In 1950, China intervened in the Korean War to save the North Koreans from being wiped out. By 1953, it succeeded but at great cost.

In 1958, China launched the **Great Leap Forward**. The idea was to mobilize the peasant masses to increase crop production by collectivizing the farms and by using the excess labor to produce steel. What ended up happening was the greatest man-made famine in human history. From 1958 to 1960, the Great Leap Forward starved 30 million people to death.

In 1966, Mao launched the Great Proletarian Cultural Revolution. Mao called upon students to rebel against authority, and they did, forming units of Red Guards. China promptly collapsed into anarchy. Schools shut down, offices closed, transportation was disrupted — it was comparable to the French Revolution.

The truth is that Chairman Mao had become Emperor Mao. While the Cultural Revolution officially ended in 1969, and the worst abuses stopped then, the politically charged atmosphere was maintained until Mao's death in 1976. Deng Xiaoping, who was purged twice during the Cultural Revolution, eventually emerged as the leader in 1978, and promptly launched his economic reform program.

Reconstruction of the important meeting between Deng Xiaoping and Margaret Thatcher in Beijing on September 24, 1984 with talks about the future of Hong Kong - at the visitors platform of the Diwang Dasha in Shenzhen (PD).

In 1982, Margaret Thatcher, then Prime Minister of Britain, went to Beijing to meet with Deng Xiaopeng. Most of the talks concerned the issue of Hong Kong. By the time she had left, the United Kingdom and the People's Republic of China had signed an agreement in principle to hand Hong Kong from the UK over to China. In 1984, the agreement was formalized in a document known as the Joint Declaration.

After June 4, progress and reform in China stopped for three years. But in 1993, Deng Xiaoping, in one of his last major public appearances, toured the Shenzhen Special Economic Zone and emphatically voiced his approval. After that, the Chinese economy exploded.[4]

Discussion Question

Why do "people" movements, movements with laudable goals of "liberty, fraternity, and justice" eventually evolve into authoritarian regimes?

---

4. http://www.snatours.com/ChineseHistory/PRC.shtml.

Christians in China:
Is the Country in Spiritual Crisis?

By Tim Gardam

It is impossible to say how many Christians there are in China today, but no-one denies the numbers are exploding. The government says . . . 25 million . . . Protestants and Catholics. Independent estimates all agree this is a vast underestimate. A conservative figure is 60 million. . . .

The new converts can be found from peasants in the remote rural villages to the sophisticated young middle class in the booming cities.

There is a complexity in the structures of Chinese Christianity which is little understood in the West. To start with, Catholicism and Protestantism are designated by the state as two separate religions.

The Haidian Christian Church in Beijing was completely re-built to cope with rising numbers.

Throughout the 20th century, Christianity was associated with Western imperialism. After the Communist victory in 1949, the missionaries were expelled, but Christianity was permitted in state-sanctioned churches, so long as they gave their primary allegiance to the Communist Party.

Mao, on the other hand, described religion as "poison," and the Cultural Revolution of the 1960s and 70s attempted to eradicate it. Driven underground, Christianity not only survived, but with its own Chinese martyrs, it grew in strength.

Since the 1980s, when religious belief was again permitted, the official churches have gradually created more space for themselves.

They report to the State Administration for Religious Affairs. They are forbidden to take part in any religious activity outside their places of worship and sign up to the slogan, "Love the country — love your religion."

In return the Party promotes atheism in schools but undertakes "to protect and respect religion until such time as religion itself will disappear."

The officially sanctioned Catholic Patriotic Association appoints its own bishops and is not allowed to have any dealings with the Vatican, though Catholics are allowed to recognize the spiritual authority of the Pope.

There is a larger Catholic underground church, supported by the Vatican. Inch by inch, the Vatican and the government have been moving towards accommodation. Most bishops are now recognized by both, with neither side admitting the greater sovereignty of the other.

> "More people go to church on Sunday in China than in the whole of Europe. . . . many of China's churches are overflowing, as the number of Christians in the country multiplies. . . ."

St. Dominic's Church in Macau is one of the oldest (AD 1587) existing churches in China built by three Spanish Dominican priests (CCA-SA2.0).

Yet in the past few months, the Chinese government has again turned tough, ordaining its bishops in the teeth of opposition from the Vatican which has in turn excommunicated one of them.

Even so, it would be wrong simply to dismiss the official church as a sham. . . .

On Easter morning, in downtown Beijing, I watched five services, each packed with over 1,500 worshipers. Sunday school was spilling on to the street.

However, these numbers are dwarfed by the unofficial "house churches," spreading across the country, at odds with the official Church which fears the house churches' fervor may provoke a backlash.

What the authorities consider non-negotiable is the house churches' refusal to acknowledge any official authority over their organization.

The State fears the influence of zealous American evangelism and some of the House Church theology has those characteristics, but, in many other respects, it seems to be an indigenous Chinese movement — charismatic, energetic, and young.

An educated young Christian described her church to me: "We have 50 young professionals in this church. Everyone is so busy working, you don't have time [to socialize], and even if you are socializing, you are putting on a fake face. But in church people feel warm, they feel welcome . . . they feel people really love them so they really want to join the community, a lot of people come for this." . . .

In some areas the state has sought to enlist Christianity into its "big idea" of a "harmonious society" — the slogan that dominates Chinese public life. There has been official interest in the Western evangelical Alpha Marriage Course, because of alarm at the escalating divorce rate among young Chinese.

What must unsettle the authorities most is the reason why so many are turning to the churches.

I heard people talking again and again of a "spiritual crisis" in China — a phrase that has even been used by the Premier Wen Jiao Bao. The old have seen the old certainties of Marxism-Leninism transmute into the most visceral capitalist society on earth.

For the young, in the stampede to get rich, trust in institutions, between individuals, between the generations, is breaking down.[5]

Discussion Question

In many nations, persecution and poverty drive people to the Lord. In China it is prosperity. Explain.

---

5. http://www.bbc.co.uk/news/magazine-14838749, September 11, 2011.

The Chinese Century

By Ted C. Fishman

China used to be far away, the country at the bottom of the world. Certainly that must be how it seemed just 20 years ago in a place like Pekin, Illinois, a city of 34,000 residents on the Illinois River that took its name from the Chinese capital in the 1820s. According to local legend, Pekin is directly opposite Beijing on the globe. The high-school teams there were still called the Chinks until 1981, when they were renamed the Dragons. A smart and forward-looking decision, it turns out: as is happening throughout the United States, the Pekinese have in their own local ways grown inextricably linked to the Chinese of today. They are now connected not by an imaginary hole through the earth but by the world's shipping lanes, financial markets, telecommunications networks and, above all, the globalization of appetites.

Follow the corn, for example. Trade deals struck between the U.S. and China in April will, farmers around Pekin hope, lead China to lower its import barriers and buy half a million metric tons of American corn this year. Illinois corn farmers get higher-than-usual prices for their exports because they have ready access to river transportation and in turn to big ports. Pekin is also home to the plant of Aventine Renewable Energy, the nation's second-largest producer of ethanol, a fuel derived from corn. (Ten percent of the American corn crop is converted to fuel.) China recently passed Japan as the world's second-largest consumer of petroleum, and growing Chinese demand has lately been pushing up oil prices worldwide. That makes ethanol an increasingly attractive alternative. And, indeed, ethanol prices climbed 40 cents a gallon this spring, dragging up U.S. corn prices as a result, a boon to Pekin's farmers and industry. . . .

In short, Pekin, Illinois, is not so different from lots of American places. China is every-where these days, influencing our lives as consumers, providers, citizens. It has by far the world's most rapidly changing large economy, and our reactions to it shift just as quickly.

Ted C. Fishman, a contributing editor for *Harper's Magazine,* is writing a book about China's place in the world. This is his first cover article for the *Times Magazine.*

The modern skyline of Hong Kong, China.

China is at one moment our greatest threat, the next our friend. It siphons off American jobs; it is essential to our competitive edge. China is the world's factory floor, and it is the world's greatest market opportunity. China's industrial might steals opportunities from the developing world, even as its booming economy pulls poorer countries up (lately it has been getting credit for helping Japan out of its slump too). China exports deflation; it stokes soaring prices. China will boom; it will bust. Or perhaps the country's economy is feeling its way right now to the soft landing that will prevent another Asian economic crash, and all the recent record numbers on trade, industrial output, consumer spending and debt are simply now in scale with China's size. The truth about China is that, like all big countries, it is full of real contradictions.

Another truth is that the current feelings about China do not fully reflect today's reality. The U.S. economy is about eight times the size of China's. Our manufacturing sector is bigger than the entire Chinese economy. Americans, per capita, earn 36 times what the Chinese do. And there is no shortage of potential roadblocks in China's path, either. Its banks may collapse. Its poor and its minorities may rebel. Uppity Taiwan and lunatic North Korea may push China to war. The U.S. could slap taxes on everything China ships to us.

Still, barring Mao's resurrection or nuclear cataclysm, nothing is likely to keep China down for long. Since 1978, its gross domestic product has risen fourfold; in straight dollar terms, China's economy is the world's sixth-largest, with a G.D.P. of around $1.4 trillion. It has gone from being virtually absent in international trade to the world's third-most-active trading nation, behind the U.S. and Germany and ahead of Japan. Tom Saler, a financial journalist, has pointed out that 21 recessions, a depression, two stock-market crashes and two world wars were not able to stop the U.S. economy's growth, over the last century, from $18 billion ($367 billion in 2000 dollars) to $10 trillion. In constant dollars, that is a 27-fold increase.

China is poised for similar growth in this century. Even if China's people do not, on average, have the wealth Americans do, and even if the United States continues to play a strong economic game and to lead in technology, China will still be an ever more formidable competitor. If any country is going to supplant the U.S. in the world marketplace, China is it.[6]

Discussion Question

Do you believe that China will replace America as the premier economic power in the world?

6. *New York Times*, July 4, 2004, http://www.nytimes.com/2004/07/04/magazine/04CHINA.html.

A view of damages to the U.S. Embassy caused by a terrorist bomb attack. Marines are here participating as members of a multinational peacekeeping force, 1983 (PD-USGOV).

Chapter 32

Terrorism: Tactics and Strategies

First Thoughts

The largest act of international terrorism to date occurred on September 11, 2001, in a set of coordinated deadly attacks on the United States, where Islamic terrorists hijacked civilian airliners and used them to attack the World Trade Center towers in New York City and the Pentagon in Washington, D.C. The operational and strategic epicenter of Islamic terrorism is now mostly centered in Pakistan and Afghanistan. Terrorism, however, has existed as a political and military intervention for thousands of years. It remains to be seen if terrorism will end in the years to come.

Chapter Learning Objectives

Terrorism has been a means and an end for extremists for thousands of years. Improved weaponry and virulent ideology combined in the 20th century to make terrorism a revived choice that would have a huge impact on world history. What is terrorism? Were American patriots terrorists? Is the War on Terrorism over?

As a result of this chapter you should be able to:

1. Discuss in what way 21st-century terrorism is different from earlier forms of terrorism

2. Explain what ominous connection existed from the beginning of terrorism

3. Understand why terrorism was utilized more freely after World War II

4. Assess if the Sons of Liberty is a terrorist organization

5. Evaluate President Obama's assessment in 2009 that the War on Terrorism was over

CONCEPTS

Terrorism

Collateral damage

Jewish zealots

Sons of Liberty

Terrorism

Terrorism:
Systematic violence against a government on behalf of a cause.

Terrorism has been applied to almost any violent counter-revolutionary act, and therefore is hard to define.

Was the French Revolution terrorism? Was the Holocaust terrorism? Was the FBI wire-tapping of anti-war demonstrators terrorism?

Most historians argue that the outcome of an action is what matters, not the intent. The retention of American sailors by Barbary Pirates in the early 19th century would be classified as terrorism because the sailors died. Otherwise, it would be a political statement or a kidnapping.

The picture was published in the Jerusalem Post after the destruction of Hotel King David by Irgoun - 1946 (PD).

Others argue that intent is everything. The assassination of John F. Kennedy was an act of terrorism because it was done without any clear political motivation.

The senseless suicide bomber in a Middle Eastern marketplace commits terrorism because he kills 25 people. **Collateral** or unintended damage to civilians from an attack by uniformed military forces on a legitimate military target is the same as a terrorist bomb directed deliberately at the civilian target with the intent of creating damage.

But things become complicated. Was the Boston Massacre in pre-Revolution America an act of terror?

Terrorists inevitably have as a primary goal to disrupt, reorder, or destroy the status quo while continuously seeking creative ways to achieve their other goals. Changes in the tactics and techniques of terrorists have been significant, but even more significant is the growth in the number of causes and social contexts where terrorism is used.

Terrorism is increasing because it works. The murder of six U.S. servicemen in 2012 in retaliation for an unintentional burning of the Koran got a docile apology from the U.S. president.

In the 19th century and early 20th century, most terrorism was tied to nationalism. These devotees were driven by the interests or culture of a group of people or a nation. A Serbian nationalist murdered the crown prince of the Austro-Hungarian Empire. Typically, nationalists share a common ethnic background and wish to establish or regain a homeland.

In the 21st century, most terrorism is connected to religion. Religious extremists often reject the authority of secular governments and view legal systems that are not based on their religious beliefs as illegitimate. They often view modernization efforts as corrupting influences on traditional culture.

Special interest groups include people on the radical fringe of many legitimate causes — e.g., people who use terrorism to uphold anti-abortion views, animal rights, radical environmentalism, and gay rights. These groups believe that violence is morally justifiable to achieve their goals.[1]

Discussion Question

In what way is 21st-century terrorism different from earlier forms of terrorism?

Terrorism, A.D. 100 to 1400

One of the earliest known organizations that exhibited aspects of modern terrorist organizations was the **Jewish zealots** of Judea. Known to the Romans as dagger-men, they carried on a successful underground campaign of assassination of Roman occupation forces, as well as any Jews they felt had collaborated with the Romans. Their motive was an uncompromising belief that they could not follow God and obey His Law while living as Roman subjects. Eventually, the Zealot revolt became open, and they were finally besieged and committed mass suicide at the fortification of Masada.

> An Islamic group called the Nizari Ismalis adopted the tactic of assassination of enemy leaders because the cult's limited manpower prevented open combat.

They were the forerunners of modern terrorists in terms of motivation, organization, targeting, and goals. Early terrorists learned something else: the effect of terrorism was compounded by the willing participation of the media. Terrorists learned to control the media and were thus able to multiply the impact of their horrible act.

The truth is, once the Roman Empire disappeared, terrorism was short of enemies to attack. Until the rise of the modern nation states after the Treaty of Westphalia in 1648, the sort of central authority and cohesive society that terrorism loves to destroy barely existed. Also, city states like the Holy Roman Empire were not in the mood to entertain terrorists. Small terrorist acts often resulted in nasty, long wars — like the 30 Year War. The truth is — and this has been a problem for terrorists since the beginning — nations have a tendency to react, some would say overreact, to terrorism acts. A few radicals bombed a couple of buildings and the United States conquered two countries. By the time kingdoms and principalities

Masada, the fortress where a group of Jewish zealots tried to survive an assault from the Roman army (CCA-SA3.0).

---

1. http://www.terrorism-research.com/history/.

The Plot of the Rue Saint-Nicaise, 1882 (PD).

The plot of the rue Saint-Nicaise, also known as the Machine infernale (English: Infernal machine) plot, was an assassination attempt on the life of the First Consul of France, Napoleon Bonaparte, in Paris on 24 December 1800. It followed the conspiration des poignards of 10 October 1800, and was one of many Royalist and Catholic plots.
The name of the Machine Infernale, the "infernal device," was in reference to an episode during the sixteenth-century revolt against Spanish rule in Flanders. In 1585, during the Siege of Antwerp by the Spaniards, an Italian engineer in Spanish service had made an explosive device from a barrel bound with iron hoops, filled with gunpowder, flammable materials and bullets, and set off by a sawed-off shotgun triggered from a distance by a string. The Italian engineer called it la macchina infernale.

became nations, they had sufficient means to enforce their authority and suppress activities such as terrorism. Modern states were not in the mood to mess around with terrorists!

The French Revolution, perhaps the first whole nation act of terrorism in history, provided the first uses of the words "terrorist" and "terrorism." Use of the word "terrorism" began in 1795 in reference to the Reign of Terror initiated by the Revolutionary government. The agents of the Committee of Public Safety and the National Convention that enforced the policies of "The Terror" were referred to as "Terrorists." The French Revolutionaries were pretty good at terrorism too and provided a macabre example to future states in oppressing their populations. Their acts also inspired a reaction by royalists and other opponents of the Revolution who employed pretty good terrorist tactics such as assassination and intimidation in resistance to the revolutionary agents. Both groups of terrorists learned how to work the crowd — an important component of terrorism. The French urban mobs played a critical role at key points before, during, and after the Revolution. Someone would chop off a head, or jump on a makeshift barricade, and the "mob" willingly joined the fun. Such extra-legal activities as killing prominent officials and aristocrats in gruesome spectacles started long before the guillotine was first used. It actually made the whole terrorist act anti-climactic.

During the late 19th century, radical political theories (e.g., anarchy) and advancements in weaponry revitalized terrorism. Anarchists killed heads of state all over Europe and the United States. However, their lack of organization and refusal to cooperate with other social movements in political efforts rendered anarchists ineffective as a political movement.

The die was cast, though. A deadly courtship and pending marriage between terrorism and ideology (religion) was to presage a world of woe for generations.[2]

Discussion Question

What ominous connection has existed from the beginning of terrorism?

---

2. http://www.terrorism-research.com/history/early.php.

Terrorism in the 20th and 21st Centuries

The truth is, the 20th century was very good to terrorist groups. It was full of new techniques of destruction — national leaders like Adolf Hitler and Josef Stalin nationalized terrorism and turned murder into a fine art. Many generations have emulated their appalling examples.

Gradually, as nations became closely tied to concepts of race and ethnicity, international political developments began to support such concepts. Members of ethnic groups whose states had been absorbed by others or had ceased to exist as separate nations saw opportunities to realize nationalist ambitions. Several of these groups chose terror as a method to conduct their struggle and make their situation known to world powers that they hoped would be sympathetic. In Europe, both the Irish and the Serbians conducted terrorist campaigns as part of their ongoing struggle for independence but had to initiate bloody uprisings to further their cause. In this, the Irish were partially successful, but the Serbians failed.

Pictured here are the remnants of a terror attack at the Erez Crossing where humanitarian aid is transferred, in which a massive bomb truck loaded with explosives was detonated. 2008 (CCA-SA2.0)

With the collapse of any limits on cultural genocide, terrorism crossed new thresholds of violence. The intensity of the conflict between starkly opposed ideologies led to excesses on the parts of all participants. New weapons and strategies that targeted the enemies' civilian population in view of destroying their economic capacity for conflict exposed virtually every civilian to the hazards of combatants and exponentially increased casualties. Everyone supported partisan and resistance organizations using terrorist tactics. Thus, murder and mayhem became *modus operandi* after World War II ended. The Viet Cong simply switched enemies: i.e., the Japanese were replaced by the French. The distinction between civilian and combatant was forever blurred.

Ironically, the very nature of nuclear weaponry redefined terrorism. Terrorists knew they could do most anything to anyone with limited consequences — no one was willing to nuke a nation state, or even an ethnic group. So terrorism saw an opportunity to expand and to form new franchises in fresh markets — especially the Middle East. Relatively minor confrontations took on significance as arenas where the superpowers could compete without risking escalation to a full nuclear war. Warfare between the East and the West took place on the peripheries, and was limited in scope to prevent escalation. It was as if terrorism became routine, almost status quo, because its significance paled in comparison to what might occur: the nuclear conflagration of the planet.

During the immediate post-war period, terrorism was more of a tactical choice by leaders of nationalist insurgencies and revolutions. Successful campaigns for independence from colonial rule occurred throughout the world, and many employed terrorism as a tactic. Again, it worked nicely. A relatively small group of dedicated fanatics could affect the policy of powerful nations; those individuals experienced feelings of euphoria and addiction. Run a stupid speedboat full of explosives into the side of an American

February 5, 2007. For the first time since the end of the 2006 conflict with Hezbollah in Lebanon, several explosive devices camouflaged as rocks planted on the international border with Lebanon in the area of Avivim, were uncovered by IDF forces (CCA-SSA2.0).

warship and one made the evening news, and even better, could drive the greatest nation on the face of the earth to remove its troops from Somalia!

When terrorism was used, it was used within the framework of larger movements, and coordinated with political, social, and military action. Even when terrorism came to dominate the other aspects of a nationalist struggle, such as the Palestinian campaign against Israel, it engendered, and fed off of, ancillary causes.

Large nation states made terrorism much easier by providing huge amounts of money and weaponry to make terrorism more effective. During the Cold War, for example, the Soviet Union provided direct and indirect assistance to revolutionary movements around the world. Of course supporting terrorism is like holding a rattlesnake — it bites the one holding the snake as well as the person next to the person holding the snake. Russia was itself attacked by Chechen terrorists.[3]

Discussion Question

Why was terrorism employed more freely after World War II?

Lesson 4

Case Study: Sons of Liberty: Patriots or Terrorists?

By Todd Alan Kreamer

During a series of protests linked to the Sons of Liberty, colonists burned and sacked the house of the Massachusetts lieutenant governor, Thomas Hutchinson.

For the American "armchair historian," this American Revolutionary organization conjures up a myriad of confusing images. But, what of this "secret" organization that played such an integral part in advancing the idea of American independence from Great Britain? What were the **Sons of Liberty**? Who were its members and how widespread was its support among the thirteen colonies comprising British America? What was the ideology and degree of political affiliation within the organization?

Shrouded in secrecy, the origins of the Sons of Liberty are in dispute. Some historical sources claim that the movement began in New York City in January 1765. A more popular claim is that the movement began in Boston, Massachusetts, through the leadership of one Samuel Adams (a well-known American Revolutionary firebrand) in

---

3. http://www.terrorism-research.com/history/recent.php.

early 1765. It is quite likely that the Boston and New York City chapters of the Sons of Liberty were organized and developed simultaneously.

Tradition has it that the Boston chapter gathered beneath the Liberty Tree for meetings while the New York City chapter met beneath the Liberty Pole for its meetings. For reasons of safety and secrecy, Sons of Liberty groups tended to meet late at night so as not to attract attention and detection of British officials and the American Loyalist supporters of the British Crown.

This secret patriotic society had its roots in the Committees of Correspondence. The "Committees" were colonial groups organized prior to the outbreak of the American War for Independence and were established for the purpose of formally organizing public opinion and coordinating patriotic actions against Great Britain. These original committees were loosely organized groups of private citizens formed in the New York, Massachusetts, and Rhode Island colonies from 1763–1764.

It was the Boston Committee of Correspondence that directed the Boston Tea Party action of December 16, 1773. Upset with the lack of redress concerning the new tax on tea established by the British government for importation of tea to Boston, a small band of the Boston Committee of Correspondence members (approximately fifty in number) led by Samuel Adams, proceeded to empty three ships worth and 342 chests of tea into Boston Harbor in protest.

Engraving depicting the burning of the Gaspee, 1883 (PD).

Was this an early terrorist action or a patriotic action? Surely, the answer lies with perspective. If you were a British official, this action was treasonous and punishable by death. If you were an American colonial citizen, this event would be seen as a glorious action of the freedom fighters worthy of praise, pride, and acclaim.

Essentially, the Sons of Liberty organized into patriotic chapters as a result of the Stamp Tax imposed by the British government on the American colonists in 1765. . . .

The Sons of Liberty organizations responded to the Stamp Act of 1765 in various ways. The New York Sons of Liberty declared in December 1765 that they would "go to the last extremity" with their lives and fortunes to prevent the enforcement of the Stamp Act. This declaration included the use of violence if necessary. Acts of rebellion against the Stamp Tax in New York City included an incident from January 9, 1766, in which ten boxes of parchment and stamped paper were delivered to City Hall and immediately confiscated, unpacked, and burned by secret leaders of the New York Sons group. . . .

While British officials accused the Sons organizations of scheming to overthrow the true and legitimate government of the American colonies, the Sons of Liberty viewed their official aims in more narrow terms, organizing and asserting resistance to the Stamp Act. Outwardly, the Sons of Liberty proclaimed their unfaltering loyalty and allegiance

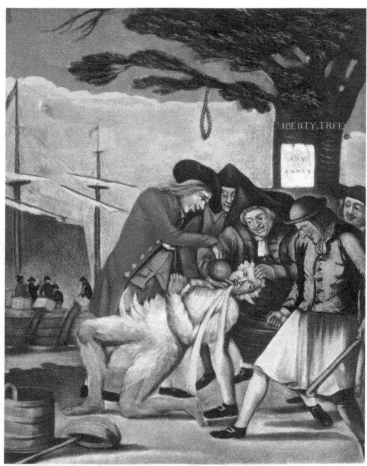

A depiction of the tarring and feathering of Commissioner of Customs John Malcolm, a Loyalist, by five Patriots on January 5, 1744, under the Liberty Tree in Boston, Massachusetts. Tea is also being poured into Malcolm's mouth. 1774 (LOC).

to King George III of Great Britain and emphasized their support of the English Constitution against the usurpation of royal officials. For eleven years, 1765 to 1776, American colonists saw British Parliament as the collective "bad guy," not the king! . . .

In the end, no universal conclusions, judgments, or definitive statements can be made about the Sons of Liberty. Were they a terrorist organization? The British certainly believed they were. After all, the Sons were advocating overthrow of the status quo government and independence for the thirteen colonies. Were they a patriotic organization? Many American colonists certainly believed they were. The Sons represented to them the American freedom fighter personified, fighting for their rights and ultimate independence. It should be noted that the Loyalists also had their version of Committees of Correspondence and Sons of Liberty namely: the United Empire Loyalists.

One thing is certain about the Sons of Liberty organization: it gave American colonists a voice and vital chance to actively participate in the independence movement.[4]

Discussion Question

How were the Sons of Liberty different from terrorist organizations of today?

4. http://www.earlyamerica.com/review/fall96/sons.html.

White House: War on Terrorism Is Over

***Washington Times*, August 6, 2009**

It's official. The U.S. is no longer engaged in a "war on terrorism." Neither is it fighting "jihadists" or in a "global war."

President Obama's top homeland security and counterterrorism official took all three terms off the table of acceptable words inside the White House during a speech Thursday at the Center for Strategic and International Studies, a Washington think tank.

"The President does not describe this as a 'war on terrorism,' " said John Brennan, head of the White House homeland security office, who outlined a "new way of seeing" the fight against terrorism.

The only terminology that Mr. Brennan said the administration is using is that the U.S. is "at war with al Qaeda."

"We are at war with al Qaeda," he said. "We are at war with its violent extremist allies who seek to carry on al Qaeda's murderous agenda."

Secretary of State Hillary Clinton said in March that the administration was not using the term "war on terror," but no specific directive had come from the White House itself. Mr. Obama himself used the term "war on terror" on Jan. 23, his fourth day as president, but has not used it since.

Mr. Brennan's speech was aimed at outlining ways in which the Obama administration intends to undermine the "upstream" factors that create an environment in which terrorists are bred.

The president's adviser talked about increasing aid to foreign governments for building up their militaries and social and democratic institutions, but provided few details about how the White House will do that.

He was specific about ways in which Mr. Obama believes words influence the way America prosecutes the fight against terrorism.

Mr. Brennan said that to say the U.S. is fighting "jihadists" is wrongheaded because it is using "a legitimate term, 'jihad,' meaning to purify oneself or to wage a holy struggle for a moral goal" which "risks giving these murderers the religious legitimacy they desperately seek but in no way deserve."

"Worse, it risks reinforcing the idea that the United States is somehow at war with Islam itself," Mr. Brennan said.

As for the "war on terrorism," Mr. Brennan said the administration is not going to say that "because 'terrorism' is but a tactic — a means to an end, which in al Qaeda's case is global domination by an Islamic caliphate."

"You can never fully defeat a tactic like terrorism any more than you can defeat the tactic of war itself," Mr. Brennan said.

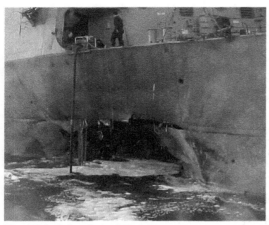

The USS *Cole* after al-Qaeda suicide attack, 2000 (PS-USNAVY).

He also said that to call the fight against al Qaeda and other terrorist groups — which he said remains "a dynamic and evolving threat" — should not be called "a global war."

While Mr. Brennan acknowledged that al Qaeda and its affiliates are active in countries throughout the Middle East and Africa, he also said that "portraying this as a 'global' war risks reinforcing the very image that al Qaeda seeks to project of itself — that it is a highly organized, global entity capable of replacing sovereign nations with a global caliphate."

The president's adviser said that in discussing counter terror operations, Mr. Obama "has encouraged us to be even more aggressive, even more proactive, and even more innovative" than they have been proposing.

But Mr. Brennan lamented "inflammatory rhetoric, hyperbole, and intellectual narrowness" surrounding the national security debate and said Mr. Obama has views that are "nuanced, not simplistic; practical, not ideological."

Juan Zarate, a former deputy national security adviser for counterterrorism to President George W. Bush, was in the audience and dismissed Mr. Brennan's speech as cosmetic in nature.

The focus on terminology, he said, is "almost a nonissue."

"It's a straw man. The question is, how do you deal with the policy?" Mr. Zarate said.

Mr. Zarate also discounted Mr. Brennan's insistence that the Obama administration is not continuing Bush-era policies. Mr. Brennan gave credit for al Qaeda's "damaged" capabilities only to front line military and intelligence personnel, while bashing the Bush administration for approving policies that green-lighted interrogation techniques such as water boarding.

Mr. Brennan also said that under the Bush administration counterterrorism became too much of an emphasis and was "defining" and "distorting" U.S. foreign and national security policy.

But critics on the left and the right have pointed out that the Obama administration has continued such Bush-era policies as extraordinary rendition, drone attacks in Pakistan, an international and domestic surveillance program that remains cloaked in mystery, and the war in Afghanistan, where Mr. Obama has increased the number of U.S. troops and the military continues to house enemy combatants at Bagram Air Base.

In addition, the White House is still considering the practice of indefinite detention of terrorist suspects.

"A challenge for John and the administration is to preserve the perception of a new approach while still continuing with counterterrorism strategies that have proven effective," said Mr. Zarate.[5]

Discussion Question

Do you agree with President Obama's assessment in 2009 that the War on Terrorism was over?

---

5. http://www.washingtontimes.com/news/2009/aug/06/white-house-war-terrorism-over/?feat=home_headlines

Tasiilaq Greenland is an icy wonderland inhabited by teams of sled dogs, colossal glaciers, and home to the world's second-largest ice sheet (CCA-SA2.0).

Chapter 33

Apocalypse: End of All Things

First Thoughts

NASA's *Ask an Astrobiologist* website received thousands of questions regarding the 2012 doomsday predictions — some of them disturbing, according to David Morrison, senior scientist with the NASA Astrobiology Institute. "A lot of [the submitters] are people who are genuinely frightened," Morrison said. "I've had two teenagers who were considering killing themselves because they didn't want to be around when the world ends," he said. "Two women in the last two weeks said they were contemplating killing their children and themselves so they wouldn't have to suffer through the end of the world."[1] How will the world end? We will look at that question and others.

Chapter Learning Objectives

The end of the world has been a topic for generations. Today, though, it is an ever-present reality. We will look at several threats: the threat of a pandemic, global warming, nuclear war, and overpopulation. We will finish by looking at biblical theology concerning the end of the world.

As a result of this chapter you should be able to:

1. Understand what a pandemic is

2. Evaluate if global warming is really a threat

3. Discuss the nuclear threat

4. Analyze the problem with overpopulation theories

5. Explain your eschatology

1. http://news.nationalgeographic.com/news/2009/11/091106-2012-end-of-world-myths.html.

Pandemic

A **pandemic** is an epidemic of infectious disease that is spreading through human populations across a large region or even worldwide. A widespread endemic disease that is stable in terms of how many people are getting sick from it is not a pandemic. Thus, it is conceivable that a pandemic could destroy the human population of the world.

There have been several pandemics in history. All eventually succumbed to interventions and ceased, or ceased by their own accord.

The very first recorded pandemic was described by Thucydides in his *History of the Peloponnesian War*. In 430 B.C., during the Peloponnesian War between Athens and Sparta, a pandemic destroyed almost two-thirds of the population of Athens.

Thucydides described the disease as such: "People in good health were all of a sudden attacked by violent heats in the head, and redness and inflammation in the eyes, the inward parts, such as the throat or tongue, becoming bloody and emitting an unnatural and fetid breath." Next came coughing, diarrhea, spasms, and skin ulcers. Historians, to this day, cannot identify exactly what this disease was.

In A.D. 165, Greek physician Galen described an ancient pandemic — smallpox that was brought to Rome by soldiers returning from duty in the Middle East. The disease killed 5,000 people. By the time the disease ran its course some 15 years later, a total of five million Romans died.

In A.D. 541–542, there was an outbreak of the bubonic plague in the Byzantine Empire. It killed 10,000 people in Constantinople every day. By the end of the outbreak, nearly half of the inhabitants of the city were dead. Overall, it killed a quarter of the human population in the Eastern Mediterranean. Ultimately, it claimed as many as 200 million.

Finally, in March 1918, in the last months of World War I, an unusually virulent and deadly flu virus was identified in a U.S. military camp in Kansas. Just six months later, the flu had become a worldwide pandemic in all continents. When the Spanish flu pandemic was over, about one billion people, or half the world's population, had contracted it. It was perhaps the most lethal pandemic in the history of humankind: between 20 and 100 million people were killed.

Could a pandemic kill everyone? Yes, it is possible. The Spanish flu infected most of the world; if it had been a more virulent strain, it could have killed most of the world.[2]

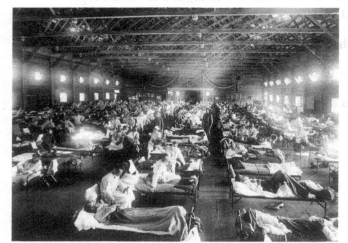

The Spanish Influenza. Emergency military hospital during influenza epidemic, Camp Funston, Kansas, United States, 1918 or 1919 (CCA-SA2.5).

Discussion Question

What is a pandemic, and is AIDS a pandemic?

2. http://www.neatorama.com/2009/04/27/5-deadliest-pandemics-in-history/.

Global Warming or Not — Two Views

Global Warming and Climate Change

Global warming has become perhaps the most complicated issue facing world leaders. Warnings from the scientific community are becoming louder, as an increasing body of science points to rising dangers from the ongoing buildup of human-related greenhouse gases — produced mainly by the burning of fossil fuels and forests.

Global emissions of carbon dioxide jumped by the largest amount on record in 2010, upending the notion that the brief decline during the recession might persist through the recovery. Emissions rose 5.9 percent in 2010, according to the Global Carbon Project, an international collaboration of scientists. The increase solidified a trend of ever-rising emissions that scientists fear will make it difficult, if not impossible, to forestall severe climate change in coming decades.

Impatient with the slow pace of international negotiations, the United States and a small group of countries — Bangladesh, Canada, Ghana, Mexico, and Sweden as well as the United Nations Environment Program — are starting a program that will address short-lived pollutants like soot (also referred to as black carbon), methane, and hydrofluorocarbons that have an outsize influence on global warming, accounting for 30 to 40 percent of global warming. Soot from diesel exhausts and the burning of wood, agricultural waste, and dung for heating and cooking causes an estimated two million premature deaths a year, particularly in the poorest countries.

Scientists say that concerted action on these substances can reduce global temperatures by 0.5 degrees Celsius by 2050 and prevent millions of cases of lung and heart disease by 2030.

The United States intends to contribute $12 million and Canada $3 million over two years to get the program off the ground and to help recruit other countries to participate. The United Nations Environment Program will run the project.

The United States has been criticized at the United Nations gatherings for years, in part because of its rejection of the Kyoto framework and in part because it has not adopted a comprehensive domestic program for reducing its own greenhouse gas emissions. President Obama has pledged to reduce American emissions 17 percent below 2005 levels by 2020, but his preferred approach, a nationwide cap-and-trade system for carbon pollution, was passed by the House in 2009 but died in the Senate the next year. United States emissions are down about 6 percent over the past five years, largely because of the drop in industrial and electricity production caused by the recession.

The debate over climate questions pales next to the fight over what to do, or not do, in a world where fossil fuels still underpin both rich and emerging economies.

Scientists learned long ago that the earth's climate has powerfully shaped the history of the human species — biologically, culturally, and geographically. But only in the last few

In a world where energy consumption is often at odds with resource availability and growing concerns for the environment, it would seem a solution like wind farms would be a popular one. However, no technology comes without issues. Complaints include reports of large numbers of birds and bats being killed by the structures, as well as health, noise, and property value issues for residents nearby. (CCA-SA3.0).

Al Gore recieving the Nobel Peace Price 2007 (CCA-SA3.0).

decades has research revealed that humans can be a powerful influence on the climate, as well.

A growing body of scientific evidence indicates that since 1950, the world's climate has been warming, primarily as a result of emissions from unfettered burning of fossil fuels and the razing of tropical forests. Such activity adds to the atmosphere's invisible blanket of carbon dioxide and other heat-trapping "greenhouse" gases. Recent research has shown that methane, which flows from landfills, livestock, and oil and gas facilities, is a close second to carbon dioxide as an impact on the atmosphere.[3]

Scientists Make Anti-Global Warming Case

Al Gore is a politician who somehow managed to win a Nobel Peace Prize. Ivar Giaever is a Nobel Laureate in Physics. When it comes to global warming one has said, "If we allow this to happen, it would be deeply and unforgivably immoral. It would condemn coming generations to a catastrophically diminished future." The other asserted, "I am a skeptic. . . . Global warming has become a new religion."

It doesn't take a rocket scientist to figure out who said what here, although one of these guys is much closer to being a rocket scientist while the other merely pretends to be one. More importantly, Ivar Giaever is only one of 650 dissenting scientists who are taking their case to the United Nations global warming conference in Poznan, Poland.

The Senate Minority Report, to be released later today

> . . . . has added about 250 scientists (and growing) in 2008 to the over 400 scientists who spoke out in 2007. The over 650 dissenting scientists are more than 12 times the number of UN scientists (52) who authored the media hyped IPCC 2007 Summary for Policymakers.

The growing skepticism is only one of many reasons why the United States shouldn't agree to any global carbon reduction treaty. The fact that cutting greenhouse gas emissions would be extremely costly and would insignificantly affect global temperatures is a pretty convincing reason, too. The Congressional Budget Office reports that a mere 15 percent cut in emissions would increase the annual average household's energy costs by $1,300. And Obama wants to cut emissions by 80 percent? Yikes.

Also frightening is the stranglehold global warming alarmists and environmental activists have on the political message. George Mason economist Walter Williams says,

> The average individual American has little or no clout with Congress and can be safely ignored. But it's a different story with groups such as Environmental Defense Fund, Sierra Club, and The Nature Conservancy. When they speak, Congress listens. Unlike the average American, they are well organized, loaded with cash, and well positioned to be a disobedient congressman's worse nightmare. Their political and economic success has been a near disaster for our nation.

---

3. Steen Ulrik Johannessen, "Global Warming & Climate Change," *New York Times*, Feb. 16, 2012.

Some of the quotes released from the skeptic scientists in the Senate Minority Report are very telling. Former NASA official, atmospheric scientist Dr. Joanne Simpson declared,

> Since I am no longer affiliated with any organization nor receiving any funding, I can speak quite frankly. . . . As a scientist I remain skeptical."

Paleontologist Dr. Eduardo Tonni, of the Committee for Scientific Research in Buenos Aires emphasized,

> The [global warming] scaremongering has its justification in the fact that it is something that generates funds.

The year 2008 has turned out to be a year of global cooling and much of the doomsday talk has dissolved. It's vitally important to understand the science before we embark on a plan that would mean doomsday for our economy. Heritage energy expert Ben Lieberman sums it up perfectly,

> "[F]ear is two-edged sword. It can be used to whip up support for action over the near term, but it is hard to sustain for long, especially if it is not well supported by fact. Eventually it could lead to a backlash. Indeed, the global-warming doomsayers may well prove to be their own worst enemy, with their credibility taking a tumble along with the prospects for cap-and-trade legislation.[4]

Discussion Question

Do you believe that global warming is a problem?

A large winter storm, classified by some as a bomb cyclone, tracked across the East Coast in February 2014, producing heavy snowfall and arctic temperatures throughout the US (NASA).

---

4. Nicolas Loris, "Scientists Make Anti-Global Warming Case," Dec. 11, 2008, http://blog.heritage.org/2008/12/11/scientists-make-their-anti-global-warming-case/.

Nuclear War

The nations with a nuclear arsenal can be counted on one hand, but the brotherhood is growing every year.

A soldier from 73 Engineer Regiment taking part in a Battle Exercise carries out personal decontamination drills. The exercise focuses on chemical defence training (PD).

In the beginning of the 21st century, a trigger-happy new addition to the nuclear bomb club is Iran, whose outspoken hatred of Israel has made the whole world, but especially Israel, uneasy. No one doubts that the fanatical Iran would blow itself up for the heroic sacrifice of destroying Israel and the United States.

One important reason for everyone's greater openness on the possibility of using nuclear arms is that the countries they threaten, with the exception of Russia, the United States, and Israel, have no nuclear retaliatory capability. In earlier years the Soviet Union, with its own large nuclear weapons arsenal, was a barrier to nuclear threats, especially to countries that were allied with the Soviets. Its termination diminished the containing force that had previously put some limits on U.S. and Israeli violence.

So ironically, what makes nuclear war more likely is the fact that small, religious radical nations are gaining the bomb and would no doubt use it at the slightest provocation.

In 2012, successful businessman Warren Buffett admitted that his biggest fear for the U.S. economy is actually a nuclear, biological, or chemical attack.

Here is a transcript from the interview by CNBC (Feb. 27, 2012).

> CNBC's Becky Quick: Overall you are very optimistic about the future not only of this country but of the stock market. But if you have a list of worries, what's at the top of that list?

> Warren Buffett: My biggest worry is nuclear, chemical, and biological attack of some sort, whether by a government or by a rogue. That will happen some day in our future and that will be a large tragedy to an unbelievable tragedy.

Quick: Right now it's not on the forefront of Americans' minds although a lot of things that are happening in the Middle East right now are creeping back up there.

Buffett: It'll happen sometime when it isn't on our minds, just like it happened on 9-11. There are people that wish us ill and they wish us a lot of ill if they can pull it off. So nuclear, chemical, and biological knowledge is spent. There are plenty of people that wish us ill, so that is the biggest worry. But in terms of the economy and all that, the luckiest person in the history of the world is the baby being born today in the United States. I mean, in terms of the outlook for their lives they are going to live better than John D. Rockefeller lived, better than I live, so our country's future is fantastic.[5]

Discussion Question

Do you share Warren Buffet's fears? Why?

Overpopulation

We've already witnessed the devastating effects of overpopulation on biodiversity: species abundant in North America two centuries ago — from the woodland bison of West Virginia and Arizona's Merriam's elk to the Rocky Mountain grasshopper and Puerto Rico's Culebra parrot — have been wiped out by growing human numbers.

Soothsayers argue that as the world's population grows unsustainably, so do its unyielding demands for water, land, trees, and fossil fuels — all of which come at a steep price for already endangered plants and animals. Most biologists agree we're in the midst of the earth's sixth mass extinction event; species are disappearing about 1,000 times faster than is typical of the planet's history. This time, though, it isn't because of geologic or cosmic forces but unsustainable human population growth. Today's global human population is over 7 billion. Every day, the planet sees a net gain of roughly 250,000 people. If the pace continues, we'll be on course to reach 8 billion by 2020 and 9 billion by 2050.

Or not. Other sociologists and ethicists show that overpopulation is a myth. In fact, the vast majority of the planet's inhabitable surface is uninhabited. There are approximately 52.5 million

Dhaka street crowds in Bangladesh (CCA-SA2.0).

5. http://www.businessinsider.com/warren-buffetts-greatest-fear-2012-2#ixzz1oZfOEkUR.

square miles of land in the world, excluding Antarctica. In 1997, the world's population was 5.9 billion. By allowing 3.5 square feet per person, all the people in the world could be brought together in an area the size of the city of Jacksonville, Florida. While everyone would admittedly be cramped in Jacksonville, it would be possible to allot each individual person 1,000 square feet (4,000 square feet of living space for a family of four) and still fit the entire world's population in the states of Nebraska, Kansas, and South Dakota, leaving the rest of the United States, plus Canada, Mexico, Central and South America, Europe, Africa, Asia, and the Australian South Pacific as areas completely uninhabited by man. There is plenty of land and plenty of food to sustain unlimited population growth (from the Roman Catholic Church).[6]

Discussion Question

The problem with the overpopulation theory is that social liberals have used it as an excuse to promote immoral practices. Explain.

Traffic congestion in Ho Chi Minh City, Vietnam (CCA-SA3.0).

6. http://www.lifeissues.net/writers/kas/kas_01overpopulation.html; https://www.biologicaldiversity.org/campaigns/over-population/7_billion_and_counting/faq.html.

Competing Views of Eschatology

Eschatology is the study of the end of time from a religious perspective. The Bible contains many prophecies about the future. The Bible talks about the "**Parousia**," or the Second Coming of Jesus Christ that either marks the end of the world or the beginning of the end. Matthew 24 is devoted to this topic, as is much of the Book of Revelation and 1 Thessalonians 4:16–18.

Revelation describes an important interval lasting for 1,000 years (called the Millennium) when Christ rules. The Tribulation is a seven-year interval when a world religious-political leader called the Antichrist will take power.

Armageddon is a terrible war provoked by the Antichrist. Most people on earth will die. A series of violent events — as prophesied in Daniel 9, Matthew 24, and Revelation 4–19 — will occur.

The Rapture or something like it is described in 1 Thessalonians 4:16–18 when Christ will descend from heaven and meet professing Christians "in the air." Likewise, Christians who have previously died will be resurrected, rise from their graves, and ascend to meet Jesus in the sky. Immediately afterward, "born-again" Christians who have not died will also ascend into the air. They will abandon cars, airplanes, factory jobs, homes, families, friends, etc. Since the vast majority of humans are not "born again," most people will remain behind on earth.

The following are popular interpretations of end times:

Premillennialism: This belief was held by a large percentage of Christians "during the first three centuries of the Christian era, and is found in the works of Papias, Irenaeus, Justin Martyr, Tertullian, Hippolytus, Methodius, Commodianus, and Lactanitus." The Antichrist first appears on earth and the seven-year Tribulation begins. Next comes the Rapture. Christ and His Church return to earth to rule for a Millennium. The faithful will spend eternity in the New Jerusalem. The New Jerusalem is also known as the Celestial City, City of God, Heavenly Jerusalem, Holy City, Shining City on a Hill, Tabernacle of God, Zion, etc. It is a gigantic cubical structure, some 1,380 miles in height, width, and depth, which will have descended to Earth. At this time the forces of evil will have been conquered. The faithful will live during these thousand years of peace in Jerusalem, while occupying spiritual bodies. After this period, all people are judged.

Dispensational Premillennialism: Most people credit John N. Darby with its resurrection. He was a minister of the Church of Ireland, a denomination in the Anglican communion, and the founder of the Plymouth Brethren. Premillennialism received general acceptance by most fundamentalists and other evangelical Christians after the publishing of the Scofield Reference Bible in 1909. All of the premillennialist beliefs teach that the Tribulation is followed by 1,000 years of peace when all live under the authority of Christ. Afterward, in a brief, final battle, Satan is permanently conquered.

Amillennialism: Amillennialists believe that the millennium is not an actual physical realm on earth. They do not believe that it will last 1,000 years. Rather it began at the time of Pentecost (circa A.D. 30) and is currently active in the world today through the

Popular interpretations of end times:

1. Premillennialism

2. Dispensational Premillennialsm

3. Amillennialism

4. Postmillennialism

5. Preterism

presence of the heavenly reign of Christ, the Bible, the Holy Spirit, and the activities of Christian faith groups. Both good and evil will continue in the world during this time. Lawlessness, a falling away from the Church, and persecution of Christians will increase in magnitude. Finally, the current Church Age will end suddenly at Christ's Second Coming. A type of Rapture will happen when Christ returns: believers will rise to meet Jesus in the sky. All will then shortly return to earth. The Day of Judgment will then occur.

Postmillennialism: This belief arose during the early 19th century. According to author Loraine Boettner, Postmillennialism involves "that view of last things which holds that the kingdom of God is now being extended in the world through the preaching of the Gospel and the saving work of the Holy Spirit, that the world eventually is to be Christianized, and that the return of Christ will occur at the close of a long period of righteousness and peace, commonly called the millennium." The theory is based on the perception of a gradual movement toward social perfection. Post-millennials predict that a massive religious revival, spiritual awakening, and purification will occur, followed by a millennium of peace and righteousness. After the millennium, Jesus will return to earth, resurrect the dead believers, and conduct the last judgment.

Preterism: Preterism is a belief that the events prophesized in the New Testament have already happened. The great war of Armageddon in the Book of Revelation occurred in the late '60s and early '70s C.E. when the temple in Jerusalem was destroyed, many Jews were killed, and the rest were driven from Palestine. When Jesus talked about the end of the world, He did not mean that the physical world would be no more. He taught that the old worldview held by various contemporary Jewish groups was coming to an end, to be replaced by a new concept, the Kingdom of God. Thus, all the major elements in the book of Revelation (Tribulation, Armageddon, Rapture, etc.) actually took place in the first century.

Discussion Question

Explain your eschatology.

Death on a Pale Horse is a version of the traditional subject, Four Horsemen of Revelation. Artist Benjamin West, 1796 (PD).

The Ghost of Christmas Yet to Come shows Scrooge his future in Dickens' *A Christmas Carol*. Illustration by John Leech, 1843 (PD).

Chapter 34

Futurology: How Should We Then Live?

First Thoughts

Futurology, the art of predicting the future, is a favorite pastime of poets and fiction writers. Only recently did it gain credibility as a science. What will be the future? What will American society look like in 2030? Can we foster a sustainable future by creating a restorative economy that protects and restores the environment while at the same time creating prosperity and a high quality of life? Futurist David Ehrenfeld has a bleak view of the future:

> A few images stick in my mind. I see huge, unsellable, suburban houses with attached three-car garages, abandoned by their owners of record, scavenged for usable parts and contents, surrounded by wild lawns filled with dandelions, brambles, dying ornamental plants, and vigorous, deep-rooted, ungainly tree of heaven saplings. I see endless shelves and display cases of "collectibles," which — like exercise machines — were a way of burning up excess wealth, and which will have reassumed their rightful monetary value: nothing.[1]

Other futurists are more optimistic. "How Should We Then Live," Francis Shaeffer quipped, and so we ask that question again in this last chapter.

Chapter Learning Objectives

As a result of this chapter you should be able to:

1. Predict what America will look like in 2030

2. Analyze the impact of the media on the American psyche

3. Discuss in what ways Orwell's society is like contemporary American society

4. Compare Aldous Huxley's vision of the future with contemporary society

5. Analyze the futuristic vision of Stephen Vincent Benet

CONCEPTS

Futurology

Globalized world

Fortress nation

---

1. http://www.colorado.edu/AmStudies/lewis/ecology/ehren.htm.

Lesson 1

Futurology

Futurists start by establishing a number of scenarios. Setting up scenarios takes place as a process with many stages. One of those stages involves the study of trends. A trend persists long term and long range. In contrast, a fad operates in the short term.

Future studies (also called **futurology**) is the prediction of future trends and the world views and myths that underlie them. Futurology seeks to understand what is likely to continue, what is likely to change, and what will be completely new. Critics call futurology "fortune telling."

Futurists are often wrong. Many 1950s futurists predicted commonplace space tourism by the year 2000, but ignored the possibilities of cheap computers. On the other hand, many forecasts have portrayed the future with some degree of accuracy. Current futurists often present multiple scenarios that help their audience envision what "may" occur instead of merely "predicting the future." They claim that understanding potential scenarios helps individuals and organizations prepare with flexibility.

Futurologist Chris Lewis, University of Colorado, offers the following scenarios for 2030 America.

Scenario 1: America as the Leader of a Globalized World

This is the future according to Thomas Friedman. The U.S. is the leader of a globalized economy and world. Wealth and the standard of living for the top 20 percent of the world (the First World) has increased. The environment is cleaner in these wealthy nations. This globalized economy is still based on fossil fuels, nuclear energy, and some renewable energy. Computer technology turns this world into a global marketplace and a global village. The First World still consumes 70 to 80 percent of global natural resources, and doing so maintains a high quality of life. In the Third World, wealth and the standard of living are declining.[2]

The quality of life in most Third World nations has declined due to overpopulation; crowded urban megacities filled with slums and refugees; increasing threats from pollution to the rural and urban poor; declining environmental quality, scarce natural resources; and the increasing inability of Third World governments to govern and manage their economies and societies.

In this globalized world there is an increasing division between the wealthy First World and the declining Third World. The economic, social, and cultural decline that began in the poor African nations in the 1990s has spread to Latin America, India, China, the Middle East, and to Southeast Asia. Global corporations dominate the economy and politics of the First World. There is an increasing tension between the declining Third World and the wealthy First World. This tension leads to increasing numbers of U.S.-led military expeditions to put down local and regional rebellions in the Third World. Even more than in the 1990s and early 2000s, Third World peoples see their only hope for a decent life as escaping to the wealthy First World. Because of the threat posed by these Third World refugees, First World nations are spending billions of dollars and using high technology to prevent these refugees from entering prosperous First

---

2. Christ Lewis, "Three Alternative Futures for 2030," http://www.colorado.edu/AmStudies/lewis/ecology/scenario.htm#Three.

World megacities. Global warming, declining soil fertility, declining fisheries, dwindling supplies of clear fresh water, increasing air and water pollution, and declining global forests threaten to undermine this increasingly divided world.

Scenario 2: America as the leader of a Global Sustainable World

The U.S. leads the world in the creation of local and regional sustainable economies that are based on the principles of a "restorative economy." Instead of being a part of a globalized economy, the U.S. tries to produce and consume products that are made in North America. Green taxes, strict environmental laws, polluter pay laws, and an emphasis on "reducing, reusing, and recycling" has improved the quality of local and regional environments. This economy is based on using renewable energy such as solar, wind, water, geothermal, and hydrogen fuel cells. This restorative economy emphasizes reducing material consumption and increasing consumption of services produced by local companies and cooperatives. The U.S. is leading the way to reduce the power of global corporations to dominate local and regional sustainable economies. Led by the United States, both the First and Third Worlds focus on creating sustainable local and regional economies. The standard of living, quality of life, and quality of the environment are slowly improving in both First World and Third World nations. Because the U.S. and other First World nations aren't supporting their economies and way of life by appropriating the natural resources and fossil fuels, and destroying the environments of Third World nations, global environmental quality, as well as the air, water, soil, forests, and fisheries, are all improving. Most of the resources needed to create this global sustainable economy came from high taxes and controls on the behavior of global corporations and the shift away from high military spending by First and Third World nations.

Instead of fighting over scarce resources and a declining global environment, First and Third World nations are cooperating to reduce their populations, restore their local and regional environments, and reduce their total impact on the earth's ecosystems. The larger goal of this U.S.-led global sustainable society is to create healthy societies with sustainable standards of living in a healthy and clean global environment that will be better able to support future generations.

Scenario 3: America as a Fortress Nation in a Troubled, Declining World

In this world the political, cultural, and environmental collapse that spread throughout Africa in the 1990s and early 2000s is spreading to the rest of the

A desire for futuristic living, design, and invention has captured the imagination since the 1930s. From private homes to public spaces, design has evolved to expand the possibilities of function within cutting-edge forms – some more commercially successful than others (CCA-SA2.0).

Quito and Guayaquil are two major cities of Ecuador. Both have economically developed areas scattered with numerous slums and shanty towns. This picture is of Guayaquil, a city on the Pacific coast, with a population of over 2 million. Shanty homes are visible on the right and right side of the picture, the city center in the middle with skyscrapers. (CCA-SA2.0).

world. We witness an increasing Third Worldization of the First World. There is increasing inequality between the top 1 to 5 percent of the global elite and the bottom 95 percent of the people in the First and Third Worlds. This economy is based on extended use of fossil and nuclear fuels, whose use is accelerating global warming and nuclear catastrophes such as Chernobyl. This is a Fortress World where the global elite who run giant global corporations and dominate First and Third World governments have to protect themselves from the majority of the population, whose quality of life and standard of living are declining. Increasing economic, cultural, and political dysfunction and anarchy spread from the Third to the First World. In such a Fortress World, the global environment is declining, damaged by global warming, destruction of forests, fisheries, and farmland, along with pollution and the destruction of natural resources. With this declining global environment, deadly diseases such as AIDS and super-resistant strains of the flu, tuberculosis, cholera, and malaria are devastating the populations of the First and Third World. With increasing threats posed by war, environmental destruction, massive refugee flows from impoverished areas to the wealthy First World enclaves, and global epidemics, First World elites increasingly rely on military and police forces to protect their Fortress communities and their privileged ways of life. In this world, a new and even more powerful form of Social Darwinism is used to justify the increasing concentration of wealth and privileges in a tiny global elite.= Threatened by increasing anarchy and disorder, this Fortress World faces a global political, economic, and environmental collapse. With this global collapse, much like with the collapse of Rome, billions of people will face increasing wars and brutal conflicts over declining global resources and the declining ability of the global environment to support massive populations. With the collapse of this Fortress World, it will take thousands of years for local and regional communities to recover from this global catastrophe. The only model for this post-collapse world is the nightmare world of "the Road Warrior" movies.[3]

Discussion Question

What do you think America will look like in 2030?

3. Ibid.

Lesson 2

War of the Worlds, Orson Welles, and the Invasion from Mars

One futuristic fear seemed to be coming to pass on Halloween Eve, 1938. Millions of Americans regularly tuned in to a popular radio program that featured plays directed by, and often starring, Orson Welles. It was the most popular radio program in America, syndicated all over the nation.

Orson Welles, 1941 (PD).

Performances were live and transmitted to substations and other places around the world. The performance that evening was an adaptation of H.G. Wells' science fiction novel *The War of the Worlds*, about a Martian invasion of the earth. But in adapting the book for a radio play, Orson Welles made an important change. Originally, H.G. Wells wrote this play as a fictional invasion of 1880 England. Orson Welles adapted the play and pretended there was a real time invasion of the eastern United States. Under Welles' direction, the play was written and performed so it would sound like a news broadcast about an invasion from Mars, a technique that, presumably, was intended to heighten the dramatic effect. It certainly did! Its real effect was spectacular!

As the play unfolded, contemporary dance music was interrupted a number of times by fake news bulletins reporting that a "huge flaming object" had dropped on a farm near Grovers Mill, New Jersey. To the average listener, it had all the markings of a legitimate news broadcast. The *Hindenburg* disaster, after all, had occurred less than a year ago. The *Hindenburg* disaster took place on May 6, 1937, as the German passenger zeppelin airship caught fire and was destroyed.

Listeners, then, expected to hear news of another Hindenburg-type disaster. What they heard was breathtaking.

As members of the audience grew increasingly interested, actors playing news announcers, officials, and other roles one would expect to hear in a news report, described the landing of an invasion force from Mars and the destruction of the United States.

The broadcast also contained a number of explanations that it was all a radio play, but if members of the audience missed a brief explanation at the beginning, the next one didn't arrive until 40 minutes into the program.

At one point in the broadcast, an actor in a studio, playing a newscaster in the field, described the emergence of one of the aliens from its spacecraft. "Good heavens, something's wriggling out of the shadow like a gray snake," he said, in an appropriately dramatic tone of voice. "Now it's another one, and another. They look like tentacles to me. There, I can see the thing's body. It's large as a bear and it glistens like wet leather. But that face. It . . . it's indescribable. I can hardly force myself to keep looking at it. The eyes are black and gleam like a serpent. The mouth is V-shaped with saliva dripping from its rimless lips that seem to quiver and pulsate. . . . The thing is rising up. The crowd falls back. They've seen enough. This is the most extraordinary experience. I can't find words. I'm pulling this microphone with me as I talk. I'll have to stop the

The landing site Grover's Mill, New Jersey. The landing site is marked by the monument in the picture at the current day Van Nest Park in West Windsor Township, New Jersey (PD).

description until I've taken a new position. Hold on, will you please, I'll be back in a minute."

America was literarily terrified! People packed the roads, ran to shelter cellars, grabbed their guns, and even wrapped their heads in wet towels as protection from Martian poison gas. Educator Ken Sanes explains, "Oblivious to the fact that they were acting out the role of the panic-stricken public, people were stuck in a kind of virtual world in which fiction was confused for fact. News of the panic (which was conveyed via genuine news reports) quickly generated a national scandal. There were calls, which never went anywhere, for government regulations of broadcasting to ensure that a similar incident wouldn't happen again. The victims were also subjected to ridicule, a reaction that can commonly be found today when people are taken in by simulations. A cartoon in the *New York World-Telegram*, for example, portrayed a character that confuses the simulations of the entertainment industry with reality. In one box, the character is shown trying to stick his hand into the radio to shake hands with Amos n' Andy. In another, he reports to a police officer that there is "Black magic!!! There's a little wooden man — Charlie McCarthy — and he's actually talking!"

In the popular newspaper *New York Tribune*, Editor Dorothy Thompson presaged that the broadcast revealed the way in which politicians could use the power of mass communications to create theatrical illusions, to manipulate the public.

"All unwittingly, Mr. Orson Welles and the Mercury Theater of the Air have made one of the most fascinating and important demonstrations of all time," she wrote. "They have proved that a few effective voices, accompanied by sound effects, can convince masses of people of a totally unreasonable, completely fantastic proposition [so] as to create a nation-wide panic. They have demonstrated more potently than any argument, demonstrated beyond a question of a doubt, the appalling dangers and enormous effectiveness of popular and theatrical demagoguery. . . . Hitler managed to scare all of Europe to its knees a month ago, but he at least had an army and an air force to back up his shrieking words. But Mr. Welles scared thousands into demoralization with nothing at all."[4]

Discussion Question

Ken Sanes writes, "We live in a time in which the ability to create deceptive simulations, especially for television, has become essential to the exercise of power. And the inability to see through these deceptions has become a form of powerlessness. Those who let themselves be taken in by the multiple deceptions of politics, news, advertising and public relations, are doomed, like the more gullible members of the radio audience in 1938, to play a role in other people's dramas, while mistakenly believing that they are reacting to something genuine." Do you agree with Mr. Sanes' assessment? Why or why not?

---

4. http://www.transparencynow.com/welles.htm.

1984

by George Orwell

Although written as a novel of the near future, to George Orwell, and now to us, the distant past, *1984* is not science fiction. It is a socio-political parable, a futuristic work whose effectiveness comes from Orwell's astute assessment of the world around him and his anticipation, and prediction, of the world that is to come.

In a **dystopian** *1984*, Winston Smith endures a terrible existence in the totalitarian Oceania under the constant surveillance of the Thought Police. The story takes place in London, the capital city of the territory of Airstrip One (formerly Great Britain).

The protagonist Winston works in a small office cubicle at the Ministry of Truth, rewriting history in accordance with the dictates of the Party and its supreme figure-head, Big Brother (who is likely simply a creation of the mind). Winston keeps a secret diary of his private thoughts, thus committing the crime of independent thought, contrary to the dictates and aims of the Party.

Eventually, the recalcitrant Winston is apprehended, "reeducated," and repentant of his crime. The novel ends with a completely changed Winston, loyal and true to "Big Brother."

The book *1984* still captures the imagination of generations of young Americans. It remains a warning about the power of a ubiquitous state.

In *1984*, the Party has a slogan: "Who controls the past controls the future; who controls the present controls the past." The past exists only in written records controlled by the Party and, therefore, in memories controlled by the Party.

Winston is a great threat because, lacking humility and self-discipline, he does not allow his memories to be controlled. "You would not make the act of submission, which is the price of sanity," he is told. "Reality exists in the human mind, and nowhere else." The mind, of course, is not the individual mind, but the mind of the Party, "which is collective and immortal." The only truth is the Party's truth. O'Brien reminds Winston of his fatal diary entry — that freedom means being able to say two and two makes four. Using torture, he tries to get Winston to say that two and two make five — because the Party says so.[5]

> **Dystopian:** Descriptive of a world that is filled with pain, human misery, oppression, and sickness; the opposite of a utopia.

Big Brother Orwell *1984* in Donetsk, Ukraine (CCA-SA3.0).

Discussion Question

Literary critic J.R. Hammond writes, "If *1984* is treated as a warning rather than a prophecy, as a satire on present tendencies rather than a forecast of the future, it can be seen that its effect has been totally salutary. Today such terms as 'doublethink,' 'newspeak,' and 'thoughtcrime' have passed into accepted usage, and for a generation of readers the book has come to be regarded as a standard treatise on the growth and influence of totalitarian trends."[6] In what ways is Orwell's society like contemporary American society?

---

5. First American edition, George Orwell, *Nineteen Eighty-Four* (New York: Harcourt, Brace, 1949).
6. J.R. Hammond, *A George Orwell Companion* (New York: St. Martin's Press, 1982).

Brave New World

By Aldous Huxley

Aldous Husley (1894-1963) was an English writer, best known for his novel *Brave New World*.

Brave New World is more a statement of ideas than a narrative or plot.

The Director of Hatcheries and Conditioning explains that this Utopia breeds people to order, artificially fertilizing a mother's eggs to create babies that grow in bottles. They are not born, but decanted. Everyone belongs to one of five classes, from the Alphas, the most intelligent, to the Epsilons, morons bred to do the dirty jobs that nobody else wants to do. The lower classes are multiplied by a budding process that can create up to 96 identical clones and produce over 15,000 brothers and sisters from a single ovary.

All the babies are conditioned, physically and chemically in the bottle, and psychologically after birth, to make them happy citizens of the society with both a liking and an aptitude for the work they will do. One psychological conditioning technique is hypnopaedia, or teaching people while they sleep — not teaching facts or analysis, but planting suggestions that will make people behave in certain ways. . . .

One is that "history is bunk" . . . society limits people's knowledge of the past so they will not be able to compare the present with anything that might make them want to change the present. Another principle is that people should have no emotions, particularly no painful emotions; blind happiness is necessary for stability. One of the things that guarantees happiness is a drug called soma, which calms you down. . . .

Bernard Marx, an Alpha of the top class, is on the verge of falling in love with Lenina Crowne, a woman who works in the Embryo Room of the Hatchery. Lenina has been dating Henry Foster, a Hatchery scientist.; her friend Fanny nags her because she hasn't seen any other man for four months. Lenina likes Bernard but doesn't fall in love with him. Falling in love is a sin . . . and she is a happy, conforming citizen of the Utopia.

Henry Ford, who has become a messianic figure to The World State. "Our Ford" is used in place of "Our Lord," as a credit to popularising the use of the assembly line. Huxley's description of Ford as a central figure in the emergence of the *Brave New World* might also be a reference to the utopian industrial city of Fordlândia commissioned by Ford in 1927. Ruins of Fordlândia (CCA-SA3.0).

Bernard is neither happy nor conforming. He's a bit odd; for one thing, he's small for an Alpha, in a world where every member of the same caste is alike. He likes to treasure his differences from his fellows, but he lacks the courage to fight for his right to be an individual. . . .

Bernard attends a solidarity service of the Fordian religion, a parody of Christianity as practiced in England in the 1920s. . . .

Bernard then takes Lenina to visit a Savage Reservation in North America. . . .

At the Reservation, Bernard and Lenina meet John, a handsome young Savage who, Bernard soon realizes, is the son of the Director.[7]

The rest of the book is somewhat confusing but Huxley is trying to make some points about the future.

"Community, Identity, Stability" is the motto of the World State. It lists the Utopia's prime goals. Community is in part a result of identity and stability. It is also achieved through a religion that satirizes Christianity. . . . And it is achieved by organizing life so that a person is almost never alone.[8]

These are values that mock and satirize early American notions of the "rugged individual" and the "American dream."

Identity is in large part the result of genetic engineering. Society is divided into five classes or castes, hereditary social groups.

Huxley wrote before there was an atomic bomb.

He was more worried about . . . misuse of biology, physiology, and psychology to achieve community. . . . Ironically . . . complete control over human activity destroys even the scientific progress that gained it such control. . . .

Every human being in the new world is conditioned to fit society's needs — to like the work he will have to do. . . .

A society can achieve stability only when everyone is happy, and the brave new world tries hard to ensure that every person is happy. It does its best to eliminate any painful emotion, which means every deep feeling, every passion.[9]

Rather than offering satisfaction, the brave new world anesthetizes its members.

This society offers its members distractions that they must enjoy in common — never alone — because solitude breeds instability. . . .

The combination of genetic engineering, bottle-birth . . . means there is no . . . marriage or family. "Mother" and "father" are obscene words that may be used scientifically on rare, carefully chosen occasions to label ancient sources of psychological problems.

The brave new world insists that death is a natural and not unpleasant process. There is no old age or visible senility. Children are conditioned at hospitals for the dying and given sweets to eat when they hear of death occurring. This conditioning does not — as it might — prepare people to cope with the death of a loved one or with their own mortality. It eliminates the painful emotions of grief and loss, and the spiritual significance of death.[10]

MR. WILLIAM
SHAKESPEARES
COMEDIES,
HISTORIES, &
TRAGEDIES.

Published according to the True Originall Copies.

LONDON
Printed by Isaac Iaggard, and Ed. Blount. 1623.

William Shakespeare, whose banned works are quoted throughout the novel by John, "the Savage." The plays quoted include *Macbeth*, *The Tempest*, *Romeo and Juliet*, *Hamlet*, *King Lear*, *Troilus and Cressida*, *Measure for Measure*, and *Othello*. Mustapha Mond also knows them because he, as a World Controller, has access to a selection of books from throughout history, including the Bible.

The title page of the First Folio of William Shakespeare's play. (PD).

7. Anthony Astrachan, *Aldous Huxley's Brave New World* (New York: Barron's Educational Series, Inc., 1984); http://www.huxley.net/studyaid/bnwbarron.html.
8. Ibid.
9. Ibid.
10. Ibid.

In other words, death is a reality. The brave new world cannot mitigate that reality. But it dilutes its effect by removing the concepts "grief" and "loss."

Discussion Question

Critic Peter Firchow writes, "For Huxley, it is plain, there is no need to travel into the future to find the brave new world; it already exists, only, too palpably, in the American Joy City, where the declaration of dependence begins and ends with the single-minded pursuit of happiness."[11] Do you agree?

Lesson 5

A Short Story — "By the Waters of Babylon"

By Stephen Vincent Benet

The first page of the story as originally published in 1937 in *The Saturday Evening Post* with the title *The Place of the Gods*.

The north and the west and the south are good hunting ground, but it is forbidden to go east. It is forbidden to go to any of the Dead Places except to search for metal and then he who touches the metal must be a priest or the son of a priest. Afterwards, both the man and the metal must be purified. These are the rules and the laws; they are well made. It is forbidden to cross the great river and look upon the place that was the Place of the Gods — this is most strictly forbidden. We do not even say its name though we know its name. It is there that spirits live, and demons — it is there that there are the ashes of the Great Burning. These things are forbidden — they have been forbidden since the beginning of time.

My father is a priest; I am the son of a priest. I have been in the Dead Places near us, with my father — at first, I was afraid. When my father went into the house to search for the metal, I stood by the door and my heart felt small and weak. It was a dead man's house, a spirit house. It did not have the smell of man, though there were old bones in a corner. But it is not fitting that a priest's son should show fear. I looked at the bones in the shadow and kept my voice still.

Then my father came out with the metal — good, strong piece. He looked at me with both eyes but I had not run away. He gave me the metal to hold — I took it and did not die. So he knew that I was truly his son and would be a priest in my time. That was when I was very young — nevertheless, my brothers would not have done it, though they are good hunters. After that, they gave me the good piece of meat and the warm corner of the fire. My father watched over me — he was glad that I should be a priest. But when I boasted or wept without a reason, he punished me more strictly than my brothers. That was right.

---

11. Ibid.

After a time, I myself was allowed to go into the dead houses and search for metal. So I learned the ways of those houses — and if I saw bones, I was no longer afraid. The bones are light and old — sometimes they will fall into dust if you touch them. But that is a great sin.

I was taught the chants and the spells — l was taught how to stop the running of blood from a wound and many secrets. A priest must know many secrets — that was what my father said.

If the hunters think we do all things by chants and spells, they may believe so — it does not hurt them. I was taught how to read in the old books and how to make the old writings — that was hard and took a long time. My knowledge made me happy — it was like a fire in my heart. Most of all, I liked to hear of the Old Days and the stories of the gods. I asked myself many questions that I could not answer, but it was good to ask them. At night, I would lie awake and listen to the wind — it seemed to me that it was the voice of the gods as they flew through the air.

We are not ignorant like the Forest People — our women spin wool on the wheel, our priests wear a white robe. We do not eat grubs from the trees, we have not forgotten the old writings, although they are hard to understand. Nevertheless, my knowledge and my lack of knowledge burned in me — I wished to know more. When I was a man at last, I came to my father and said, "It is time for me to go on my journey. Give me your leave."

He looked at me for a long time, stroking his beard, and then he said at last, "Yes. It is time." That night, in the house of the priesthood, I asked for and received purification. My body hurt but my spirit was a cool stone. It was my father himself who questioned me about my dreams.

He bade me look into the smoke of the fire and see — I saw and told what I saw. It was what I have always seen — a river, and, beyond it, a great Dead Place and in it the gods walking. I have always thought about that. His eyes were stern when I told him he was no longer my father but a priest. He said, "This is a strong dream."

"It is mine," I said, while the smoke waved and my head felt light. They were singing the Star song in the outer chamber and it was like the buzzing of bees in my head.

He asked me how the gods were dressed and I told him how they were dressed. We know how they were dressed from the book, but I saw them as if they were before me. When I had finished, he threw the sticks three times and studied them as they fell.

"This is a very strong dream," he said." It may eat you up."

"I am not afraid," I said and looked at him with both eyes. My voice sounded thin in my ears but that was because of the smoke.

He touched me on the breast and the forehead. He gave me the bow and the three arrows.

"Take them," he said. "It is forbidden to travel east. It is forbidden to cross the river. It is forbidden to go to the Place of the Gods. All these things are forbidden."

"All these things are forbidden," I said, but it was my voice that spoke and not my spirit. He looked at me again.

"My son," he said. "Once I had young dreams. If your dreams do not eat you up, you may be a great priest. If they eat you, you are still my son. Now go on your journey."

I went fasting, as is the law. My body hurt but not my heart. When the dawn came, I was out of sight of the village. I prayed and purified myself, waiting for a sign. The sign was an eagle. It flew east.

Sometimes signs are sent by bad spirits. I waited again on the flat rock, fasting, taking no food. I was very still — I could feel the sky above me and the earth beneath. I waited till the sun was beginning to sink. Then three deer passed in the valley going east — they did not mind me or see me. There was a white fawn with them — a very great sign.

I followed them, at a distance, waiting for what would happen. My heart was troubled about going east, yet I knew that I must go. My head hummed with my fasting — I did not even see the panther spring upon the white fawn. But, before I knew it, the bow was in my hand. I shouted and the panther lifted his head from the fawn. It is not easy to kill a panther with one arrow but the arrow went through his eye and into his brain. He died as he tried to spring — he rolled over, tearing at the ground. Then I knew I was meant to go east — I knew that was my journey. When the night came, I made my fire and roasted meat.

It is eight suns' journey to the east and a man passes by many Dead Places. The Forest People are afraid of them but I am not. Once I made my fire on the edge of a Dead Place at night and, next morning, in the dead house, I found a good knife, little rusted. That was small to what came afterward but it made my heart feel big. Always when I looked for game, it was in front of my arrow, and twice I passed hunting parties of the Forest People without their knowing. So I knew my magic was strong and my journey clean, in spite of the law.

Toward the setting of the eighth sun, I came to the banks of the great river. It was half-a-day's journey after I had left the god-road — we do not use the god-roads now for they are falling apart into great blocks of stone, and the forest is safer going. A long way off, I had seen the water through trees but the trees were thick. At last, I came out upon an open place at the top of a cliff. There was the great river below, like a giant in the sun. It is very long, very wide. It could eat all the streams we know and still be thirsty. Its name is Ou-dis-sun, the Sacred, the Long. No man of my tribe had seen it, not even my father, the priest. It was magic and I prayed.

Then I raised my eyes and looked south. It was there, the Place of the Gods.

How can I tell what it was like — you do not know. It was there, in the red light, and they were too big to be houses. It was there with the red light upon it, mighty and ruined. I knew that in another moment the gods would see me. I covered my eyes with my hands and crept back into the forest.

Surely, that was enough to do, and live. Surely it was enough to spend the night upon the cliff. The Forest People themselves do not come near. Yet, all through the night, I knew that I should have to cross the river and walk in the places of the gods, although the gods ate me up. My magic did not help me at all and yet there was a fire in my bowels, a fire in my mind. When the sun rose, I thought, "My journey has been clean. Now I will go home from my journey." But, even as I thought so, I knew I could not. If I went to the Place of the Gods, I would surely die, but, if I did not go, I could never be at peace with my spirit again. It is better to lose one's life than one's spirit, if one is a priest and the son of a priest.

Nevertheless, as I made the raft, the tears ran out of my eyes. The Forest People could have killed me without fight, if they had come upon me then, but they did not come.

When the raft was made, I said the sayings for the dead and painted myself for death. My heart was cold as a frog and my knees like water, but the burning in my mind would not let me have peace. As I pushed the raft from the shore, I began my death song — I had the right. It was a fine song.

"I am John, son of John," I sang. "My people are the Hill People. They are the men.

I go into the Dead Places but I am not slain.

I take the metal from the Dead Places but I am not blasted.

I travel upon the god-roads and am not afraid. E-yah! I have killed the panther, I have killed the fawn!

E-yah! I have come to the great river. No man has come there before.

It is forbidden to go east, but I have gone, forbidden to go on the great river, but I am there.

Open your hearts, you spirits, and hear my song.

Now I go to the Place of the Gods, I shall not return.

My body is painted for death and my limbs weak, but my heart is big as I go to the Place of the Gods!"

All the same, when I came to the Place of the Gods, I was afraid, afraid. The current of the great river is very strong — it gripped my raft with its hands. That was magic, for the river itself is wide and calm. I could feel evil spirits about me, I was swept down the stream. Never have I been so much alone — I tried to think of my knowledge, but it was a squirrel's heap of winter nuts. There was no strength in my knowledge any more and I felt small and naked as a new-hatched bird — alone upon the great river, the servant of the gods.

Yet, after a while, my eyes were opened and I saw. I saw both banks of the river — I saw that once there had been god-roads across it, though now they were broken and fallen like broken vines. Very great they were, and wonderful and broken — broken in the time of the Great Burning when the fire fell out of the sky. And always the current took me nearer to the Place of the Gods, and the huge ruins rose before my eyes.

I do not know the customs of rivers — we are the People of the Hills. I tried to guide my raft with the pole but it spun around. I thought the river meant to take me past the Place of the Gods and out into the Bitter Water of the legends. I grew angry then — my heart felt strong. I said aloud, "I am a priest and the son of a priest!" The gods heard me — they showed me how to paddle with the pole on one side of the raft. The current changed itself — I drew near to the Place of the Gods.

When I was very near, my raft struck and turned over. I can swim in our lakes — I swam to the shore. There was a great spike of rusted metal sticking out into the river — I hauled myself up upon it and sat there, panting. I had saved my bow and two arrows and the knife I found in the Dead Place but that was all. My raft went whirling down-stream toward the Bitter Water. I looked after it, and thought if it had trod me under, at least I would be safely dead. Nevertheless, when I had dried my bowstring and re-strung it, I walked forward to the Place of the Gods.

It felt like ground underfoot; it did not burn me. It is not true what some of the tales say, that the ground there burns forever, for I have been there. Here and there were the marks and stains of the Great Burning, on the ruins, that is true. But they were old marks and old stains. It is not true either, what some of our priests say, that it is an island covered with fogs and enchantments. It is not. It is a great Dead Place — greater than any Dead Place we know. Everywhere in it there are god-roads, though most are cracked and broken. Everywhere there are the ruins of the high towers of the gods.

How shall I tell what I saw? I went carefully, my strung bow in my hand, my skin ready for danger. There should have been the wailings of spirits and the shrieks of demons, but there were not. It was very silent and sunny where I had landed — the wind and the rain and the birds that drop seeds had done their work — the grass grew in the cracks of the broken stone. It is a fair island — no wonder the gods built there. If I had come there, a god, I also would have built.

How shall I tell what I saw? The towers are not all broken — here and there one still stands, like a great tree in a forest, and the birds nest high. But the towers themselves look blind, for the gods are gone. I saw a fishhawk, catching fish in the river. I saw a little dance of white butterflies over a great heap of broken stones and columns. I went there and looked about me — there was a carved stone with cut — letters, broken in half. I can read letters but I could not understand these. They said UBTREAS. There was also the shattered image of a man or a god. It had been made of white stone and he wore his hair tied back like a woman's. His name was ASHING, as I read on the cracked half of a stone. I thought it wise to pray to ASHING, though I do not know that god.

How shall I tell what I saw? There was no smell of man left, on stone or metal. Nor were there many trees in that wilderness of stone. There are many pigeons, nesting and dropping in the towers — the gods must have loved them, or, perhaps, they used them for sacrifices. There are wild cats that roam the god-roads, green-eyed, unafraid of man. At night they wail like demons but they are not demons. The wild dogs are more dangerous, for they hunt in a pack, but them I did not meet till later. Everywhere there are the carved stones, carved with magical numbers or words.

I went north — I did not try to hide myself. When a god or a demon saw me, then I would die, but meanwhile I was no longer afraid. My hunger for knowledge burned in me — there was so much that I could not understand. After a while, I knew that my belly was hungry. I could have hunted for my meat, but I did not hunt. It is known that the gods did not hunt as we do — they got their food from enchanted boxes and jars. Sometimes these are still found in the Dead Places — once, when I was a child and foolish, I opened such a jar and tasted it and found the food sweet. But my father found out and punished me for it strictly, for, often, that food is death. Now, though, I had long gone past what was forbidden, and I entered the likeliest towers, looking for the food of the gods.

I found it at last in the ruins of a great temple in the mid-city. A mighty temple it must have been, for the roof was painted like the sky at night with its stars — that much I could see, though the colors were faint and dim. It went down into great caves and tunnels — perhaps they kept their slaves there. But when I started to climb down, I heard the squeaking of rats, so I did not go — rats are unclean, and there must have been many tribes of them, from the squeaking. But near there, I found food, in the heart of a ruin, behind a door that still opened. I ate only the fruits from the jars — they had a very sweet taste. There was drink, too, in bottles of glass — the drink of the gods was strong and made my head swim. After I had eaten and drunk, I slept on the top of a stone, my bow at my side.

When I woke, the sun was low. Looking down from where I lay, I saw a dog sitting on his haunches. His tongue was hanging out of his mouth; he looked as if he were laughing. He was a big dog, with a gray-brown coat, as big as a wolf. I sprang up and shouted at him but he did not move — he just sat there as if he were laughing. I did not like that. When I reached for a stone to throw, he moved swiftly out of the way of the stone. He was not afraid of me; he looked at me as if I were meat. No doubt I could have killed him with an arrow, but I did not know if there were others. Moreover, night was falling.

I looked about me — not far away there was a great, broken god-road, leading north. The towers were high enough, but not so high, and while many of the dead-houses were wrecked, there were some that stood. I went toward this god-road, keeping to the heights of the ruins, while the dog followed. When I had reached the god-road, I saw that there were others behind him. If I had slept later, they would have come upon me asleep and torn out my throat. As it was, they were sure enough of me; they did not hurry. When I went into the dead-house, they kept watch at the entrance — doubtless they thought they would have a fine hunt. But a dog cannot open a door and I knew, from the books, that the gods did not like to live on the ground but on high.

I had just found a door I could open when the dogs decided to rush. Ha! They were surprised when I shut the door in their faces — it was a good door, of strong metal. I could hear their foolish baying beyond it but I did not stop to answer them. I was in darkness — I found stairs and climbed. There were many stairs, turning around till my head was dizzy. At the top was another door — I found the knob and opened it. I was in a long small chamber — on one side of it was a bronze door that could not be opened, for it had no handle. Perhaps there was a magic word to open it but I did not have the word. I turned to the door in the opposite side of the wall. The lock of it was broken and I opened it and went in.

Within, there was a place of great riches. The god who lived there must have been a powerful god. The first room was a small ante-room — I waited there for some time, telling the spirits of the place that I came in peace and not as a robber. When it seemed to me that they had had time to hear me, I went on. Ah, what riches! Few, even, of the windows had been broken — it was all as it had been. The great windows that looked over the city had not been broken at all though they were dusty and streaked with many years. There were coverings on the floors, the colors not greatly faded, and the chairs were soft and deep. There were pictures upon the walls, very strange, very wonderful — I remember one of a bunch of flowers in a jar — if you came close to it, you could see nothing but bits of color, but if you stood away from it, the flowers might have been picked yesterday. It made my heart feel strange to look at this picture — and to look at the figure of a bird, in some hard clay, on a table and see it so like our birds. Everywhere there were books and writings, many in tongues that I could not read. The god who lived there must have been a wise god and full of knowledge. I felt I had a right there, as I sought knowledge also.

Nevertheless, it was strange. There was a washing-place but no water — perhaps the gods washed in air. There was a cooking-place but no wood, and though there was a machine to cook food, there was no place to put fire in it. Nor were there candles or lamps — there were things that looked like lamps but they had neither oil nor wick. All these things were magic, but I touched them and lived — the magic had gone out of them. Let me tell one thing to show. In the washing-place, a thing said "Hot" but it was not hot to the touch — another thing said "Cold" but it was not cold. This must have been a strong magic but the magic was gone. I do not understand — they had ways — I wish that I knew.

It was close and dry and dusty in the house of the gods. I have said the magic was gone but that is not true — it had gone from the magic things but it had not gone from the place. I felt the spirits about me, weighing upon me. Nor had I ever slept in a Dead Place before — and yet, tonight, I must sleep there. When I thought of it, my tongue felt dry in my throat, in spite of my wish for knowledge. Almost I would have gone down again and faced the dogs, but I did not.

I had not gone through all the rooms when the darkness fell. When it fell, I went back to the big room looking over the city and made fire. There was a place to make fire and a box with wood in it, though I do not think they cooked there. I wrapped myself in a floor-covering and slept in front of the fire — I was very tired.

Now I tell what is very strong magic. I woke in the midst of the night. When I woke, the fire had gone out and I was cold. It seemed to me that all around me there were whisperings and voices. I closed my eyes to shut them out. Some will say that I slept again, but I do not think that I slept. I could feel the spirits drawing my spirit out of my body as a fish is drawn on a line.

Why should I lie about it? I am a priest and the son of a priest. If there are spirits, as they say, in the small Dead Places near us, what spirits must there not be in that great Place of the Gods? And would not they wish to speak? After such long years? I know that I felt myself drawn as a fish is drawn on a line. I had stepped out of my body — I could see my body asleep in front of the cold fire, but it was not I. I was drawn to look out upon the city of the gods.

It should have been dark, for it was night, but it was not dark. Everywhere there were lights — lines of light — circles and blurs of light — ten thousand torches would not have been the same. The sky itself was alight — you could barely see the stars for the glow in the sky. I thought to myself, "This is strong magic," and trembled. There was a roaring in my ears like the rushing of rivers. Then my eyes grew used to the light and my ears to the sound. I knew that I was seeing the city as it had been when the gods were alive.

That was a sight indeed — yes, that was a sight: I could not have seen it in the body — my body would have died. Everywhere went the gods, on foot and in chariots — there were gods beyond number and counting and their chariots blocked the streets. They had turned night to day for their pleasure — they did not sleep with the sun. The noise of their coming and going was the noise of the many waters. It was magic what they could do — it was magic what they did.

I looked out of another window — the great vines of their bridges were mended and god-roads went east and west. Restless, restless, were the gods and always in motion! They burrowed tunnels under rivers — they flew in the air. With unbelievable tools they did giant works — no part of the earth was safe from them, for, if they wished for a thing, they summoned it from the other side of the world. And always, as they labored and rested, as they feasted and made love, there was a drum in their ears — the pulse of the giant city, beating and beating like a man's heart.

Were they happy? What is happiness to the gods? They were great, they were mighty, they were wonderful and terrible. As I looked upon them and their magic, I felt like a child — but a little more, it seemed to me, and they would pull down the moon from the sky. I saw them with wisdom beyond wisdom and knowledge beyond knowledge. And yet not all they did was well done — even I could see that ? and yet their wisdom could not but grow until all was peace.

Then I saw their fate come upon them and that was terrible past speech. It came upon them as they walked the streets of their city. I have been in the fights with the Forest People — I have seen men die. But this was not like that. When gods war with gods, they use weapons we do not know. It was fire falling out of the sky and a mist that poisoned. It was the time of the Great Burning and the Destruction. They ran about like ants in the streets of their city — poor gods, poor gods! Then the towers began to fall. A few escaped — yes, a few. The legends tell it. But, even after the city had become a Dead Place, for many years the poison was still in the ground. I saw it happen, I saw the last of them die. It was darkness over the broken city and I wept.

All this, I saw. I saw it as I have told it, though not in the body. When I woke in the morning, I was hungry, but I did not think first of my hunger for my heart was perplexed and confused. I knew the reason for the Dead Places but I did not see why it had happened. It seemed to me it should not have happened, with all the magic they had. I went through the house looking for an answer. There was so much in the house I could not understand — and yet I am a priest and the son of a priest. It was like being on one side of the great river, at night, with no light to show the way.

Then I saw the dead god. He was sitting in his chair, by the window, in a room I had not entered before and, for the first moment, I thought that he was alive. Then I saw the skin on the back of his hand — it was like dry leather. The room was shut, hot and dry — no doubt that had kept him as he was. At first I was afraid to approach him — then the fear left me. He was sitting looking out over the city—he was dressed in the clothes of the gods. His age was neither young nor old — I could not tell his age. But there was wisdom in his face and great sadness. You could see that he would have not run away. He had sat at his window, watching his city die — then he himself had died. But it is better to lose one's life than one's spirit — and you could see from the face that his spirit had not been lost. I knew, that, if I touched him, he would fall into dust — and yet, there was something unconquered in the face.

That is all of my story, for then I knew he was a man — I knew then that they had been men, neither gods nor demons. It is a great knowledge, hard to tell and believe. They were men — they went a dark road, but they were men. I had no fear after that — I had no fear going home, though twice I fought off the dogs and once I was hunted for two days by the Forest People. When I saw my father again, I prayed and was purified. He touched my lips and my breast, he said, "You went away a boy. You come back a man and a priest." I said, "Father, they were men! I have been in the Place of the Gods and seen it! Now slay me, if it is the law — but still I know they were men."

He looked at me out of both eyes. He said, "The law is not always the same shape — you have done what you have done. I could not have done it my time, but you come after me. Tell!"

I told and he listened. After that, I wished to tell all the people but he showed me otherwise. He said, "Truth is a hard deer to hunt. If you eat too much truth at once, you may die of the truth. It was not idly that our fathers forbade the Dead Places." He was right — it is better the truth should come little by little. I have learned that, being a priest. Perhaps, in the old days, they ate knowledge too fast.

Nevertheless, we make a beginning. It is not for the metal alone we go to the Dead Places now — there are the books and the writings. They are hard to learn. And the magic tools are broken — but we can look at them and wonder. At least, we make a beginning. And, when I am chief priest we shall go beyond the great river. We shall go to the Place of the Gods — the place New York — not one man but a company. We shall look for the images of the gods and find the god ASHING and the others — the gods Lincoln and Biltmore and Moses. But they were men who built the city, not gods or demons. They were men. I remember the dead man's face. They were men who were here before us. We must build again.[12]

Discussion Question

Did you figure out the ending of this futuristic short story before reading the end? Write a fictional short story of what life would be like if the world was destroyed.

---

12. http://www.tkinter.smig.net/outings/rosemountghosts/babylon.htm.

Abley, Mark. *Spoken Here: Travels Among Threatened Languages.* Boston, MA: Houghton Mifflin, 2003.

Abu-Lughod, Janet. *The World System in the Thirteenth Century: Dead End or Precursor?* Washington, DC: American Historical Association pamphlet, 1994.

Abu-Lughod, Janet. "The World-System Perspective in the Construction of Economic History." Michael Adas. *Machines as the Measure of Men: Science, Technology, and the Ideologies of Western Dominance.* Ithaca, NY: Cornell University, 1989.

Adas, Michael, ed. *Islamic & European Expansion: The Forging of a Global Order.* Philadelphia, PA: Temple University, 1993.

Bairoch, Paul. *Economics and World History: Myths and Paradoxes.* Chicago, IL: University of Chicago Press, 1993.

Balakrishnan, Gopal, ed. *Debating Empire.* London; New York: Verso Books, 2003.

Barber, Benjamin R. *Jihad vs. McWorld: How the Planet Is Both Falling Apart and Coming Together.* New York: Ballantine Books, 1996.

Bentley, Jerry H. "Cross-Cultural Interaction and Periodization in World History." *American Historical Review* 101 (1996), 749–770.

Bentley, Jerry H. "Myths, Wagers, and Some Moral Implications of World History." *Journal of World History* 16 (2005), 51–82.

Bentley, Jerry H. *Old World Encounters: Cross-Cultural Contacts and Exchanges in Pre-Modern Times.* New York: Oxford University Press, 1993.

Bentley, Jerry H. *Shapes of World History in 20th Century Scholarship.* American Historical Association, 1995.

Benton, Lauren. "From the World-Systems Perspective to Institutional World History: Culture and Economy in Global Theory." *Journal of World History* 7 (1996).

Berg, Maxine, and Kristine Bruland, eds. *Technological Revolutions in Europe: Historical Perspectives.* Northhampton, MA: Edward Elgar, 1998.

Bernal, Martin. *Black Athena: The Afroasiatic Roots of Classical Civilization.* New Brunswick, NJ: Rutgers University Press, 1987.

Black, Jeremy. *Maps and History: Constructing Images of the Past.* New Haven, CT: Yale University Press, 2000.

Black, Jeremy. *Maps and Politics.* Chicago, IL: University of Chicago Press, 1997.

Blaut, James M. *Eight Eurocentric Historians.* New York: Guilford, 2000.

Bobbitt, Philip. *The Shield of Achilles: War, Peace and the Course of History.* New York: Alfred A. Knopf, 2002.

Braudel, Fernand. *Civilization and Capitalism, 15th–18th Century,* Vol. 3. New York: Harper and Row, 1984.

Close-up view of an American major in the basket of an observation balloon flying over territory near front lines during World War 1, 1918 (PD).

Titanic life boats on way to *Carpathia*, 1912 (LOC).

Braudel. *Civilization and Capitalism, 15th–18th Century,* Vol. 3. "Economies in Space: The World Economies," excerpt from Ross E. Dunn, ed. *The New World History: A Teacher's Companion.* New York: Bedford/St. Martin's, 2000, 246–252.

Bull, Hedley, and Adam Watson, eds. *The Expansion of International Society.* Oxford, UK; New York: Oxford University Press, 1986.

Burke, Edmund III. *Global Crises and Social Movements: Artisans, Peasants, and Populists and the World Economy.* Boulder, CO: Westview Press, 1988.

Burke, Edmund III. "Marshall G.S. Hodgson and the Hemispheric Interregional Approach to World History." *Journal of World History* 6 (1995), 237–250.

Cameron, Rondo. *A Concise Economic History of the World from Paleolithic Times to the Present.* Oxford, UK; New York: Oxford University Press, 1997.

Cavalli-Sforza, Luigi Luca. *Genes, Peoples, and Languages.* New York: North Point Press, 2000.

Cavalli-Sforza, Luigi Luca, and Francisco Cavalli-Sforza. *The Great Human Diasporas: The History of Diversity and Evolution.* Reading, MA: Addison-Wesley, 1995.

Chakrabarty, Dipesh. *Provincializing Europe: Postcolonial Thought and Historical Difference.* Princeton, NJ: Princeton University Press, 2000.

Chase-Dunn, Christopher, Thomas D. Hall, Charles Tilly, eds. *Rise and Demise: Comparing World-Systems.* Boulder, CO: Westview Press, 1997.

Chatterjee, Partha. *The Nation and Its Fragments: Colonial and Postcolonial Histories.* Princeton, NJ: Princeton University Press, 1993.

Chomsky, Noam. "Free Trade and Free Markets: Pretense and Practice." Fredric Jameson, ed. *The Cultures of Globalization.* Durham, NC: Duke University Press, 1998, 356–370.

Christian, David. *Maps of Time: An Introduction to Big History.* Berkeley, CA: University of California Press, 2004.

Cohen, Joel E. *How Many People Can the World Support?* New York: W.W. Norton, 1995.

Cohen, Robin. "Diasporas, the Nation-State, and Globalization." Wang Gungwu, Raymond Grew, eds. *Global History and Migrations.* Boulder, CO: Westview Press, 1997, 117–143.

Cohen, Robin, and Zig Layton-Henry, eds. *The Politics of Migration.* Cheltenham, UK; Northampton, MA: Elgar, 1997.

Cooper, Frederick, Allen F. Isaacman, Mallon Florencia E. *Confronting Historical Paradigms: Peasants, Labor, and the Capitalist World System in Africa and Latin America.* Madison, WI: University of Wisconsin Press, 1993.

Cosgrove, Denis. *Apollo's Eye: A Cartographic Geneology of the Earth in the Western Imagination.* Baltimore, MD: Johns Hopkins University Press, 2001.

Costello, Paul. *World Historians and Their Goals: Twentieth-Century Answers to Modernism.* DeKalb, IL: Northern Illinois University Press, 1993.

Crosby, Alfred W. *Ecological Imperialism.* Cambridge, UK; New York: Cambridge University Press, 1993.

Crosby, Alfred W. *The Measure of Reality: Quantification and Western Society, 1250–1600.* Cambridge, UK; New York: Cambridge University Press, 1997.

Curtin, Philip D. *Cross-Cultural Trade in World History.* Cambridge, UK; New York: Cambridge University Press, 1984.

Davis, Mike. *Late Victorian Holocausts: El Nino Famines and the Making of the Third World.* New York: Verso Books, 2001.

Diamond, Jared M. *Collapse: How Societies Choose to Fail or Succeed.* New York: Penguin Books, 2011.

Diamond, Jared M. *Guns, Germs, and Steel: The Fates of Human Societies.* New York: Norton, 2005.

Diamond, Jared M. *The Third Chimpanzee.* New York: HarperCollins, 1992.

Dore, Ronald. "Unity and Diversity in World Culture." Hedley Bull and Adam Watson, eds. *The Expansion of International Society.* Oxford, UK; New York: Oxford University Press, 1986, 408–424.

Dunn, Ross E., ed. *The New World History: A Teacher's Companion.* New York: Bedford/St. Martin's, 2000.

Durham, William H. *Coevolution: Genes, Culture, and Human Diversity.* Stanford, CA: Stanford University Press, 1991.

Featherstone, Mike, and Scott Lash, eds. *Spaces of Culture: City, Nation, World.* London: Sage, 1999.

Featherstone , Mike, ed. *Global Culture: Nationalism, Globalization and Modernity.* London; Newbury Park: Sage Publications, 1990.

Fernandez-Armesto, Felipe. *Civilizations: Culture, Ambition, and the Transformation of Nature.* New York: Free Press, 2001.

Fernandez-Armesto, Felipe. *Millennium: A History of the Last Thousand Years.* New York: Scribner, 1995.

Fernandez-Armesto, Felipe. *Near a Thousand Tables: A History of Food.* New York: The Free Press, 2002.

Fernandez-Armesto, Felipe. *The Americas: A Hemispheric History.* New York: Modern Library, 2003.

Foner, Eric. "American Freedom in a Global Age." *American Historical Review* 106 (2001), 1–16.

Fracchia, Joseph, and Richard Lewontin. "Does Culture Evolve?" *History and Theory* 38 (1999), 52–78.

Fracchia, Joseph, and Richard Lewontin. "The Price of Metaphor," *History and Theory* 44 (2005), 14–29.

A homeless veteran in New York (CCA-SA2.0).

A close-up camera view shows Space Shuttle Columbia as it lifts off from Launch Pad 39A on mission STS-107, 2003 (NASA).

Frank, Andre Gunder. *ReOrient: Global Economy in the Asian Age.* Berkeley, CA: University of California Press, 1998.

Fredrickson, George. *The Comparative Imagination: On the History of Racism, Nationalism and Social Movements.* Berkeley, CA: University of California Press, 1997.

Friedman, Jonathan. *Culture Identity and Global Process.* London: Sage, 1994.

Fukuyama, Francis. "Reflections on the End of History, Five Years Later." Philip Pomper, Richard H. Elphick , Richard T. Vann, eds. *World History: Ideologies, Structures, and Identities.* Oxford, UK; Cambridge, MA: Blackwell Publishers, 1998, 199–216.

Fukuyama, Francis. *The End of History and the Last Man.* New York: Free Press, 1992.

Fukuyama, Francis. "The End of History." *The National Interest* 16 (1989), 3–18.

Galtung, Johan, and Sohail Inayatullah, eds. *Macrohistory and Macrohistorians: Perspectives on Individual, Social, and Civilizational Change.* New York: Praeger, 1997.

Geyer, Michael, and Charles Bright. "World History in a Global Age." *American Historical Review* 100 (1995), 1034–1060.

Goldstone, Jack A. *Revolutions and Rebellions in the Early Modern World.* Berkeley, CA: University of California Press, 1991.

Goody, Jack. *The East in the West.* Cambridge, UK; New York: Cambridge University Press, 1996.

Goudsblom, Johan. *Fire and Civilization.* New York: Penguin, 1995.

Goudsblom, Johan, Stephen Mennell, E.L. Jones. *The Course of Human History: Economic Growth, Social Process, and Civilization.* Armonk, NY: M.E. Sharpe, 1996.

Grafton, Anthony, with April Shelford and Nancy Sirasi. *New Worlds, Ancient Texts: The Power of Tradition and the Shock of Discovery.* Cambridge, MA: Belknap Press of Harvard University Press, 1992.

Greenblatt, Stephen. *Marvelous Possessions: The Wonder of the New World.* Chicago, IL: University of Chicago Press, 1991.

Gunn, Geoffrey C. *First Globalization: The European Exchange, 1500–1800.* Lanham, MD: Rowman and Littlefield, 2003.

Guthrie, Stewart Elliott. *Faces in the Clouds: A New Theory of Religion.* New York: Oxford University Press, 1993.

Headley, John M. "The Universalizing Principle and Process: On the West's Intrinsic Commitment to a Global Context." *Journal of World History* 2002 (13), 291–320.

Hedrick, Charles W. "The Ethics of World History." *Journal of World History* 16 (2005), 33–49.

Held, David, Anthony G. McGrew, David Goldblatt, Jonathan Perraton, eds. *Global Transformations: Politics, Economics and Culture.* Stanford, CA: Stanford University Press, 1999.

Helms, Mary W. *Ulysses' Sail: An Ethnographic Odyssey of Power, Knowledge, and Geographical Distance.* Princeton, NJ: Princeton University Press, 1988.

Hobhouse, Henry. *Forces of Change: An Unorthodox View of History.* New York: Arcade, 1989.

Hobson, John M. *The Eastern Origin of Western Civilization.* Cambridge, UK; New York: Cambridge University Press, 2004.

Hodgson, Marshall. *Rethinking World History: Essays on Europe, Islam, and World History.* New York: Cambridge University Press, 1993.

Holt, Thomas C. "Race, Race-Making, and the Writing of History." *American Historical Review* 100 (1995), 1–20.

Horsman, Mathew. *After the Nation-state: Citizens, Tribalism, and the New World Disorder.* London: HarperCollins, 1994.

Iriye, Akira. *China and Japan in the Global Setting.* Cambridge, MA: Harvard University Press, 1992.

Jameson, Fredric. "Notes on Globalization as a Philosophical Issue." Fredric Jameson, ed. *The Cultures of Globalization.* Durham, NC: Duke University Press, 1998, 54–77.

Jones, E.L. *Growth Recurring: Economic Change in World History.* Oxford, UK: Clarendon Press, 1988.

Jones, E.L. *Growth Recurring: Economic Change in World History.* Ann Arbor, MI: University of Michigan Press, 2000.

Jones, Martin. *The Molecule Hunt: Archaeology and the Search for Ancient DNA.* New York: Arcade, 2002.

Pair of 12 inch guns on HMS Dreadnought. 2 QF 12 pounder 18 cwt anti-torpedo boat guns are mounted on the turret roof.

Karttunen, Frances E. *Between Worlds: Interpreters, Guides, and Survivors.* New Brunswick, NJ: Rutgers University Press, 1994.

Karttunen, Frances E., and Alfred W. Crosby. "Language Death, Language Genesis, and World History." *Journal of World History* 6 (1995), 157–174.

Keeley, Lawrence H. *War before Civilization.* New York: Oxford University Press, 1996.

Kelley, Donald R. "The Rise of Prehistory." *Journal of World History* 14 (2003), 17–36.

King, Anthony D., ed. *Culture, Globalization and the World-System: Contemporary Conditions for the Representation of Identity.* Minneapolis, MN: University of Minnesota Press, 1997.

Kuper, Adam. *The Invention of Primitive Society.* London; New York: Routledge, 1988.

Lal, Deepak. *Unintended Consequences: The Impact of Factor Endowments, Culture, and Politics on Long-Run Economic Performance.* Cambridge, MA: MIT, 1998.

Lambropoulos, Vassilis. *The Rise of Eurocentrism: Anatomy of Interpretation.* Princeton, NJ: Princeton University Press, 1993.

Landes, David S. *The Wealth and Poverty of Nations: Why Some Are So Rich and Some So Poor.* New York: W.W. Norton, 1998.

Automobiles lining up for fuel at a service station in Maryland, in June 1979 (LOC).

Lefkowitz, Mary. *Not Out of Africa: How Afrocentrism Became an Excuse to Teach Myth as History*. New York: HarperCollons, 1997.

Levathes, Louise. *When China Ruled the Seas: The Treasure Fleet of the Dragon Throne, 1405–1433*. New York: Simon & Schuster, 1994.

Lewis, Archibald R. *Nomads and Crusaders, A.D. 1000–1368*. Bloomington, IN: Indiana University Press, 1988.

Lewis, Martin W. *The Myth of Continents: A Critique of Metageography*. Berkeley, CA: University of California Press, 1997.

Liu, Alan. "Local Transcendence: Cultural Criticism, Postmodernism, and the Romanticism of Detail." *Representations* No. 32 (Autumn 1990): 75–113.

Lockard, Craig A. "The Contribution of Philip Curtin and the 'Wisconsin School' to the Study and Promotion of Comparative World History." *Journal of Third World Studies* 11 (1994), 180–223.

MacNeil, J.R. *Something New under the Sun: An Environmental History of the Twentieth Century*. New York: W.W. Norton, 2000.

Maier, Charles S. " Consigning the Twentieth Century to History: Alternative Narratives for the Modern Era." *American Historical Review* 105 (2000), 807–31.

Manning, Patrick. "The Problem of Interactions in World History." *American Historical Review* 101 (1996), 770–782.

Marks, Robert B. *The Origins of the Modern World: A Global and Ecological Narrative*. Lanham, MD: Rowman and Littlefield, 2002.

Marx, Anthony W. *Making Race and Nation: A Comparison of South Africa, the United States, and Brazil*. Cambridge, MA: Cambridge University Press, 1998.

Mazlish, Bruce. "Crossing Boundaries: Ecumenical, World, and Global History." Philip Pomper, Richard H. Elphick , Richard T. Vann, eds. *World History: Ideologies, Structures, and Identities*. Oxford, UK; Cambridge, MA: Blackwell Publishers, 1998, 41–52.

Mazlish, Bruce, and Akira Iriye. *The Global History Reader*. New York: Routledge, 2005.

Mazlish, Bruce, and Ralph Buultjens, eds. *Conceptualizing Global History*. Boulder, CO: Westview Press, 1993.

McClellan, James E., and Harold Dorn. *Science and Technology in World History*. Baltimore, MD: Johns Hopkins University Press, 1999.

McDougall, Walter A. " 'Mais century n'establish pas d'histoire': Some Thoughts on Toynbee, McNeill, and the Rest of Us." *Journal of Modern History* 58 (1986), 19–42.

McGrew, Tony, Anthony G. McGrew, Paul G. Lewis, eds. *Global Politics: Globalization and the Nation State*. Cambridge, UK; New York: Cambridge University Press, 1992.

McNeill, William. "History and the Scientific Worldview." *History and Theory* 37 (1998), 1–13.

McNeill, William. *The Human Web: A Bird's-Eye View of World History*. New York: W.W. Norton, 2002.

McNeill, William H. *Plagues and Peoples*. New York: Doubleday Anchor, 1989.

McNeill, William H. *The Global Condition*. Princeton, NJ: Princeton University Press, 1992.

McNeill, William H. *The pursuit of Power: Technology, Armed Force, and Society Since A.D. 1000*. Chicago, IL: University of Chicago Press, 1982.

McNeill, William H. *The Rise of the West: A History of the Human Community with a Retrospective Essay*. Chicago, IL: University of Chicago Press, 1991.

McNeill, William H. "World History and the Rise and Fall of the West." *Journal of World History* 9 (1998), 215–36.

Melko, Matthew. "The Nature of Civilizations." Stephen K. Sanderson, ed. *Civilizations and World Systems. Studying World-Historical Change*. Walnut Creek, CA: Altamira Press, 1995, 25–44.

Mignolo, Walter D. *The Darker Side of the Renaissance: Literacy, Territoriality, and Colonization*. Ann Arbor, MI: University of Michigan Press, 2003.

Mokyr, Joel. "Eurocentricity Triumphant." Review essay of Landes, *The Wealth and Poverty of Nations. American Historical Review* 104 (1999), 1240–1246.

Mokyr, Joel, Donna J. Guy, Charles Tilley. Forum on Landes, *The Wealth and Poverty of Nations: Why Some Are So Rich and Some So Poor. American Historical Review* 104 (1999), 1240–57.

Nettle, Daniel. *Linguistic Diversity*. Oxford; New York: Oxford University Press, 1999.

Nettle, Daniel, and Suzanne Romaine. *Vanishing Voices: The Extinction of the World's Languages*. Oxford; New York: Oxford University Press, 2000.

Nichols, Johanna. *Linguistic Diversity in Space and Time*. Chicago, IL: University of Chicago Press, 1992.

Offen, Karen, Ruth Roach Price, Jane Rendall, eds. *Writing Women's History: International Perspectives*. Bloomington, IN: Indiana University Press, 1991.

Olson, Steve. *Mapping Human History: Discovering the Past through Our Genes*. Boston, MA: Houghton Mifflin, 2002.

Osterhammel, Jürgen. *Colonialism: A Theoretical Overview*. Princeton, NJ: Princeton University Press, 1997.

Pacey, Arnold. *Technology in World Civilization*. Cambridge, MA: MIT, 1990.

Parker, Geoffrey. *The Military Revolution: Military Innovation and the Rise of the West, 1500–1800*. Cambridge, UK; New York: Cambridge University Press, 1988.

Passavant, Paul A. ed. *Empire's New Clothes: Reading Hardt and Negri*. London; New York: Routledge, 2003.

Pomeranz, Kenneth. *The Great Divergence: China, Europe, and the Making of the Modern World Economy*. Princeton, NJ: Princeton University Press, 2000.

Pomeranz, Kenneth, ed. *The World that Trade Created: Culture, Society and the World Economy, 1400 to the Present*. Armonk, NY: M.E. Sharpe, 1999.

Manning the port lookout station, a Seaman wears a MCU-2/P gas mask during a simulated chemical, biological and radiological (CBR) warfare attack at a General Quarters (GQ) drill aboard USS *Nimitz* (USNavy).

Nanjing Road, a major shopping street in Shanghai, China (CCA-SA3.0).

Pomper, Philip, Richard H. Elphick, Richard T. Vann, eds. *World History: Ideologies, Structures, and Identities.* Oxford, UK; Cambridge, MA: Blackwell Publishers, 1998.

Ponting, Clive. *A Green History of the World: The Environment and the Collapse of Great Civilizations.* New York: Penguin, 1993.

Pratt, Mary Louise. *Imperial Eyes: Travel Writing and Transculturation.* London; New York: Routledge, 1992.

Richmond, Anthony H. *Global Apartheid: Refugees, Racism, and the New World Order.* Oxford, UK; New York: Oxford University Press, 1995.

Robertson, Roland. *Globalization: Social Theory and Global Culture.* London: Sage Publications, 1992.

Runciman, W.G. "Culture Does Evolve." *History and Theory* 44 (2005), 1–13.

Runciman, W.G. "Rejoinder to Fracchia and Lewontin." *History and Theory* 44 (2005), 30–41.

Sakai, Nakoki. "Modernity and Its Critique: The problem of Universalism and Particularism." Masao Miyoshi and H.D. Harootunian, eds. *Postmodernism and Japan.* Durham, NC: Duke University Press, 1989; London: Sage Publications, 1992, 93–122.

Sanderson, Stephen K., ed. *Civilizations and World Systems: Studying World-Historical Change.* Walnut Creek, CA: Altamira Press, 1995.

Service, Elman R. *Origins of the State: The Process of Cultural Evolution.* New York: W.W. Norton, 1975.

Skocpol, Theda. *States and Social Revolutions: A Comparative Analysis of France, Russia, and China.* Cambridge, UK; New York: Cambridge University Press, 1979.

Smil, Vaclav. *Energy in World History.* Boulder CO: Westview Press, 1994.

Snooks, Graeme Donald. *The Dynamic Society: Exploring the Sources of Global Change.* London; New York: Routledge, 1996.

Snooks, Graeme Donald. *The Ephemeral Civilization.* London; New York: Routledge, 1997.

Snooks, Graeme Donald. *The Laws of History.* London; New York: Routledge, 1998.

Spence, Jonathan. *The Chan's Great Continent: China in Western Minds.* New York: W.W. Norton, 1998.

Spier, Fred. *The Structure of Big History from the Big Bang until Today.* Amsterdam: Amsterdam University Press, 1996.

Stearns, Peter N. *The Industrial Revolution in World History.* Boulder, CO: Westview Press, 1993.

Stokes, Gale. "The Fates of Human Societies: A Review of Recent Macrohistories." *American Historical Review* 106 (2001), 508–525.

Strange, Susan. *States and Markets.* New York: Pinter Publishers, 1988.

Stuart-Fox, Martin. "Evolutionary Theory of History." *History and Theory* 38 (1999), 33–51.

Swartz, Stuart B., ed. *Implicit Understandings: Observing, Reporting, and Reflecting on the Encounters between Europeans and Other Peoples in the Early Modern Era.* Cambridge, UK; New York: Cambridge University Press, 1994.

Tilly, Charles. "A Grand Tour of Exotic Landes." Review essay of Landes, *The Wealth and Poverty of Nations. American Historical Review* 104 (1999), 1253–1257.

Tracy, James D., ed. *The Rise of Merchant Empires: Long-distance Trade in the Early Modern World, 1350–1750.* Cambridge, UK; New York: Cambridge University Press, 1990.

Van Der Veer, Peter. *Nation and Migration: The Politics of Space in the South Asian Diaspora.* Philadelphia, PA: University of Philadelphia Press, 1995.

Voll, John Obert. "Islam as a Special World System." Ross E. Dunn, ed. *The New World History: A Teacher's Companion.* New York: Bedford/St. Martin's Press, 2000, 276–284.

Vries, P.H.H. " Are Coal and Colonies Really Crucial? Kenneth Pomeranz and the Great Divergence." *Journal of World History* 12 (2001), 407–55.

Wallerstein, Immanuel. *The Essential Wallerstein.* New York: New Press, 2000.

Wallerstein, Immanuel. "The Ideological Tensions of Capitalism: Universalism vs Racism and Sexism." *The Essential Wallerstein.* New York: New Press, 2000, 344–352.

Wallerstein, Immanuel. "The National and the Universal: Can There Be Such a Thing as World Culture?" Anthony D. King, ed. *Culture, Globalization and the World-System: Contemporary Conditions for the Representation of Identity.* Minneapolis, MN: University of Minnesota Press, 1997, 91–105.

Wallerstein, Immanuel. "The Rise and Future Demise of the World Capitalist System: Concepts for Comparative Analysis." *The Essential Wallerstein.* New York: New Press, 2000, 71–102.

Wallerstein, Immanuel. "World Systems Analysis." *The Essential Wallerstein.* New York: New Press, 2000, 129–148.

Wallerstein, Immanuel. *World-Systems Analysis: An Introduction.* Durham, NC: Duke University Press, 2004.

Wang, Gungwu, Raymond Grew, eds. *Global History and Migrations.* Boulder, CO: Westview Press, 1997.

Watts, Sheldon. *Epidemics and History: Disease, Power and Imperialism.* New Haven, CT: Yale University Press, 1998.

Whitrow, G.J. *Time in History.* Oxford, UK; New York: Oxford University Press, 1988.

Chuck Berry, 1957 (PD).

Wilkinson, David. "Central Civilization." *Comparative Civilizations Review* 17 (1987), 31–59.

Wilkinson, David. "Civilizations Are World Systems!" Stephen K. Sanderson, ed. *Civilizations and World Systems: Studying World-Historical Change.* Walnut Creek CA: Altamira Press, 1995, 248–258.

Wilson, Allan C., and Rebecca L. Cann. "The Recent African Genesis of Humans." *Scientific American* (April 1992), 68–73.

Wolf, Eric R. "Connections in History." Ross E. Dunn, ed. *The New World History: A Teacher's Companion.* New York: Bedford/St. Martin's Press, 2000, 131–137.

Wolf, Eric R. *Envisioning Power: Ideologies of Dominance and Crisis.* Berkeley, CA: University of California Press, 1999.

Wong, R. Bin. *China Transformed: Historical Change and the Limits of European Experience.* Ithaca, NY: Cornell University Press, 1997.

Wood, Denis. *Five Billion Years of Global Change: A History of the Land.* New York: Guilford Press, 2004.

Atomic bombing of Nagasaki on August 9, 1945 (USArmy).

"One Big Union for All": Was the goal of the radical labor leaders and Socialists who met in Chicago in 1905.

18th Amendment: Outlawed the sale of alcohol products in the U. S. A.

20th Century movement: The nation's population shifted from the Northeast to the Sunbelt.

A constitutional monarchy: In effect a democracy, and in Britain's case it also had a huge empire.

American Civil Liberties Union: A private, liberal organization devoted to upholding the Constitution.

Andrew Melendrez: Sergeant in the US Army fighting in Europe during World War II.

Anti-Semitism: Systematic prejudice against Jewish people.

Antioch Church: A city church that welcomed diversity of all types.

Apollo: NASA efforts to go to the moon.

Art for Art's Sake: A view that art should not be analyzed or judged for its composition, form, or worldview.

Assassination: Murder of a political official.

Avant-Garde: Forward thinking, modern.

Ben Horry: From Murrells Inlet, South Carolina, and told his account of slavery.

Biplanes: Early airplanes with dual wings that helped them maneuver.

A french biplane returning from a bombing run in 1916 (PD).

Black Nationalism: African-American movement that celebrated African-American exclusionism.

Blues: The name given to both a musical form and a music genre that originated in African-American communities of primarily the "Deep South" of the United States.

Bolshevism: Russian Communism.

Brain Trust: Franklin Roosevelt's advisors.

Butler Act: Tennessee law that made the teaching of evolution illegal.

Cabaret: A burlesque show.

Carlisle Evans: Fought with the Marines in the Pacific.

Chaplain George T. McCarthy: Roman Catholic chaplain who made an effort to focus on the Lord in the midst of danger and death.

Chiang Kaishek: Nationalist leader of China.

Christo et Ecclesiae: Harvard's motto for 300 years, which meant "for Christ and church."

City of God, City of Satan: Terms coined to describe a notion that Satan wants to own the city.

Clarence Darrow: The successful lawyer at the Scopes Trial.

Two local German women file past piles of corpses outside the crematorium in the newly liberated Buchenwald concentration camp, 1945 (PD).

Clive Staples (C.S.) Lewis: Professor of Medieval and Renaissance English literature at Cambridge University.

Collateral Damage: Injury to non-combatant civilians.

Common Market: Advances free trade and uniform standards.

Concentration camps: Massive prison-holding facilities often used to slaughter large groups of people.

Crew of Battleship Potemkin: Russian participants in the 1905 Revolution.

Crucicentrism: Cross-centered theology.

Czar Nicholas II: Czar when the Russian Revolution arrived.

Daguerreotype: The first commercially successful photographic process.

Deism: Belief system that posits that God is alive but not present.

Distinctive food: Became a defining symbol of national identity in the 19th century.

Dixieland: Dixieland music, sometimes referred to as Hot jazz, Early Jazz or New Orleans jazz, is a style of jazz music which developed in New Orleans at the start of the 20th century.

Dreadnoughts: Large battleships thought to be unsinkable.

Duma: The Russian Parliament.

Edward Gibbon: Author of *The Decline and Fall of the Roman Empire*.

Einsatzgruppen: Mobile killing units in Russia.

Epistemology: The study of knowledge.

Eschatology: Study of the end times.

European Parliament: The governing body of the European Union.

European Union: The union of continental Europe after the Iron Curtain fell in 1990.

Executive Branch: Composed of the president and his cabinet.

Fascism: Totalitarianism.

Fatherhood: A movement to save fathers' roles in families.

Federal Government of the United States: Composed of the executive branch, the legislative branch, and the judicial branch.

Federal Income Tax: The first federal tax based on income.

Federal Writers' Project (FWP): Sent writers into 17 states to interview ordinary people in order to write down their life stories.

Feminism: An assertive women's rights movement.

Field hospitals: Emergency medical centers set up out where the battles ensued.

Final Solution: German plan to kill all the Jews in Europe.

Fortress Nation: A concept of a world that is paraochial and self-serving.

Francis Schaeffer: Moved to Switzerland in 1948 as a missionary, and founded L'Abri (the Shelter) Fellowship with his wife, Edith.

Free-market capitalists: Assert that government intervention merely drags out recessions and depressions.

Futurology: The prediction of the future.

Galatians 3:28: Biblical passage that speaks of the equal status of all who are in Christ.

Gemini: NASA efforts to understand space travel.

Geopolitical Conflict: A world-wide conflict between two different political ideologies.

German Reich: A German government.

Ghettoization: A term to describe the movement of African-Americans into poor sections of the city.

Ghettoization: Placing Jews in containment areas for later deportation.

Gleichschaltung: Take over by Nazis of the civil services.

Global Warming: A theory that the world is warming.

Globalized World: A world who draws its vision and resources from the entire globe.

Government: Refers to the way people arbitrate, control, and live their lives.

Grant Wacker: Insists that the growth of the Church has, and must, employ whatever tools God provides — including the media.

Great Depression: A time of great economic stress, 1929-1940.

Great Leap Forward: Economic and social revolution in the 1960s.

Harold Ockenga: A great evangelist who founded Fuller Seminary.

Harvard University Charter: A charter stating the mission and purpose of Harvard University.

Herb Block: A political cartoonist.

Hindenburg: The German passenger zeppelin airship that caught fire and was destroyed in 1937.

History Maker: A term to describe someone who really changes history.

Holocaust: Murder of 5 million Jews during World War II.

Homeschooling: A movement that has existed through all of American history but has become more popular since the 1970s.

Horace Mann: Early leader in public education.

Immanuel Kant: A philosopher who saw experience as the primary core reality.

Inflation: Increased prices.

Iranian Hostages: The Iran hostage crisis was a diplomatic crisis between Iran and the United States where 52 Americans were held hostage for 444 days from November 4, 1979 to January 20, 1981.

Iron Curtain: A metaphor for the closing of the borders between free, democratic Europe and Soviet-controlled Eastern Europe.

Jazz: A musical style that originated at the beginning of the 20th century in African American communities in the Southern United States.

Jeremy Rifkin: A controversial New Left historian.

Jewish Zealots: Radical Jewish Zionists who sought freedom for Israel.

John A. Lomax: National Advisor on Folklore and Folkways for the FWP.

John Holt: Educator who was critical of orthodox education.

Polish children in Warsaw Ghetto, 1941 (PD).

Sign of the energy crisis in 1973 (NARA).

John Wesley: The founder of Methodism.

John William Manix: Fought with the US Army in the Pacific.

Jonathan Edwards: American philosopher and theologian.

Judicial Branch: The Court system.

King Belshazzar's Feast: A metaphor based on the Book of Daniel to explain the university.

Kulturkampf: Stuggles in culture.

Leave It to Beaver: A successful sit-com television show in the 1950s.

Legislative Branch: Congress and its influence.

Lenin: Leader of the Russian Revolution.

Leona Cox: A Red Cross nurse during World War II.

Limited War: As opposed to limited war, combatants intentionally limit the extent and scope of warfare.

Lt. Col. George Brenton Laurie: From Nova Scotia; appointed a special service officer, including the command of a mounted infantry battalion for the South African War.

Manchus: Late 19th-century ruling Chinese family.

Mao Zedong: Communist leader of Chinia.

Margaret Sanger: A racist advocate of birth control.

Mary Reynolds: Born in slavery to the Kilpatrick family, she claimed to be more than a hundred years old.

Mass communication: Forms of media that reach a broad, national audience.

McCarthy Era: A time of heightened fear against Communism in the U. S. A.

Mercury Projects: Early NASA efforts to put a man in space.

Militarism: National philosophy of military power.

Mischlinge: A German designation for a Jewish person.

Moral Relativism: Morality based on circumstances.

Morrill Act: Federal act to set up lend lease colleges.

Mother Teresa: Her Missionaries of Charity grew from 12 to thousands serving the "poorest of the poor" in 450 centers around the world.

National Recovery Administration: A New Deal agency committed to oversight of labor and management.

National Socialist government: Nazi government.

National Stumping: To hold informal mass rallies in support of a position or ideology.

Nativist: A group who opposed immigration of all sorts.

Neurasthenia: National anxiety.

Nuremberg Laws of 1935: Determined who was Jewish and who was not.

Oil Crisis: Shortages of oil that caused spiked oil prices.

Orson Welles: Gave a live performance of H.G. Wells' science fiction novel *The War of the Worlds*.

Oswald Bölcke: Joined the German Air Corps in 1914 and fought in every major engagement until he went missing in action in 1916.

Oswald Chambers: Early 20th-century saint who wrote a very popular devotional, *My Utmost for His Highest.*

Pandemic: A worldwide disease epidemic.

Parousia: The Second Coming of Jesus Christ.

Phenakistiscope: The phenakistoscope was an early animation device that used the persistence of vision principle to create an illusion of motion.

Placing concrete and erecting of gates, lower main lock chamber looking upstream, Mississippi River Lock #18, a Public Works Aministration Project, Amry Corps of Engingeers, 1934 (NARA).

Positive Liberal State: A state with a lot of government intervention.

Post-modern architecture: Created new designs and new visions in buildings.

Post-Modernism: Post-1990 movement that emphasizes the subjective.

Pragmatism: Philosophical view that argues for ordinary, common sense.

Premillennialism: A belief of the end times held by a large percentage of Christians during the first three centuries of the Christian era.

Progressives: A reform movement in the United States, 1880-1920.

Prohibition: Banning the production and sale of alcohol.

Protective Tariffs: Duties placed on goods to protect indigenous industries.

Public Works Administration: Job creation agency in the New Deal.

Racial separatism vs. Racial accommodation: In the face of racial prejudice, separatism is a theory of gaining rights through separation from one's adversaries. Accommodation is a view of gaining rights by learning to live among one's adversaries.

Racism: A belief system based on the concept that people are divided into races, and that certain races are superior to others.

Ragtime: Ragtime is an original musical genre that enjoyed its peak popularity between 1900 and 1918.

Ralph Nader: An early leader of the consumer movement.

Raymond Moore: Pioneer in home education.

Recession of 2008: The most serious economic downturn since the Great Depression.

Religious extremists: Often view modernization efforts as corrupting influences on traditional culture.

Reparation: Money paid as punishment for the loss of a war.

Richard Rorty: A philosopher who emphasized the use of language.

Robert Stobaugh: Author of *Future Energy.*

Rock n' Roll: A type of music emerging in the 1950s.

Rough Riders: Roosevelt's Spanish American troops who took San Juan Hill.

Satosphere: A modern multi-dimensional film.

Scientific Revolution: Dynamic changes in technological progress, including fields of medicine and media.

Second Great Awakening: The great revival in American in the 19th century.

The Burj Khalifa, tallest skyscraper in the world since 2010, with a height of 2,722'. Skyscrapers taller than 985' are also called Supertalls, those taller than 1,968' are called Megatalls (CCA-SA3.0).

Skyscraper: Tall buildings to accommodate the maximum number of people within a minimum space.

Social Gospel: A theory of helping the needy and poor based on human good, not the Bible.

Social Revolution: Dynamic changes in family, government, and society.

Sons of Liberty: Organized into patriotic chapters as a result of the Stamp Tax of 1765.

Soviet: A group of Communists.

Space Shuttle Columbia disaster: The Space Shuttle Columbia disaster occurred on February 1, 2003, when shortly before it was scheduled to conclude its 28th mission.

Sputnik: Russian satelitte—the first one in space.

Surrealism: Out of the real of ordinary experience.

T. S. Eliot: Perhaps the best poet and dramatist of the 20th century.

Tea Party Movement: A conservative political movement whose main purpose is to decrease government control of American life.

Terrorism: Systematic violence against a government on behalf of a cause.

Thaumatrope: a card with different pictures on either side so that when the card is rapidly twirled, the images appear to combine.

The New Deal: Roosevelt's legislation intervention for the New Deal.

The Nuclear Age: A period that of nuclear power that gained prominence at the end of World War II.

The Socialist Party: Represented the middle class; became important in the German Empire.

The Woman's Christian Temperance Union (WCTU): Organized by women concerned about the destructive power of alcohol.

Theodore Roosevelt: Great progressive president.

Thomas Merton: One of the most influential American spiritual writers of the 20th century.

Tiananmen Square: Historical gathering place of radicals and revolutionaries.

Tom Mix: Early cinema cowboy star.

Traditional family: A typical family from the 1960s that comprised a working father, a homemaker mother, and their two kids.

UFOs: Unidentified Flying Objects.

United States of Europe: A term used by Victor Hugo during a speech at the International Peace Congress in 1849.

University of Bologna: The first university.

University: An institution of advanced education and research that grants academic degrees.

Unschooling: The educational philosophy of John Holt's followers; what he called "learning by living."

Urbanization: A movement in history toward a majority of world dwellers living in the city.

Vaudeville: A form of comedy entertainment.

Vietnamization: An attempt by the Americans to leave the conduct of the War to South Vietnam.

Vitascope: Vitascope was an early film projector first demonstrated in 1895.

Volstead Act: Defined intoxicating beverages as anything with more than 0.5 percent alcohol.

Walter Calloway: Lived to be 89, with most of his life spent on the south side of Birmingham.

Wannsee Conference: A German conference to deal with the extermination of the Jews.

Weimar Republic: A period of German democracy after WWI and before the Nazis took power.

Wernher Von Braun: Former Nazi German space scientist who helped the Americans.

White Guilt: A term to describe white guilt over racial relations.

William Jennings Bryan: A great American statesman.

Winston Churchill: British prime minister during World War II.

Woodstock: Huge rock concert in the summer of 1969.

Yellow journalism: Sensational, salacious writings to persuade an audience to buy into a lie.

Youth Culture: A term that describes the growing influence of youth.

Winston Churchill giving his famous 'V' sign — on May 20, 1940, just ten days after Churchill became Prime Minister, German troops reached the English Channel. (PD).

Tea Party protesters walk toward the United States Capitol during the Taxpayer March on Washington, September 12, 2009 (PD).